Southern Living Party Cookbook

Complete Menus and Entertaining Guide

by

Celia Marks

and

The Editors of Southern Living Magazine

Library of Congress Catalog Card Number: 72-85026
Manufactured in the United States of America
First Printing 1972

Contents

Introduction

"Pleasantest of all ties is the tie of host and guest." — *Aeschylus, 500 B. C.*

It is the purpose of this book to help you in all seasons, on all occasions, to be at your best while entertaining.

A good party doesn't just happen, not even for the hostess who is regarded as having an inborn flair for entertaining. The successful party is the result of careful planning of the food to be offered, as well as an awareness of just what makes an occasion memorable.

So often in organizing our entertaining, we tend to forget why we're doing it at all. We're so busy with the mechanics of the affair, we overlook the real purpose of entertaining — the pleasure of dispensing hospitality. It should be our aim that afterwards, our guests will be warmed by the memory of a happy, exciting party; that they'll think back on an interesting discussion, a challenging turn of the conversation, an exciting newcomer with a different viewpoint — and wonder, too, what magic you worked with the food you served. These intangibles are so much more important than the guest's seeing his reflection in the shine on your furniture.

The old French proverb puts it succinctly: "The company makes the feast." But you as hostess can create the climate surrounding the feast, the climate that promotes the enjoyment of people when they get together.

It's impossible to bring about this ambience if you're in the kitchen tasting and fussing instead of being with your guests, seeing that the shy are not ignored, that the glasses are refilled before you hear the ice rattle, that everyone gets a chance at the nibbles you've prepared ahead of time (for as a famous American columnist once complained, "There's someone at every party who eats all the celery.").

The day of "the little maid who helps out" is gone. So, too, are the lavish refreshments of the past. Any cookbook that pretends otherwise is no friend of yours. Today the need is for a straightforward, realistic approach to a servant-less society.

If entertaining is to be done with confidence and pleasure — and often if it is to be done at all — much of the food should be prepared ahead of time, allowing for catastrophes and recovery therefrom. Because where entertaining is concerned, most of us feel we operate according to Murphy's Law, anyhow: "If anything can go wrong, it will go wrong."

Equal to the problem of timing is that greatest stumbling block in the path of even veteran hostesses — what goes with what. Many women may be great at producing one superb dish; but however wonderfully constructed, to exploit its virtues, the entrée must be surrounded by dishes which complement rather than compete with it. As an artist is concerned with relationships in a painting, so you, an artist in your own kitchen, are concerned with the relationship of one dish to another, with the creation of a harmonious unit rather than a heterogeneous assortment of parts, good as each may be.

That subject — the harmony of one dish with another — we have dealt with in this book. Although the complete menus are planned primarily to show off the star of the performance — the entrée — we hope you'll have fun skipping about from one menu to another, matching a dish from one with something you like from another, giving full vent to your own imagination and ingenuity.

We hope the menus we've selected will solve your entertaining problems so that when the last guest has departed and you lock up, take off your shoes, and turn to your mate and ask, "Well, how do you think it went?" you'll know the happy answer before you get it.

Celia Marks

Chattanooga
August 1972

Dispensing Southern Hospitality

Hospitality, a synonym for the South, comes from the heart. Even the most discerning disciple of etiquette may fall short as a hostess if she fails to bestow this gift upon her guests. For hospitality is a gift: it is the giving of oneself, the opening of one's home to create a warm and welcoming spot where friends or near strangers may be completely at their ease. When a guest leaves feeling he brought joy to his hostess and happiness to the household, he himself has received hospitality.

In addition to this intangible quality that may be so readily felt, there exist the guidelines of etiquette and "behind-the-scene" activities that help the party run smoothly. The ambience of a party should announce to the guest upon arrival that a good time is to be had. Nothing can be duller than waiting for the action to begin. How to create this ambience is the question. Be prepared: do as much work ahead as possible. Do something unusual: decorate the house and the table to the mood of the party. Even a flickering candle may softly announce a warm welcome. The simplest extra touch tells guests that they are special and that the hours ahead will be, too.

Entertaining is easy and always fun when you approach it with interest and individuality. And it is our goal to guide and give ideas that may help you entertain in a manner suited perfectly to you.

Let a plate of Bacon Roll-Ups (page 381) be the focal point for your cocktail party.

THE SIZE OF YOUR PARTY

If you want to entertain 8 to 12 people you know well, the dinner party is preferable to the cocktail party. Groups of 10 to 16 seem to be the most difficult to handle at a cocktail party unless the group plans to go on together to another gathering of some kind. Perhaps this is because a group of this size so easily breaks up into two or three small clusters. In a small space, têté-a-têtés are difficult to break up.

A big party has the advantage of allowing people to talk in small groups, to explore new acquaintances, to do their own mixing tactfully and easily.

Whatever size party you decide on, include several guests who will carry part of the entertainment load. Naturally, you won't limit your list only to life-of-the-party types; that way lies bedlam as each clamors for the spotlight. On the other hand, several of these personalities can save a party which seems to be drearily winding down.

Never make the mistake of trying to do away with all your social obligations at one party by inviting everyone who ever sent you a get-well card. Ask those who will most likely enjoy being with one another; that's what entertaining is all about. Don't fling strangers at each other indiscriminately just because you've managed to incur obligations and you can't live with yourself any longer and see the big bash as a chance to wipe the slate clean. You'll have an unforgettable party in that case — remembered for all the wrong reasons.

For the hostess with limited space and a long guest list, the best solution is to divide the list, invite them for different days — and do the ahead-of-time cooking for both at the same time. No hostess can be relaxed and effective if she must preside at a mob scene; the size of the group must be manageable, though not so small as to be uncomfortable for guests standing around sparsely in what may be a large room. Elbow-to-elbow is preferable to that!

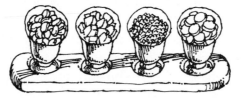

SPUR-OF-THE-MOMENT ENTERTAINING

When spur-of-the-moment guests are sprung on you, don't panic. Put your time to use. Relax, take stock of what food you have or can prepare to serve with speed and facility.

Such guests are well aware that their arrival is unexpected and should have any apprehensions quickly dispelled by a warm, welcoming hostess.

So, as you ponder the menu, tidy up the house, (the guests will not expect a showplace), clean the guest bath, and set the table or buffet appropriately for what you plan to serve.

Don't try to prepare a gargantuan feast. A simple yet well planned meal will embarrass guests less and impress them more. Use what you have: it's wise to keep a supply of staples, canned goods, and various non-spoiling ingredients for your quick specialties.

Begin with a soup to give a touch of elegance to an otherwise routine meal. Add zest to the flavor of canned soup by combining two or garnishing with a tangy twist of lemon, a sprinkle of parsley, or a scattering of crusty croutons.

Then, perhaps whip up an omelet, Welsh rarebit, or quiche. Or take out the frozen asparagus, boil it lightly, roll it in sizzled ham slices, cover with a cheese-flavored white sauce and serve. Toss a quick salad for a side dish, bring out the frozen dessert, homemade ahead, or bought for just such an occasion. Or, for an off-season surprise, serve fruitcake that's been rummed, wrapped and stored.

Do what preparations you can for the meal then slip back and spruce up (if there's time, relax in a quick shower or bath). You'll look better, feel prettier, and smile readily.

ISSUING INVITATIONS

For most home entertainment, informal invitations are sufficient and correct. Today's relaxed lifestyle and spur-of-the-moment planning makes engraved invitations impractical except for truly special occasions. Engraved or handwritten invitations are most certainly issued for very formal and official entertainment, formal receptions, dances, weddings, and wedding receptions, but we are concerned here with everyday hospitality in Southern homes.

Informal invitations may be used for formal occasions such as teas, christenings, formal dinners, and small dances. The reverse is not true. You may telephone guests for a sit-down dinner but you would not send an engraved invitation for a pool-side picnic.

This relaxing of formality is an example of etiquette changing to become more helpful in given situations. But by no means does it mean etiquette is turning topsy-turvy. Far from being fossilized, etiquette is evolving quietly and efficiently giving guidelines to put people at their ease. As contemporary demands render obsolete many formalities, new ones take their place. Visiting cards, once an important adjunct to a lady's day, are now primarily used as gift enclosures or note cards for informal invitations.

Every invitation, formal or informal, should indicate the precise time, date, place, and degree of formality. If the dinner is "black tie" tell your guests, else they will be justified in assuming evening clothes are not necessary. And, equally embarrassed is the guest who comes dressed for dinner to find the party gathered informally on the terrace. Over the phone, you might suggest what you and your husband will be wearing and on a written invitation, write the information on the lower right corner. It is also considerate to give full directions to the house for a guest who is unfamiliar with the town or area.

An acceptance should repeat the hour, day, and place of the event as a double check. The hostess will then be able to catch a mistake in case the guest misunderstood.

It is only courteous for the guest to answer an invitation promptly and with the same degree of formality. An informal letter may be answered either by telephone or in the same form of letter, but a response to an engraved invitation should always be written out in the third person on formal writing paper.

Informal invitations include all verbal invitations, those written on cards, informals or various notes, and those telegraphed.

Spoken invitations are given by the hostess to the wife of the couple to be invited. If the husband issues an invitation, it is considered tentative until confirmed by his wife by telephone or note. In like manner, the wife accepts the invitation. A husband may tentatively accept but his wife should confirm the acceptance.

When giving a face-to-face invitation avoid speaking within hearing of someone who may not be invited. Be precise. A casual or tentative invitation may leave your guest unsure as to whether he has been invited or not. In return the guest should avoid giving a delayed answer. If he isn't certain he can accept, he should give his regrets and give the reason. Allow the hostess the right to say, "Let me know tomorrow."

When a face-to-face invitation is issued during the confusion of another party or a meeting, a reminder card is a wise follow-up.

The wording of spoken invitations, whether face to face or by telephone, depends on the closeness of the person to be invited. If a party is to have a guest of honor, save the words "in honour of" for an engraved invitation. Say instead, "We're giving a luncheon for Judy Sullins, Saturday noon, and hope you can come."

Telephone invitations are most helpful when an immediate reply is needed and an exact person count is important to the menu planning. Telephoning also gives a hostess time to find a replacement in case a guest regrets or drops out.

Invitations by card indicate a large gathering. So, in a sense they are less formal than those given over the telephone for an intimate seated dinner. Cards are most often used for a crowd of 20 or more when an immediate reply is not necessary and there is more leeway in the guest count. They are used less often for luncheons or dinners, though they may be, and are most frequently used for a tea, cocktail party, or buffet.

An invitation sent on a visiting card is written in by hand in ink above and below the engraved name. For close friends or for a personal touch, the hostess may draw a line through her engraved name and sign her first or full name. An unmarried man or woman often draws the line through the title only. Cards engraved for Mr. and Mrs. are reserved for occasions when both will be present. An informal note card or letter is sent to the wife. Only engraved invitations are issued to the husband and wife.

*Two favorite brunch dishes are Crepes Fitzgerald (page 111)
and Eggs Benedict (page 119).*

INVITATION	ACCEPTANCE OR REGRET
Tea, Saturday *April 20th, Four o'clock* Mrs. John Teal Smith *R.s.v.p.* *1410 North 20th Street*	*delighted to come to Tea,* *April 20th, Four o'clock* Mrs. James Arron Jones *many thanks*
Joint card is not used for a tea where Mr. is not invited.	May be written on an informal note as well.
Won't you join us for egg-nog *Xmas Eve, 5-7* ~~Mr. and Mrs. William Creech~~ *Love,* *Susan*	*Dear Susan,* *We would love to come* *for Xmas Eve egg-nog. See* *you around five.* *Love,* *Margaret*
Line drawn through name for close friend.	Openhouse invitation requires no response but one is always appreciated.
Buffet Supper *New Year's Day at seven o'clock* Mr. and Mrs. William Creech *R.s.v.p. regrets only.* *879-5592* *12 Lakeview Road*	*Dear Mrs. Creech,* *We are sorry to miss your* *New Year's party but John and* *I will be visiting his parents.* *You were so thoughtful* *to include us. Sincerely,* *Marianne Johnson*
Regrets only for a large party saves answering many calls.	Regret should always give a reason. Formality of response depends on intimacy of friends.

In accepting an informal note, telephoning or sending a visiting card is correct and need only be responded to if an "R.S.V.P." is requested. But an answer is always a courtesy particularly if it should be a regret. A written response shows more consideration, however, the telephone is prompt when time is important.

The degree of formality used in responding depends on closeness of the correspondents rather than the wording of the invitation. A card response may be as simple as "delighted to come" with the date and time and perhaps a "thank you." A close friend might draw a line through the engraved name and sign her first name.

An informal note could read: "Dear Joan, Tom and I would love to come to the buffet but Sally's recital is Saturday evening, too. Perhaps we'll be through in time to drop by for dessert. Love, Anne." Or a regret after the fact: "Dear Helen, Regret upon regret. We just returned from a week at the beach and found your invitation waiting for us. We promise not to miss the next one. Love, Sylvia."

The folded informal card is also used for written invitations and replies. The name is engraved on the outside and the message is written either above and below the name or inside on the lower half of the note.

Purchased printed invitations, gaily decorated or plain, are available but are preferable for less formal occasions if used. An ingenious hostess may create an invitation to carry out her party theme. A catchy jingle written across a small brown paper sack could send out the news of a chuckwagon barbecue. Or for a Shakespearean party, a large square of parchment-type paper hand printed, folded and secured with sealing wax could announce a special event for guests.

A telegram indicates an impromptu affair which is apt to be informal and fairly large. It is often used when there are several people giving the party and when an immediate response is required. The form is precise but accurate as to information: "Won't you come to the reunion at the Blake Farm on Tohoe Lake, Saturday, June 24th? Swimming begins at 10 a.m., the picnic at 12 p.m. R.S.V.P. Mrs. William Blake, Tohoe Lake, Clinton." A list of the hosts follows: Julie and Bill Blake, Grace and David Blake, Faith and Steve Thornton.

As time is obviously important responses should be phoned or telegraphed: "Looking forward to coming to the reunion on Lake Tohoe, June 24th. Susan and Scott Blake." Or, "Our luck — Jim's in a golf tournament all day June 24th. Will hate to miss the reunion but thanks for asking us. Tish and Stuart Thornton."

Both written and spoken forms are basically informal so convenience to the hostess and to her guests should determine which is to be used. In following given rules it is helpful to remember that the purpose of etiquette has been to inform and help, to give an accepted mode of behavior in a situation where questions often arise. But a considerate hostess puts the pleasure and ease of her guests above adherence to form for form's sake.

A HOST OF HOSTESSES

Several hostesses often join efforts for larger parties, receptions, teas, showers, children's parties, or buffet luncheons. As decisions must be agreeable to all involved, it is often wise (for the sake of friendship) to keep the number to no more than three. Together the hostesses must decide in whose home the party is to be held or where outside the home. They collaborate on the guest list and share the task of sending invitations. All names appear on the invitation and the address is clearly indicated. Guests are greeted by all hostesses as they arrive. Duties should be either shared or allocated so that each has equal responsibility in the planning and production of the party.

A TIME TO COME AND A TIME TO STAY

Meal and party times do vary in different areas but within standard schedules. The hostess, of course, follows the customs of her community.

Brunch: Between 10:30 a.m. and 1:00 p.m.

Luncheon: Begins at 12:30 or 1:00 p.m. and lasts from one and a half to two hours.

Buffet luncheon: Begins at 12:30 and is served until 2:00 p.m.

Dinner: More than any meal, the time depends on the location. For metropolitan areas 8:00 p.m. is the usual time, but with moved up theater and symphony hours earlier dining is becoming a fashionable necessity. In smaller communities dinner is customarily earlier than in cities, the time being from 6:30 to 7:00 p.m. Dinner means from three to three and a half hours. A good time to leave is 40 minutes to an hour after coffee or liqueur has been served depending upon the other guests and upon the plans of the hostess. If entertainment has been planned, the hours are longer. A guest should never leave before the guest of honor. For this reason the guest of honor should hold to the prescribed three to three and one half hours unless the occasion indicates otherwise.

Buffet suppers: Begin at 8:30 or 9:00 p.m. There is more leeway here, particularly if the buffet is served before or after a special occasion.

Morning coffees: Between 10:00 a.m. and noon.

Tea parties: From 4:00 p.m. (not later than 4:30) to 5:00 p.m. or 5:30 p.m.

Cocktail parties: Begin around 5:00 p.m. and last until 7:00 p.m. On working days, the party may be moved up to 6:00 p.m. to 8:00 p.m. Guests should stay a minimum of 45 minutes to an hour unless the party is so large that departure will not be noticed. The maximum length to stay depends upon the party — just don't be the lingering last when the dinner hour approaches.

Guests are allowed a few minutes beyond the stated hour unless the dinner party precedes a concert, theatre, or some special event. Ten to fifteen minutes is acceptable. A half an hour, even in cities is a maximum. Often, if the dinner needs to be served promptly, the hostess may so indicate in the wording of the invitation, "Come around 7:30, dinner will be served at 8:00."

What better way to announce the coming of spring than with a garden tea. Our Garden Tea Menu is on page 64.

If a guest is unavoidably detained he should by all means telephone the hostess, give a reason for the delay, a time of expected arrival and add that she should not hold dinner. If it is possible to wait for his arrival, the hostess will indicate. A hostess should wait longer for older guests or a guest of honor than for an intimate friend.

If the dinner has begun, a guest should apologize to the hostess quietly and without vivid details, take his seat and cause as little disruption as possible. If the first course is finished, the late arrival should decline it, even though offered, rather than keep the rest waiting.

Being punctual means on time coming and going. Early guests can interfere with a hostess' last minute preparations, although the hostess should be ready. And the guest who repeatedly overstays the party hour may receive fewer invitations — not because he isn't wanted but because he isn't wanted for quite so long.

When guests do linger the hostess has no recourse but to entertain them. The host and hostess may decline to join them in that "last" drink. Or they may drop subtle hints saying that the next day begins early and is a busy one, in which case one of you may be excused. As a last resort, ask the most tenacious guest to keep you company while you clean up in the kitchen. At least you will be getting some of the work done and the movement will keep you awake.

ENTERTAINING IN LIMITED SPACE

When there's no space to spare you'll use your ingenuity to entertain with utmost confidence and calm. Let the entire house entertain your guests. Be innovative. A change gives spark to a party and makes the occasion guests remember.

Perfect planning is your key to getting the maximum use of minimum space. Have everything ready beforehand so last minute doings are minimal. Before your serenity and poise your guests will relax and have a good time.

If your area is extremely limited, two small dinner parties given in the same week could be less hassle for you and pleasanter for your guests. Cocktail parties thrive on variety but even elbow-bumping becomes old after a few spilled drinks. So hold the guest list to a comfortable number.

When giving a large party there will be congested areas around the bar, the buffet, and probably near the entrance. Scatter these areas and scatter the crowd. Set the bar up in a hallway — possibly leading to the outdoors and send guests on their way. If food is "pick-up at your leisure" set each course in a different room. Station snacks handily throughout; hor d'oeuvres in the den; main course in the dining room (so it may easily be replenished and kept warm); and desserts perhaps in a bedroom. If you've prepared food in advance — desserts, snacks and cold buffet — set it out before guests arrive.

To serve in other rooms, use the furniture that is already there — the desk, a chest, coffee tables — and bring in moveable carts, folding tables, and makeshift buffets. Brightly covered cloths cover whatever you need to hide and also protect your good furniture. Trays also protect the tabletop and are unobtrusively removed to the kitchen for refills.

Snacks are best limited to finger foods so there is no need for dishes or utensils. And tiered serving trays hold a lot of food compactly.

Cook food that can be served and handled easily. Cold buffets are ideal, but a hot dish — stew, meat pie, or casserole — can be prepared ahead and reheated just before serving.

Small trays before a buffet are handy for guests who must sit where they may. Other helpers that can be brought out when guests begin to serve themselves are folding tables, stacking stools, collapsible fiber boards to place over card tables, oversized pillows, and rented chairs. They're just as readily removed once supper is over.

For a sit-down dinner, use a piece of plywood across two saw-horses. Hide it under a decorative cloth. Set up a picnic on the floor with bright runners for a "table," pillows for sitting, and cold suppers stashed in sand buckets. Use a low coffee table with plush cushions for an exotic dinner. Let an old chest or a raised hearth serve as a buffet.

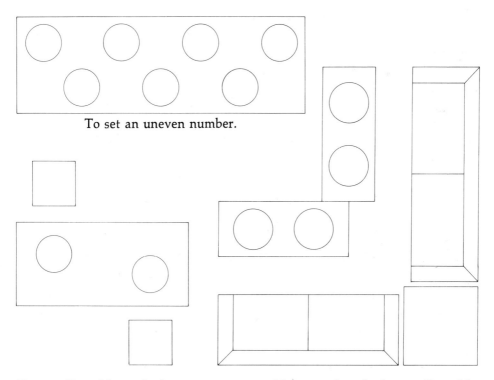

To set an uneven number.

Use a coffee table in the living room.   Use a couch and a long coffee table.

Make an indoor cafe with several round, knock down tables, appropriately covered, of course. Let an old armoire become a bar. Serve a large party in a long hallway — seat them at a long table or on the floor, Indian fashion. Obscure an imbalance of guests with tables that seat an odd number. And give an outdoor picnic using bright red wagons to hold utensils and wheel the food about.

Now, with these few suggestions as a starter, turn your imagination free to find the solutions that best suit your needs. Even the space shy can be gregarious hostesses.

SEATING ARRANGEMENTS

Seating is secondary at a gathering of intimate friends but certain guidelines do help for formal and informal meals. As a courtesy to new acquaintances, the elderly and the distinguished, the order of precedence would be (1) guest of honor, (2) a guest invited for the first time to a meal, (3) a stranger brought by a guest, (4) an older person or one who warrants particular recognition, a clergyman or retired judge, (5) guests who have visited the house infrequently, (6) constant guests, houseguests, and relatives, (7) children.

Changes in this order would be made to place an older person above a young first-time guest, a foreign first-time guest above an American first-time guest, a child first on his birthday.

Host and hostess take their places at opposite ends of the table with the hostess nearest the kitchen door. The hostess faces the host at all tables (round or otherwise) except when there are eight or a higher multiple of four. In this case she relinquishes her seat to the man guest of honor and moves to his left or right. If she sits on the left, the lady guest of honor is seated on the hosts' left, otherwise on the hosts' right. If there is no host the lady guest of honor sits to the right of the man guest of honor unless they are married. If they are, she is placed to the left of the gentleman to the hostess' left. In all other cases, the lady guest of honor is seated on the hosts' right, the gentleman guest of honor on the hostess' right. The second guests of honor go on the left, respectively. Husbands and wives are never seated side by side but engaged couples are never separated. Men and women alternate unless the number is uneven.

At family dinners, the eldest are given top seating and children who need help are placed by their mothers. Often a special children's table (set up nearby) with seats for a favorite aunt or uncle makes the meal more enjoyable for children and adults.

In placing guests, the hostess should consider congeniality of dinner partners. An out-of-town guest would appreciate sitting by a close but infrequently seen friend. But close friends who see each other frequently should be separated to give each an opportunity to entertain and be entertained by others.

SERVING A BUFFET

When setting up a buffet table the prime consideration should be traffic flow. Placement should allow easy circulation before, during, and after the meal. Movement through the serving line should be such that guests who have served themselves need not cross paths with those still in line. Food should be placed on the table in logical serving order to avoid the necessity of back tracking. Proximity to the kitchen is important so dishes may be unobtrusively replenished with ease. If food is to be kept in electric warmers, sufficient outlets will need to be close at hand.

A buffet dinner or luncheon may be seated and semi-served or guests may serve and seat themselves. At a seated buffet dinner or luncheon, for more formal or sophisticated gatherings, one large table or several smaller ones are used. The tables are covered and entirely set except for dinner plates. A first course such as soup or melon may be served as may be the dessert. For a buffet meal where guests seat themselves wherever they may, every consideration should be taken to make guests comfortable. Clear coffee and end tables and set up folding tables for guests. Small trays placed before the buffet are helpful for holding filled plates, silver, and drinks.

The table is most often set up in the dining room though guests may be served wherever most convenient. Outdoors, however, is precarious for all but the smallest informal gatherings as one can never count on the weather.

A table for an informal lunch is rarely set with a cloth — unless you wish to hide a makeshift table or contribute to the decor with a novelty covering. For dinner it may be bare or decoratively covered. Linen damask for dinners and embroidered organdy for luncheon are always appropriate for formal buffets.

The table covering should complement the mood and style of the serving dishes, centerpiece, and other elements. And all should be in keeping with the occasion.

Centerpieces contribute a great deal to the atmosphere but must not dominate the table. Otherwise, with many serving dishes an overcrowded look might detract from the overall view. Decorations are best placed in the center of an away-from-the-wall table but create an interesting asymmetric effect when placed at one end of a buffet against the wall.

Place food on the buffet in logical progression following the guests' need. Plates, flatware, and napkins come first. Silver is most readily accessible when laid out in simple rows. A fork may be placed on an individual napkin for easy pick up.

Food is arranged so that guests may scan the dishes and make a decision at a glance. Vegetables should be in a grouping. If the entrée is to be served over rice, the rice should precede it. Place all sauces next to the dish they are to garnish. Salads, cheeses, and desserts come last.

Dishes requiring one large spoon or fork for serving facilitate movement and help guests with their juggling act. Leave space before a tossed salad for guests to set their plate down as both hands are needed for serving. Offer salt and pepper shakers — grinders take two hands. Serve drinks in light pitchers or carafes for one-handed pouring.

Desserts may be at one end of the table with the rest of meal, but an elaborate dessert makes a better showing if given a table to itself. All desserts are served after the main courses have been removed. For a small gathering a hostess might like to pass a simple dessert, saving the guests the trouble of getting up — particularly if they are seated on a couch where one person getting up would disturb the others.

Drinks are most efficiently served from a separate side table. As guests often prefer to find a seat and come back for drinks, the separate table cuts down on traffic confusion.

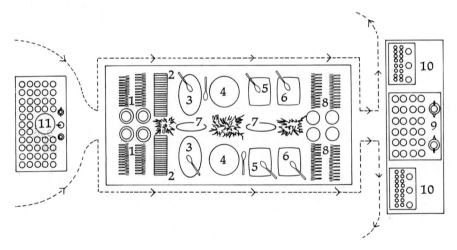

Duplicate Servings for a Large Buffet

For a large party two duplicate lines speed service. Each guest takes a plate, fork (1) (knives usually not needed), and napkin (2), then makes his way down the line; entrée (3), alternate entrée (4), vegetable (5), second vegetable (6), buttered biscuits (7), dessert plates and forks (8), and stops for beverages at the sideboard; water pitchers and glasses (9), and wine bottles and glasses (10). After the main course has been cleared away, two desserts will be placed on either side of the table and guests will proceed in the opposite direction from the main course, to end up at the coffee service (11).

Buffet Served from a Sideboard

When the buffet is small and seated, the sideboard is most convenient for serving. The dining table is completely set with napkins, silver, drinks, condiments, and breads — everything except the dinner plates (1). Guests proceed down the line: dish of rice (2) served under meat dish (3) with sauce (4) conveniently at hand. Salad (5) has space next to it for setting down plate (6) for serving. Cheese board (7) comes last. Candlesticks, figurines, or whatever ornaments decorate back (8). Arrangement at side gives asymmetric interest and doesn't crowd food. Dessert and plates will be brought after main course has been cleared.

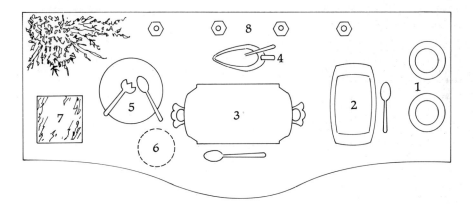

Buffet in the Round

A round buffet works well for a small gathering of eight where guests sit about the room. Dinner plates and forks (1). Meat dish (2). Pepper and salt shakers (3). Vegetable (4). Place to put plate (5) while serving salad (6). Bread (7). Napkins (8). Dessert plates and spoons (9). Demitasses (10). After the main course has been removed, dessert plates and spoons will be moved to position (1). Coffee pot, cream, and sugar will fill void between demitasses.

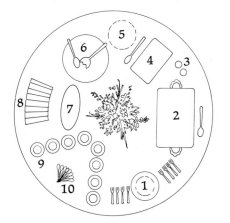

TANTALIZING TEA TABLES AND TRAYS

A tea can be as elegant as a formal reception to entertain a great number of people or as cozy as cinnamon toast before a fire with close friends. The secret is to brew a good pot, and set a tempting tray or table.

An afternoon tea at home is served by the hostess and is usually brought in from the kitchen already made. A bare tray, (never use a covering for tea), is arranged to make serving easy for the hostess. The teapot is at hand in the lower right and a jug of hot water nearby for those who like their tea weakened. Grouped behind the pot are a small plate of lemon slices, a small pitcher of milk (not cream for a serious tea drinker), and a bowl of lump sugar to its left. If loose tea is used, a strainer and waste bowl may be included on the tray. The tea plates with napkins between each and butter knives placed with handles facing the guests are stacked in the upper left. Teacups with saucers and spoons to the right may be stacked in two's (but not more), if necessary. Hot buttered toast, cake, or other tea fare are brought in afterward and put on the table.

For a formal at home tea, the tea is brewed at the table if one has a large hot-water kettle of silver or copper (1). The large water pot is kept warm over an alcohol burner so each guest gets a fresh cup of tea. A small amount of tea is taken from the caddy (2) and placed in the teapot (3) and hot water is added from the kettle. When a new pot of tea is needed the waste is turned into the dregs bowl (4). The lemon (5), sugar (6), milk (7), and strainer (8) remain on the tea tray which rests on a covered table. Teacups, saucers, and plates (9) are brought in on the tray then arranged around the table. They are stacked as follows: the plate with a small folded napkin on top, then the saucer, cup upside down, and spoon. If honey or butter are served (10), butter knives are placed on the plates parallel to the spoons. Buttered toast (11), jam or honey, and cookies or tea cakes (12) are traditional tea food. When cake is served, about a quarter of the whole cake is sliced and the knife left nearby so guests can cut the rest. Forks should not be necessary as most food is neatly eaten with the fingers but should be provided if icing is sticky.

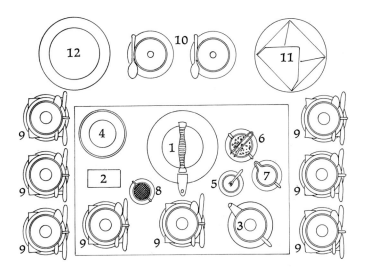

A table for a formal afternoon reception is usually the center of attraction and should be set accordingly. It may be bare or covered in a fine white or pastel cloth with an attractive arrangement of flowers, fruit, or decorative object. The food should be arranged for looks and convenience. If the table is small, it is better to place some food on a buffet or side table or bring it in as needed, than it is to overcrowd the table. The drawing below suggests an arrangement that allows guests to walk around the table. Tea (1) is served at one end and coffee or hot chocolate (2) at the other. Both trays are flanked by cups, saucers, and teaspoons. Tea plates (3) and tea napkins (4) arranged for easy pick up. Sandwiches, cookies, and small cakes (5) are conveniently located. A square cake cut for serving (6). Muffins or toast are kept warm in covered dishes (7).

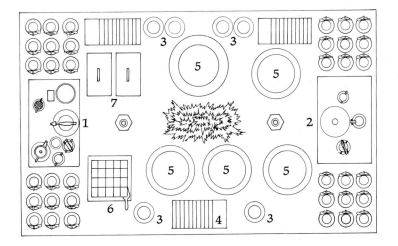

SELECTING AND CARING FOR TABLE LINENS

The table coverings you use may be as individual as you are imaginative. There are rules for table settings but none so rigid as to hamper your creativity. Your choice of table coverings is determined by the time of day, the formality of the occasion, the menu, the surroundings, and by you.

A covered table imparts a feeling of hospitality traceable, perhaps, to the 15th century when sharing the cloth with one's host indicated complete acceptance and equality. But use throughout history has tended more to the functional and decorative. A covering protects a beautiful table surface or hides a marred one. It ensures quieter service and reflects light. (In candlelight, pink is most becoming; in daylight, choose yellow.) Coverings, mats, or cloths, create a desired atmosphere and unify the components of the table setting.

A tablecloth is best when the meal is large and the dishes many. It gives a continuous background and prevents a cluttered look. By the same token, mats are preferable for intimate luncheons or when there are fewer guests and less food. The mats break the continuity, adding design and interest.

The size of the meal and the occasion should thus be a guide in the choice between mats or cloth. A flowered sheet might spread a table for a weekend brunch whereas embroidered mats of the finest linen could set a formal dinner for four. You can also achieve spectacular effects by using flowered, colored, or gaily bordered napkins with a plain cloth.

The innovators often prefer informal entertaining which gives them free reign on table appointments — provided all elements work as an ensemble. Patch work and paper plates are fine for picnics, homespun and pewter set a provincial table, and Chinese print runners and fine china complement a Chippendale decor. But a mix and match rarely will do.

Informal settings are fun and add variety and charm to entertaining, but the simplicity of a fine damask cloth is always in good taste. Formal settings should be distinguished and are best made so with damask for dinner, lighter linens for luncheons, and organdies and laces for teas.

Consider the purchase of linen an investment — one good is worth two mediocre — because the durability of fine linen offsets the cost. If colored linens are chosen for luncheons, check that they are vat-dyed or guaranteed colorfast. Linen is a difficult fiber to penetrate with a dye. For the same reason designs should be handblocked rather than printed.

The size cloth depends, of course, on your table but be sure to allow for the proper overhang — for buffet, 20 inches; formal dinners, 18 to 20 inches; formal luncheon or tea, 12 to 15 inches.

Napkin size varies as well. Formal dinner napkins may be a 22-inch square. Breakfast, luncheon, and tea napkins vary from 18 inches and smaller. The large dinner napkins are folded in thirds to form a rectangle not longer than the diameter of the service plate. All napkins are placed to the left of the fork, not under it. The luncheon, tea, or informal napkin is folded in a triangle and the two edges folded again to form a wedge.

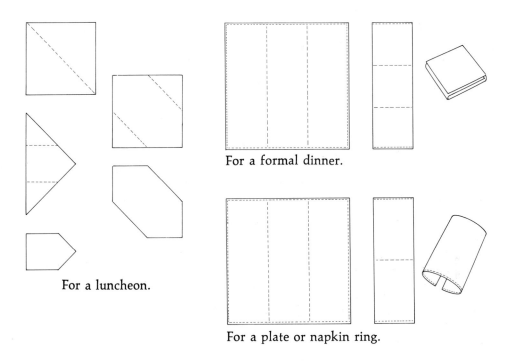

For a formal dinner.

For a luncheon.

For a plate or napkin ring.

Nowadays, many people use napkin rings as a means of dressing up napkins for an informal dinner party. But they are for decoration only. By all means, serve guests clean napkins at each meal.

Once you've chosen your fine linen, use it. It's tough. (It's the stuff mummies are wrapped in.) Linen is made from the long fiber inside the stalk of the flax plant. Due to the length of the fibers, linen is lint free: no short ends work out of the fabric to cling. The long fibers create a smooth unbroken surface which gives linen its luster and resiliency. Given the proper care linen will take on a lustrous finish that intensifies with use.

To ensure their permanence, never over starch your linens. The fibers are likely to crack. Extreme amounts of sunlight or bleach will cause the fibers to rot. And remember plant fibers tend to tear when rubbed or twisted and they prefer mild soaps to detergents.

For that lustrous sheen, iron your linens while damp on the wrong side with a moderately hot iron. Then turn them over and press lightly on the right side to "polish." Embroidered or lace inserts may be pressed wrong side up on a terrycloth towel. Never iron folds for fear of cracking fibers and shift the center crease to prevent a worn line. Often it is easiest to iron the cloth on the table, provided you have adequate padding. Table ironing also rids the cloth of storage folds. Only a center crease is permissable for a perfect formal table.

To prevent creasing, it is best to roll linens on a large dowel for storage. This can be done as you iron. If rolling is impossible, fold the linen, wrap it in blue paper and store it in a dark drawer to prevent yellowing. Napkins should be stored flat. If linens do yellow, restore whiteness by boiling in plain water. And to restore an antique look, dip linens in coffee.

Since linen does not possess a natural affinity for dyes it gives up stains readily. But do try to remove stains before laundering. Fresh stains are usually removed by soaking the fabric in cool water before washing in warm suds. Set stains may require special treatment.

Alcohol and soft drinks. Wash old stains in warm suds using a bleach.

Wine. Cover at once with salt and wash thoroughly afterwards. If the stains are old, rub with suds of laundry soap, coat thickly with powdered starch and bleach 2 hours in the sun. Repeat. Another solution is to soak the stain in milk.

Blood and baby foods. Use an enzyme presoak product of diluted ammonia, then wash the fabric in warm suds. Fresh blood stains should be soaked in cold water. If possible, do not launder beforehand since hot water sets the stain.

Butter, grease, and oil including foods with grease such as eggs, coffee with cream, and chocolate. Spray with a laundry pretreatment spray or sponge with cleaning agent, then wash as usual. To sponge, have an absorbent material under the cloth and drive the stain into it from above.

Catsup and tomato sauce. Soak fresh stains in cool water or use an enzyme presoak before washing. If stain persists, use a bleach. Rinse and rewash.

Candle wax. Remove excess wax with dull knife. Then place between two blotters and press with a warm iron. If stain remains, sponge with a dry cleaning fluid.

Tea and coffee without cream. Pour boiling water over stain and launder. Use bleach for any remaining stains.

Fruit juice. Stretch material over bowl and pour boiling water through stain. If stain remains, bleach.

Ink. Test first in lukewarm water for water-soluble ink. Soak out stain, then launder. If not water-soluble, sponge with a dry-cleaning agent or ink remover.

Lipstick or rouge. With a heavy stain, sponge with a dry cleaning agent. Brush with soap solution and launder.

Mildew. Launder and bleach.

Milk, cream, or ice cream. Soak in lukewarm water, then launder. If grease mark remains, sponge with dry-cleaning agent.

Rust. Treat with oxalic acid (available at pharmacy) or rub with salt and lemon juice and allow to set in the sun.

Scorch. First launder, then bleach. A deep scorch cannot be removed.

Grass stain. Sponge with dry-cleaning agent. Rub soap into fabric, then launder. Bleach if necessary.

It is nice to have a fine linen wardrobe but the lack of one should never prevent one from entertaining with elegance. Just remember to suit the setting to the menu and the mood.

DECORATING THE TABLE

One of the happiest aspects of modern entertaining is the relaxation of the old, rigid rules about table decorations.

No longer does the hostess feel compelled to phone the florist well in advance of a party to order a formal centerpiece, giving him the description of her china and linens, the color of her walls, draperies, and carpets. Nowadays the use of her ingenuity and imagination, and often whimsy or wit, are likely to elicit as many compliments as the food she serves.

Most hostesses have certain favorite decorative pieces — containers, bowls, figurines, carvings. Today's informal entertaining provides a wonderful opportunity for displaying originality in using whatever is at hand — tastefully and creatively.

If a party is served buffet-style where guests serve themselves and then are seated at a large table, a central table decoration is appropriate.

If the service is buffet-style and guests are seated at small tables set up wherever room permits, the main decoration may be placed at one end of the long buffet, provided there is room for it without crowding the platters of food. If the buffet table is pushed against the wall, a front-view arrangement (back to the wall) is practical.

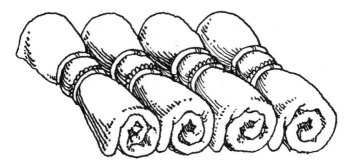

When guests are seated at small, set tables, decorations are unnecessary unless some theme is being carried out and appropriate accessories are used — but don't let them monopolize the eating space.

One of the loveliest table decorations I have ever seen was at the home of a talented hostess who had used an elaborately carved picture frame (minus the glass) which she had painted a flat blue-white. Inside the frame, completely filling the area, she had mounded clusters of deep blue hydrangeas in a shallow, invisible container. Magnificent! After the impact of that show-stopper, the food came in for some compliments too — but only afterwards.

Another hostess I know keeps a permanent centerpiece on her large cherry dining table, a beautiful handmade pottery candle lantern, surrounded by greens from her yard. When guests come, all she has to do is replenish the greens and light the candle. Instant decor!

One of my favorite centerpieces for a seated informal dinner when the entire party is seated at the same table is a centerpiece that is to be eaten as dessert. The washed and polished fresh fruit, any kind available, is piled high in a boat-shaped wooden bowl; everything in it is edible. During grape season it is especially beautiful, the bunches of grapes spilling over the oranges and pears and apples, giving a bountiful look even when the fruit underneath is not as varied as I would like it to be. A pair of fruit shears (for the grapes) is placed nearby as a mute reminder that the fruit is to be eaten. Sometimes a bowl of unshelled walnuts (warmed in a slow oven about an hour), with nutcracker provided, also lends informality as well as variety to the dessert. The cheese tray to accompany the fruit used as centerpiece and the small dessert plates with fruit knives may be brought in at dessert time, then everyone invited to help himself.

For formal entertaining, the lighted candles should be tall enough not to obstruct the view of the diners on the opposite side of the table. For casual entertaining an arrangement of short, chubby, lighted candles is not only practical but beautiful.

Most important of all is that whatever you plan to use, let that decision be made almost simultaneously with your decision to have a party. Regardless of how simple your decorations are to be, they should be thought through, then written down — for there is nothing so frustrating to the novice hostess as to awaken on party-day and start scurrying around trying to find something in bloom in the yard — or inexpensive greens at the florist. I have found that sudden inspiration seldom arrives on the day of a party — and last-minute table arrangements usually reflect the frustration and panic that inspired them.

SETTING THE TABLE

It has been said that in the study of painting one should know the rules so he can feel free to break them. Perhaps the same can be said about setting a table properly. Nevertheless, there are times in every hostess's life when she feels inclined to go a step or two beyond forks-to-the-left-knives-to-the-right. The following suggestions are designed to be helpful for both everyday table setting and those times when the hostess polishes up the silver and prepares to entertain with all the elegance at her command.

The knife, sharp edge inward, then the spoon should always be placed to the right of the dinner plate; the fork or forks to left. A general rule to follow is to place the silver according to how it is to be used, starting at the outside, away from the plate.

A dinner setting when salad is to be served as a first course should have a salad fork on the far left, since it will be used first. If the salad is to be served with the entrée on its own plate or as a separate course following the entrée (this custom is widely practiced in Europe), the salad fork should be on the inside, next to the plate. If an appetizer is served, an appetizer fork would go to the outside of the teaspoon or soup spoon, on the right.

The dessert fork or spoon is usually brought in with the dessert; another method is to place dessert silver (sometimes spoon and fork) at the top of the place setting, parallel with edge of table, with handle of spoon toward the right and handle of fork toward the left.

Bread-and-butter plates are set at the tip of the fork. The butter spreader is placed on the butter plate parallel to edge of the table with handle toward the right and blade toward edge of table.

All silver, napkins, and dishes are placed with bottom edge 1 inch from edge of table.

Properly set table. The salad fork placement indicates salad will be served following entrée.

Serving Salad: Some hostesses prefer to serve the salad following the main course. There are at least two good reasons for this: A classic green salad serves to "cleanse the palate", just as the old custom of serving a non-sweet sherbet following the main course (but before dessert) was used. Another reason is that while a salad served at this point in the dinner doesn't exactly constitute dessert, for those watching their diets, it could serve the purpose.

If salad is to be served in this manner, remove the dinner plate and used silver. In this case, the salad fork is logically placed next to the plate, to the right of the dinner fork.

When salad is served with the main course, on its own plate, the salad fork is placed to the left of the dinner fork.

Serving Coffee: Serve coffee with dessert at dinner table or later as demitasse in the living room. Coffee spoons are brought in with cups and saucers, wherever you choose to serve coffee.

SAYING GRACE

In the household where the custom is to say grace before meals and where dinner is being served buffet style, it seems awkward for the first guest seated to wait until he gets a cue from the hostess that dinner may begin.

I have found this a practical way of solving the problem: Just after dinner is announced but before the first guest in line has served himself, ask for a moment of silence. A brief word of grace is then pronounced, and from that moment on, it is understood that one may begin eating as soon as he is seated, whether at a large dining table where the entire company will be gathered or at a small table set up elsewhere. — C.M.

GIFTS FROM GUESTS

A token of appreciation, a thank-you-for-an-enjoyable-evening need be no more than a telephone call or a written note, but one should be given — at the very least when saying good night after the event. Houseguests should reply promptly with a written thank you.

Flowers sent the following day are also a nice gesture especially for first-time or out-of-town guests. Sent on the day of the occasion, flowers could be an inconvenience as they probably would not fit into the hostess' decorative plans, yet she may feel obligated to use them. However, a small bouquet offered upon arrival need not inconvenience her as she obviously has the house decorated. She may quickly arrange the flowers and place them on a table. Candy is often taken and a European custom is to offer a bottle of wine or "des petits fours," a variety of delicate bakery cookies.

Weekend guests usually take, or send later, a small gift for the house or something for the children. A bottle of liquor or wine could be offered to the host. A gift sent later often reflects a thoughtful guest who noticed something the hostess admired or needed. Large gifts are inappropriate and often embarrassing to the hostess who offers hospitality without expecting payment. Try instead to find a gift that will be useful or ornamental and that will make the hostess think fondly of a perfect guest.

CONVERSATION

If conversation lags it is the host's responsibility to get it going again. It's good to have a few subjects in mind to bring up for deadly lulls. But a new topic must be interjected so casually that conversation follows naturally. A question and debate forum will frighten all but the most outgoing and these may tend to dominate the conversation in any event.

If possible, draw a guest into conversation by talking about a subject which particularly interests him or her. Again, outright questions have a negative reaction. Instead, an opener might be an article, book, or late development you've read about the subject, then let the knowledgable guest respond and carry the conversation from there. In return, a guest should never indulge in a monologue but should try to bring others into the discussion.

When talk takes a turn to the controversial or unpleasant, the hosts should be there to guide it back. A conversation may be stimulating but never heated for the hosts are responsible for every guest's feelings and none should be insulted or demeaned while visiting in their home.

At larger parties the hosts should watch that no one is left out or that one of a tête-a-têté is less than interested. If one appears trapped, the host may take a third party over, engage him in the conversation with the unhappy member then adroitly lead the other to another group. On the other hand, don't be a hawk-eye or a hummingbird, let your guests move on their own initiative, too.

The secret of the strategy is subtlety. Never let the guests be aware that they're being maneuvered. Simple phraseology can make the difference. "Have you had an opportunity to meet . . ." is more inviting than "Come talk to . . ."

In a manner so facile as to be unnoticed, a host must engage the guests in order that they contribute their best. In this way, each gains and enjoys the knowledge of others and has the satisfaction of giving the same.

GREETINGS AND GOOD NIGHTS

Host and hostess should be ready to receive guests five or ten minutes before the hour. So if a guest is early, he need not feel his entry is inopportune. A good idea is to set your schedule up fifteen minutes. Say you invited guests for 6:30, plan and work throughout the day as if you were expecting them at 6:15 (except for last minute foods). That way you've a backlog of time in case of emergencies or simply more minutes to dress yourself and let a relaxed smile come through.

When guests arrive the host or hostess gives the opening greeting of welcome and invites the guest in. If there are wraps, the host hangs the men's in a hall closet and the hostess leads the ladies to a guest bedroom. Then the couples rejoin in the hall and enter the living room together. At a small party it is important for one, host or hostess, to remain with guests while the other greets new arrivals. The host usually tends to the drinks while the hostess introduces guests. For a large party, introductions about the room are unnecessary but a hostess should see that a newcomer is properly integrated with a group before leaving him to mingle further on his own. If there is a guest of honor, new arrivals are always introduced to them. Out-of-towners, newcomers, or particularly shy guests should be given special attention throughout the evening but a hostess should never be overbearing or insistent upon guiding these guests about.

When the hour to leave arrives, the guests express their thanks for the evening and take their leaves. (The guest of honor is first to go at a formal dinner.) Host and hostess should always notice when a guest departs, even at a large party. If they are engaged in conversation, they should excuse themselves and move to say good-bye. Both may accompany the guest to the door but in all events the host does. He should walk a single lady to her car and help her in or call a taxi if need be, or arrange for another guest to give her a ride home. In an apartment building the host walks guests to the elevator, rings for it and waits until it arrives. At a house, the host may walk to the drive with guests and does not shut the door until guests are in the car and on their way. The hostess need not join her husband.

GLASS SELECTION GUIDE

A. All-purpose 18-ounce glass is used for all wines.
B. Tulip-shaped champagne glass may also be used for aperitifs with soda.
C. Large 22-ounce burgundy glass may also be used for iced tea or beer.
D. Standard 12-ounce bordeaux glass may be used for other wines or mixed drinks.
E. Tapering 10-1/2-ounce burgundy glass is often used for a Bloody Mary or a cold vichyssoise.
F. Rounded 6-ounce sherry glass may be used as a cocktail glass.
G. Delicate 6-1/2-ounce champagne flute may be used to serve fruit juice.
H. Brandy inhaler could hold cocktails.
I. Chimney-shaped 5-ounce brandy glass may be used for liqueurs or straight whiskies.
J. Large 19-ounce tumbler is used for long drinks.
K. The 13-ounce tumbler serves any mixed drink.
L. Slender 19-ounce tumbler serves fruit punches or iced tea.
M. Large 13-ounce old-fashioned glass is used for any drink on the rocks.

Cocktail Parties and Cocktail Suppers

The cocktail party is possibly the easiest and most misunderstood way to entertain a large group of people. The party may begin anywhere from 5 o'clock on, and the invitation may or may not state the hour. If the guest list is large, groups may be invited for a two hour period, but don't be surprised if a few guests have such a good time that they stay through the first list and mingle with the second group of guests.

Guests are given a choice of food, the hors d'oeuvres may be placed on one table, or at several vantage points for better serving of guests. Since guests usually have to stand at cocktail parties, pick-up foods are served. It's wise to have a choice of these tidbits, and be sure to have plenty of each kind.

A cocktail supper is usually held for a specific group; guests at a wedding reception, or for friends who are going to a concert afterwards. Hot foods are often served from chafing dishes at this type party, and in addition to these hot foods the hostess may serve the usual dips and open-face sandwiches.

In both type entertainments the bar, serving both alcoholic and non-alcoholic beverages, should be set apart from the table serving the hors d'oeuvres.

Deep South Cocktail Party

COCKTAIL PARTY FOR TWENTY

Chicken Magnolia with Toast Points
Cold Sliced Peppered Beef with Thin-Sliced Rye Bread

Mustard Sauce   **Cherry Tomatoes**

Pickled Okra

Dill Pickle Slices   **Celery Curls**

Bertha Marks's Cucumbers

Olives   **Green Onions**

Assorted Cheeses with Crackers

Marzipan Cupcakes   **Chocolate-Walnut Squares**

Coffee

Provide a pitcher of chilled tomato juice or similar non-sweet, non-alcoholic beverage for diet-conscious guests.

CREAMED CHICKEN MAGNOLIA
(may be prepared the day before)

This is an excellent, old-fashioned creamed chicken that is ideal for buffet service. Small toast triangles make a good foundation.

Cook a 5- to 6-pound hen or small turkey the day before using. Cut meat into 1-inch pieces, pour about a cup or more chicken broth over it to retain moisture and refrigerate until ready to use.

3 tablespoons butter	1/4 teaspoon ground nutmeg
7 tablespoons all-purpose flour	1/8 teaspoon cayenne pepper
2 cups warm chicken broth	1/2 teaspoon paprika
2 cups warm light cream or milk	4 hard-cooked eggs, diced
Salt and pepper to taste	About 4 cups cooked chicken
1 teaspoon dry mustard	1 (8-ounce) can water chestnuts, drained and sliced
1/8 teaspoon Accent	1/4 cup Madeira or sherry
1/2 teaspoon sugar	*mushrooms*
1 teaspoon seasoned salt	

Melt butter in saucepan; blend in flour until smooth. Slowly add broth and cream, stirring until smooth. Cook until thickened, stirring constantly. Add all seasonings. Cook for a minute or two to blend; then place over hot water. Fold in eggs, chicken, water chestnuts, and wine; mix well. Keep warm until serving time, then transfer to large chafing dish (or to a casserole placed over heating device). Yield: 8 to 10 servings; double the recipe for a cocktail party for about 20.

Note: For a luncheon, chicken may be served in patty shells. It may be extended by adding a pound of sliced fresh mushrooms sautéed in butter, or canned mushrooms, drained and sautéed.

PEPPERED BEEF

1/4 cup coarsely ground black pepper	Marinade
1 teaspoon ground cardamom (optional)	Thin-sliced rye bread
1 (4- to 5-pound) boneless brisket of beef	

Combine pepper and cardamom and spread evenly on sheet of waxed paper. Place beef firmly over the mixture, press down; turn beef over. With heel of hand, press pepper mixture firmly down into the meat. Try to cover both sides evenly and thoroughly, using all the pepper mixture.

Marinade

2/3 cup soy sauce	1 teaspoon paprika
1/2 cup vinegar	1 clove garlic, crushed
1 tablespoon tomato paste or catsup	

Combine all ingredients. Place meat in shallow dish and pour marinade over it, cover and refrigerate overnight, turning meat occasionally. (You may place meat in a heavy plastic bag and pour marinade over it. Tie top of bag securely and turn occasionally.)

When ready to cook, remove meat from marinade and wrap securely in aluminum foil. Place in shallow pan and bake at 300° for about 3 hours, or until meat is quite tender. You'll be astonished how well the pepper remains on the surface of the meat. Excellent served cold. Yield: about 8 servings. For a cocktail party for about 20, where a variety of hors d'oeuvres will be offered, 1 (6-pound) roast should be enough — sliced very thin.

Variation: This method is also excellent for a rib eye of beef. The same proportions of pepper and marinade may be used for a 4- to 6-pound cut. In this case, for medium-rare beef, remove from oven after 1-1/2 hours (or use a meat thermometer). Place the meat under broiler for a minute or two for a more attractive crust.

MUSTARD SAUCE FOR COLD ROAST BEEF

1/2 cup mayonnaise	1/2 cup heavy cream, whipped
2 tablespoons prepared yellow mustard	Salt to taste

Fold mayonnaise and prepared yellow mustard into heavy cream. Add salt to taste. Yield: 10 servings; double the recipe to serve 20.

PICKLED OKRA

Garlic (1 clove for each jar)
Hot pepper (1 for each jar)
Okra
Dill seed (1 teaspoon for each jar)

1 quart white vinegar
1 cup water
1/2 cup salt

Place the garlic and hot pepper in the bottom of clean, hot pint jars. Pack firmly with clean, young okra pods from which only part of the stem has been removed. Stem end must be open. Add dill seed.

After packing jars, bring vinegar, water, and salt to a boil. Simmer about 5 minutes and pour, while boiling hot, over the okra. Seal the jars immediately. This amount of pickling solution will fill from 5 to 7 pint jars.

BERTHA MARKS'S CUCUMBERS

3 large cucumbers
2 teaspoons salt
1 large onion, quartered and sliced
2 tablespoons salad oil

1/4 teaspoon black pepper
1/4 teaspoon sugar
2/3 cup vinegar

Peel cucumbers and slice very thin. Place in layers in shallow bowl, sprinkling salt between layers. Cover with a plate and weight the plate down with a heavy object. Allow to stand at room temperature for about 2 hours. Drain well, gently pressing liquid from the cucumbers with palms of hands. Put in large jar with tight-fitting cover and add onions. Combine oil, pepper, sugar, and vinegar; stir well and pour over cucumbers and onions. If dressing does not cover the vegetables, add vinegar until it does. Chill for 12 hours before serving. Excellent with beef. Yield: 6 to 8 servings as a condiment; double the recipe for a cocktail party for about 20.

MARZIPAN CUPCAKES
(may be prepared ahead of time)

1/3 cup butter (no substitute)
1/4 cup powdered sugar
1 egg yolk

1/4 teaspoon almond extract
1 cup all-purpose flour

Cream butter and sugar well in bowl of electric mixer; add egg yolk and almond extract; mix well. Blend in flour, then chill about an hour for easier handling. Pinch off marble-size pieces and press into bottom and sides of tiny ungreased muffin tins. Bake at 375° for 7 to 8 minutes.

Filling

1/3 cup butter (no substitute)
1/2 (8-ounce) can almond paste
1/2 cup granulated sugar
2 eggs

1/2 teaspoon almond extract
3/4 cup powdered sugar
Orange or lemon juice
1/4 teaspoon almond extract

Cream butter with almond paste until well blended; beat in 1/2 cup granulated sugar thoroughly. Blend in eggs and 1/2 teaspoon almond extract. Spoon into each baked shell, then bake at 350° for 20 minutes. While tarts bake, prepare a thin frosting by combining 3/4 cup powdered sugar with orange or lemon juice and about 1/4 teaspoon almond flavoring. Drizzle over outer edges of warm cakes. Bake ahead of time and freeze. Yield: 36 tiny cupcakes; double the recipe for a cocktail party for about 20.

CHOCOLATE-WALNUT SQUARES
(may be prepared ahead of time)

Crust

3/4 cup finely chopped walnuts	3 tablespoons sugar
3 tablespoons all-purpose flour	3 tablespoons soft butter

Combine walnuts, flour, and sugar in a bowl. Blend in soft butter. Press mixture over bottom of ungreased 9-inch square pan.

Filling

1/2 cup butter or margarine	1 teaspoon vanilla extract
1 cup sugar	1/3 cup all-purpose flour
3 eggs	1/2 teaspoon baking powder
2 squares unsweetened chocolate, melted	1/8 teaspoon salt

Place all ingredients in large bowl of electric mixer. Mix at low speed until smooth; pour over Crust. Bake at 325° for 35 to 40 minutes.

Chocolate Glaze

1/2 cup semi-sweet chocolate bits	1/4 teaspoon vanilla extract
2 tablespoons butter or margarine	

Melt chocolate with butter over warm water. Add vanilla and stir until smooth. Spread over cooled cake. Sprinkle top with more chopped nuts if desired. When Glaze has set, cut into 1- or 1-1/2-inch squares. Yield: about 36 squares.

ASHTRAY TIP

If you own large decorative ashtrays which aren't easily identifiable as ashtrays, before guests come take a puff or two of a cigarette, extinguish it and leave it on the tray.

Party Meatballs Cocktail Party

COCKTAIL PARTY FOR TWENTY

Party Meatballs in Chafing Dish

Salmon Ball with Melba Rounds

Sesame Pork Strips　　　　　　　**Hot Cheese Toast**

Curried Crabmeat with Toast Triangles

Filled Date Bars　　　　　　**Butterscotch Brownies**

Coffee

Provide a pitcher of chilled tomato juice or similar non-sweet, non-alcoholic beverage for diet-conscious guests.

A Silk Purse Menu — Looks and tastes expensive, but isn't.

PARTY MEATBALLS
(may be prepared ahead of time)

2 tablespoons butter or margarine	1 teaspoon seasoned salt
1/2 cup finely minced onion	1/2 teaspoon grated lemon rind
1-1/2 pounds ground meat (equal parts beef, veal, and pork)	1 teaspoon freshly squeezed lemon juice
2 slices white bread	1 tablespoon Worcestershire sauce
2 eggs	1/2 teaspoon anchovy paste
3 tablespoons minced fresh parsley, or 1 tablespoon dried parsley	About 2 tablespoons salad oil
1/4 teaspoon paprika	3-1/2 cups beef broth (bouillon cubes and hot water may be used)
1/4 teaspoon freshly ground black pepper	Sauce

Heat butter in large skillet or Dutch oven. Add onion and sauté until yellow. Put meat in large bowl. Soak bread in water, squeeze dry and add to meat. Add onions and all other ingredients except oil and broth. Mix thoroughly, using a wooden spoon or your hands. Form into 1-inch balls and brown in heated oil. Remove to paper towels to drain. Strain fat from skillet, reserving the "crustlings" (brown bits that cling to the skillet) if they aren't scorched.

Heat the broth in same skillet and bring to boiling point. Add meatballs, cover and simmer for 15 minutes. Remove meatballs and prepare Sauce. Place balls in Sauce and heat gently for about 30 minutes. Transfer to chafing dish just before serving.

Sauce
(may be prepared ahead of time)

4 tablespoons butter or margarine	1 tablespoon minced parsley
4 tablespoons all-purpose flour	1 teaspoon freshly squeezed
2-1/2 cups meatball liquid	lemon juice
1 tablespoon drained capers	

Heat butter or margarine in large skillet. Blend in flour until smooth and barely golden. Gradually add 2-1/2 cups of the liquid left from cooking meatballs. Cook, stirring constantly, until smooth. Add drained capers and minced parsley, then lemon juice. May be prepared ahead and frozen. Yield: 6 to 8 servings; double the recipe to serve 20. That amount should be sufficient for this menu, since a variety of other hors d'oeuvres will be served.

SALMON BALL
(may be prepared the day before)

1 (1-pound) can red salmon	1/2 teaspoon salt
1 (8-ounce) package cream cheese	Dash Worcestershire sauce
2 tablespoons freshly squeezed lemon juice	Several dashes cayenne pepper
3 teaspoons grated onion	1/4 teaspoon commercial liquid smoke
2 teaspoons horseradish	1/2 cup chopped pecans
	3 tablespoons minced fresh parsley

Drain salmon, remove skin and bones, and flake with fork. In small bowl of electric mixer, cream cheese and blend in lemon juice, onion, horseradish, salt, Worcestershire sauce, cayenne pepper, and liquid smoke (this is important). When well blended, stir in the flaked salmon. Check seasonings; it might require a little more salt.

Combine pecans and parsley and spread on a sheet of waxed paper. Turn salmon out onto this mixture and turn it this way and that until all sides of the mound are coated. Wrap in the waxed paper and chill thoroughly before using. The mixture will not be sliceable but will spread nicely when chilled. Yield: 10 servings; make two rolls for a cocktail party of about 20.

WHO TO INVITE

A thoughtful hostess tries to invite groups who may have something in common, people she feels will be compatible even though they may not know each other well. If she knows that the views of a certain person are distasteful to the group as a whole, she should omit him from that party and perhaps invite him for another time — or as a guest to a large party where guests will be varied and he will probably be more comfortable.

SESAME PORK STRIPS

About 1-1/2 pounds pork steak or pork
  filets, cut about 1/2 inch thick
1/4 cup soy sauce
  1 tablespoon honey
  2 to 3 tablespoons dry sherry
  Several grinds black pepper

1/2 teaspoon powdered ginger
  1 clove garlic, crushed
  2 tablespoons toasted sesame seed
  Chicken broth (bouillon cube and
  hot water)

Trim all fat from pork. Place in shallow glass dish. Combine all ingredients
except broth. Pour over pork and marinate for 2 to 3 hours at room temperature,
turning often. Drain off liquid, saving the seed to pat on meat. Roast uncovered
at 350° for about 45 minutes, turning frequently and basting with chicken
broth. Do not use marinade for basting; it's too salty.

When pork is tender, remove from oven and cut into small diagonal slices
to be speared on cocktail picks and served with drinks. The pork is best served
at room temperature; don't chill it unless you must prepare it the day before.
If so, remove from refrigerator and allow to warm to room temperature.
Yield: 6 to 8 servings; double or triple the recipe to serve 20.

Note: To toast sesame seed, put in shallow pan and bake at 275° for
about 20 minutes.

HOT CHEESE TOAST
(may be prepared for baking the day before)

  8 slices bacon
1/3 cup mayonnaise
  1 cup shredded sharp Cheddar cheese
  1 small onion, grated
  1 egg, lightly beaten

Freshly ground black pepper
1/8 teaspoon dry mustard
1/2 teaspoon Worcestershire sauce
  Several dashes Tabasco sauce
  8 slices firm white day-old bread

Cook bacon by placing on a rack over a shallow pan and bake at 350° for
about 20 minutes, or until crisp. Drain on paper towels and set aside.

Combine all ingredients except bread in a bowl. Crumble bacon and add
to mixture; set aside.

Cut crusts from bread slices and toast on both sides. Spread each slice
generously with cheese mixture; then cut each slice into three long strips.
Sprinkle with paprika; place on baking sheet, cover with waxed paper and
refrigerate. This may be done the day before. Remove from refrigerator 30
minutes before ready to bake; bake at 350° for about 20 minutes, or until light
brown and puffy. Serve hot. Yield: 24 strips; double the recipe for a cocktail
party of 20.

Note: These strips are quite filling. For a daintier appetizer, cut strips in half
before baking. These are delicious and versatile, providing a good luncheon or
brunch dish. They should be served with sliced tomatoes and garnished with
parsley clusters; in which case, serve two whole bread slices per person,
not cutting into strips.

CURRIED CRABMEAT SPREAD

1/2 pound crabmeat (fresh, or canned, drained)	2 teaspoons grated onion
1/4 cup mayonnaise	1 tablespoon minced fresh parsley
2 tablespoons commercial sour cream	1 teaspoon curry powder
	Salt and pepper to taste

Pick over crabmeat, discarding any cartilage. Shread the meat, then blend with all ingredients. Taste for seasoning; serve with thin buttered toast, crisp crackers, or melba rounds. Yield: 10 servings; double recipe for a cocktail party for 20.

TOAST TRIANGLES
(see Index)

FILLED DATE BARS

2 cups all-purpose flour	1 teaspoon soda
2 cups quick-cooking oatmeal	1 cup brown sugar
1/4 teaspoon salt	3/4 cup butter or margarine

Put all ingredients except butter into bowl. Cut in butter until mixture resembles cornmeal. Pat half of mixture in an ungreased 12- x 8- x 2-inch pan.

Filling

1 (8-ounce) package pitted dates, chopped	1 cup granulated sugar
	1 cup water

Combine all ingredients in a saucepan; heat until sugar has dissolved and dates are soft; the mixture should be thick and mushy. Spread over dough in pan, then cover with remaining dry mixture, patting the top layer smoothly. Bake at 325° for about 40 minutes, or until lightly browned. Watch carefully as they will scorch easily. Cut into bars while warm. Yield: 24 bars.

BUTTERSCOTCH BROWNIES

2 (6-ounce) packages butterscotch bits	1-1/4 teaspoons salt
1/2 cup butter or margarine	1 teaspoon baking powder
4 eggs	2 cups chopped nuts (pecans, walnuts, or mixed)
1 cup light brown sugar	
1-1/2 cups all-purpose flour, sifted	

Melt butterscotch bits with butter over hot (not boiling) water. Remove from heat. Beat eggs with sugar in large bowl of electric mixer until light and fluffy. Sift in flour, salt, and soda; beat until blended. Add melted butterscotch mixture, then stir in nuts. Pour into lightly greased 15- x 10- x 1-inch jellyroll pan and bake at 350° for 25 minutes. Cool and cut into squares or bars. Yield: about 50 brownies.

Sausage Balls Cocktail Supper

COCKTAIL SUPPER FOR FIFTY

Sausage Balls

Rice Salad with Caviar and Sour Cream Topped Deviled Eggs

Olives   Cauliflower Flowerets

Celery Sticks with Tomato-Horseradish Sauce

Cherry Tomatoes   Sesame Seed Sticks

Clam Dip with Toast Fingers

Toffee Bars   Walnut Balls

Coffee

Provide a pitcher of chilled tomato juice or similar non-sweet, non-alcoholic beverage for diet-conscious guests.

SAUSAGE BALLS
(may be prepared ahead of time)

1 pound hot or mild bulk pork sausage
1 egg, slightly beaten
1/3 cup seasoned breadcrumbs (dry packaged herbed stuffing)
1/4 teaspoon ground sage
1/4 cup catsup
1/4 cup chili sauce
1 tablespoon soy sauce
2 tablespoons brown sugar
1 tablespoon vinegar
1/2 cup water

Combine first four ingredients and mix thoroughly. Shape into balls the size of a quarter. Brown on all sides in dry skillet; drain on paper towels. Drain fat from skillet, then add catsup, chili sauce, soy sauce, brown sugar, vinegar, and 1/2 cup water. Stir well, return meatballs to skillet, cover and simmer for 30 minutes. Refrigerate or freeze. When ready to serve, reheat, place in chafing dish and serve with cocktail picks. Yield: approximately 36 balls; triple the recipe for a cocktail supper for about 50.

Note: The first time I made these I used half mild and half hot sausage; the next time, one part hot to three parts mild and that seemed perfect.—C.M.

RICE SALAD
(may be prepared the day before)

2 cups regular rice
2 stalks celery, minced
2 green onion tops, minced
2 tablespoons minced ripe olives

1/2 green pepper, diced
Slivered almonds
Cooked shrimp (optional)
Dressing

Boil rice using your favorite method and refrigerate. When chilled, combine with all other ingredients and refrigerate until time to combine with Dressing.

Dressing

1/2 cup mayonnaise
1 tablespoon soy sauce
1/2 teaspoon freshly squeezed lemon juice

1/4 teaspoon curry powder
Tomato wedges
Parsley clusters

Mix dressing ingredients and pour over rice. Toss well and serve garnished with tomato wedges and parsley clusters. Yield: 8 to 10 servings; double the recipe but omit shrimp for this cocktail supper for about 50.

DEVILED EGGS
(may be prepared ahead of time)

8 eggs
3 tablespoons mayonnaise
1/2 teaspoon seasoned salt
1 teaspoon prepared yellow mustard

1/2 teaspoon freshly squeezed lemon juice
Several dashes Tabasco sauce
Salt and pepper to taste
Paprika and minced parsley (optional)

Boil eggs for 20 minutes; plunge into cold water. When cool enough to handle, shell and slice in half lengthwise. Scoop out yolks and mash with fork. Add remaining ingredients except paprika and parsley and blend well. Replace in whites and garnish if desired. Yield: 8 servings; triple the recipe to serve 50.

Variation: For caviar and sour cream-topped eggs, add 2 teaspoons scraped onion to filling mixture and after stuffing the whites, spread top of egg with a little sour cream and top with a tiny peak of red or black caviar.

TOMATO-HORSERADISH SAUCE
(may be prepared ahead of time)

1 cup catsup
1/2 cup mayonnaise
2 tablespoons horseradish
2 teaspoons Worcestershire sauce

2 tablespoons freshly squeezed lemon juice
Several dashes cayenne pepper
Salt to taste

Combine all ingredients, chill and use as a dip for raw vegetables or seafood. May be made a day or two before party. Yield: about 1-3/4 cups; double the recipe to serve 50.

SESAME SEED STICKS
(may be prepared ahead of time)

3/4 cup butter or margarine
2 cups all-purpose flour
1 teaspoon salt

2 dashes cayenne pepper
Ice water
1 cup sesame seed

Cut shortening into flour sifted with salt and pepper. Sprinkle ice water over dough and toss with fork until dough holds together, as for pastry. Roll out on floured board to 1/8-inch thickness and cut into strips 1 x 3 inches. Place on ungreased baking sheet, sprinkle generously with sesame seed and bake at 325° for about 15 minutes. Before removing from pan and while still hot, sprinkle with a little salt. May be frozen. For a cocktail supper for about 50, triple the recipe.

CLAM DIP
(may be prepared the day before)

2 (7-ounce) cans clams
1/2 cup mayonnaise
2 tablespoons freshly squeezed
   lemon juice
Salt and Tabasco sauce to taste

12 ounces cream cheese
2 tablespoons minced chives
2 tablespoons minced green
   stuffed olives
Toast fingers

Drain clams. Combine mayonnaise and lemon juice; add salt and Tabasco to taste. Mash cheese; blend in mayonnaise mixture. Stir in chives, clams, and olives; mix well and chill before serving with thin toast fingers. May be made the day before using. For a cocktail supper for about 50, prepare 1-1/2 times the recipe.

TOFFEE BARS
(may be prepared ahead of time)

1 cup butter or margarine
1 cup brown sugar
1 teaspoon vanilla extract
1 teaspoon maple extract (optional)
2 cups all-purpose flour, sifted
   after measuring

Dash salt
1 (6-ounce) package semi-sweet
   chocolate bits
1 cup coarsely chopped walnuts
   or pecans

Cream butter, sugar, and flavorings thoroughly in large bowl of electric mixer. Add flour and salt; mix well. Stir in chocolate bits and nuts and spread in ungreased 15- x 10- x 1-inch pan. Bake at 325° for 25 minutes, or until lightly browned. While warm, cut in 1- x 2-inch bars and cool in pan.

These are delicious cookies, remaining crisp in an airtight tin. In spreading dough in pan, be sure that edges of dough are slightly thicker than in center; when edges are thin they tend to brown more quickly than rest of dough. Yield: about 56 bars; double the recipe for a cocktail supper for about 50.

WALNUT BALLS
(may be prepared ahead of time)

1 **cup butter or margarine**	1 **teaspoon vanilla extract**
1/4 **cup granulated sugar**	2 **cups coarsely chopped walnuts**
2 **cups all-purpose flour**	**Powdered sugar**

Cream butter in large bowl of electric mixer, add sugar and beat until light and fluffy. Sift in flour, add vanilla and beat until smooth. Stir in walnuts. Form into balls about the size of a quarter; place on greased baking sheet. Bake at 300° for 25 to 30 minutes, watching carefully to avoid overbaking. The cookies should not be allowed to brown. When done, roll in powdered sugar and store in airtight container. Freezes beautifully. Yield: 60 to 65 cookies; double the recipe for cocktail supper for about 50.

DOUBLE THE RECIPE

Throughout this book you will find recipes with proportions that will not serve the number of guests for which the menu is planned. At the end of these recipes you will see the suggestion "double the recipe," sometimes "triple the recipe."

In planning the section on serving a number of guests, I was tempted to increase the original recipes in order to agree with the number of guests. And then I remembered; not all kitchens are equipped to handle large quantities of food; the utensils and other equipment available are not always large enough to accommodate a doubled recipe; even when they are, and assuming your arm holds out, it is harder to blend flavors thoroughly, achieve desired texture, season subtly and fold in uniformly when you are handling a large volume of foods. I therefore resisted the temptation to tamper with what I knew to be manageable quantities for the average home kitchen, especially when the hostess must do the work herself.

You may find it practicable to double or triple a recipe with the utensils (and strength) you have. But in some cases you may find it easier to prepare the recipe several times in order to end up with an adequate amount to serve a sizeable group. Also, this will allow you to better control the seasoning. — C.M.

Traditional Cocktail Supper

COCKTAIL SUPPER FOR TWENTY

Poached Sausage Slices

Sliced Baked Ham Piquante with Party Rye Bread and Dijon Mustard

Mrs. Chandler's Potato Salad   **Swiss Cheese Slices**

Dill Pickle Slices

Tomato Stacks in Italian Dressing

Congo Squares   **Overnight Meringues**

Coffee

Provide a pitcher of chilled tomato juice or similar non-sweet, non-alcoholic beverage for diet-conscious guests.

POACHED SAUSAGE

Place a 2-1/2- to 3-pound sausage (I use one marked "summer sausage;" any kind may be used) in a heavy pot. Cover with cold water; bring to boil, cover and simmer for 45 minutes. Remove, drain on paper towels, and slice thinly.

I find this sausage infinitely better if served just warm or at room temperature and suggest that it be poached about 2 hours before serving. For a cocktail supper menu, unmold potato salad and surround with sliced Poached Sausage.— C. M.

BAKED HAM PIQUANTE

1 (16-pound) whole, tenderized ham
3 tablespoons peanut butter
3 tablespoons prepared yellow mustard
1-1/2 cups brown sugar
About 2 tablespoons sweet pickle juice
Pineapple slices
About 24 whole cloves

First, remove most of the skin from the ham, leaving only a small portion at the hock end. Soften peanut butter with wooden spoon and gradually blend in mustard, brown sugar, and pickle juice. Taste to be sure no one flavor predominates, least of all the peanut butter. Spread over entire ham and place in covered roaster. Do not add water or other liquid. Bake at 350° until tender, about 15 minutes to the pound.

When ham is done, remove cover and place pineapple slices over top. (Anchor the slices with wooden picks and remove them before serving.) Stick whole cloves into the slices, using about 2 dozen. Bake 30 minutes longer uncovered, just until pineapple is slightly brown. Baste with the liquid that has collected in the roaster.

MRS. CHANDLER'S POTATO SALAD
(must be prepared the day before)

8 boiled medium potatoes (in jackets)	1/2 teaspoon salt
1-1/2 cups mayonnaise	1 cup fresh chopped parsley (do not
1 cup commercial sour cream	omit or decrease)
1-1/2 teaspoons horseradish	2 medium onions, finely minced;
1 teaspoon celery seed	or 1 (2-ounce) carton frozen chives

Peel potatoes; cut in 1/8-inch slices. Combine mayonnaise, sour cream, horseradish, celery seed, and salt; set aside. In another bowl mix parsley and onion.

In large serving bowl arrange layer of potatoes; salt lightly; cover with layer of mayonnaise-sour cream mixture, then layer of onion mixture. Continue layering, ending with parsley and onion. Do not stir! Cover and refrigerate at least 8 hours before serving; the salad is better if made the day before. Yield: 8 to 10 servings; double the recipe for a cocktail supper for about 20.

TOMATO STACKS
(prepare ahead of time)

Peel large ripe tomatoes and slice about 1/4 inch thick, allowing half a tomato per person. Place in large shallow dish; sprinkle each slice with half a teaspoon minced chives. Drizzle sparingly with Italian Dressing; repeat layering of tomatoes, chives, and dressing until you have three layers.

The stacks of three are to be served as a salad on a bed of lettuce, the platter garnished with clusters of parsley. Provide a flat serving piece for easy handling.

ITALIAN DRESSING
(may be prepared ahead of time)

1/3 cup tarragon vinegar	2/3 cup salad or olive oil
1 teaspoon salt	1 clove garlic, slashed
1 teaspoon dry mustard	2 teaspoons drained capers
1 teaspoon paprika	1/2 teaspoon dried oregano
1/4 teaspoon freshly ground black pepper	1/2 teaspoon minced parsley

Combine vinegar, salt, dry mustard, paprika, and pepper in a jar with tight cover. Shake until salt is dissolved. Add oil, shake again, then garlic, capers, oregano, and parsley. Give the jar a good final shake, then let dressing stand until needed. Before using, remove garlic and shake the jar again. Yield: about 1 cup.

CONGO SQUARES

2-1/2 cups all-purpose flour, measured
    before sifting
1-1/2 teaspoons baking powder
  1/2 teaspoon salt
  2/3 cup butter or margarine
2-1/4 cups light or dark brown sugar

3 eggs
2 teaspoons freshly squeezed
  lemon juice
1 cup broken pecans
1 (6-ounce) package semi-sweet
  chocolate bits

Combine flour, baking powder, and salt; set aside. Melt butter in large saucepan; remove from heat. Stir in sugar, then eggs, one at a time, beating well after each addition. Beat in lemon juice, then sifted dry ingredients, pecans, and chocolate bits. Blend well. Spread in greased 12- x 8- x 2-inch pan and bake at 350° for 25 to 30 minutes. Do not overbake; remove as soon as done. Cut into 1-1/2-inch squares while warm; remove from pan when cool. Freezes well. Yield: 35 squares; double the recipe for a cocktail supper for about 20.

OVERNIGHT MERINGUES
(see Index)

OUR SECRET — THE SILK PURSE MENUS

Let's conspire, you and I; let's engage in a little harmless conspiracy, secure in the belief that: "It takes much cleverness to know how to conceal cleverness."

This book doesn't claim that elegance can be produced from pennies or that you can make a silk purse of a menu from a sow's ear of provisions. This is an honest and realistic book; no evasions and no euphemisms, so let's face it. There are times when all of us must consider cost in planning our entertaining. The *silk purses* (menus that look and taste expensive, but aren't) are planned for just such times.

Remember, the successful party is one where food, important as it undoubtedly is, plays a secondary role to the general atmosphere created by the welcoming hostess. When such warmth and graciousness are present, then the choice of a menu may be governed by considerations of cost with no sacrifice of either good taste or pride. Certainly, the specter of an overdrawn bank account won't contribute to the serenity of a hostess. Agreed?

So for those times when we all look for menus planned with an eye toward "frugal elegance," we have designed the *silk purse* menus. They're scattered throughout the book, in most categories. Have fun with them. — C.M.

Beef Filet Cocktail Party

COCKTAIL PARTY FOR TWENTY

Sliced Filet of Beef with Horseradish Sauce

Fine White Bread   **Thin-Sliced Dark Rye Bread**

Whipped Butter

Assorted Cheeses and Crackers

Frosted Fudge Squares   **Creole Porcupines**

Coffee

Provide a pitcher of chilled tomato juice or similar non-sweet, non-alcoholic beverage for diet-conscious guests.

FILET OF BEEF
(may be prepared the day before)

Marinate a 3- to 4-pound beef filet at room temperature for several hours, using a marinade of red wine (Burgundy or Madeira), Worcestershire sauce, juice of 1 lemon, and some freshly ground black pepper. (The exact proportions aren't important; I would suggest a cup of wine and a tablespoon Worcestershire sauce along with the other ingredients.)

Heat 1/2 cup butter (no substitute) in skillet and brown filet well on all sides. Remove to shallow roasting pan, insert a meat thermometer into thickest part and place in a 375° oven uncovered, and bake until desired degree of doneness.

This beef is served to best advantage at room temperature, sliced very thin. If this is not practical, prepare the meat the day before serving, chill and slice cold, then let it attain room temperature. For a cocktail supper for about 20, double the recipe.

HORSERADISH SAUCE

1/4 cup drained prepared horseradish   **1 cup commercial sour cream**
1/2 teaspoon salt

Combine horseradish, salt, and sour cream. Cover and chill until ready to serve. Yield: 6 to 8 servings; double the recipe for a cocktail supper for about 20.

FINE WHITE BREAD
(see Index)

FROSTED FUDGE SQUARES

3-1/2 ounces unsweetened chocolate
3/4 cup butter or margarine
4 eggs
2 cups sugar
1/2 teaspoon salt

1 teaspoon vanilla extract
1 cup all-purpose flour, sifted
1-1/2 cups broken pecans (or pecans and walnuts mixed)

Melt chocolate and butter together in top of double boiler; cool. Using wooden spoon, beat eggs slightly, gradually adding sugar, salt, and vanilla. Stir in cooled chocolate. Sift flour over nuts, mix thoroughly, then add to batter. Stir only enough to combine; pour into greased 12- x 8- x 2-inch pan and bake at 325° for 35 to 40 minutes. Frost with Quick Frosting or Favorite Brownie Frosting and cut into squares while warm. Yield: 40 (1-1/2-inch) squares.

Quick Frosting

Immediately after removing cake from oven, place eight small thin milk chocolate bars over top. Cover with flat pan for a few minutes to hasten melting, then smooth the chocolate over surface of brownies.

Favorite Brownie Frosting

1-1/2 squares unsweetened chocolate
2 tablespoons butter or margarine
1/4 cup cream
1/3 cup firmly packed dark brown sugar

Pinch salt
1/2 teaspoon vanilla extract
1/2 teaspoon sherry extract
About 1-1/2 cups powdered sugar

Combine chocolate, butter, cream, brown sugar, and salt in small saucepan. Bring to a boil and cook, stirring constantly until chocolate is melted. Remove from heat, add flavorings, then powdered sugar to yield spreading consistency. Yield: enough to thinly glaze two 8-inch square pans of brownies or a slightly thicker glaze for a 12- x 8- x 2-inch pan.

CREOLE PORCUPINES
(a traditional New Orleans cookie)

3 tablespoons butter (no substitute)
1 cup firmly packed brown sugar
2 eggs, well beaten

1-1/2 cups chopped pecans
1 cup chopped dates
3 cups shredded coconut

Melt butter and stir into sugar; beat in eggs. Add pecans, dates, and 1 cup of the coconut. Form into small balls and roll in the remaining 2 cups of coconut. Place on greased baking sheet and bake at 300° until cookies just begin to brown lightly, about 25 minutes. Yield: about 4 dozen little cookies.

Chicken Tetrazzini Cocktail Supper

COCKTAIL SUPPER FOR TWENTY

Party Chicken Tetrazzini

Asparagus-Almond Mold   **Pineapple Pickles**

Baked Canadian Bacon

or

Sliced Baked Ham

Party Rye Bread   **Thin-Sliced White Bread**

Dijon Mustard   **Brown Mustard**

Apricot Bars   **Chocolate-Walnut Meringues**

Coffee

Provide a pitcher of chilled tomato juice or similar non-sweet, non-alcoholic beverage for diet-conscious guests.

PARTY CHICKEN TETRAZZINI
(may be prepared ahead of time)

1 (6-pound) hen, stewed, reserve 4 cups of broth
1/4 pound butter
8 tablespoons all-purpose flour
1 cup heavy cream
3/4 pound processed yellow cheese, cut in small chunks
1 (1-pound) can ripe olives, pitted and sliced

1 (4-ounce) can mushroom slices or stems and pieces, drained
1 (3-ounce) package slivered toasted almonds
3 tablespoons finely minced onion
3 tablespoons minced green pepper
3 tablespoons minced celery
Salt and pepper to taste
8 ounces thin noodles, cooked; or chow mein noodles

Stew hen until tender; reserve 4 cups of the broth. Cut meat into bite-size pieces; set aside.

Heat butter in large saucepan and gradually blend in flour. Slowly add the 4 cups chicken broth, then cream. Stir over low heat until mixture has thickened. Add cheese and stir until melted. Combine with chicken and all other ingredients except noodles.

Boil noodles according to package directions, drain well and stir into chicken mixture. Turn into two buttered 1-1/2-quart casseroles and refrigerate until ready to bake. Bake at 350° until bubbly and heated through. It will freeze nicely if prepared ahead of time — and any leftovers will also freeze. Yield: 12 servings. Prepare the recipe twice for a cocktail supper for about 20.

ASPARAGUS-ALMOND MOLD

1 envelope unflavored gelatin
1/4 cup cold water
    1 (1-pound) can cut asparagus, drained, reserve liquid
    1 cup mayonnaise

1 cup sliced blanched almonds
1 cup chopped celery
    Freshly squeezed lemon juice to taste
    Salt if needed

Soak gelatin in cold water for 5 minutes. Drain asparagus; heat asparagus liquid to boiling and dissolve gelatin in it. Gradually blend into mayonnaise; add other ingredients including asparagus and pour into mold which has been greased with a little mayonnaise; chill until set. Yield: 4 to 6 servings; triple the recipe for a cocktail supper for about 20. If made in a very large mold, use 4 packages gelatin instead of 3, for added firmness.

PINEAPPLE PICKLES
(prepare ahead of time)

1 (29-ounce) can pineapple chunks
3/4 cup cider vinegar
1 cup granulated sugar
6 whole allspice berries
3 whole cloves
1 (3-inch) stick cinnamon

1 teaspoon powdered coriander seed
    Dash salt
2 teaspoons tiny red cinnamon candies (or substitute a drop or two of red coloring)

Drain pineapple, reserving 3/4 cup of the syrup. Put the 3/4 cup syrup and all ingredients except pineapple chunks (and coloring if you're using it) in a large saucepan. Cook uncovered for 15 minutes. Add pineapple chunks and bring to a brisk boil; cook for 5 minutes. Remove from heat, add coloring if desired. Cool, pour into jar with tight-fitting cover and refrigerate at least 24 hours before using. Serve very cold in a clear crystal bowl. Yield: 20 servings.

BAKED CANADIAN BACON

Remove outer wrapping from stick of Canadian bacon and wrap bacon loosely in aluminum foil. Bake in shallow pan at 325° for 1-1/2 hours.

This method of baking Canadian bacon requires no embellishments. The time given is the same for any size piece, as the diameter remains the same regardless of the length. A 5-pound stick usually serves 10 to 12. For a cocktail supper of 20 where the bacon is to augment a heartier dish, a 5-pound stick, sliced very thin, should suffice.

BAKED HAM
(see Index)

APRICOT BARS

1-1/2 cups all-purpose flour, sifted
1 teaspoon baking powder
1/4 teaspoon salt
1-1/2 cups quick-cooking oatmeal

1 cup firmly packed brown sugar
3/4 cup butter or margarine
3/4 cup apricot preserves or jam

Combine flour, baking powder, and salt in a bowl; stir in oatmeal and sugar. Cut in butter until crumbly; pat two-thirds of mixture into an ungreased 11- x 7- x 1-inch pan. Spread with preserves; cover with remaining crumb mixture, press down lightly and bake at 350° for 30 to 35 minutes, or just until lightly browned. Cool, cut into bars or squares. Yield: about 24 (1- x 3-inch) bars; double the recipe for a cocktail supper for about 20.

Variation: Follow directions, substituting raspberry jam for apricot preserves.

CHOCOLATE-WALNUT MERINGUES
(prepare ahead of time and freeze)

1 (6-ounce) package semi-sweet
   chocolate bits
2 egg whites
1/2 cup sugar

1/2 teaspoon vinegar
1/8 teaspoon salt
1/2 teaspoon vanilla extract
3/4 cup chopped walnuts

Melt chocolate over warm water. Beat egg whites until foamy; gradually add sugar, beating until stiff peaks form. Beat in vinegar, salt, and vanilla. Fold in slightly cooled chocolate and walnuts. Drop by teaspoonfuls onto well greased baking sheet and bake at 300° for about 20 minutes. May be made far ahead of time and frozen. Yield: about 36; double the recipe for a cocktail supper for about 20.

Note: These meringues may be made larger, with centers indented somewhat, to serve as a dessert with a scoop of ice cream placed in center and a chocolate sauce poured over it.

TIP FOR CRISP MERINGUES

Crisp meringues are delicious filled with ice cream, but not if they go soggy on you. If you are baking the meringues for a party and they soften during an overnight stay in a covered container, reheat them in a very slow oven for 15 minutes or so; then cool. They should regain their lovely crispness.

Old-Fashioned Hot Pot

COCKTAIL SUPPER FOR TWENTY

Tennessee Hot Pot with Toast Cups

Jellied Cucumber-Shrimp Salad   **Blue Cheese Mayonnaise**

Assorted Cheeses and Crackers (optional)

Chocolate-Date Bars   **Birdie Cookies**

Coffee

Provide a pitcher of chilled tomato juice or similar non-sweet, non-alcoholic beverage for diet-conscious guests.

TENNESSEE HOT POT
(prepare the day before)

Don't be discouraged by the formidable list of ingredients in this recipe. Just have faith; you won't regret having gone to the trouble.

2 tablespoons salad oil	1 teaspoon chili powder
3 tablespoons butter or margarine	1/8 teaspoon ground ginger
3 medium onions, chopped	1 tablespoon Worcestershire sauce
2 cloves garlic, crushed	1 tablespoon freshly squeezed lemon juice
1 pound lean beef, cut in 2/3-inch cubes	2 teaspoons soy sauce
1 pound pork, cut in 2/3-inch cubes	1 bay leaf
1 pound veal, cut in 2/3-inch cubes	1/8 teaspoon ground cloves
2 teaspoons salt	1/8 teaspoon dried oregano
Black pepper to taste	1/8 teaspoon dried thyme
1/2 teaspoon cayenne pepper	1-1/2 tablespoons dried parsley
1 (10-ounce) can beef bouillon	1/2 teaspoon dry mustard
2 (10-ounce) cans tomato puree	1 teaspoon commercial liquid smoke
2 tablespoons vinegar	

Heat oil and butter in heavy Dutch oven. Add onions and garlic and sauté until yellow. Remove to paper towels to drain. Place meat in pot and sear quickly, adding salt and black pepper while browning. Return onions and garlic to pot; add all other ingredients. Stir well, cover and simmer gently for 3 hours. If mixture cooks down, add a small amount of hot water. This should be made the day before serving so flavor can mellow and also to enable you to remove congealed fat from the surface. Freezes beautifully. Yield: 10 servings; double the recipe for a cocktail supper for about 20.

TOAST CUPS

Cut slices of fresh white bread into rounds, using a biscuit cutter. Melt butter or margarine and brush inside of small muffin tins. Fit bread rounds into cups, handling carefully to avoid tearing. Brush inside of bread cups with butter. Bake at 375° for about 15 minutes, or just until lightly and evenly browned. Remove from muffin tins immediately. These little cups are excellent for using with any creamed dish or meat mixture with sauce. For a cocktail supper for about 20, prepare about 4 dozen toast cups.

JELLIED CUCUMBER-SHRIMP SALAD

5 envelopes unflavored gelatin
1 cup cold water
3 cups boiling water
1 tablespoon salt
1/2 teaspoon pepper
1/2 teaspoon Tabasco sauce
   Juice of 4 lemons

6 medium cucumbers, peeled and grated (including juice)
2 medium onions, grated
4 pounds raw shrimp in the shell, cooked and cleaned
   Blue Cheese Mayonnaise
   Paprika
   Lettuce

Soften gelatin in cold water for 5 minutes; dissolve in boiling water, add seasonings and lemon juice. Cool; stir in cucumbers and onion and taste for seasoning. Allow to partially congeal, then stir in cooked shrimp. Pour into lightly oiled, large ring mold and chill until set. Unmold onto lettuce-lined platter and fill center with Blue Cheese Mayonnaise. Sprinkle paprika generously over top of mayonnaise. Yield: 20 servings.

BLUE CHEESE MAYONNAISE
(may be prepared ahead of time)

1 (4-ounce) package blue cheese
1/4 cup hot water
1/2 teaspoon salt
   Generous amount freshly ground black pepper

Dash red pepper
1 clove garlic, crushed
1/4 cup dry sherry
   About 1 cup mayonnaise

Crumble cheese into small bowl; pour hot water over it and stir until melted. Add dry ingredients, garlic, and sherry. Gradually blend this into mayonnaise until smooth. Chill thoroughly before serving. Keeps well. Excellent over wedges of iceberg lettuce or cold asparagus. Yield: about 1-3/4 cups; double the recipe for a party of about 20.

CHOCOLATE-DATE BARS

1 (8-ounce) package dates, chopped	1-1/4 cups all-purpose flour, sifted
3/4 cup firmly packed brown sugar	3/4 teaspoon soda
1/2 cup water	1/2 teaspoon salt
1/2 cup butter or margarine	1/3 cup orange juice
1 (6-ounce) package semi-sweet chocolate bits	1/4 cup milk or cream
2 eggs	1 cup broken walnuts or pecans (not ground)

Combine dates, sugar, water, and butter in large saucepan. Cook over low heat, stirring constantly, until dates soften, about 5 minutes. Remove from heat; stir in chocolate until melted. Beat in eggs.

Sift flour with soda and salt; add to first mixture alternately with orange juice, then milk, blending well after each addition. Stir in nuts and turn into well greased 15- x 10-inch pan. Bake at 350° for 25 minutes or just until cake tests done. Cool for 5 minutes, then spread with Orange Glaze. Let cake finish cooling after glazing.

While still warm use a sharp knife to cut into 1- x 1-1/2-inch bars. Remove from pan when cool. Freezes beautifully. Yield: 56 bars.

Orange Glaze

2 tablespoons soft butter or margarine	2 teaspoons freshly squeezed lemon juice
1-1/4 cups sifted powdered sugar	3 tablespoons orange juice
Dash salt	2 tablespoons grated orange rind

In small bowl of electric mixer combine soft butter or margarine, powdered sugar, salt, lemon juice, and about 3 tablespoons orange juice. When smooth, stir in 2 teaspoons grated orange rind by hand.

BIRDIE COOKIES
(may be prepared ahead of time)

1/2 pound butter (no substitute)	1 teaspoon vanilla extract
1 cup sugar	2 cups all-purpose flour
2 egg yolks	1 egg white, unbeaten
1 teaspoon grated lemon rind	Ground almonds or pecans
2 teaspoons freshly squeezed lemon juice	

Cream butter and sugar thoroughly in large bowl of electric mixer. Add egg yolks, lemon rind, lemon juice, and vanilla, blending well. Beat in flour; chill dough. When ready to bake, remove a small portion of dough at a time from refrigerator; roll out to 1/4-inch thickness on lightly floured board. Cut into desired shapes. Place on ungreased baking sheet, brush with unbeaten egg white and sprinkle with ground nuts. Bake at 325° for about 15 to 20 minutes.

These cookies should be removed from oven as soon as edges start to color; if you bake then until brown all over, they're ruined. May be made ahead and frozen. Yield: about 5 dozen cookies.

Cocktail Party with Baked Eye-of-Round

COCKTAIL PARTY FOR TWENTY

Baked Eye-of-Round with Rosemary

Toast with Presto Spread   **Caper-Stuffed Eggs**

Assorted Cheeses with Salted and Unsalted Crackers (optional)

Layered Nut Bars   **Satin-Top Brownies**

Coffee

Provide a pitcher of chilled tomato juice or similar non-sweet, non-alcoholic beverage for diet-conscious guests.

BAKED EYE-OF-ROUND WITH ROSEMARY
(may be prepared ahead of time)

Eye-of-round beef	Black pepper
Seasoned salt	About 1 teaspoon rosemary, crushed
Garlic salt	1 teaspoon shortening

If convenient, season meat 2 days before cooking; otherwise, the night before. However, don't let the time element deter you; I have seasoned this beef just before cooking, with excellent results.

Rub entire surface of meat liberally with a mixture of the seasonings. Wrap tightly in aluminum foil and refrigerate. About an hour before cooking, remove from refrigerator to attain room temperature. Brown on all sides in a teaspoon of shortening, just enough to grease the skillet. Place meat in shallow pan; insert meat thermometer into the thickest part of meat. Bake at 300° until desired doneness. If you don't use a thermometer, bake for 15 minutes to the pound for rare, 20 minutes to the pound for medium, and 22 minutes to the pound for well done.

This beef is delicious served at room temperature and therefore may be prepared several hours ahead of serving. Or it may be prepared and frozen, then thawed and placed in a slow oven for 20 minutes. A thinly sliced 5-pound roast will serve 8 to 10; for a cocktail supper for about 20, prepare 2 (5-pound) roasts.

PRESTO SPREAD FOR TOAST
(may be prepared ahead of time)

2 tablespoons minced fresh parsley
1 tablespoon dried basil
1 cup grated Parmesan cheese
1 cup butter, slightly softened

1/2 teaspoon anchovy paste; or 2 anchovy
  filets, mashed
2 tablespoons freshly squeezed
  lemon juice

Combine parsley, basil, and cheese in a bowl, and stir, mashing well as you stir. Add to butter in small bowl of electric mixer and beat until fluffy. Beat in anchovy paste and lemon juice. Refrigerate until ready to use. Spread on slices of French bread and bake at 250° for about 30 minutes, until crisp. This is an excellent spread to use when the bread accompanies bland meat. Or you could cut bread into strips and use as an appetizer. Yield: about 2-1/4 cups.

CAPER-STUFFED EGGS

4 hard-cooked eggs
3 anchovy filets, drained; or 2 teaspoons
  anchovy paste
1 tablespoon drained capers
4 ripe olives, pitted

2 tablespoons mayonnaise
1/2 teaspoon anchovy liquid
  Black pepper to taste
  Freshly squeezed lemon juice
  Paprika

Cut eggs in half; mash yolks through a fine sieve. Grind anchovies, capers, and olives in food grinder or chop finely in a wooden bowl. Combine with mayonnaise and sieved yolks. Add anchovy liquid, pepper, and about 2 teaspoons lemon juice. Fill shells and sprinkle with paprika. Yield: 8 stuffed halves; for a cocktail supper for about 20, make the recipe four times.

LAYERED NUT BARS
(may be prepared ahead of time)

1/2 cup butter (no substitute)
1 cup all-purpose flour
3 tablespoons ice water

Filling
Frosting

Cut butter into flour with pastry blender; gradually add water. When dough holds together, form into a ball, remove to floured surface and roll out to fit a 12- x 8- x 2-inch pan loosely. Place in pan, bringing dough up on sides about 1/2 inch, as it will shrink in baking. You want to end up with the entire bottom

FROSTING TIP

Before you start frosting your cake, place two knives in a glass of very hot water. Keep the glass handy and if frosting hardens too quickly while you're working, one of the hot, wet knives will spread the frosting smoothly.

of pan covered with a layer of pastry. Bake at 325° for 20 minutes; after 5 minutes baking, prick any bubbles that form. While pastry bakes, prepare Filling.

Filling

3 eggs	1/8 teaspoon salt
1-1/2 cups firmly packed light brown sugar	1-1/2 cups chopped pecans or walnuts (or mixed)
6 tablespoons all-purpose flour	
3/4 teaspoon baking powder	1 cup shredded coconut

Beat eggs, gradually add sugar, then sifted dry ingredients. Stir in nuts and coconut. Pour into baked shell and bake at 325° for 25 minutes. Cool 5 minutes, then frost.

Frosting

1 tablespoon melted butter	1/2 teaspoon orange extract
1-1/2 cups powdered sugar	1 tablespoon freshly squeezed lemon juice
3 tablespoons orange juice	

Blend all ingredients in small bowl of electric mixer. Spread on cake, allow to cool for about 10 minutes, then cut into 1- x 2-inch bars with a hot knife. Remove from pan while slightly warm. These freeze beautifully. Yield: 42 bars.

SATIN-TOP BROWNIES

Do not use an electric mixer. In fact, I have found it best never to use an electric mixer for brownies; the texture is adversely affected.

1/2 cup all-purpose flour, measured before sifting	2 eggs
1/2 teaspoon salt	1 cup sugar
1/2 cup coarsely chopped walnuts	1/4 cup salad oil
2 (1-ounce) squares unsweetened chocolate, melted	1 teaspoon vanilla extract

Spread sheet of waxed paper on table; sift onto it flour and salt. Add nuts and stir to coat thoroughly. Melt chocolate in small saucepan over hot (not boiling) water; set aside. Beat eggs slightly, using wooden spoon; add sugar; stir well. Add oil, then vanilla and stir vigorously for a minute. Now add melted chocolate, then flour-nut mixture. Stir only until traces of flour are no longer visible. Turn into greased 8- x 8- x 2-inch pan and bake at 350° for 25 to 30 minutes, just until brownies test done; do not overbake. While warm, cut in squares; cool before removing from pan. Yield: 16 brownies; this recipe may be doubled and baked in a greased 8- x 12- x 2-inch baking pan for 35 to 40 minutes.

Note: A nice variation is to sprinkle a few coarsely chopped walnuts over the top before baking if you do not wish to frost the brownies.

Southern Cocktail Supper

COCKTAIL SUPPER FOR TWENTY

Sliced Baked Kentucky Ham and Small Buttered Biscuits

New Orleans Diablotins

Mixed Olives   **Celery Sticks with Les's Seasoned Salt**

Chicken-Wild Rice Casserole

Avocado-Cucumber Salad

Party Macaroon Muffins   **Natchez Cookies**

Coffee

Provide a pitcher of chilled tomato juice or similar non-sweet, non-alcoholic beverage for diet-conscious guests.

BAKED KENTUCKY HAM

Scrub country ham thoroughly with a brush, changing water often. Soak overnight in cold water to cover. Next day, put ham in a very large container with enough cold water to more than cover it. (You may have a "lard stand," an empty can in which lard was packed; this makes an excellent boiler.) Slowly bring to the boiling point, then simmer very, very gently for 5 to 6 hours, depending on size of ham (about 28 minutes to the pound). Turn off heat and allow ham to cool in the cooking water, then remove from water and take off rind; it will peel off easily. Put ham in an open roaster, spreading over it a mixture of 4 teaspoons prepared mustard, 1/4 cup vinegar, and 2 cups brown sugar. Insert whole cloves into ham and bake at 375° for about 45 minutes. When cold, carve into small, thin slices and provide a tray of small buttered biscuits.

NEW ORLEANS DIABLOTINS

1 cup crumbled Roquefort cheese
1/4 pound butter or margarine, softened
1/2 cup finely ground walnuts (do not substitute)

Generous pinch cayenne pepper
16 slices French bread

Trim crusts from slices of French bread, then cut into three long strips about 1 inch wide. Spread butter lightly on one side and toast. Then spread cheese mixture generously on unbuttered side and broil briefly, until very lightly browned. Yield: 48 strips.

LES'S SEASONED SALT
(see Index)

CHICKEN-WILD RICE CASSEROLE
(may be prepared ahead of time)

2 (3-pound) whole broiler-fryer chickens
1 cup water
1 cup dry sherry
1-1/2 teaspoons salt
1/2 teaspoon curry powder
1 medium onion, sliced
1/2 cup sliced celery

1 pound fresh mushrooms
1/4 cup butter or margarine
2 (6-ounce) packages long-grain and wild rice with seasonings
1 cup commercial sour cream
1 (10-1/2-ounce) can cream of mushroom soup

Place chickens in deep kettle; add water, sherry, salt, curry powder, onion, and celery. Cover and bring to a boil; reduce heat and simmer for 1 hour. Remove from heat; strain broth. Refrigerate chicken and broth at once, without cooling first.

When chicken is cool, remove meat from bones; discard skin. Cut meat into bite-size pieces. Rinse mushrooms and pat dry; slice and sauté in butter until golden, about 5 minutes, stirring constantly. (Reserve enough whole caps to garnish top of casserole; they may be sautéed along with sliced mushrooms.)

Measure chicken broth; use as part of liquid for cooking rice, following directions for firm rice on the package. Combine chicken, mushrooms, and rice in 3-1/2- or 4-quart casserole. Blend in sour cream and mushroom soup and toss with chicken-rice mixture. Arrange reserved mushroom caps in a circle over top of casserole. Cover; refrigerate overnight if desired. To heat, bake covered at 350° for 1 hour. The casserole may be completely prepared and frozen ahead of time. Yield: 8 to 10 servings; double the recipe for a cocktail supper for about 20.

AVOCADO-CUCUMBER MOLD

1 (3-ounce) package lemon-flavored
  gelatin
2 tablespoons cold water
1/2 cup boiling water
1 cup commercial sour cream
3/4 teaspoon salt

2 tablespoons freshly squeezed lemon
  juice
1/2 cup minced or coarsely grated
  unpeeled cucumber
1 cup diced avocado
2 tablespoons minced chives or onion

Soften gelatin in cold water for 5 minutes. Dissolve in hot water. Blend into sour cream, beating until smooth. Add all other ingredients and pour into mold. Chill until set. Yield: 4 servings; for a cocktail supper for about 20, make four times the recipe. To lend added firmness to a very large, heavy mold, add 1 package of plain unflavored gelatin to the 4 packages of lemon-flavored gelatin.

PARTY MACAROON MUFFINS
(may be prepared ahead of time)

1 cup soft butter (no substitute)
1/2 cup sugar
1 egg
1/2 teaspoon vanilla extract

1/2 teaspoon almond extract
2 cups all-purpose flour, measured
  before sifting

Cream butter and sugar thoroughly in large bowl of electric mixer. Beat in egg, flavorings, and flour. Drop with teaspoon into tiny greased muffin cups, pressing dough over bottom and up around sides. Chill. Heat oven to 325°; fill little cups with Almond Macaroon Filling. Bake about 25 to 30 minutes. Freezes well. Yield: 3 dozen tiny muffins; double the recipe for a cocktail supper for about 20.

Almond Macaroon Filling

Beat 2 eggs until light and foamy. Gradually beat in 1/2 cup sugar until well blended. Fold in 1-1/4 cups finely chopped blanched almonds and 1 teaspoon almond extract.

NATCHEZ COOKIES

1 cup unsalted butter
1 cup sugar
1 egg, separated

2 cups all-purpose flour
Juice and grated rind of 1/2 lemon
1 cup chopped pecans or walnuts

Cream butter and sugar thoroughly in large bowl of electric mixer. Add egg yolk, flour, lemon juice, and rind, mixing until well blended. Pat dough evenly onto ungreased 15- x 10- x 1-inch baking sheet; dough should be about 1/4-inch thick. Brush with slightly beaten egg white, sprinkle with nuts. Bake at 325° for 25 to 30 minutes; cut into strips while hot. Yield: about 36 bars.

Chicken Almondine Cocktail Supper

COCKTAIL SUPPER FOR SIXTEEN TO TWENTY

Chicken Almondine

Baked Rice with Peas

Tarragon Baked Ham with Hot Biscuits

Hot Caramel Fruit with Walnut-Stuffed Dates

Kipfel   **Chocolate-Nut Bars**

Coffee

Provide a pitcher of chilled tomato juice or similar non-sweet, non-alcoholic beverage for diet-conscious guests.

CHICKEN ALMONDINE

3 tablespoons butter or margarine	1 small bay leaf
2-1/2 tablespoons all-purpose flour	2 egg yolks
1-1/2 cups warm milk	1/4 cup heavy cream
1 cup good chicken broth (from cooking chicken)	3 tablespoons dry sherry
	Dash Angostura bitters (optional)
Salt and pepper to taste	4 cups chopped cooked chicken
1 tablespoon finely minced onion	1/2 cup toasted slivered almonds
2 teaspoons butter or margarine	Buttered breadcrumbs

Melt the 3 tablespoons butter in saucepan, blend in flour, remove from heat and gradually blend in milk, then chicken broth. Add salt and pepper to taste, return to stove and cook, stirring constantly, until thick and smooth. Lightly sauté onion in 2 teaspoons butter in small skillet; stir into sauce, add bay leaf and simmer gently for about 5 minutes.

In the meantime, combine egg yolks with cream, sherry, and bitters. Remove bay leaf from sauce, then begin blending hot sauce into egg mixture. Do this slowly to avoid curdling eggs. When mixed, add chicken and almonds; pour into buttered casserole, sprinkle with buttered crumbs and bake uncovered at 325° for 25 minutes. Serve with rice to absorb the wonderful sauce. Yield: 8 servings; double the recipe for a cocktail party for 16 to 20.

BAKED RICE WITH PEAS

1-1/2 cups long-grain regular rice
   3 tablespoons butter or margarine
   1 teaspoon salt
1-3/4 cups water

1 (10-ounce) can chicken bouillon
1 (10-ounce) package frozen peas, thawed

Combine all ingredients except peas in a 1-1/2-quart casserole. Cover and bake at 350° for 1 hour, or until rice is done. Ten minutes before serving, stir in thawed peas. (Do not add peas before that time, as they should be crisp.) Yield: 6 servings; triple the recipe for a cocktail supper for about 16 to 20.

TARRAGON BAKED HAM
(prepare ahead of time)

6 to 8 pounds tenderized ham
1/2 cup brown sugar
   1 teaspoon dry tarragon, crumbled
1/2 teaspoon dry mustard

1/2 teaspoon ground cloves
1/4 cup tarragon vinegar
   3 to 4 juniper berries, mashed (optional)

Mix all ingredients thoroughly and pour into glass dish. Turn ham cut-side down into the sauce. Cover with aluminum foil or waxed paper and refrigerate overnight, spooning sauce over ham occasionally. When ready to bake, turn ham over with fat-side up, cover loosely with aluminum foil and bake at 300° until fork-tender, about 20 minutes per pound, basting now and then with sauce in bottom of baking pan. Allow to rest a few hours before slicing. Yield: 10 servings. For a cocktail supper for about 20, marinate a whole ham for 2 days and double all ingredients.

HOT CARAMEL FRUIT
(prepare ahead of time)

2 (29-ounce) cans Elberta peaches
1 (1-pound) can dark sweet pitted cherries
1 (11-ounce) package dried apricots
   Juice of 1/2 orange
   Juice of 1/2 lemon

1/4 teaspoon grated orange rind
1/4 teaspoon grated lemon rind
   1 cup firmly packed brown sugar
12 pitted dates
12 walnut halves

Drain peaches and cherries separately; reserve peach juice. Mix all other ingredients except dates and walnuts, stir in peach juice, turn into buttered baking dish and bake uncovered at 325° for 1-1/2 hours basting several times. While fruit bakes, stuff about 12 pitted dates with walnut halves. About 15 minutes before fruit is done, arrange dates around the casserole, baste with syrup in bottom of baking dish and allow to finish baking. Yield: about 10 to 12 servings; double the recipe for a cocktail supper for about 20.

KIPFEL
(prepare ahead of time)

2 eggs, separated
1 cup commercial sour cream
1/2 cup sugar
2-1/2 cups all-purpose flour, sifted
1/2 pound butter (no substitute)

Extra softened butter for rolling pastry
Filling
Powdered sugar

Combine egg yolks with sour cream. Mix sugar and flour in a bowl and cut in butter with pastry blender until texture resembles coarse meal. Add egg-cream mixture and beat until smooth. Cover and chill overnight. Dough may be kept a week if necessary.

When ready to bake, work with a fourth of the dough at a time, keeping the remainder refrigerated. On floured board, roll dough very thin — as thin as you can — lightly, however, to prevent sticking. Spread with softened butter; fold in thirds* and roll again. Repeat twice, spreading with butter each time. Chill between rolling if necessary to keep dough manageable.

Cut into 3-inch squares. Fill with 1 rounded tablespoon Filling and roll tightly. Pinch ends to seal, form into crescents; seal edges with slightly beaten egg whites. Place, sealed-side down, on ungreased baking sheet and bake at 400° for 5 minutes, then at 350° for 15 to 20 minutes, or until pale golden. Remove and while hot, sift powdered sugar over top. Yield: 48.

*To fold any pastry dough in thirds, roll into a rectangle; fold top third of dough toward you; fold bottom third up over this. Now fold right third over toward left, then left third over that making a neat square.

Filling

4 cups finely ground nuts (pecans and walnuts, mixed)
1/2 teaspoon grated lemon rind
1/2 teaspoon grated orange rind
2 tablespoons freshly squeezed lemon juice
5 teaspoons freshly squeezed orange juice

4 tablespoons sweet cream
4 tablespoons brown sugar
6 tablespoons granulated sugar
15 crumbled vanilla wafers
6 tablespoons jelly
1 teaspoon almond extract

Mix all ingredients. Filling should be moderately firm; if it seems too loose, add more crumbled cookies.

Kipfels freeze beautifully. To serve after freezing, thaw and bake at 200° for 15 to 20 minutes. Sprinkle with a little sifted powdered sugar.

ORANGE TIP

Whenever a recipe calls for both orange juice and rind, wash and grate the orange before juicing.

CHOCOLATE-NUT BARS
(prepare ahead of time)

1/3 cup butter or margarine	1/4 teaspoon soda
1 cup brown sugar	1/4 teaspoon salt
1 egg	1 cup semi-sweet chocolate bits
1 teaspoon vanilla extract	1/2 cup chopped pecans or walnuts
1 cup all-purpose flour, measured before sifting	

Cream butter and sugar in large bowl of electric mixer. Add egg and vanilla; beat well. Combine flour, soda, and salt; add to creamed mixture and mix well. Stir in chocolate bits and nuts. Spread in greased 11- x 7- x 1-inch pan. Bake at 350° for 20 to 25 minutes. Cut into bars while warm. Will freeze. Yield: 2 dozen; double the recipe for a cocktail supper menu for about 20.

STOCKING THE BAR

For a large party, an experienced bartender should be hired. For a smaller group (20 or so) your co-host or a friend may be asked to tend bar for the first hour, after which time he may leave his post to join other guests, leaving bottles, ice, and mixers out so guests may help themselves to refills.

How much liquor to buy? There are seventeen 1-1/2-ounce drinks in a fifth of liquor; roughly 200 drinks to a case (12 bottles to a case). To be on the safe side, allow three drinks per guest. Some guests will have only one drink, but it's better to have too much than not enough.

If your party is a sizeable one, you'll undoubtedly have some non-drinkers. For them, it's thoughtful to have a large pitcher of chilled fruit juice and another of chilled tomato or V-8 juice. Scotch, bourbon or rye, vodka, gin, plenty of mixers (tonic, ginger ale, club soda) and lots and lots of ice are necessary for stocking the bar.

You can start making ice a week before the party and store the cubes in plastic bags in the freezer. If you don't have a freezer, buy the ice during the afternoon of party-day and keep it in a tub out of sight.

And, oh yes, provide plenty of lemon wedges. And please provide a tray or table for used glasses!

Teas, Receptions, and Coffees

A coffee or tea table draped in delicate organdy and lace linens and set with trays of cakes and sandwiches is the epitome of elegance and a tribute to the guest of honor. Surprisingly, a tea or coffee requires less planning than most people may think. The table follows a set pattern (see diagrams in the chapter, "Dispensing Southern Hospitality"), and the fare varies within a standard.

Actually, a coffee and tea are interchangeable. A coffee usually refers to a morning affair, while a tea is more often held in the afternoon. Afternoon biscuits and dainty sandwiches might replace morning muffins and pastries, but coffee and tea are offered at both times.

When a tea grows in number of guests it becomes a reception and is usually given in honor of someone or some occasion. Food is, of course, more plentiful and varied for a large reception. And punch may be added to the beverages.

Garden Tea

TEA FOR FORTY TO FIFTY

Whole Wheat Sandwiches with Olive Filling

Dainty Sandwiches of Homemade Bread

with

Seafood-Cucumber Filling

Horns of Plenty Filled with Chicken Salad

Toasted Almond Balls   **Croesus Bars**

Strawberry Cookies

Brownies Deluxe   **Chocolate-Pecan Meringues**

Swiss Doubles

Filled Pastries   **Caramel Meringue Cookies**

Tea   **Coffee**

WHOLE WHEAT SANDWICHES WITH OLIVE FILLING
(may be prepared ahead of time)

1/2 cup slivered almonds or pecans	Seasoned salt to taste
1 (4-1/2-ounce) can chopped ripe olives	Lemon juice to taste
Mayonnaise (as needed for spreading consistency)	2 or 3 teaspoons salad dressing (optional)
About 1/2 teaspoon Worcestershire sauce	1 loaf whole wheat sandwich bread

Chop almonds until fine; combine with other ingredients. Trim crust from bread, spread one slice with filling, top with another slice of bread; cut into finger sandwiches. Yield: 32 sandwiches.

FINE WHITE BREAD
(may be prepared ahead of time)

1 cake compressed yeast or 1 package active dry yeast	9 cups all-purpose flour
1 teaspoon sugar	1 tablespoon salt
1/2 cup lukewarm water (very warm for dry yeast)	3 tablespoons sugar
2 cups milk	1/2 cup melted butter or margarine
	4 eggs, beaten slightly

Combine yeast, 1 teaspoon sugar, and lukewarm water (very warm if dry yeast is used); stir until dissolved; set aside.

Put milk and 4 cups of the flour in large bowl of electric mixer; beat thoroughly. Add salt, the 3 tablespoons sugar, melted butter, eggs, and yeast mixture. Combine thoroughly, then add remainder of flour. (The last cup or two will probably have to be added by hand, as dough becomes too stiff to behave with the average mixer. This is no problem if you have a mixer equipped with a dough hook attachment.)

Turn dough out onto floured surface and knead well for 8 to 10 minutes, until it becomes smooth and elastic. Place in well greased bowl, turn to grease all sides, cover with cloth and let rise in warm spot until double in bulk. If not ready to use, punch air out with your fist, oil top of dough, cover and refrigerate until ready to use.

To make bread, divide dough in fourths. Roll each portion out into a rectangle about 9- x 7- x 1-inch. Fold long ends of dough toward the center, overlapping slightly. Pinch ends and overlapped side slightly, then place loaf, sealed-edge down, in greased breadpan. Let rise until double in bulk; bake at 350° for about 50 minutes, or until done.

About 5 minutes before removing from oven, spread top of loaves with melted butter and return to oven. Turn out loaves and allow to cool on wire racks. Freezes beautifully. Yield: 4 loaves.

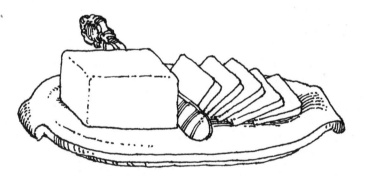

SEAFOOD-CUCUMBER FILLING
(may be prepared ahead of time)*

1 cup crabmeat or chopped cooked shrimp

1/3 cup grated peeled cucumber, drained (press moisture out between paper towels)

2 teaspoons minced chives

1 to 2 teaspoons freshly squeezed lemon juice

1/4 teaspoon salt

1/8 teaspoon dried dill weed

4 tablespoons mayonnaise or commercial sour cream

Combine all ingredients and chill thoroughly. Yield: about 1-1/2 cups; double the recipe for a tea for 40 to 50.

*If you make up sandwiches ahead of time, be sure to spread bread lightly with soft butter before filling sandwiches; the butter will prevent the filling from seeping in and causing sogginess.

HORNS OF PLENTY
(may be prepared ahead of time)

First, cut clean white paper into 2-1/2-inch squares.

Prepare your favorite pastry dough. Roll out to about 1/8-inch thickness and cut into 2-1/2-inch squares. Roll into cornucopia shape; secure with wooden picks. Place paper, also rolled into cornucopia shape, inside the opening to prevent collapsing. Bake on ungreased baking sheet at 425° for about 10 minutes, or until lightly browned. When cool, slip paper out. Fill with chicken salad a short while before serving.

These little pastries may be filled with sweetened, flavored whipped cream, or custard, or jam — anything that appeals to you — but the filling should be moderately stiff and not go running about all over your beautifully arranged tea tray. Prepare about 6 dozen cornucopias for a tea for 40 to 50.

CHICKEN SALAD
(see Index)

TOASTED ALMOND BALLS
(may be prepared ahead of time)

1 (6-ounce) package semi-sweet chocolate bits	1-1/2 teaspoons grated orange rind
1 (6-ounce) package butterscotch bits	1/4 teaspoon salt
1/2 cup sifted powdered sugar	2 cups dry cakecrumbs, or crushed plain cookies
1/2 teaspoon almond extract	1 cup almonds, toasted and ground*
1/2 cup commercial sour cream	

Melt chocolate and butterscotch bits together over hot (not boiling) water; remove from heat. With wooden spoon blend in powdered sugar, almond extract, sour cream, orange rind, and salt. Stir in cakecrumbs and chill until firm enough to handle, about 1 hour. Shape into 1-inch balls and roll in chopped toasted almonds. Store in tightly covered container. Yield: 4 to 5 dozen; double the recipe to serve 40 to 50.

*Place 1 cup whole unblanched almonds in shallow pan in a 275° oven for about 20 to 25 minutes. Remove, cool and grind with small nut grinder.

CROESUS BARS
(may be prepared ahead of time)

1 cup butter or margarine	2 cups all-purpose flour, sifted
2/3 cup light brown sugar	1/4 teaspoon soda
1/2 cup granulated sugar	1/2 teaspoon salt
3 eggs, separated	12 ounces semi-sweet chocolate bits
1 tablespoon water	1 cup chopped black walnuts or pecans
1 teaspoon vanilla extract	Pinch cream of tartar
1/2 teaspoon almond extract	1/2 cup brown sugar

Cream butter with the 2/3 cup brown sugar and 1/2 cup granulated sugar in large bowl of electric mixer. Beat egg yolks lightly and add, then beat in water and flavorings. Sift flour with soda and salt and blend in well. Spread in ungreased 15- x 10- x 1-inch jellyroll pan; sprinkle with chocolate bits, then walnuts; press down lightly with palm of hand. Beat egg whites until foamy; add cream of tartar; continue beating until stiff. Fold in the 1/2 cup brown sugar, spread over chocolate bits and bake at 300° for 50 to 55 minutes. Cool, cut in squares (small for cookies; larger as base for ice cream dessert). Freezes well. Yield: 60 small cookies; make the recipe twice for a tea for 40 to 50.

STRAWBERRY COOKIES
(may be prepared ahead of time)

5 tablespoons butter or margarine	1 cup chopped pecans or walnuts
1 cup sugar	2-1/2 cups rice cereal
Pinch salt	Red sugar crystals
2 eggs	Powdered sugar
1-1/2 cups chopped dates	Milk
1 teaspoon vanilla extract	

Melt butter or margarine in electric skillet set at 300°. Combine 1 cup sugar, salt, and eggs in a bowl and add to skillet. Cook, stirring constantly, until mixture thickens to consistency of a medium white sauce. Add chopped dates and continue cooking until a spoon drawn through the mixture leaves an open path. Cut off heat; stir in vanilla, chopped pecans or walnuts, and rice cereal.

Pinch off small portions and roll into balls the size of a quarter. Form into shape of strawberry. Roll in red sugar crystals (available at most markets).

Make a simple icing of powdered sugar and milk; tint pale green. Using a pastry tube (you can improvise one with a sheet of white paper), form caps on berries.

If mixture cools while you are forming the berries, reheat slightly and it will become manageable again. Use to garnish platters of cookies and assorted confections. Yield: 5 to 6 dozen.

BROWNIES DELUXE
(may be prepared ahead of time)

1 cup butter or margarine	1-1/2 cups all-purpose flour
4 (1-ounce) squares unsweetened chocolate	1 teaspoon baking powder
	2 teaspoons vanilla extract
4 eggs	1 cup chopped pecans or walnuts (or mixed)
1 cup granulated sugar	
1 cup brown sugar	5 ounces miniature marshmallows

Melt chocolate and butter over warm water in top of double boiler. Beat eggs; add granulated and brown sugar, then flour sifted with baking powder. Stir in flavoring and nuts, then chocolate mixture. Turn into greased and lightly floured 15- x 10- x 1-inch pan and bake at 325° for about 25 to 30 minutes. Remove from oven; immediately spread marshmallows over top. While cake bakes, prepare Frosting.

Frosting

1/2 cup butter or margarine	2/3 cup evaporated milk (1 small can)
1 cup sugar	1 (1-pound) box powdered sugar
3 (1-ounce) squares unsweetened chocolate	1 teaspoon vanilla extract

Do not wash the chocolate pot; add to it 1/2 cup butter or margarine, sugar, unsweetened chocolate, and evaporated milk. Cook over boiling water until well blended. Beat in powdered sugar and vanilla extract. Pour immediately over hot marshmallow-covered brownies. Let set for 24 hours before cutting into 1-inch squares. Freezes beautifully. Yield: about 6 dozen; make the recipe twice for a tea for 40 to 50.

CHOCOLATE-PECAN MERINGUES
(may be prepared ahead of time)

2 egg whites	1 (6-ounce) package semi-sweet chocolate bits
1/8 teaspoon salt	
1/8 teaspoon cream of tartar	2/3 cup chopped pecans
3/4 cup sugar	1 teaspoon vanilla extract

Line cookie sheets with plain white paper. Beat egg whites, salt, and cream of tartar until frothy. Add sugar gradually, beating until stiff peaks form. Fold in chocolate, nuts, and flavoring. Drop by heaping teaspoonfuls 2 inches apart onto paper. Bake at 300° about 25 minutes. Remove with sharp spatula. Store in airtight container. Yield: 36; double the recipe for a tea for 40 to 50.

SWISS DOUBLES
(may be prepared ahead of time)

Make Birdie Cookies* with this exception: Do not brush with egg white or sprinkle with nuts. Bake the cookies plain and when cool, put two together (flat-sides together) with raspberry jam or apricot preserves as filling, to make sandwiches. Dust liberally with sifted powdered sugar. Freezes well. Yield: about 3 dozen; triple the recipe for a tea for 40 to 50.

*See Index for Birdie Cookies recipe.

FILLED PASTRIES
(see Index)

CARAMEL MERINGUE COOKIES
(may be prepared ahead of time)

1 **egg white**	1/2 **teaspoon vanilla extract**
Pinch cream of tartar	1/2 **teaspoon almond extract**
3/4 **cup light brown sugar, not packed**	3/4 **cup chopped pecans or walnuts**
1 **tablespoon all-purpose flour**	**(or mixed)**

Beat egg white with cream of tartar until soft peaks form. Beat in sugar and flour until stiff. Fold in flavorings and nuts; drop by teaspoonfuls onto greased baking sheet and bake at 325° for about 10 minutes. These cookies spread in baking, so allow for it. Store in airtight container. Freezes well. Yield: about 2 dozen; triple the recipe for a tea for 40 to 50.

MAKE TWO LISTS

Here's a suggestion which may appear to be kindergarten stuff, but it is born of sad experience, for I have been known to get halfway through a company dinner before realizing that one of the courses was still waiting in the refrigerator.

When planning a party, however informal, make two schedules: a daily order of battle made simultaneously with selection of the menu; and an hourly plan written down early on the day of the party.

The first schedule lists those dishes that may be prepared ahead of time, and how far ahead, even the separate steps which, though minor, are pure nuisance — toasting breadcrumbs, chopping nuts, mincing parsley.

The second timetable is the real countdown. It stipulates the time to remove the appetizers from refrigerator or freezer; when to drain the celery sticks; the time to plug in the coffee pot. It's a good idea, too, that the time for each operation not be too critical for with gremlins lurking about, it's wise not to cut your cloth too fine.

Old South Tea
TEA FOR TWENTY-FIVE

Chicken-Almond Sandwiches on Homemade Bread

Herb Bread Sandwiches

Nut Shortbread   **Coconut Meringue Cupcakes**

Almond Fingers

Brown-Eyed Susans   **Seven-Layer Cookies**

Gelatin Strawberries

Quick Petits Fours

Tea   **Coffee**

DAINTY CHICKEN-ALMOND SANDWICHES

Combine finely chopped almonds, minced cooked chicken, and diced celery with homemade mayonnaise. Spread on thinly sliced white bread with crusts removed. Cut into small squares and garnish with finely chopped parsley.

HOMEMADE BREAD
(see Index)

HERB BREAD

1 cake compressed yeast or 1 package active dry yeast	3/4 cup milk, scalded
1/4 cup warm water (very warm water for dry yeast)	About 3 to 3-1/2 cups sifted all-purpose flour
2 tablespoons sugar	1/2 teaspoon ground nutmeg
2 tablespoons shortening or margarine	1 teaspoon ground sage
1-1/2 teaspoons salt	1 teaspoon celery seed
	1 egg, slightly beaten

Dissolve yeast in warm water; set aside. Combine sugar, shortening, and salt in large bowl of electric mixer; stir in hot milk. Cool to lukewarm. Add about half the flour and mix well, then add nutmeg, sage, celery seed, egg, and yeast mixture. Beat until smooth; add remaining flour, or enough to make a moderately soft dough. Turn onto floured surface and knead until smooth, about 8 minutes. Place in lightly greased bowl, turn to grease other side. Cover and let rise in warm place until double, about 1-1/2 hours. Punch down, cover and let rest 10 to 15 minutes. Shape into round or rectangular loaf; put in greased 8- or 9-inch pieplate or rectangular loafpan. Cover with light cloth and let rise until almost double, about 1 hour. Bake at 375° for about 35 minutes, or until done. Just before removing from oven, brush surface with melted butter and let bake 5 minutes longer. Yield: 1 loaf.

Variation: Dill or caraway seed may be used instead of celery seed. Poultry seasoning may be used instead of sage.

Note: For tea sandwiches, fill thin slices with one of suggested fillings. I like a mixture of cream cheese, olives, and walnuts. — C. M.

NON-SWEET SANDWICH FILLINGS

1. Thinly sliced peeled cucumber and minced green pepper on bread spread with sour cream and prepared mustard.
2. Ground cooked lamb, chopped fresh mint, minced onion, mayonnaise, salt, and pepper.
3. Ground cooked ham, sweet pickle, and mayonnaise or whipped cream cheese.
4. 1-1/4 cups ground cooked beef, 1 teaspoon prepared horseradish, 1 tablespoon chili sauce, and about 2 tablespoons mayonnaise.
5. 1 cup ground cooked chicken, 1/4 cup each minced celery and cucumber, 1 tablespoon chopped capers, and 1/4 cup mayonnaise.
6. 1 cup minced or ground smoked salmon mixed with 1 teaspoon each lemon juice, chopped capers, and dill weed. Season to taste and add enough mayonnaise for spreading.
7. 4 ounces cream cheese with 1/4 cup chopped stuffed olives and 2 tablespoons chopped walnuts. Beat in a little cream to yield spreading consistency.

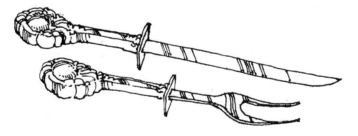

NUT SHORTBREAD
(may be prepared ahead of time)

1/2 cup powdered sugar	1/2 cup chopped pecans or walnuts
2-1/2 cups sifted all-purpose flour	1 cup butter or margarine
1/8 teaspoon salt	Nut halves for decorating

Combine sugar, flour, salt, and nuts in a bowl; cut in butter, then blend thoroughly with hands. Roll out to 1/3-inch thickness, cut with pastry wheel into 1-1/2-inch squares. Place on ungreased baking sheet; decorate with nut halves; bake at 275° for 45 minutes. Do not allow to brown. Freezes well. Yield: about 40.

COCONUT MERINGUE CUPCAKES
(may be prepared ahead of time)

3 egg whites
1/4 teaspoon cream of tartar
2/3 cup sugar
1/2 teaspoon almond extract

6 tablespoons all-purpose flour
1 (3-1/2 ounce) can coconut or 1-1/2 cups dry shredded coconut

Place fluted paper cups in a 12-muffin tin, the 2-1/2-inch size. Put egg whites and cream of tartar in small bowl of electric mixer; beat until frothy. Gradually add sugar, continuing to beat until stiff peaks form and sugar is thoroughly blended. Add almond extract, then flour, sprinkling a little at a time on the meringue, beating at low speed only until flour is blended. Fold in coconut; fill paper liners almost to top (these don't rise much). Bake at 325° for 30 minutes, or until golden brown. Freezes well. Yield: 12 muffins 2-1/2-inches across top. For a tea they should be made in smaller, tiny muffin cups and baked about 15 minutes. The recipe would then yield about 24 tiny cakes. Double the recipe for a tea for 25.

Note: If baked in 2-1/2-inch muffin tins, the cakes may be used in several ways. They may be used for a strawberry shortcake, the cakes split horizontally and sweetened strawberries spooned over the halves, then topped with vanilla ice cream. They may also be used topped with ice cream and hot sherry-flavored chocolate sauce spooned over them for a luscious dinner dessert.

ALMOND FINGERS
(may be prepared ahead of time)

1 cup butter, softened (no substitute)
1/2 cup powdered sugar
1-1/2 cups sifted all-purpose flour

Pinch salt
1 teaspoon almond extract
2 cups chopped toasted almonds

In large bowl of electric mixer cream together the butter and sugar thoroughly. Add flour sifted with salt, blend well, then beat in flavoring. Stir in almonds; chill about an hour for easier handling.

To bake, pinch off about a tablespoon of the mixture and roll between palms of hands into a 2-inch long cylinder about 1/2 inch thick. Place on lightly greased baking sheet and bake at 325° for 20 minutes, or until very lightly browned. Remove cookies to a flat pan onto which you have sifted powdered sugar, then sift more sugar over top of the cookies. Store in airtight container with waxed paper between layers. Freezes well. Yield: about 6 dozen.

BROWN-EYED SUSANS
(may be prepared ahead of time)

1 cup butter or margarine
6 tablespoons powdered sugar
1 teaspoon almond extract

2 cups all-purpose flour
1/2 teaspoon salt

Cream the butter in large bowl of electric mixer. Blend in sugar, flavoring, flour, and salt. Roll level tablespoons of this dough into balls; place on greased baking sheet and flatten slightly. Bake at 350° for about 12 to 15 minutes.

Frosting

1 cup sifted powdered sugar
2 tablespoons cocoa
2 tablespoons hot water

1/2 teaspoon vanilla extract
Almond halves

Combine sugar and cocoa; add water and vanilla. Put 1/2 teaspoon on each cookie; place an almond half in the center. Yield: about 5 dozen small cookies.

SEVEN-LAYER COOKIES
(may be prepared ahead of time)

5 tablespoons butter or margarine
1-1/2 cups graham cracker crumbs
1 cup coconut
1 cup semi-sweet chocolate bits
1 cup butterscotch bits

1 cup chopped nuts (pecans, walnuts, or mixed)
1 (15-ounce) can sweetened condensed milk

Put butter in a 9-inch square pan in a 325° oven. When butter has melted, spread crumbs evenly over butter. Now spread coconut, then chocolate bits, butterscotch bits, then nuts. Do not mix layers. Spread or pour condensed milk over all and bake at 325° for about 30 minutes (25 minutes if using glass dish). Cut into 1-1/2-inch squares. Freezes well. Yield: 36 squares; double the recipe for a tea for 25.

GELATIN STRAWBERRIES
(may be prepared ahead of time)

1 (15-ounce) can sweentened condensed milk
1 pound coconut, ground (be sure the package is marked fine; otherwise you'll have to grind it yourself)

2 (3-ounce) packages strawberry-flavored gelatin
1 cup finely ground almonds
1 tablespoon granulated sugar
1 teaspoon vanilla extract
1/2 teaspoon almond extract

Combine condensed milk, coconut, 1 package of the dry gelatin, almonds, sugar, and flavorings. Mix well, then with hands shape to form strawberries. Roll berries in the remaining package of gelatin to coat thoroughly. Allow to dry before storing.

For the leaves, use any kind of green-tinted frosting piped through a pastry tube to form leaf or stem. A piece of green candied cherry may be used, if desired.

To make small oranges, follow same directions, using orange gelatin.

These confections do not need refrigeration. They keep well for some time stored in a box or covered tin. They are delicious served as candy or to garnish fruit salads, tea trays, etc. Yield: 25 servings.

QUICK PETITS FOURS
(may be prepared ahead of time)

Make cake using pound cake mix or bake a pound cake in two 8-inch square pans. Cut slices about 3/4 inch thick. Then if desired cut slices in fancy shapes with small cutters. Put together sandwich-fashion with jam or jelly between.

To frost and decorate, put Petits Fours on rack with tray underneath to catch drippings. Spoon Petits Fours Frosting over cakes until coated, scraping frosting up from tray to reuse. When firm, decorate, using a pastry tube, with Decorating Frosting. If you have no pastry tube, you can improvise one with a sheet of stiff white paper. Freezes beautifully. Two 8-inch square cakes will yield about 50 small squares.

Petits Fours Frosting

1 cup granulated sugar
1/16 teaspoon cream of tartar
1/8 teaspoon salt
1/2 cup water
Sifted powdered sugar

Flavoring (1/2 teaspoon vanilla, almond, rum, brandy — any flavor you like)
Food coloring (optional)

Bring sugar, cream of tartar, salt, and water to a boil; cook to 236° on a candy thermometer (soft-ball stage). Cool to lukewarm (100°). Gradually beat in enough powdered sugar until thick enough to almost hold its shape. Add flavoring. Divide into four parts. If desired, leave one part white and tint others pink, yellow, green, etc.

Decorating Frosting

Mix until smooth two parts powdered sugar to one part butter or margarine. Flavor and color as desired. Or buy tubes of colored frostings which are available with decorating tips to fit the tubes.

NUTS

Scattered throughout this book you will find recipes that have nuts as an ingredient. Sometimes the recipes will stipulate the one kind of nut to be used, but more often, especially in pastry fillings, they will suggest "pecans or walnuts (or mixed)." This doesn't mean that I am uncertain about the kind that best suits the purpose; it means that some years ago I found that many of the best European pastry cooks mixed pecans and walnuts to yield an intriguing flavor which captured the best of both pecans and walnuts — and left one to wonder at the heavenly, indefinable results. — C.M.

Hearty Coffee

COFFEE FOR SIXTEEN TO TWENTY

Curried Meat Turnovers

Cheese Wafers

Vanilla Crumb Coffeecake

Filled Brownies   **Butterscotch Bars**

Orange-Almond Sweet Rolls

Coffee   **Tea**

CURRIED MEAT TURNOVERS
(may be prepared ahead of time)

Pastry

1 (8-ounce) package cream cheese, softened

1/2 cup butter or margarine, softened

2 cups all-purpose flour, sifted

1/2 teaspoon salt

Combine cream cheese, butter, flour, and salt; blend with fingertips until mixture holds together. Form into a ball, wrap in waxed paper and chill at least 4 hours, or overnight.

Filling

2 tablespoons butter or margarine

1 medium onion, chopped

1/4 pound fresh mushrooms, chopped

1-1/2 cups coarsely ground cooked pork (leftover roast pork is fine; any cooked meat or poultry may be used)

1 tablespoon sherry

1 tablespoon soy sauce

1/2 teaspoon sugar

1/2 teaspoon curry powder (or more, to taste)

About 2 to 3 tablespoons sweet or sour cream

Heat butter in skillet; add onion and mushrooms and sauté until onion is transparent. With slotted spoon, remove to bowl. Add pork to skillet and heat, stirring a minute or two. Add sherry, soy sauce, sugar, and curry powder. Mix well and cook over low heat for 2 to 3 minutes. Combine with mushrooms and onions, mix well, then add enough cream to moisten mixture. Allow to cool before using.

Roll dough as thin as possible on lightly floured board, about 1/8-inch thickness. Cut into 3-inch circles. Place scant teaspoon Filling on one side of circle; moisten edge of circle with water, fold dough over, moisten top edge with water, then press edges with fork to seal. Prick top with fork; place on ungreased baking sheet and bake at 400° for about 15 minutes, or until lightly browned. Yield: about 40 turnovers.

CHEESE WAFERS
(may be prepared ahead of time)

1 cup butter or margarine, softened	3 dashes cayenne pepper
1/2 pound sharp Cheddar cheese, shredded, softened	1 teaspoon steak sauce
	1 rounded tablespoon chives
1/2 teaspoon dry mustard	2-2/3 cups all-purpose flour, measured before sifting
1 teaspoon caraway seed	

Cream butter in large bowl of electric mixer, gradually beat in cheese and all other ingredients except flour. Beat thoroughly, then gradually blend in flour. Shape into four rolls about 1-1/2 inches in diameter. Wrap in waxed paper and refrigerate several hours.

To bake, cut slices 1/4 inch thick; place on ungreased baking sheet and bake at 350° for 12 to 15 minutes, or until just done. Freezes well. Yield: about 9 dozen wafers.

VANILLA CRUMB COFFEECAKE
(may be prepared ahead of time)

3 tablespoons sugar	2 eggs
1/2 cup chopped pecans	1 teaspoon vanilla extract
1 cup crushed vanilla wafers (about 28 wafers)	1/2 teaspoon almond extract
	2 cups sifted all-purpose flour
1/4 cup butter or margarine, melted	1 teaspoon baking powder
1/2 cup butter or margarine	1/4 teaspoon salt
1 cup sugar	1/2 cup milk

Put 3 tablespoons sugar, pecans, and crushed wafers into a bowl. Add 1/4 cup melted butter and mix well. Press mixture on bottom and sides of greased 9-inch tubepan, covering sides to within 1-1/2 inches from top of pan. Set aside.

Cream 1/2 cup butter with 1 cup sugar until light and fluffy in large bowl of electric mixer. Add eggs, flavorings, then sifted flour, baking powder, and salt, adding alternately with milk, beginning and ending with dry ingredients. Pour into prepared pan and bake at 350° for 1 hour or until cake is golden and cake tester inserted in center comes out clean.

Cool in pan for 10 minutes; invert to remove, then turn top-side up.

To freeze: Wrap cooled cake in foil and freeze. To serve, thaw 1 hour at room temperature.

FILLED BROWNIES

1 cup butter or margarine	1 teaspoon soda
2 cups firmly packed dark brown sugar	3/4 teaspoon salt
	2 cups coarsely crushed cornflakes
2 eggs	2 cups oatmeal
1 teaspoon vanilla extract	1 cup chopped pecans
1-1/2 cups all-purpose flour	

Cream butter and sugar in large bowl of electric mixer. Add eggs, one at a time, beating well after each addition. Add vanilla and beat thoroughly. Blend in flour, soda, and salt, which have been sifted together. Stir in cornflakes, oatmeal, and nuts. Press half this dough into bottom of greased 15- x 10- x 1-inch jellyroll pan and set aside. This dough is sticky; flour your fingers repeatedly to press down easily.

Filling

2 cups semi-sweet chocolate bits	3/4 cup sweetened condensed milk
2 tablespoons butter or margarine	1/2 teaspoon salt
2 teaspoons vanilla extract	1 cup finely chopped pecans

Melt chocolate and butter over hot water. Remove from heat; stir in flavoring, condensed milk, and salt. Add nuts, stir until smooth, then spread evenly over dough in pan. (A small spatula dipped repeatedly in hot water helps.) Spread reserved half of dough over chocolate filling, again using the hot spatula. Bake at 350° for 30 to 35 minutes. (The usual test for doneness won't work here as filling remains moist, but cake shrinks slightly from edges of pan when done.)

Let rest about 5 minutes, then using a sharp knife cut into 1-1/2-inch squares. Cool completely before removing from pan. These freeze well — and incidentally are excellent for shipping. Yield: 54 squares.

BUTTERSCOTCH BARS
(may be prepared ahead of time)

1-1/2 cups sifted all-purpose flour	1/4 teaspoon salt
3/4 cup brown sugar	1/2 cup soft butter

Combine all ingredients until blended; press into 13- x 9- x 1-inch ungreased pan. Bake at 375° for 10 minutes.

Frosting

1 (6-ounce) package butterscotch bits	1 tablespoon water
1/4 cup dark corn syrup	1 teaspoon salt
2 tablespoons butter or margarine	2 cups coarsely chopped walnuts

Combine butterscotch bits, corn syrup, butter or margarine, water, and salt in top of double boiler. Heat over boiling water and stir until smooth. Remove from heat; blend in chopped walnuts. Spread evenly over top of baked layer and bake for 10 minutes. Cut into bars while warm, cool and freeze if desired. Yield: about 4 dozen (2- x 1-inch) bars.

ORANGE-ALMOND SWEET ROLLS
(may be prepared ahead of time)

2 cakes compressed yeast or 2
  packages dry yeast
1/4 cup lukewarm water
  (very warm water for dry yeast)
1/2 cup soft butter or margarine
1 cup milk, scalded

1/2 cup granulated sugar
2 teaspoons grated orange rind
1 teaspoon almond extract
4 to 4-1/2 cups all-purpose flour,
  measured before sifting

Crumble yeast into lukewarm water in a small bowl and stir until dissolved. Put butter in large bowl of electric mixer. Pour over it the hot milk; stir until lukewarm. Add sugar, orange rind, yeast mixture, and flavoring. Beat well, then add flour, using just enough to yield a soft dough. Cover and let rise until almost double in bulk.

If you aren't ready to make rolls, punch dough down, cover and refrigerate. Dough will keep a day or two.

To bake: On floured surface roll out dough to a 24- x 12-inch rectangle. Spread lower half of the 24-inch side with filling; fold top dough over filling and press edges lightly to seal. Cut into 1-inch strips (crosswise); twist the strip several times; then, holding one end down on greased baking sheet, curl strip around the core or center and tuck the end under. Cover with light cloth and let rise until double in bulk (about an hour). Bake at 350° for 15 to 20 minutes, until light golden.

There are two ways of glazing these rolls. Combine 1/3 cup orange juice and 4 tablespoons sugar. Mix well, brush over top of rolls, return to oven and bake for 5 minutes longer.

Make a simple frosting by combining a tablespoon of butter, 3 or 4 tablespoons orange juice, 1/2 teaspoon almond extract, and about 3/4 cup powdered sugar. Drizzle over warm rolls a few minutes after removing from oven. Freezes well. Yield: about 32 rolls.

Neighborhood Coffee

COFFEE FOR SIXTEEN TO TWENTY

Hot Sesame-Cheese Rolled Sandwiches

Spiced Apricot Bread Dainty Sandwiches

Marzipan Cupcakes **Cherry Coffeecake**

Chocolate-Frosted Toffee Bars

Coffee **Tea**

SESAME-CHEESE ROLLED SANDWICHES

16 slices white bread, crusts removed
1 (6-ounce) jar processed yellow
  cheese spread

3 tablespoons sesame seed, toasted

Use a rolling pin to flatten slices of bread. Spread each with cheese; sprinkle with sesame seed. Roll each slice, jellyroll fashion; brush with melted butter; cover with waxed paper or plastic wrap; chill several hours.

Cut rolls in half crosswise and place on baking sheet, seam-side down; bake at 425° about 10 minutes, or until lightly browned. Yield: 32 small sandwiches.

SPICED APRICOT BREAD DAINTY SANDWICHES

1-1/2 cups dried apricots, diced
  1 cup sugar
  1/2 teaspoon cloves
  1/4 teaspoon ground nutmeg
  1/2 teaspoon ground cinnamon
  1/2 teaspoon salt
  6 tablespoons melted butter
    or margarine

1 cup water
1 egg, beaten
2 cups all-purpose flour,
  measured before sifting
1 teaspoon soda
1 cup chopped pecans or
  walnuts (or mixed)

Combine apricots, sugar, spices, butter, and water in saucepan. Cook 5 minutes and cool thoroughly. Add beaten egg, then flour sifted with soda. Stir in nuts, mix well and turn into greased 9- x 5- x 3-inch loafpan. Bake at 350° for 1 hour. Freezes beautifully.

For a party, chill bread, then slice thinly and make small dainty sandwiches. For filling use one of the following:

Sandwich Fillings

1. Softened cream cheese flavored with honey and lemon juice.
2. 1 cup chopped dates mixed with 1/4 cup orange juice and 1/4 cup finely chopped hazlenuts or walnuts.
3. 4 ounces cream cheese mixed with 1 tablespoon grated orange rind, 1/4 cup chopped raisins, 2 tablespoons chopped pecans, and 2 tablespoons orange juice.

MARZIPAN CUPCAKES
(see Index)

CHERRY COFFEECAKE

1/2 cup milk	1 (20-ounce) can cherry pie filling
2 tablespoons sugar	3/4 cup sugar
1 teaspoon salt	1 teaspoon ground cinnamon
2 tablespoons butter or margarine	1/4 teaspoon ground nutmeg
1 package active dry yeast	2 tablespoons butter or margarine, softened
1/4 cup very warm water	1 egg, slightly beaten
1 egg	1/3 cup light cream or evaporated milk
2 cups sifted all-purpose flour	

Put milk, 2 tablespoons sugar, salt, and 2 tablespoons butter in saucepan. Heat until just under boiling point; remove and cool to lukewarm.

Sprinkle yeast into warm water in large bowl of electric mixer. Stir until dissolved; add cooled milk mixture and egg. Gradually beat in flour. Cover with a damp towel; let rise in warm spot until double in bulk (about 1 hour). Punch dough down. Spread in greased 13- x 9- x 2-inch pan; spoon pie filling evenly over dough; you may have to do this in dabs, but never mind; do the best you can. Combine the 3/4 cup sugar with cinnamon, nutmeg, and soft butter. Reserve 2 tablespoons; sprinkle the rest over cherries. Cover with light cloth and let rise until double in bulk.

Bake at 375° for 20 minutes, or until golden. Mix beaten egg and cream; pour over cake, then sprinkle with reserved sugar mixture. Bake 20 minutes longer. Should be served warm from baking dish. Yield: 16 small servings.

CHOCOLATE FROSTED TOFFEE BARS
(may be prepared ahead of time)

1 (8-ounce) bar semi-sweet chocolate or 8 ounces semi-sweet bits
1 cup butter or margarine
1 cup firmly packed brown sugar
1 egg yolk

1/2 teaspoon vanilla extract
2 cups all-purpose flour, measured before sifting
1 cup finely chopped pecans

Start melting chocolate over warm water when you start mixing cookies. In large bowl of electric mixer cream butter and sugar until light and fluffy. Add egg yolk, vanilla, then flour. Mix well; spread in ungreased 15- x 10- x 1-inch pan. (You may find the spreading easier with flour-dipped fingers.) Bake at 325° for 20 to 25 minutes. Remove from oven and spread melted chocolate over surface while still warm. (A knife dipped repeatedly in very hot water keeps icing smooth while spreading.) Sprinkle immediately with nuts, pressing down lightly. Cut into 1- x 1-inch bars and remove from pan while slightly warm. Freezes well. Yield: about 56 bars.

Note: If chocolate becomes too stiff to spread, blend in a bit of vegetable shortening until smooth and manageable. Spread gently to avoid tearing surface of cake.

FOR THE CONVENIENCE OF GUESTS WHO SMOKE

Place several lighted candles around the room if you've invited guests who smoke. For some unknown reason they help to clear the air of smoke. Specially treated candles which do this little job even more effectively are available at most variety stores. They come in multicolored glass containers and also add to the overall decorative effect in the room. But most important, they ensure the comfort of non-smoking guests.

Set out your extra ashtrays the day before the party. There is nothing more discomforting to a smoker than a room without an ashtray, so always have plenty of them around. Be sure, too, that your ashtrays are large and comfortably spaced throughout the room.

Empty the ashtrays at regular intervals. It's easier to empty small ashtrays into one large one than it is to stack up several little ashtrays for emptying. A thoughtful hostess always provides filter and non-filter cigarettes in several convenient places throughout the room.

Farewell Coffee
COFFEE FOR SIXTEEN TO TWENTY

Hot Rolled Sandwiches

Herbed Cheese Dollars

Dainty Sandwiches of Orange, Date, and Pecan Bread

Gingersnaps   **Snickerdoodles**

Party Coffeecake   **Luscious Squares**

Coffee   **Tea**

HOT ROLLED SANDWICHES
(may be prepared ahead of time)

1 loaf thinly sliced white bread
  (about 16 slices)
1 (8-ounce) package cream cheese
  About 2 teaspoons anchovy paste

2 heaping tablespoons commercial
  sour cream
  Dash garlic powder

Trim crusts from bread; flatten with a rolling pin. Combine other ingredients with spread on bread slices. Roll up, jellyroll fashion. Cut each in half crosswise.

To freeze, place rolls, seam-side up, in shallow plastic freezer container with tight-fitting lid. Brush with melted butter; turn over; brush other side. Freeze.

To bake, remove rolls from freezer; let stand in container at room temperature 1 hour. Broil, 4 inches from heat, turning often, until hot and golden brown, 3 to 4 minutes. Yield: 32 sandwiches.

HERBED CHEESE DOLLARS
(may be prepared ahead of time)

1/4 cup butter or margarine, softened
1/2 pound sharp Cheddar
    cheese, shredded
  1 (3-ounce) package cream cheese
1-1/4 cups all-purpose flour, measured
    before sifting

1/4 teaspoon dried basil
1/4 teaspoon ground sage
1/4 teaspoon powdered thyme
  3 shakes cayenne pepper
  2 tablespoons dry white wine

Combine butter, Cheddar, and cream cheese in bowl of electric mixer. Beat until thoroughly blended. Add other ingredients, form into a long roll about the size of a silver dollar. Wrap in waxed paper and chill until firm.

To bake, slice 1/8 inch thick, place on lightly greased baking sheet and bake 10 minutes at 400°. Store in airtight tin. Freezes beautifully. Yield: about 6 dozen wafers.

Note: These wafers may be served with fruit salad or as an appetizer — or just any time you need a delicious nibble.

ORANGE, DATE, AND PECAN BREAD
(may be prepared ahead of time)

1 orange
About 1/2 cup boiling water
1 cup chopped dates
1 cup sugar
2 tablespoons melted butter
  or margarine
1 egg, beaten

2 cups all-purpose flour,
  measured before sifting
1 teaspoon baking powder
1/4 teaspoon salt
1 teaspoon soda
2/3 cup chopped pecans or walnuts
  (or mixed)

Wash and squeeze orange and add to the juice enough boiling water to yield 1 cup. Remove pulp from orange and put peeling through food grinder. Combine with dates, orange liquid, sugar, butter, and egg. Sift dry ingredients together three times and add; mix well; stir in nuts. Turn into greased loafpan and bake at 350° (325° for glass pan) about 50 minutes, or until bread tests done. Cool in pan. Freezes beautifully. Yield: 1 loaf.

To make dainty sandwiches, freeze or refrigerate bread and slice thinly. Fill with 8 ounces softened cream cheese blended with honey, lemon juice, 2 teaspoons orange juice, dash salt, and a few drops almond extract.

NEW ENGLAND GINGERSNAPS

3/4 cup butter or margarine
1 cup sugar
1 egg
4 tablespoons molasses
2 cups all-purpose flour,
  measured before sifting

2 teaspoons soda
1 teaspoon ground cinnamon
1 teaspoon ground cloves
1 teaspoon ground ginger
Granulated sugar

Cream butter and sugar together thoroughly in large bowl of electric mixer. Add egg, then molasses; beat well. Sift dry ingredients together, add to creamed mixture and beat until smooth. Refrigerate about 2 hours. Roll in small balls about the size of a quarter; drop into a bowl of granulated sugar, turn to coat well, then place 2 inches apart on greased baking sheet. Bake at 350° for 11 to 12 minutes. Allow to cool a minute before removing from pan. Freezes well. Yield: about 6 dozen.

Note: These cookies puff up while baking, then flatten. Don't be alarmed when they collapse; they're supposed to.

SNICKERDOODLES
(may be prepared ahead of time)

1 cup butter (no substitute)
1-1/4 cups sugar
2 eggs
1/2 teaspoon vanilla extract
1/2 teaspoon almond extract
1 teaspoon freshly squeezed lemon juice

2-3/4 cups all-purpose flour, measured before sifting
2 teaspoons cream of tartar
1 teaspoon soda
1/2 teaspoon salt
1 teaspoon grated orange rind (optional)

Beat butter and sugar thoroughly in large bowl of electric mixer. Add eggs one at a time, beating after each addition, then add flavorings and lemon juice. Sift dry ingredients together and add, then by hand stir in orange rind. Refrigerate 1 hour.

Drop by teaspoonfuls into bowl of granulated sugar, roll into balls and place about 1-1/2 inches apart on greased baking sheet. Bake at 350° for about 14 minutes, or until lightly browned. Remove from pan immediately. Freezes well. Yield: about 7 dozen cookies.

Note: It is the nature of Snickerdoodles to rise spectacularly during baking, then collapse as they brown. For a crisp cookie, allow to bake until this falling occurs. If you prefer a chewy cookie, you may underbake them.

PARTY COFFEECAKE
(may be prepared ahead of time)

1/2 pound butter or margarine
1 cup sugar
3 eggs
1 cup commercial sour cream
2-1/2 cups all-purpose flour, measured before sifting

2 teaspoons baking powder
1 teaspoon soda
1 teaspoon freshly squeezed lemon juice
1 teaspoon vanilla extract
1/2 teaspoon almond extract

Cream butter and sugar thoroughly in large bowl of electric mixer. Add eggs one at a time, beating after each addition. Beat in sour cream, then dry ingredients which have been sifted together three times. Blend in lemon juice, vanilla, and almond flavorings.

While cake bakes, prepare Filling. Spread half the batter in bottom of a
12- x 8- x 1-inch greased pan (or two 8-inch round pans). Sprinkle half the
Filling over batter; spoon remaining batter over Filling, spreading carefully with
small spatula or spoon to smooth. Sprinkle remaining Filling over top and bake
at 350° for about 35 minutes, or until cake tests done. Freezes beautifully.
Yield: 1 large rectangular or 2 round 8-inch cakes.

Filling

Combine 1-1/2 cups chopped pecans with 2/3 cup sugar and 1-1/2
teaspoons ground cinnamon.

LUSCIOUS SQUARES
(may be prepared ahead of time)

1 cup all-purpose flour, measured before sifting	2 tablespoons all-purpose flour
2 tablespoons sugar	1 teaspoon baking powder
1/2 cup butter (no substitute)	1 cup chopped pecans
3 eggs	1/2 cup flaked coconut
1-1/2 cups brown sugar	1 teaspoon vanilla extract
	Frosting

Sift 1 cup flour and sugar together into a bowl. With hands, blend in butter
until dough is smooth. Pat into bottom of a greased 9-inch square baking dish or
pan; bake at 325° for 10 to 15 minutes.

Meanwhile, in bowl of mixer beat eggs with brown sugar, 2 tablespoons
flour, and baking powder. Stir in pecans, coconut, and vanilla. Pour over baked
crust; return to oven for 25 minutes. Let remain in pan; when cool, frost and cut
into squares. Remove from pan carefully to avoid breaking bottom crust.
Freezes well. Yield: 36 (1-1/2-inch) squares.

Frosting

Combine 2 tablespoons melted butter with 1-1/2 cups powdered sugar
(more if needed) and 2 tablespoons light cream.

THE TREND SETTERS

Sometimes guests are reluctant to be the first to help themselves to a
spectacular, edible table arrangement like grapefruit shells filled with strawberries,
cantaloupe shells filled with green and pink melon balls, or other beautiful fruit.
Conspire with a friend to wait until the crowd around the table is at its height,
then have her casually spear a piece of the fruit with a cocktail pick. Once the
trend is started, your fruit centerpiece will be enjoyed to the hilt.

Holiday Reception
RECEPTION FOR FORTY TO FIFTY

Champagne Punch

or

Blushing Rose Punch

Holiday Eggnog

Thumbprint Cookies   Rocky Road Clusters

Coconut Chews

Tiny Pecan Tarts   Coconut Balls

Sherried Cupcakes

Holiday Fruit Bars   Cherry Delectables

Rum Squares

Brazil Nut Sticks   Meringue Fruit Drops

Salted Nuts

For a gala holiday tea or an open house, several of the above might be omitted and a selection of small sandwiches added. Some of these items are especially suited to holiday entertaining.

CHAMPAGNE PUNCH

1-1/2 cups powdered sugar	1 quart pineapple sherbet
1/2 cup curacao	3 bottles champagne
1/2 cup cognac	1 orange, sliced
1/2 cup maraschino cherry juice	1 lemon, sliced

Chill the punch bowl. Mix sugar and curacao thoroughly in a pitcher. Stir in cognac and cherry juice. Pour into punch bowl; gently place block of sherbet in center. Slowly add champagne and garnish with fruit slices. (Fruit will be prettier if small notches are cut in outer rim of rind to resemble flower petals.) Do not stir the punch after champagne is added. Yield: about 25 (punch-cup) servings; triple or quadruple recipe for a reception for 40 to 50.

Note: If it's a warm day and a convivial crowd, it might be wise to be prepared for everyone to require refills, so count on 8 ounces per guest.

BLUSHING ROSE PUNCH

1 pint cranberry juice cocktail	1 quart raspberry sherbet
1-1/2 cups freshly squeezed lemon juice	Ice Ring*
1 cup sugar	Lemon or lime slices
2 (28-ounce) bottles chilled ginger ale	

Combine cranberry juice cocktail, lemon juice, and sugar; blend well and chill. To serve, pour over ice ring in punch bowl, add chilled ginger ale, then gently stir in sherbet, garnish with lemon slices. Yield: about 30 (punch-cup) servings; double the recipe for a reception for 40 to 50.

*See Index for Ice Ring recipe.

HOLIDAY EGGNOG

3/4 cup sugar	1 quart heavy cream, unwhipped
10 egg yolks	10 egg whites, stiffly beaten
1 pint bourbon	Ground nutmeg
1 cup rum	

Cream sugar and yolks thoroughly. Add bourbon slowly stirring constantly, then add rum. Add unwhipped cream, then stiffly beaten egg whites. Stir lightly. Serve in punch cups with a dash of nutmeg sprinkled on top of each. Yield: 20 to 25 servings; make the recipe twice to serve 40 to 50.

THUMBPRINT COOKIES

1/2 cup soft butter or margarine	1/4 teaspoon salt
1/4 cup brown sugar	Finely ground pecans or walnuts (or mixed)
1 egg, separated	Chopped candy, fruit, jelly, or powdered sugar icing
1/2 teaspoon vanilla extract	
1 cup all-purpose flour	

Beat butter and brown sugar until blended in large bowl of electric mixer. Beat in egg yolk and vanilla. Sift together flour and salt and add to first mixture.

Prepare two bowls, one containing the slightly beaten egg white and the other the finely ground nuts. Roll dough into 1-inch balls and dip first in the egg white, then in nuts. Place about 1 inch apart on ungreased baking sheet. Bake at 350° for 5 minutes. Remove from oven and quickly press thumb down on each cookie, making a depression in center. Return to oven and bake 10 minutes longer. Cool and place in the little valley in the center a bit of chopped candy, candied fruit, jelly, or tinted powdered sugar. Freezes well. Yield: about 2 dozen cookies; triple the recipe to serve 40 to 50.

Note: The little cookies are beautiful placed in paper bonbon cups and used on a tray of assorted sweets.

ROCKY ROAD CLUSTERS
(may be prepared ahead of time)

2 cups semi-sweet chocolate bits	16 marshmallows, cut in pieces
3/4 cup white raisins	1-1/2 cups chopped walnuts

Melt chocolate over warm (not hot) water, stirring to keep smooth. Add remaining ingredients and when coated, drop by teaspoonfuls onto waxed paper. Let cool. Yield: 3 dozen; triple the recipe to serve 40 to 50.

COCONUT CHEWS

3/4 cup butter or margarine
1-1/2 cups all-purpose flour,
    sifted before measuring

3 tablespoons granulated sugar

Blend all ingredients together, pat into greased 8- x 12-inch pan; bake at 375° for 15 minutes. Prepare Filling.

Filling

3 eggs, separated
1-3/4 cups brown sugar
1 (3-1/2-ounce) can coconut

1 cup coarsely chopped pecans
    or walnuts (or mixed)

Beat egg whites until stiff; set aside. Combine other ingredients and fold in whites thoroughly. Pour over first layer; bake at 350° for 30 minutes. While hot cut into bars of desired size; replace pan in oven with heat turned off for 30 minutes. Yield: about 25 servings; double the recipe to serve 40 to 50.

TINY PECAN TARTS
(may be prepared ahead of time)

1 (3-ounce) package cream cheese
1/2 cup butter or margarine

1 cup sifted all-purpose flour

Combine cream cheese and butter; blend in flour; chill about 1 hour. Shape into balls about 1 inch in diameter and press into tiny ungreased muffin tins.

Filling

1 egg
3/4 cup brown sugar
1 tablespoon butter or
    margarine, melted

1 teaspoon vanilla extract
2/3 cup coarsely chopped pecans

Beat egg with wooden spoon; add brown sugar, melted butter, and vanilla. Mix well and stir in pecans. Pour into prepared shells and bake at 325° for about 25 minutes, cool before removing from pans. Yield: about 20; quadruple the recipe to serve 40 to 50.

COCONUT BALLS
(may be prepared ahead of time)

1 cup butter or margarine, softened
1/4 cup sifted powdered sugar
2 teaspoons vanilla extract
1 tablespoon water

2 cups all-purpose flour
1 cup chopped pecans
1 (8-ounce) package finely
    shredded coconut

Cream butter and sugar in large bowl of electric mixer. Blend in vanilla and water, then flour. Mix well and stir in nuts. Form into 1-inch balls and bake on ungreased baking sheet at 300° for 20 minutes, or until delicately browned. Cool thoroughly before removing from pan. Dip in Frosting, then roll some in white coconut, others in coconut tinted pink, yellow, or other colors of choice. Freezes! Yield: about 4 dozen; double the recipe to serve 40 to 50.

Frosting

4 cups sifted powdered sugar
1/2 cup milk or cream

1/2 teaspoon vanilla or almond extract
Dash salt

To sifted powdered sugar gradually add 1/2 cup milk or cream, blending until smooth. Add extract and a dash salt.

To tint coconut: Place shredded coconut in jar. Add a few drops food coloring. Cover and shake until coconut is uniform in color.

SHERRIED CUPCAKES

2 cups all-purpose flour, measured
    before sifting
3/4 teaspoon baking powder
1/2 teaspoon salt
1 cup chopped candied fruit (orange,
    pineapple, and cherries)
1 cup chopped pecans or walnuts
    (or mixed)

2/3 cup butter or margarine
1/2 cup granulated sugar
2/3 cup white corn syrup
  2 eggs
2/3 cup sherry
1/2 teaspoon almond extract

Sift flour, baking powder, and salt together. Put fruit and nuts on a sheet of waxed paper and sift over them 1/2 cup of the dry mixture; stir well to coat and set aside.

Cream butter and sugar together thoroughly in large bowl of electric mixer. Blend in corn syrup, then eggs one at a time, beating after each addition. Add dry ingredients alternately with sherry and flavoring, beginning and ending with dry ingredients. Fold in fruit-nut mixture. Turn into tiny greased muffin tins and bake at 325° for about 20 minutes. When cakes are cool, frost with a drizzle of powdered sugar frosting, flavored with almond extract and a few drops of sherry extract. Freezes well. Yield: 4 dozen tiny cakes; make this recipe twice to serve 40 to 50.

PUNCH TIP

Instead of using an ice block for your punch bowl, try this: Well ahead of time prepare a mixture of orange juice with any other fruit juice desired; it should be quite strong. Pour into a large round plastic container and freeze. You may add a few whole strawberries.

Before serving, remove ice block from container and place in punch bowl; pour punch over it. It will prevent punch from becoming watery and insipid during a long serving period.

HOLIDAY FRUIT BARS
(may be prepared ahead of time)

2 eggs
1 cup sifted powdered sugar
1/3 cup butter or margarine, melted
3/4 cup all-purpose flour, measured before sifting
1-1/2 teaspoons baking powder

1/4 teaspoon salt
1 cup coarsely chopped pecans or walnuts (or mixed)
1 cup chopped dates
3/4 cup candied fruit (cherries, candied pineapple, and orange peel)

Beat eggs until light in large bowl of electric mixer; gradually beat in sugar, then melted butter. Sift dry ingredients together; sift 1/2 cup over the nuts and fruit which have been spread on a sheet of waxed paper. Turn to coat thoroughly. Add remaining dry ingredients to first mixture, beat well, then stir in flour-coated fruit and nuts. Turn into greased 9-inch square pan and bake at 325° for about 35 minutes. Cut into bars and while warm spread thin glaze of powdered sugar icing (almond-flavored) over bars. If desired, decorate with a nut or piece of candied cherry. Freezes well. Yield: about 2 dozen small bars; make the recipe three times to serve 40 to 50.

CHERRY DELECTABLES
(may be prepared ahead of time)

1 (8-ounce) package cream cheese
1 cup soft butter (no substitute)
2 cups sifted all-purpose flour

1/4 cup brandy
1 (8-ounce) jar maraschino cherries
Powdered sugar

Blend cheese and butter; work in flour until stiff dough is formed; chill overnight. Combine brandy and cherries, with their juice, and let stand overnight.

When ready to bake, drain cherries thoroughly. Roll dough to 1/8-inch thickness on a surface sprinkled with powdered sugar. (Work with half the dough at a time, keeping remainder refrigerated.) Using a pastry wheel, cut into strips about 1 x 3 inches. Place a well drained cherry on each strip and roll up, pinching end of strip to seal. (The cherry will be exposed on both sides of the pastry strip.) Place, folded-side down, on lightly greased baking sheet and bake at 350° for about 15 minutes, or until very lightly browned. Remove; dust immediately with sifted powdered sugar. Freezes well. Yield: 10 dozen.

Variation: Pecan halves may be substituted for cherries, omitting soaking in brandy.

Note: This is a beautiful small cookie, ideal for glamorizing a tray of assorted fancy cakes.

RUM SQUARES
(prepare a long time ahead)

Cut angelfood cake into 3/4-inch squares. (A loaf cake is easiest for this purpose.) Dip cake squares into frosting made of 1/2 pound melted butter blended with powdered sugar and flavored with 1/2 cup rum. Roll in shredded toasted almonds and set aside until frosting hardens. These cake squares freeze beautifully.

The variations are infinite; cream and almond extract may be substituted for rum; cakes may be rolled in shredded coconut, plain or tinted; they may be made larger (similar to Petits Fours) and decorated in any way desired. Yield: 3 to 4 dozen squares.

BRAZIL NUT STICKS

2 eggs	1/2 teaspoon baking powder
2 cups brown sugar	1/2 teaspoon salt
1 teaspoon vanilla extract	1 pound ground Brazil nuts
1-3/4 cups all-purpose flour	

Beat eggs until light in large bowl of electric mixer. Gradually add sugar, beating well after each addition. Add vanilla. Sift flour, baking powder, and salt over nuts; mix well and add to first mixture, blending thoroughly; chill several hours.

Roll small pieces of dough no thicker than a pencil and about 2 inches long. Place on a well greased baking sheet and bake at 350° for 12 to 15 minutes. If desired, roll in powdered sugar. Freezes well. Yield: 150 sticks.

Variations: Reserve 1/2 to 3/4 cup of the ground nuts. After rolling sticks to desired shape, dip in slightly beaten egg white, then roll in ground nuts. Bake as directed.

Dip ends of baked sticks first in melted semi-sweet chocolate bits, then in ground nuts — or dip one end in chocolate and the other in nuts.

MERINGUE FRUIT DROPS

3 egg whites	1 cup chopped dates
1/2 teaspoon salt	1 teaspoon vanilla extract
1 cup sugar	1/2 teaspoon almond extract
1 cup flaked coconut	
1 cup chopped pecans or walnuts (or mixed)	

Beat egg whites with salt until stiff. Fold in all other ingredients. Drop on buttered baking sheet and bake at 325° for about 20 minutes; do not overbake. Yield: about 3 dozen; triple the recipe to serve 40 to 50.

Gala Reception

RECEPTION FOR FIFTY

Summer Party Punch

or

Citrus Cream Punch

Date-Nut Fingers   **Swedish Melting Moments**

Butter Meringue Squares

Bourbon Balls   **Millionaire Tarts**

Austrian Hazelnut Cookies

Chocolate Cherries   **Commercial Mints**

Assorted Petits Fours

Streusel Cake Squares   **Salted Nuts**

SUMMER PARTY PUNCH

1 cup freshly squeezed lemon juice	1 (28-ounce) bottle sparkling water, chilled
4-1/2 cups fresh orange juice	
1-3/4 cups medium-dry or sweet sherry	1 orange, sliced (notch edges of peeling to resemble flower petals)
1/2 cup brandy	
1/2 cup light rum	1 lemon, sliced (notch edges of peeling to resemble flower petals)
3/4 cup sugar	
	Fresh mint

Combine lemon juice, orange juice, sherry, brandy, rum, and sugar, stirring until sugar is dissolved. Chill well. To serve, pour over ice in punch bowl; stir in sparkling water. Float orange and lemon slices in the punch and garnish with fresh mint. Yield: 3 quarts, or 25 (punch-cup) servings. Triple the recipe to serve 50.

ICE RING FOR PUNCH BOWL

Fill a 6- or 8-cup ring mold with water; set in freezer for 4 hours, or overnight, or until frozen solid. To unmold, let stand at room temperature about 5 minutes, or until ice ring is movable in mold. Invert onto a cookie sheet and slide carefully into punch bowl.

Variation: For a colorful Strawberry Ice Ring, pour water to a depth of 1/4 inch into a 6- or 8-cup ring mold; freeze about 20 minutes, or until firm. Arrange about 8 whole strawberries on top of frozen layer; pour in 3/4 cup water; freeze. To keep berries in place, keep adding water, a little at a time, freezing after each addition, until mold is filled. Freeze until solid. To unmold, let stand at room temperature about 5 minutes or until ice ring is movable in mold. Invert onto a cookie sheet and slide carefully into punch bowl. The same method may be used with fresh mint leaves, pineapple cubes, and other small fruits.

CITRUS CREAM PUNCH

1 (12-ounce) can frozen
  lemonade concentrate
1 (6-ounce) can frozen orange
  juice concentrate

9 (6-ounce) cans cold water
5 pints pineapple sherbet
1 quart vanilla ice cream

Combine lemonade concentrate, orange concentrate, and cold water in large pitcher. Place the pineapple sherbet and ice cream in punch bowl; pour contents of the pitcher over these and stir until sherbet and ice cream are fairly well incorporated into the liquid punch. Yield: about 5 quarts, or 40 (punch-cup) servings. Double the recipe to serve 50.

    Note: For a sparkling, more tangy punch, add to the punch bowl a 28-ounce bottle of ginger ale.

DATE-NUT FINGERS
(may be prepared ahead of time)

1 cup chopped dates
1 cup chopped pecans or walnuts
  (or mixed)
1 cup sugar
1/2 cup butter or margarine

1 tablespoon light corn syrup
1 egg, well beaten
2 cups rice cereal (bits, not squares)
1/4 teaspoon almond extract
1/2 teaspoon vanilla extract

Combine all ingredients except cereal bits and flavorings in a deep saucepan. Cook for 10 minutes, stirring constantly. Do not overcook. Remove from heat; stir in cereal and flavorings and set aside to cool. Mixture will be sticky, but never mind; dust hands with powdered sugar and form small finger-size rolls. Drop into bowl of powdered sugar or finely grated coconut; roll until well coated. Yield: about 5 dozen.

SWEDISH MELTING MOMENTS
(may be prepared ahead of time)

1/2 pound butter or margarine
5-1/2 tablespoons powdered sugar
1-1/4 cups all-purpose flour

1/2 cup cornstarch
1/4 teaspoon almond extract
1/4 teaspoon orange extract

Cream butter with sugar in large bowl of electric mixer; sift in flour and cornstarch and mix thoroughly. Add flavorings and chill for 1 hour. Shape into balls the size of a walnut and place on greased baking sheet. Flatten with bottom of a small wet glass; bake at 350° for 10 minutes.

    These cookies do not brown. Carefully remove from pan and while warm spread with Cookie Glaze. Yield: 25 servings; double the recipe to serve 50.

Cookie Glaze

Beat together 1 cup powdered sugar, 1 tablespoon melted butter, 1 tablespoon lemon juice, and 1 tablespoon orange juice.

Note: This is a very special, delicate party cookie and should not be used just to fill a cookie jar for casual nibbling.

BUTTER MERINGUE SQUARES
(may be prepared ahead of time)

1 cup butter or margarine	2 eggs, separated
1 cup sugar	2/3 cup sugar
2 cups all-purpose flour, measured after sifting	1-1/2 teaspoons ground cinnamon
1 tablespoon ground cinnamon	1 cup chopped walnuts

Cream butter and 1 cup sugar thoroughly in large bowl of electric mixer. Add egg yolks and beat well. Blend in flour sifted with the 1 tablespoon cinnamon. Spread on ungreased 15- x 10-inch pan.

Beat egg whites lightly with fork and pour over surface of dough. Mix the 2/3 cup sugar with 1-1/2 teaspoons cinnamon and nuts; sprinkle evenly over egg whites. Bake at 325° for 30 to 35 minutes. Cut into squares while hot and allow to cool in pan, then remove with spatula. These may be frozen or stored for some time in a tin with tight-fitting cover. Place sheets of waxed paper between layers. Yield: about 4 dozen bars or squares.

BOURBON BALLS
(may be prepared ahead of time)

2 tablespoons cocoa	2 cups crushed vanilla wafers (or similar plain cookie)
1 cup powdered sugar	
1/4 cup bourbon (rum may be substituted)	1 cup finely chopped pecans or walnuts (or mixed)
2 tablespoons light corn syrup	

Sift cocoa and sugar into a bowl. Stir in bourbon which has been combined with syrup. Mix well; add crumbs and nuts and mix well again. Roll into small balls about 3/4 inch in diameter. Drop into a bowl of powdered sugar, roll around to coat on all sides, and allow to dry several hours before using. Freezes well. Yield: 3 dozen; triple the recipe to serve 50.

MILLIONAIRE TARTS

4 tablespoons water	1 cup chopped pecans or walnuts (or mixed)
1 cup white raisins	
3 eggs, beaten	1 teaspoon ground cinnamon
1-1/2 cups sugar	1/4 teaspoon ground allspice
2 tablespoons butter or margarine	1/2 teaspoon ground nutmeg
1 tablespoon vinegar	24 baked Tiny Tart Shells*

Put water and raisins in saucepan; boil 5 minutes. Add all other ingredients except nuts and cook until thick, stirring constantly. Cool; stir in nuts.

Pour into baked Tiny Tart Shells. Top with a bit of brandy-flavored whipped cream. Yield: 24 tiny tarts.

These small rich tarts are an excellent substitution for fruitcake or mincemeat tarts, ideal for winter teas and receptions.

*See Index for Tiny Tart Shells recipe.

AUSTRIAN HAZELNUT COOKIES
(may be prepared ahead of time)

First, toast 1 cup sliced hazelnuts (filberts) for about 20 minutes in a 250° oven. Cool and grind, reserving a few whole nuts for decorating.

1 cup all-purpose flour	1/4 teaspoon almond extract
1/3 cup sugar	Ice water
3/4 cup ground hazelnuts	Chocolate Butter Filling
1/2 cup soft butter (no substitute)	Chocolate Frosting

Sift flour and sugar into bowl; stir in nuts. With pastry blender cut in butter; sprinkle with ice water and flavoring until dough holds together. Form into a ball, wrap in waxed paper and chill for 1 to 2 hours.

When ready to bake, roll out dough on floured surface to 1/8-inch thickness. Cut into 2-inch rounds, using a scalloped cutter if you have one. Place on ungreased baking sheet and bake at 375° for 7 to 10 minutes, only until light golden.

Have filling and frosting ready before baking the cookies as they should be frosted while warm. Spread filling between two cookies, bottoms together, as for sandwiches. Spread top with frosting and sprinkle with a few sliced reserved nuts. Press nuts down lightly to anchor them to the frosting. Yield: 36 single cookies, or 18 sandwich cookies; triple the recipe to serve 50.

Chocolate-Butter Filling

Cream 2 tablespoons butter with 1/3 cup sifted powdered sugar. Blend in 1 (1-ounce) square melted and cooled chocolate; add 1/4 teaspoon almond extract.

If you prefer, you may substitute raspberry, cherry, or strawberry jelly or jam for the Filling.

Chocolate Frosting

Cream 1 tablespoon butter with 1/3 cup sifted powdered sugar. Add 1 egg yolk, 1 ounce melted and cooled chocolate and 1/2 teaspoon almond extract. Freezes well.

CHOCOLATE CHERRIES
(may be prepared ahead of time)

1 (7-1/4-ounce) package vanilla wafers, finely crushed
1/2 cup powdered sugar
1/2 cup chopped walnuts
1/4 cup boiling water
2 tablespoons butter or margarine
1 tablespoon light corn syrup
2 teaspoons instant powdered coffee

30 maraschino cherries with stems
2 (6-ounce) packages semi-sweet chocolate bits
Flaked coconut (optional)
Multi-colored sprinkles (optional)
Chocolate sprinkles (optional)
Chopped nuts (optional)

Mix vanilla wafer crumbs, powdered sugar, and walnuts. Combine water, butter, corn syrup, and instant coffee. Add to first mixture. Shape approximately 1/2 tablespoon of this mixture around each cherry. Cover and refrigerate at least 1 hour.

Melt chocolate over warm water. Holding stem, dip coated cherries into chocolate, coating carefully and completely. Place on wire rack over waxed paper. After about 5 minutes, garnish with coconut, sprinkles, or nuts if desired. Refrigerate until chocolate has hardened. Yield: 2-1/2 dozen; double the recipe to serve 50.

ASSORTED PETITS FOURS
(may be prepared ahead of time)

Petits Fours are not hard to make, despite these lengthy, detailed instructions. The important fact is that to make proper ones that resemble the commercially produced cakes, you must allow plenty of time and be reconciled to making the authentic Fondant Frosting, which should be made at least 2 days before the little cakes. Happily, these freeze beautifully, so just set aside some time when you're not preoccupied with trivialities and you'll be more than compensated when your guests wonder how you could ever have afforded a whole table-full of Petits Fours. This recipe makes 50 delicious Petits Fours; double the recipe to serve 50 guests. — C.M.

Fondant

2 cups boiling water
6 cups sugar

1/4 teaspoon cream of tartar

Put ingredients in a deep heavy saucepan; stir until sugar has dissolved, then cook quickly without stirring until syrup reaches 236° on a candy thermometer (or to soft-ball stage when a little is dropped into cold water). Occasionally wash off crystals that form on sides of pan, using a brush dipped in cold water.

Pour onto a buttered marble slab, large pan, or platter. Cool until lukewarm, then using a spatula pull sides into middle repeatedly until mixture turns white and thick. Let stand 5 minutes, then knead with buttered hands until creamy enough to form a firm ball. At first it will be crumbly, but butter hands heavily and often. Store Fondant in a tightly covered container for at least 2 days before using. Yield: 1 quart. This is too much for the recipe that follows, but it keeps well, refrigerated or frozen, and it's advisable to have enough on hand for more than one batch of cakes.

To prepare Fondant for frosting cakes, warm 1 or 2 cups slowly over hot water (do not allow water to boil or Fondant will lose its shine and become dull and unattractive). If you wish, tint desired share with a few drops of food coloring. Stir in flavoring to taste, such as vanilla, rum, almond, or other extracts. Thin Fondant to heavy cream consistency by adding a few drops of hot water at a time.

Chocolate Fondant

Melt 2 (1-ounce) squares unsweetened chocolate; cool. Add it to 1 cup Fondant and stir mixture over a low flame until it is warm to the touch. Add 1/2 teaspoon vanilla and thin to the right consistency with a little warm water.

Pound Cake

Pound cake is most satisfactory for Petits Fours as it cuts cleanly and does not crumble.

1 cup butter (no substitute)	2-1/4 cups all-purpose flour, sifted before measuring
1 cup sugar	1/8 teaspoon salt
6 eggs	
1 teaspoon vanilla extract	

Cream butter thoroughly in large bowl of electric mixer. Beat in sugar until mixture is light and fluffy. Add eggs one at a time, blending well after each addition. Add vanilla, then sifted dry ingredients. Butter two 8-inch square pans; line bottoms with waxed paper, butter the paper, then dust with flour. Pour equal amount of batter in each pan and spread evenly. Bake at 300° for about 40 minutes or until cakes test done. Cool in pans about 5 minutes, invert onto wire racks and peel off paper. Let cool and if desired wrap in foil and freeze until ready to use.

To complete the Petits Fours: Trim edges from cakes and cut into 1-1/4-inch squares or rectangles about 2 x 1-1/4 inches. The little cakes may now be frosted; however, the most elegant Petits Fours are filled with a butter cream before frosting. Here's the way: Cut a 1/3-inch slice from top of each cake and lay it aside. Hollow out the center of cake, fill with Butter Cream Filling and replace top. Place cakes on a wire rack on a pan and work quickly to coat top and sides with Fondant. Decorate tops with nuts, chocolate shots, silver dragees, or candied fruit. Put in paper bonbon cups and arrange beautifully on silver tray.

Basic Butter Cream Filling

Combine 3/4 cup sugar, 1/4 cup water, and 1/8 teaspoon cream of tartar in saucepan; stir until dissolved. Cook rapidly to 240° on candy thermometer, or until syrup spins a thread. Meanwhile, beat 5 egg yolks until very light. Pour syrup in a slow steady stream into yolks, beating constantly until mixture is thick and cool. Whip 1 cup soft butter and blend thoroughly into yolk mixture; flavor with any extract or liqueur desired. Keep at room temperature to use immediately or store covered in refrigerator, or freeze, for later use. Yield: about 2 cups; enough for about 50 square Petits Fours or 30 rectangular ones cut from the two square 8-inch pound cakes.

Filling Variations: For Orange Butter Cream, blend 1/2 cup Basic Butter Cream with 2 teaspoons thawed frozen orange juice concentrate and 1/4 teaspoon grated orange rind.

For Mocha Butter Cream, dissolve 2 teaspoons cocoa and 1/2 teaspoon powdered coffee in 1-1/2 teaspoons hot water. Blend with 1/2 cup Basic Butter Cream Filling.

STREUSEL CAKE SQUARES
(may be prepared ahead of time)

1/2 cup butter or margarine	2 cups all-purpose flour, measured after sifting
1 (8-ounce) package cream cheese	2 teaspoons baking powder
1-1/4 cups sugar	1/2 teaspoon soda
2 eggs	1/2 teaspoon salt
1 teaspoon vanilla extract	1/2 cup milk
1/2 teaspoon almond extract	

Cream butter and cheese thoroughly in large bowl of electric mixer. Add sugar gradually, beating after each addition. Add eggs one at a time, beating well after each addition, then flavorings. Sift dry ingredients together three times; add to batter alternately with milk, beginning and ending with dry ingredients. Pour into greased 13- x 9- x 2-inch pan; sprinkle with crumb topping and bake at 350° for 35 to 40 minutes. Cut in small squares and arrange attractively on tray. Yield: 7 or 8 dozen small squares.

Topping

Mix 1/2 cup flour with 1/2 cup sugar. Cut in 1/4 cup butter or margarine; add 1/2 cup coarsely chopped pecans.

Brunches

A brunch starts the day in a relaxed festive way. It's a time to appreciate an especially good morning, whether it's just the family on a lazy Saturday or a crowd before the ball game.

The time is as flexible as the feeling, and the hostess is left to choose which hour best suits her, her guests, and the activities that follow. As the noon hour approaches, the dishes move from the egg and bacon sphere to luncheon fare. But for those who can't fathom a brunch without eggs, there are several variations on the ever-popular fluffy scrambled ones.

A brunch suggests a hearty meal, as it is intended to take the place of breakfast and lunch. The heartiness depends on the function. Before a hunt you may see several meats, a variety of eggs and breads, grits and stewed tomatoes. But after a morning wedding, a brunch would most likely resemble a light but elegant luncheon.

For a start, those who really haven't had breakfast appreciate something refreshing, a juice or fruit perhaps. And to add a bit of the unexpected, serve an unusual bread, salad, or your own special creation.

Chicken Casserole Brunch

BRUNCH FOR TEN

Vegetable-Clam Juice Cocktail

Continental Chicken Casserole with Buttered Toast Points

Sliced Ham and Scrambled Eggs   **Asparagus with Cashew Butter**

Hungarian Coffeecake

Sliced Oranges Acapulco with Cornelia's Cookies

or

Cantaloupe or Melon with Wedge of Lemon or Lime

Coffee

VEGETABLE-CLAM JUICE COCKTAIL
(may be prepared the day before)

4 cups V-8 juice	1 teaspoon Worcestershire sauce
4 cups bottled clam juice	1/4 teaspoon salt
1/4 cup freshly squeezed lemon juice	Several grinds white pepper

Combine all ingredients in large pitcher and refrigerate until serving time. Serve in old-fashioned glasses with a celery stick for stirring. Yield: 10 servings.

CONTINENTAL CHICKEN CASSEROLE
(may be prepared ahead of time)

3 tablespoons butter	1/2 teaspoon sugar
6 tablespoons all-purpose flour	1/8 teaspoon cayenne pepper
2 cups chicken broth	1/2 teaspoon paprika
1 cup light cream	1/2 teaspoon seasoned salt
1 teaspoon prepared yellow mustard	1/4 cup dry sherry
1/2 teaspoon salt	4 hard-cooked eggs, cubed
Dash pepper	4 cups cooked chicken, chopped
1/8 teaspoon allspice	Buttered breadcrumbs
1/8 teaspoon ground nutmeg	

Melt butter in saucepan and stir in flour until smooth. Over low heat, slowly blend in broth, then cream. Cook over medium heat until thick, stirring constantly. Combine all seasonings, then blend into sauce. Stir in wine; fold in eggs and chicken. Turn into buttered 3-quart casserole, top with crumbs and bake at 350° for 30 minutes. Leftover turkey may be substituted for chicken with excellent results. Yield: 10 to 12 servings.

HEAT-AND-HOLD SCRAMBLED EGGS
(see Index)

ASPARAGUS WITH CASHEW BUTTER

3 pounds fresh asparagus, or 3 (10-ounce) packages frozen

1/2 cup butter or margarine

6 teaspoons freshly squeezed lemon juice

1/2 teaspoon dried marjoram

1/2 cup salted cashew nuts, coarsely chopped

Cook asparagus in salted water in large covered skillet until tender, about 18 minutes; or if using frozen asparagus, cook as directed on package. Drain and arrange on heated platter. While asparagus cooks, melt butter in small saucepan; add lemon juice, marjoram, and cashew nuts. Simmer over low heat for about 3 minutes. Pour over cooked asparagus. Yield: 10 servings.

HUNGARIAN COFFEECAKE

Prepare Coffeecake Dough. When ready to bake, make a little assembly line consisting of bowl of chilled dough; 1 stick butter or margarine, melted; 1-1/2 cups brown sugar mixed with 1-1/2 teaspoons cinnamon; and 1 cup chopped pecans.

Grease a deep tubepan well. With teaspoon, scoop out balls of dough about the size of a walnut; dip in butter, then in sugar-cinnamon mixture; place in pan. Continue until bottom of pan is full, then sprinkle with nuts. (If you like white raisins, add a layer at this point; do not use them on top of cake; they scorch.)

Make another layer in same manner; there should be two layers. If you have any butter left, drizzle over top. Cover with light cloth and allow to rise until double in bulk. Bake at 350° for about 45 minutes, or until done.

To glamorize this beautiful cake, you may invert it very carefully so it will hold its shape, then invert again to bring top-side up. Drizzle simple icing over top, allowing it to run down sides.

Caution: This is a rich, buttery, tender dough. When you invert pan to remove cake, some of the balls of dough may threaten to break loose from main body of cake. To avoid this, arm yourself with several tall objects (a pitcher, a vase, a tall pepper grinder) to quickly support the balls until the cake cools and filling between layers has a chance to solidify and glue the whole together. Freezes well.

COFFEECAKE DOUGH

1 cup milk	4 to 4-1/2 cups all-purpose flour
6 tablespoons sugar	1/2 cup melted butter or margarine
1/2 teaspoon salt	1/2 teaspoon vanilla extract
2 cakes compressed yeast	1/2 teaspoon almond extract
2 eggs, lightly beaten	Extra softened butter or margarine

Scald milk; cool to lukewarm. Put sugar, salt, and crumbled yeast into large mixer bowl. Pour in milk, stir until yeast is dissolved. Add eggs, then sift in 2 cups of the flour. Beat well; add melted butter, flavorings, then remaining 2 (or more) cups flour, scraping the bowl often. Add only enough flour to yield a soft dough. Beat a minute or two with wooden spoon, cover with light cloth and allow to rise in warm spot until double in bulk. Punch dough down, cover and refrigerate several hours or overnight.

SLICED ORANGES ACAPULCO
(may be prepared the day before)

7 or 8 ripe juicy oranges	Ground cinnamon
7 or 8 tablespoons powdered sugar	

Peel and section oranges. Arrange attractively on large platter; sift powdered sugar over all, then sprinkle with cinnamon. Oranges may be prepared the day before, with sugar and cinnamon added just before serving. Yield: 10 servings.

CORNELIA'S COOKIES
(prepare for baking the day before)

1 cup light brown sugar	1 cup all-purpose flour, sifted
1/2 cup butter, melted (no substitute)	Pinch soda
1 egg, lightly beaten	1 cup pecans, cut or broken, not ground

Combine sugar, butter, and egg. Beat well. Combine flour, soda, and nuts and blend into first mixture. Form into a roll and wrap in waxed paper; refrigerate overnight.

To bake: Slice very thin and bake on greased baking sheet for 8 to 10 minutes at 375°. Watch these cookies; they burn easily. Remove from pan immediately. Yield: about 30 to 36 cookies.

ASK A FRIEND TO HELP

If you're hostessing a party without help, ask a friend to keep you posted on when trays need replenishing. Better yet, ask her to refill them herself. I have never known a guest who wasn't pleased to be asked to help in this way.

He-Man Brunch

BRUNCH FOR SIX

Tomato Cocktail

or

Rum Bob Newell

Corned Beef Hash Patties

or

Ham with Red-Eye Gravy

Double-Boiler Scrambled Eggs

Celery, Cauliflower Flowerets, Cherry Tomatoes, Radishes, and Green Onions

Served with

Sour Cream, Lemon Juice, and Dill Weed

Baked Southern Grits

Fresh Fruit   **Viennese Schnecken**

Coffee

A Silk Purse Menu — Looks and tastes expensive, but isn't.

TOMATO COCKTAIL
(prepare ahead of time)

4 cups tomato juice

1 medium cucumber, peeled and chopped fine (save a small chunk to mince for garnish)

2 tablespoons minced scallions, including green stems

1 teaspoon Worcestershire sauce

Juice of 1 lemon

1/2 teaspoon grated lemon rind

2 teaspoons prepared horseradish

1 clove garlic, peeled and crushed

1/4 teaspoon freshly ground black pepper

3 drops Tabasco sauce

8 lemon wedges

Place all ingredients except lemon wedges in large bowl or pitcher and mix well. Cover and refrigerate for 2 to 3 hours. Strain and check seasoning; it may need salt. Serve in chilled glasses and garnish top with a bit of finely chopped cucumber and a sprig of watercress if desired. Serve with lemon wedges. Yield: 8 servings.

RUM BOB NEWELL
(see Index)

CORNED BEEF HASH PATTIES

1 pound cooked or canned corned beef	1 small stalk celery
2 cups cooked potatoes (3 to 4 medium potatoes)	1/2 teaspoon black pepper
1 small onion	3/4 cup light cream
1/2 green pepper	4 tablespoons butter or margarine
	Minced parsley

Put beef (leftover home corned beef is fine), potatoes, onion, green pepper, and celery through coarse blade of food grinder (or chop in wooden bowl). Add black pepper, then gradually the cream, until well blended. The mixture should hold together but not be overly moist. Turn out onto a sheet of waxed paper and pat out about 1 inch thick. Using a 3-inch cutter (if you don't have one, improvise, using a large glass or anything else of proper size). Cut six patties. Heat butter in large skillet and brown patties on both sides. Scatter minced parsley over top to serve. Yield: 6 servings.

HAM WITH RED-EYE GRAVY

6 slices Smithfield country-cured ham (1/2-inch thick)	2 cups boiling water

Soak ham slices in cold water at least 6 hours (it is very salty). Dry on paper towels. Remove hard black rind. Put slice into ungreased heavy skillet at fairly high heat. Fry each side 5 to 7 minutes to a good brown, but do not burn.

Remove slices to platter, pour off all but 3 tablespoons of fat. Put pan back on stove so it is smoking hot. Add boiling water. Let boil up and be sure to scrape all "fry" from the bottom to blend into the gravy. Pour over the ham slices and serve with grits.

DOUBLE-BOILER SCRAMBLED EGGS

12 eggs	Dash pepper
1/2 cup milk	3 tablespoons butter
3/4 teaspoon salt	

Break eggs into bowl. Add milk, salt, and pepper; beat thoroughly with fork. Melt butter in top of double boiler over boiling water. Add eggs; cover, and stir now and then until eggs thicken. Remove from heat; continue stirring until eggs are set. They should be soft, fluffy — and completely digestible! Yield: 6 servings.

BAKED SOUTHERN GRITS

1 teaspoon salt
4 cups water
1 cup hominy grits
1/2 cup butter or margarine

1 cup milk
4 eggs, slightly beaten
1/2 cup shredded Cheddar cheese

Add salt to water; bring to a boil. Stir in grits slowly, keeping water at a brisk boil. Cover and cook slowly for 1 hour, or until grits are soft, stirring occasionally. Remove from heat; stir in butter and milk. Cool to lukewarm; beat in eggs and turn into greased 2-quart casserole. Bake at 350° for 1 hour or until knife inserted in center comes out clean. Ten minutes before dish is done, sprinkle cheese over top and bake until golden. Yield: 6 servings.

Variations: For more pronounced cheese flavor, stir in 1-1/2 cups shredded Cheddar cheese before baking. And for garlic cheese grits, stir in a 6-ounce roll of garlic cheese before baking. For a sharp, tangy casserole, 1/4 teaspoon cayenne pepper may be added. If you're a grits fancier, anything you do to the dish is right!

VIENNESE SCHNECKEN
(may be prepared ahead of time)

2 cakes compressed yeast or 2 packages
    dry yeast
2 teaspoons sugar
2 cups warm milk
1/2 pound butter or margarine
1 cup sugar

3 egg yolks
1 whole egg
1/2 teaspoon vanilla extract
1/2 teaspoon almond extract
7 cups all-purpose flour
1 cup white raisins (optional)

Dissolve yeast and 2 teaspoons sugar in warm milk (use very warm water for dry yeast); set aside. Cream butter in large bowl of electric mixer, gradually add sugar, and mix thoroughly. Beat in egg yolks and whole egg. Add extracts, then flour alternately with yeast-milk mixture. If using raisins, add them at this point. (If you're using an electric mixer, the last cup of flour may have to be added by hand as the dough stiffens and causes the mixer to balk.) Beat well with wooden spoon until blisters form on the dough; cover with cloth and let rise until double in bulk. If you aren't ready to use dough, punch down, cover and refrigerate several hours or overnight.

When ready to bake, have the following ready: 1-1/2 cups brown sugar mixed with 1-1/2 teaspoons cinnamon; pecan halves; 3/4 cup butter or margarine, melted; some maple syrup.

Grease small muffin tins. (I use tins measuring 1-3/4 inches across top and 3/4 inch deep.) Place 1 teaspoon butter, 1 teaspoon sugar-cinnamon mixture, 1 teaspoon syrup and 1 or 2 pecan halves in bottom of each muffin cup.

Schnecken Filling

2 cups finely chopped pecans	2 tablespoons freshly squeezed lemon juice
1/2 cup brown sugar	
1/2 cup granulated sugar	2 teaspoons grated orange rind
2 teaspoons ground cinnamon	1 teaspoon grated lemon rind
1 cup strawberry preserves	1 cup dry cake or plain cookie crumbs
4 tablespoons orange juice	

Mix all together thoroughly; filling should be firm enough so none pours off the side of a spoon.

To make the Schnecken: On floured board roll out one-third the dough at a time. Roll into a rectangle about 20 x 10 inches, 1/4 inch thick. Spread with a little melted butter and one-third of the filling. Roll tightly and using a sharp knife and quick strokes, cut into 1-inch pieces. Place cut-side down in prepared muffin tins. Repeat with rest of dough. Cover with cloth and let rise until almost double. Bake at 350° for 15 to 20 minutes; for tiny muffins, 15 minutes should suffice. Remove from tins immediately, invert on rack and spoon remaining syrup from pans over the little cakes. They may be frozen and reheated before serving. Yield: 6 to 7 dozen.

LES'S SEASONED SALT

There are certain preparations every good hostess makes when the idea of entertaining changes from a gleam in her eye to a firm decision to "have some people in."

I have found one of the best timesavers is to make sure there are plenty of little stores on hand — spice blends, seasoned salt, frozen minced parsley and chives, dry and buttered breadcrumbs (both frozen), ground nuts, etc. — so you won't have to stop and *prepare the ingredients* before you can prepare the recipe that calls for them!

One of the most important of these last-minute items is seasoned salt. Various processors produce different blends, and despite the uniformity of their names, they are not always interchangeable. I have found it easy and practical to make up my own general-purpose seasoning salt, and the one I call Les's Seasoned Salt is my standard; it works very well in all the recipes in this book calling for seasoned salt. It is especially good for meat dishes of all kinds. — C.M.

2 tablespoons celery salt	1-1/4 teaspoons chili powder
2 tablespoons garlic salt	1/2 teaspoon black pepper (scant)
2 tablespoons onion salt	1/8 teaspoon cayenne pepper
1-1/2 teaspoons paprika	

Combine all ingredients and sift together three or four times. Put in a jar with a tight lid, preferably one with inside shaker-top.

Crab Casserole Brunch

BRUNCH FOR EIGHT

Tomato Frappé

or

Bee-Bites

Crab Casserole

Heat-and-Hold Scrambled Eggs

Baked Sausages

Fresh Grapefruit Sections with Sour Cream Topping

Cornmeal Crisps

Lemon Squares

Coffee

TOMATO FRAPPÉ

1 (46-ounce) can tomato juice
1/4 teaspoon Tabasco sauce
2 teaspoons Worcestershire sauce
2 teaspoons freshly squeezed lemon juice
1/4 teaspoon celery salt
1 large egg white (or 2 small ones)

Pour half the tomato juice into freezer trays (without the dividers) and freeze until partially frozen. Chill the remainder. When ready to serve, pour chilled juice into a shaker; add all other ingredients and shake until frothy (or put in electric blender half a minute). Spoon partially frozen juice into tumblers (larger than old-fashioned glasses); fill with seasoned juice. If desired, these may be spiked with vodka or other spirits. Yield: 8 servings.

BEE-BITES
(see Index)

HEAT-AND-HOLD SCRAMBLED EGGS
(see Index)

BAKED SAUSAGES
(see Index)

CRAB CASSEROLE

2 (7-1/4-ounce) cans crabmeat
   or 1 pound frozen
8 slices bread
1/2 cup mayonnaise
1 cup chopped celery
1 green pepper, chopped
1 medium onion, chopped

1/2 teaspoon salt
4 eggs, slightly beaten
3 cups milk
1 (10-1/2-ounce) can cream of
   mushroom soup
1/2 cup shredded Cheddar cheese

Drain and cut crabmeat into chunks. Dice half the bread into bottom of large buttered casserole. Combine crab, mayonnaise, celery, green pepper, onion, and salt. Spread over diced bread. Trim crusts from remaining bread, dice, and place over crab mixture. Mix eggs and milk together and pour over bread. Cover and refrigerate several hours or overnight. Bake at 325° for 15 minutes. Remove from oven and spoon undiluted mushroom soup over top; sprinkle with shredded cheese. Return to oven and bake for 1 hour longer. Yield: 8 to 10 servings.

Note: For an additional touch of elegance, half a cup of slivered blanched almonds may be added to the mixture and/or a can of water chestnuts, drained and sliced, may be stirred in with the other vegetables.

CORNMEAL CRISPS
(see Index)

LEMON SQUARES
(prepare the day before)

2/3 cup butter or margarine
1-1/2 cups all-purpose flour, measured
   before sifting
4 eggs
2 cups firmly packed brown sugar
1-1/2 cups shredded coconut

1/4 teaspoon baking powder
1 teaspoon vanilla extract
1-1/3 cups powdered sugar
2 tablespoons grated lemon rind
3 tablespoons freshly squeezed
   lemon juice

Cut butter into flour until mixture holds together. Pat out evenly into an ungreased 12- x 8- x 2-inch pan. Bake at 350° for 20 minutes.

Meanwhile, beat eggs; add brown sugar, coconut, baking powder, and vanilla extract. Spread over baked base, return to oven and bake for 25 to 30 minutes longer. (Actually, about 28 minutes is right.)

Blend together powdered sugar, lemon rind, and lemon juice. Frost cookies while they are very hot, immediately on removing from oven. Cut into 2-inch squares. Leave uncovered, at least overnight, before storing in airtight container. Yield: about 24.

Note: Lemon Squares can be served as cookies, cut smaller than 2 inches; or they can be cut larger and topped with vanilla ice cream for dessert.

Ham and Artichoke Casserole Brunch

BRUNCH FOR SIX

Orange Spritzers

Ham and Artichoke Casserole

Double-Boiler Scrambled Eggs

Baked Thick-Sliced Bacon

Marinated Tomatoes with Celery Curls

Riz Biscuits   Whipped Sweet Butter

Strawberry or Raspberry Preserves

Crepes Fitzgerald

or

Glazed Peaches with Cream

Coffee

ORANGE SPRITZERS
(see Index)

HAM AND ARTICHOKE CASSEROLE

4 tablespoons butter or margarine
4 tablespoons all-purpose flour
2 cups warm milk
Generous dash seasoned salt
Generous dash cayenne pepper
1/4 teaspoon ground nutmeg
Paprika

Pinch white pepper
2/3 cup shredded Swiss and Parmesan cheese, mixed
4 tablespoons dry sherry
2 (1-pound) cans artichoke hearts, drained
12 thin slices boiled or baked ham

Melt butter in saucepan over medium heat; blend in flour; when smooth remove from heat. Gradually stir in warm milk; when smooth return to heat. Stir constantly until thickened. Add seasonings, then cheese; stir over low heat until melted. Remove from heat; stir in sherry.

If artichoke hearts are large, cut in half and wrap two halves in a slice of ham, allowing two rolls per person. Arrange in buttered casserole with sides touching; pour sauce over all. Sprinkle with Topping and bake at 350° for 25 to 30 minutes, until brown and bubbly.

Topping

2/3 cup buttered breadcrumbs mixed with 2/3 cup grated Parmesan and Swiss cheese, mixed. Yield: 6 servings.

Note: You may not need two cans of artichoke hearts. The size of the artichokes varies according to the processor. Best to buy two, open one and see.

DOUBLE-BOILER SCRAMBLED EGGS
(see Index)

BAKED THICK-SLICED BACON
(see Index)

MARINATED TOMATOES
(prepare the day before)

2 tablespoons salad oil	1/2 teaspoon seasoned salt
2 tablespoons vinegar	1/4 teaspoon dried leaf thyme, crushed
1/2 clove garlic, crushed	6 fresh peeled, or canned, tomatoes

Combine oil, vinegar, and seasonings thoroughly, pour over tomatoes, cover and refrigerate 24 hours before using; baste with marinade several times. May be used as salad, served on a bed of leaf lettuce, as a garnish, or as a vegetable course. Yield: 6 servings.

RIZ BISCUITS
(may be prepared ahead of time)

5 cups all-purpose flour	3/4 cup vegetable shortening
2 teaspoons baking powder	1 cake compressed yeast
1-1/2 teaspoons salt	1/4 cup lukewarm water
1 teaspoon soda	2 cups buttermilk
2 tablespoons sugar	

Sift all dry ingredients into bowl; cut in shortening with a pastry blender. Dissolve yeast in lukewarm water and add to buttermilk. Pour into first mixture and stir with wooden spoon just until blended. Refrigerate overnight, or until ready to use.

Roll out dough to 1/2-inch thickness; cut with biscuit cutter. Place on greased baking sheet, brush with melted butter and let rise until double in bulk (usually 1 to 1-1/2 hours). Bake at 400° for about 15 minutes.

When time is an important factor, you may roll out biscuits, brush with butter, place on pan in which they are to be baked and refrigerate until about 1-1/2 hours before baking. In this case, be sure to place chilled biscuits in warmest spot in the kitchen to speed the rising.

This dough is easy to make and keeps beautifully in the refrigerator. You might like to stir it up as soon as you're alerted to the prospect of guests, or better yet, make it up for the family and use as needed. Leftover biscuits are excellent buttered and toasted for breakfast.

Note: These biscuits are almost identical to Angel Biscuits in ingredients and proportions, but these require rising and are more like rolls than biscuits.

CREPES FITZGERALD

12 crepes at room temperature or warmed*
8 ounces cream cheese, softened
3/4 cup commercial sour cream
6 tablespoons sugar

2 teaspoons grated lemon peel
3 cups strawberries, sliced
4 tablespoons butter (no substitute)
About 1/4 cup strawberry liqueur
About 1/4 cup kirsch

Make crepes. Beat softened cream cheese with sour cream and 2 tablespoons of the sugar until light and smooth. Stir in grated lemon rind. Spoon the mixture onto crepes and roll them up, leaving ends open. Place on a platter and keep warm in a very slow oven.

Cook strawberries in a saucepan with remaining sugar and the butter just until sugar has dissolved and berries are heated through. Transfer to chafing dish and pour the strawberry liqueur over them, then the kirsch. Ignite, and when flames die down, spoon over crepes which have been placed on serving plates. Garnish with whole berries. Yield: 6 servings.

*See Index for Crepes recipe.

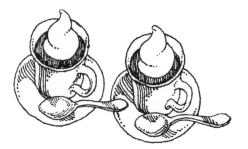

GLAZED PEACHES

Use good quality canned peaches; allow two halves per person. Drain peaches. To the syrup add 2 teaspoons grated orange rind, 1 teaspoon grated lemon rind, then the juice of both orange and lemon. Simmer uncovered until the syrup is reduced to about half. Place fruit in syrup and poach gently for about 15 minutes, spooning the syrup over the fruit constantly. Be careful not to break the fruit. Pour into bowl and chill. Serve with or without a pitcher of heavy cream as a sauce, or a bowl of lightly whipped cream (flavored with sugar and almond flavoring, if desired).

Ladies Gala Brunch

BRUNCH FOR EIGHT

Daiquiris

Crepes with Chicken Filling

In-and-Out-of-Season Fruit Salad

Whipped Dream Dressing   **Honey Dressing**

Sesame Seed Sticks

Almond Squares

Coffee

DAIQUIRIS
(see Index)

CREPES
(may be prepared ahead of time)

3 eggs
1-1/2 cups all-purpose flour
1 teaspoon sugar
1/8 teaspoon salt

1-1/2 cups milk
2 tablespoons melted butter or oil, cooled

Using a rotary beater or electric mixer, beat eggs about a minute (medium speed on a mixer), until yolks and whites are well blended. Add half the dry ingredients and mix well, then add remaining dry ingredients. (If mixture is too thick for your beaters, add a small amount of the milk.) Now add milk a little at a time until half is used, then pour in remainder and beat until smooth. Beat in melted butter; cover and set aside at room temperature for 1 or 2 hours. (Batter may be refrigerated overnight if more convenient.)

To cook crepes: Over medium heat place a small skillet measuring 5 or 6 inches across bottom. Brush with butter or oil; lift off heat and with a ladle pour in 1-1/2 to 2 tablespoons batter, only enough to coat bottom of the pan. Swirl the pan quickly and pour off any excess, then return to heat. When crepe is golden brown on bottom (you can lift the edge and peep under it), flip it over quickly and cook on reverse side for about half a minute. Turn crepes out onto a clean cloth towel and continue cooking additional crepes over medium heat, adding a little more butter or oil to pan if needed.

If you plan to use the crepes immediately, stack them on a plate and keep warm in a slow oven. If they are to be used later (or the next day), stack with waxed paper between them after they have cooled; then cover. If they are to be frozen, wrap in foil or put in freezer bag, with waxed paper between crepes. Yield: 24 (6-inch) crepes.

Variation: The above is the standard recipe recommended for the novice crepe-maker. A more delicate crepe can be made using these proportions: 7/8 cup flour, 1/8 teaspoon salt, 3 eggs, 2 tablespoons melted butter, and 1-1/2 cups milk.

CHICKEN FILLING

2 cups chopped cooked chicken or turkey, do not grind

1 tablespoon chopped fresh parsley

1 teaspoon grated onion

1/2 cup light cream

1 egg yolk

3 cups Medium Cream Sauce using chicken broth instead of milk*

Large pinch ground sage

3 strips bacon cooked crisp, then crumbled

1/2 cup shredded Swiss and Parmesan cheese, mixed

In a saucepan simmer the chicken, parsley and onion in cream for about 10 minutes. Combine egg yolk with half the cream sauce, add sage, then add to chicken mixture. Cook over low heat just a few minutes until mixture is thickened a little more, then stir in crumbled bacon and half the cheese.

Spread a generous tablespoon of the filling down center of each crepe; roll up, leaving ends open, and place seam-side down in a buttered baking dish. Stir in a tablespoon or two of cream to the remaining sauce to thin it slightly and pour over top of crepes. Sprinkle with remaining cheese. Bake at 350° for about 20 minutes, or until golden brown. This dish freezes well; defrost completely before baking, then follow baking instructions above. Yield: 8 servings.

Note: This recipe will fill 14 to 16 (6-inch) crepes. Allow two or three crepes per serving. Bacon may be cooked on a wire rack at 350° for 20 minutes.

*See Index for Sauce Preparation Guide.

IN-AND-OUT-OF-SEASON FRUIT SALAD

1 (1-pound) can peach halves, drained

1 (1-pound) can pineapple chunks, drained (spears are prettier if available)

1 (1-pound) can pear halves, drained

2 cups fresh grapes, seeded and cut

2 cups cantaloupe or melon balls

4 to 5 cups sliced fresh peaches

1 cup fresh blueberries, if in season

1/2 honeydew melon, cut into balls or chunks

2 cups any other fruit in season

Combine all fruit in large, lettuce-lined bowl; toss gently to mix. Serve dressing separately. Yield: 8 to 10 servings.

WHIPPED DREAM DRESSING FOR FRUIT SALAD

1 (3-ounce) package cream cheese, softened

2 tablespoons mayonnaise

6 ounces pineapple, peach, or apricot preserves

1 tablespoon freshly squeezed lemon juice

1/4 teaspoon curry powder

1/2 cup heavy cream, whipped

Blend cream cheese and mayonnaise by hand until smooth. Stir in preserves, lemon juice, and curry powder. Chill until about an hour before serving. Stir in whipped cream and refrigerate until serving time. Yield: about 1-1/2 cups.

Note: This is an unusual, delicious dressing for all kinds of fruit salads.

HONEY DRESSING FOR FRUIT SALAD

2 tablespoons sugar

1 teaspoon salt

1 teaspoon paprika

1 teaspoon dry mustard

1/4 teaspoon pepper

1/4 cup freshly squeezed lemon juice

3/4 cup salad oil

Few drops onion juice or 1/2 teaspoon scraped onion

1/3 cup honey

1 teaspoon celery seed

Combine all ingredients in jar with tight-fitting lid. Shake vigorously until thoroughly blended and chill before serving. Yield: about 1-1/2 cups.

SESAME SEED STICKS
(see Index)

ALMOND SQUARES

1 cup butter (no substitute)

3/4 cup sugar

1 egg, separated

1/2 cup almond paste

1 teaspoon almond extract

2 cups all-purpose flour, sifted

1/2 cup sliced almonds

Cream butter and sugar thoroughly in large bowl of electric mixer. Add egg yolk, then almond paste, and extract. Beat well; add flour and beat just until blended; do not overbeat. Smooth with a spatula into an ungreased 12- x 8- x 2-inch pan or ovenproof baking dish. Beat egg white until foamy and brush over surface of dough. Scatter almonds over top and bake at 350° (325° for glass) for 40 minutes, until cake tests done. Cool and cut into squares. Yield: 2 to 2-1/2 dozen squares.

Note: This is a fine little cake, its almond-butter flavor guaranteed to bring back memories to all who have tasted the famous pastries of Vienna.

Celebration Brunch

BRUNCH FOR EIGHT

Orange-Champagne Cocktail

Chicken Kiev

Walnut-Mushroom Asparagus   **Chafing Dish Fruit**

Poppy Seed Butter Crescents   **Whipped Butter**

Sour Cream-Raisin Coffeecake

Coffee

ORANGE-CHAMPAGNE COCKTAIL
(see Index)

CHICKEN KIEV
(may be prepared ahead of time)

Chicken Kiev does not deserve its reputation for being hard to prepare. It's a practical and versatile dish and quite easy to do. Don't be intimidated by it.

1/4 cup very finely minced onion, or minced chives

1/2 cup plus 2 tablespoons butter (no substitute)

3 tablespoons minced fresh parsley

8 flattened chicken breasts (4 whole ones, boned, split and pounded; ask butcher to do this for you)

Salt and pepper

All-purpose flour

2 eggs, lightly beaten

About 24 buttery round crackers, finely crushed

Shortening

Sauté onion in the 2 tablespoons butter in large skillet just until tender but not brown; combine with parsley. Sprinkle chicken lightly with salt and pepper. Place equal portions of onion mixture on each piece of chicken, and 1 tablespoon butter over onion mixture; roll up chicken, tucking in sides, making a neat little package. Secure with wooden picks. Roll in flour, dip in egg, then roll in crumbs. Refrigerate at least 1 hour (overnight isn't too long). Fry in 1/2 inch vegetable shortening until golden brown; drain on absorbent paper; remove wooden picks before serving. Yield: 8 servings.

Note: Chicken may be frozen after frying. Wrap individually to freeze. To serve, unwrap frozen chicken; let stand at room temperature for 1 hour, then bake on rack in shallow pan at 425°, about 20 to 25 minutes, or until heated through and crisp.

WALNUT-MUSHROOM ASPARAGUS

4 small green onions, chopped	Salt to taste
2 cups sliced fresh mushrooms	3 pounds fresh asparagus, cooked; or 2
6 tablespoons butter or margarine	(1-pound) cans, drained; or 2 (10-
1/2 cup toasted walnuts, coarsely ground	ounce) packages frozen

Sauté onions and mushrooms in butter until tender but not brown. Add walnuts and salt to taste. Spoon over hot cooked asparagus spears that have been well drained. Yield: 8 servings.

Note: To toast walnuts, bake in a shallow pan at 250° for about 20 minutes.

CHAFING DISH FRUIT

1 (1-pound) can apricot halves	Juice of 2 oranges
1 (1-pound) can cling peach halves	Grated rind of 1 orange
1 (1-pound) can pear halves	Grated rind of 1 lemon
1 (1-pound) can pineapple slices	1 (8-ounce) package pitted dates, cut
or spears	in half

Drain fruit. Combine 2/3 cup syrup of each of the fruits in a saucepan. Add orange juice and grated rinds; simmer uncovered until reduced by half. Taste the syrup; if it is cloying sweet, stir in the juice of half a lemon. Transfer to top of double boiler, add drained fruit and dates, and cook for about 15 minutes. When ready to serve, transfer to a chafing dish and serve hot. Yield: 8 to 10 servings.

BUTTER CRESCENTS

1 cake compressed yeast or 1 package	3/4 cup butter or margarine
dry yeast	1/3 cup sugar
1 teaspoon sugar	3/4 teaspoon salt
3/4 cup milk, scalded	4 cups all-purpose flour
2 eggs, beaten	

In a small bowl dissolve yeast and 1 teaspoon sugar in 1/4 cup of milk which has been cooled to lukewarm (very warm for dry yeast). Add eggs; mix well. Cream butter with 1/3 cup sugar and salt in large bowl of electric mixer; combine with first mixture. Add half the flour, then remaining milk, then rest of flour. Beat until dough is smooth. Turn into greased bowl, grease top of dough lightly, cover with light cloth and place in warm spot to rise until double in bulk. Punch dough down, cover and chill for an hour or two for easier handling.

Divide dough in half. Roll out each portion into a 16-inch circle about 1/4 inch thick. Cut into quarters; then cut each quarter into four parts, yielding 16 triangular pieces from each half of dough.

Beginning at wide edge of triangle, roll tightly toward the point, shape into crescents and place, pointed-end down, on greased baking sheet. Cover with light cloth and let rise until not quite double in bulk. Bake at 375° for about 15 minutes, or until light golden. Serve warm. Yield: 32 rolls.

Note: If poppy seed rolls are desired, after shaping dough into crescents, brush lightly with melted butter and sprinkle generously with poppy seed.

SOUR CREAM-RAISIN COFFEECAKE
(may be prepared ahead of time)

1/2 cup butter or margarine	1 teaspoon baking powder
1 cup sugar	1 teaspoon soda
2 eggs	1/4 cup sugar
1 cup commercial sour cream	1 teaspoon ground cinnamon
1 teaspoon vanilla extract	1/2 cup white raisins
2 cups all-purpose flour	

Cream together butter and 1 cup sugar in large bowl of electric mixer. Add eggs, beating well after each, then add sour cream and vanilla. Sift flour, baking powder, and soda together three times; add to batter and mix well.

Spread half the batter in greased 12- x 8- x 2-inch ovenproof baking dish. Sprinkle with mixture of 1/4 cup sugar, the cinnamon, and raisins. Carefully spread remaining batter over that. (I find a small spatula does this best, without tearing up the layers underneath.)

Topping

Combine 1/4 cup light brown sugar, 1 tablespoon all-purpose flour, 1/2 teaspoon ground cinnamon, and 1/3 cup chopped pecans or walnuts. Sprinkle evenly over batter, then drizzle 1-1/2 tablespoons melted butter over top. Bake at 325° (350° if using a metal pan) for about 40 minutes, or until cake tests done. Freezes beautifully. Yield: 1 coffeecake.

WHO TO INVITE

A thoughtful hostess tries to invite groups who may have something in common, people she feels will be compatible even though they may not know each other well. If she knows that the views of a certain person are distasteful to the group as a whole, she should omit him from that party and perhaps invite him for another time — or as a guest to a large party where guests will be varied and he will probably be more comfortable.

Scrambled Eggs Brunch

BRUNCH FOR EIGHT

Bloody Mary

Heat-and-Hold Scrambled Eggs

with

Baked Thick-Sliced Bacon

or

Eggs Benedict

with

Baked Pork Sausages

Fruit Platter

or

Curried Baked Fruit

Croissants   **Whipped Sweet Butter**

Strawberry Preserves   **Sweet Orange Marmalade**

Quick Streusel Coffee Bars

Coffee

BLOODY MARY
(see Index)

HEAT-AND-HOLD SCRAMBLED EGGS
(ideal method for serving a crowd)

1/4 cup butter (no substitute)	1/8 teaspoon pepper
12 eggs	2 tablespoons all-purpose flour
1-1/3 cups milk	1 tablespoon chopped pimiento
1 teaspoon salt	1 tablespoon chopped parsley

Melt butter in large skillet over low heat. Combine remaining ingredients in large bowl; beat with rotary beater until smooth and well blended. Pour into skillet and stir from outside edge toward center, allowing uncooked egg in center to flow to outer edge of skillet. Continue stirring until all eggs have been cooked and the mixture has a creamy appearance. Yield: 8 servings.

Note: Eggs may be covered and kept warm for 2 hours in a chafing dish or an electric skillet set at 200°. Or if size of oven permits, the skillet in which eggs are cooked may be covered and baked at 200°. To serve 50, use 8 dozen eggs.

BAKED THICK-SLICED BACON

Arrange thick slices of bacon on a rack over a pan; do not overlap slices. Bake at 375° for 20 to 25 minutes, or until well browned and dry. Allow 3 or 4 slices per serving.

Note: This is also an excellent method for thin-sliced bacon. It should be baked at 300° for about 20 to 25 minutes.

EGGS BENEDICT

This is the classic dish reputed to have been created in the Vatican kitchen around 1760 for Pope Benedict XIII. Its excellence depends on the freshness and flavor of the various ingredients and also your ability to "bring the dish to a head" at the point of perfection of each of the ingredients. Following is the recipe for one portion; multiply for the number of servings required.

1/2 **English muffin**	1 **poached egg**
1 **slice ham, lightly sautéed (Canadian bacon round is also used because of its suitable shape)**	1-1/2 **tablespoons Hollandaise Sauce***

Toast the muffin lightly; place ham on the cut-side, top with the poached egg and cover all with the sauce. Yield: 1 serving.

*See Index for Hollandaise Sauce recipe.

BAKED PORK SAUSAGES
(see Index)

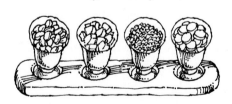

EGGS BENEDICT TIP

No matter how you poach an egg, you can put it immediately into a bowl or jar of cold water, cover and refrigerate it for up to 2 days, no longer. To reheat, immerse the egg in a generous amount of water just hot to the touch but not hot enough to cook the egg further. Let the egg stand for 5 to 10 minutes in the hot bath, adding more hot water if necessary to keep the temperature up until serving time.

PLATTER OF MIXED FRUIT
(including watermelon chunks, cantaloupe, fresh peaches,
blueberries, grapes, etc.)

CURRIED BAKED FRUIT
(prepare the day before)

1 (1-pound) can pear halves	12 maraschino cherries
1 (1-pound) can cling peaches	3/4 cup light brown sugar
1 (1-pound) can pineapple chunks or spears	3 teaspoons curry powder
	1/3 cup butter or margarine, melted
1 (1-pound) can apricot halves	2/3 cup blanched slivered almonds

Drain all fruit. Add sugar and curry powder to melted butter. Arrange fruit and nuts in layers in casserole, pour butter mixture over all and bake at 325° for 1 hour. Refrigerate overnight; reheat at 350° before serving. Yield: 10 to 12 servings.

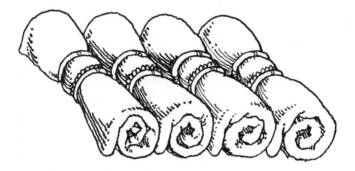

CROISSANTS

Although the French are considered to take their meals seriously, breakfast is regarded as rather unimportant. Invariably the French breakfast consists of café au lait, a Croissant with jam, maybe a piece of fresh fruit. But always a Croissant.

Americans traveling in France easily fall in love with the custom, the object of their affection centered around the Croissant. And why not? Basically, Croissants are crescent-shaped yeast rolls made with a very rich dough, thoroughly delectable. They may sound tricky but actually are quite simple if you follow directions explicitly. I have looked and looked — and never found a shortcut! — C.M.

3/4 cup butter (no substitute)	1 teaspoon salt
1/4 cup all-purpose flour, unsifted	1 egg, beaten
3/4 cup milk	3 cups all-purpose flour, unsifted
1/4 cup warm water	1 egg mixed with 1 tablespoon milk
1 package dry or compressed yeast	Sugar
3 tablespoons sugar	

Using a wooden spoon, blend butter into the 1/4 cup flour until mixture is a smooth paste. Put between two sheets of waxed paper and roll lightly to a 10- x 4-inch rectangle. Chill for 1 hour.

When butter mixture is chilled, prepare dough: Scald milk; cool to lukewarm. Warm large mixing bowl by pouring hot water into it and letting it stand for a few minutes. Pour it out, then add to the bowl the 1/4 cup warm water. Crumble in yeast, stir until dissolved. Add warm milk; stir in 3 tablespoons sugar, salt, beaten egg, and 1 cup flour; beat until smooth. Stir in remaining flour until completely blended.

Turn dough out onto well floured board. Roll into a 12-inch square. Carefully peel waxed paper from slab of cold butter; place on center of dough. Fold bottom third of dough over butter; then bring top third of dough down over that fold. Turn the dough a quarter way 'round and roll out into a 12-inch square. Fold in thirds, just as before, and roll out. Do this two more times. Wrap in waxed paper and chill for 2 hours (longer if more convenient).

When ready to make Croissants, divide chilled dough in thirds. Work with one-third at a time, keeping remainder in refrigerator. Roll out on floured board into a circle 12 to 14 inches in diameter. Cut into eight pie-shaped wedges. Brush the point of each wedge with a little of the egg-milk mixture. Now roll each piece tightly, beginning at wide end. Seal point and place on greased baking sheets, point down. Curve to form a crescent; brush with egg mixture; sprinkle with sugar. Let rise in warm place free from drafts until light, for about 1 hour. Bake at 350° for about 15 minutes, or until golden brown. Yield: 24.

Note: Croissants should always be served warm. To reheat, bake at 350° for 10 minutes; turn off heat, open oven door and allow rolls to remain in oven for 5 more minutes. To freeze Croissants, wrap tightly in aluminum foil. To thaw, heat in unopened foil wrapping at 400° for about 15 minutes. Open foil and heat for another 5 to 10 minutes.

QUICK STREUSEL COFFEE BARS
(may be prepared ahead of time)

1/2 cup butter or margarine	1 cup sifted all-purpose flour
1/2 cup sugar	1/3 cup sugar
1 egg, beaten	1 teaspoon ground cinnamon
1 teaspoon vanilla extract	1 cup chopped pecans

Cream butter and 1/2 cup sugar thoroughly in large bowl of electric mixer. Add egg and vanilla; mix well. Blend in flour. Spread in well greased 11- x 8- x 1-inch pan. Combine 1/3 cup sugar with cinnamon, mix well, and sprinkle over surface of batter; then sprinkle nuts over top. Press down lightly with hand (so Streusel won't fall off when inverted). Bake at 350° for 25 to 30 minutes. While warm cut into 2- x 1-inch bars. Freezes well. Yield: about 25 bars.

Cheese Cloud Brunch
BRUNCH FOR SIX

Orange Blush

or

Scorpions

Cheese Cloud

Baked Pork Sausages

Thick Slices Peeled Tomatoes Sprinkled with Dill Weed

or

Bibb Lettuce and Cherry Tomatoes with Herbed French Dressing

Warm Danish Pastry Slices

Coffee

A Silk Purse Menu — Looks and tastes expensive, but isn't.

ORANGE BLUSH

1 (6-ounce) can frozen orange juice
concentrate, thawed
1 cup cranberry juice

4 tablespoons sugar
1 pint sparkling water (club soda)

Combine undiluted orange juice, cranberry juice, and sugar. Chill thoroughly. Just before serving stir in sparkling water and pour over crushed ice in old-fashioned glasses. Yield: 6 servings.

SCORPIONS
(see Index)

CHEESE CLOUD
(may be prepared the day before)

12 slices day-old white bread
1/2 pound Cheddar cheese, sliced (use
bulk cheese, not processed)
4 eggs
2-1/2 cups milk
1/2 teaspoon prepared yellow mustard

1 tablespoon grated onion
1/4 teaspoon salt
Dash cayenne pepper
Dash black pepper
1 teaspoon seasoned salt

Trim crusts from bread and arrange six slices in bottom of a 12- x 8- x 2-inch greased baking dish. Cover with cheese slices, then with remaining bread slices. Beat eggs, add milk, mustard, onion, and seasonings. Pour over casserole and let stand at room temperature for 1 hour. This dish may be prepared the day before and refrigerated overnight if more convenient. Bake at 325° for 1 hour; serve immediately. Yield: 6 servings, but no seconds.

BAKED PORK SAUSAGES

Allow at least two link pork sausages for each serving. Drop sausages into boiling water to cover. Simmer for 5 minutes and drain. Arrange on a rack over a shallow pan; brush with melted butter or margarine. Bake at 350° for 30 minutes. Slash each sausage with a few diagonal cuts (as for French bread) just before arranging on platter. This method may be used for any link sausage.

HERBED FRENCH DRESSING

The French are probably outraged at the things we do to the classic French dressing, which simply consists of good olive oil, vinegar, salt, and freshly ground pepper — 3 tablespoons of oil to 1 of vinegar. Nevertheless, the following is an excellent dressing regardless of nationality. — C. M.

1/2 cup best quality olive oil	1/4 teaspoon dried basil
3 tablespoons cider vinegar	1/4 teaspoon dried tarragon
1 tablespoon freshly squeezed lemon juice	1 tablespoon minced onion
	1/2 teaspoon tomato paste (or paprika)
1/4 teaspoon dried oregano	1/4 teaspoon freshly ground black pepper

Beat all ingredients together in a bowl, pour into jar with tight-fitting lid and shake well several times before using. Serve over Bibb lettuce and cherry tomatoes. Yield: about 3/4 cup.

DANISH PASTRY
(may be prepared ahead of time)

Despite the popular suspicion that Danish pastry can be made in only fine bakeries, you can turn out the real article in your own kitchen if you follow directions carefully and refuse to be intimidated. This recipe will make three coffeecakes.

Butter Layer

6 tablespoons all-purpose flour	1-1/2 cups butter (no substitute)

Blend flour into butter, using a wooden spoon. Roll out between sheets of waxed paper to a rectangle 12- x 6- x 1-inches. Leave the mixture in the waxed paper and chill thoroughly. (On occasion I have gotten side-tracked and left the butter layer refrigerated for as long as 3 days; no ill effects.)

Dough

1 **cup milk**	2 **eggs, beaten**
1/4 **cup sugar**	1/2 **teaspoon almond extract**
1 **cake compressed yeast, or 2 packages dry yeast**	1/4 **teaspoon ground nutmeg**
1/4 **cup warm water (very warm water for dry yeast)**	**About 4 cups all-purpose flour**

Scald milk mixed with sugar. Pour into large mixer bowl and cool to lukewarm. Dissolve yeast in warm water (very warm water for dry yeast); add to milk, then add eggs. Beat in flavoring, nutmeg, and 2 cups flour. Beat thoroughly. Beat in remaining flour, until you have a stiff dough. It may take a little more flour to achieve this.

Turn out onto floured board and knead for about 5 minutes, until dough looks smooth. Roll out to a 14-inch square. Peel waxed paper from butter layer and place on half the dough. Fold dough over and seal edge by pressing down with fingers. Roll out to about 1/3-inch thickness and fold to make three layers. ("Folding in thirds" is described elsewhere. See Index.) Repeat this folding and rolling two more times, using as little additional flour as possible. If dough becomes unmanageable, chill it a short while.

Cut dough in thirds and work with one portion at a time, keeping rest refrigerated. Roll out to a rectangle 1/4 inch thick. Spread with one-third of the Filling. Roll up as for jellyroll and place on greased pan; form into a crescent. Using a sharp knife, make slashes in surface about 1 inch deep to indicate serving portions; cover with light cloth and let rise for about an hour, or until puffy but not quite double in bulk. Bake at 350° for 30 to 35 minutes. It is unnecessary to frost, but a thin glaze of powdered sugar, cream, and flavoring may be applied.

Dry Filling

Mix 1 teaspoon ground cinnamon with 1-1/2 cups light brown sugar; stir in 1 cup chopped pecans.

Moist Filling

2 **eggs**	1 **cup sugar**
2 **cups finely ground pecans or almonds**	1/2 **teaspoon almond extract**

Beat eggs in small bowl of electric mixer; gradually add sugar, then flavoring, beating until thick. Fold in nuts.

Note: Danish pastry should always be served warm. To heat, cover loosely with aluminum foil and bake at 350° for 10 minutes. The pastry may be frozen satisfactorily, thawed in freezer wrapping, then reheated as suggested.

Luncheons

Luncheons will most likely bring to mind fine linen, glimmering silver, and rainbow-casting crystal — and a meal that is elegant, appetizing, and light. This would be a formal luncheon given perhaps in honor of an out-of-town guest, for an engagement, or just because that is the way you like to entertain. But luncheon may also be informal — perhaps a terrace setting with bandana napkins and denim place mats given for a child's birthday or an after-tennis foursome. And weekend luncheons allow couples to gather to enjoy a companionable Saturday afternoon.

Since a luncheon focuses on the noon meal, the setting is nearly as important as the food to be served. Special care should be taken to ensure that centerpiece and table appointments are appealing and appropriate to the formality of the meal and to the menu itself.

Summertime Bridge Luncheon

LUNCHEON FOR FOUR

Chicken and Carrot Salad

or

Polynesian Chicken Salad

Lime-Grape Gelatin Molds

Commercial Butter Crescents

Coffee Tortoni

Iced Tea   **Coffee**

CHICKEN AND CARROT SALAD

1 tablespoon freshly squeezed lemon juice	3/4 cup diced celery
1 cup homemade mayonnaise	1/2 cup slivered blanched almonds
2 cups diced cooked chicken	2 tablespoons finely chopped onion
1 cup shredded carrot	Salt to taste
	Lettuce

Stir lemon juice into mayonnaise. Toss with chicken, carrot, celery, almonds, onion, and salt. Chill and serve on lettuce. Yield: 4 servings.

POLYNESIAN CHICKEN SALAD

2 cups cooked chicken, cut into small pieces	1/4 cup commercial sour cream
1-1/2 cups diced celery	1 teaspoon curry powder
1-1/2 cups diced canned pineapple, or white seedless grapes	1 teaspoon freshly squeezed lemon juice
1/4 cup shredded carrot (not grated)	1/2 teaspoon salt
1/2 cup toasted almond halves	Salad greens
1/2 cup mayonnaise	Minced parsley

Combine chicken, celery, pineapple or grapes, carrots, and almonds. Blend mayonnaise with sour cream and seasonings; pour over chicken and toss lightly. Chill thoroughly; arrange on greens and garnish with minced parsley. Yield: 6 servings.

Note: This is an unusual, delightful chicken salad. Sometimes I prepare it with pineapple and sometimes with grapes — and to stretch it, sometimes with both. It's grand anyway you choose to do it. To use in this menu, you would of course include only the pineapple. — C. M.

MY STANDARD MAYONNAISE

1 **whole egg**
1 **teaspoon dry mustard**
1/2 **teaspoon salt**
1/2 **teaspoon powdered sugar**
1/8 **teaspoon cayenne pepper**

1 **teaspoon seasoned salt**
3 **tablespoons freshly squeezed lemon juice**
2 **cups salad oil**

Beat egg well in small bowl of electric mixer. Add mixed dry ingredients; blend thoroughly. Add half the lemon juice, then add oil very slowly at first — 1/2 teaspoon at a time, beating well after each addition and scraping sides of bowl frequently with rubber spatula. As mixture begins to thicken, increase amount of oil — a tablespoon at a time now. When three-fourths of oil has been added, gradually beat in remaining lemon juice, then rest of oil. Chill before using. Yield: 1 pint.

Note: Half the recipe may be made by using the yolk of 1 small egg.

LIME-GRAPE GELATIN MOLDS

1 **(3-ounce) package lime-flavored gelatin**
1/4 **cup freshly squeezed lime juice**

1 **cup small green seedless grapes**
Lettuce

Prepare gelatin according to directions on package, substituting lime juice for part of water. When partially set, fold in grapes and pour into four individual molds. Chill until set; unmold on bed of lettuce, parsley, or watercress. Serve with Dressing.

Dressing

2-1/2 **tablespoons mayonnaise**
1/3 **cup commercial sour cream**

Salt and sugar to taste
Strawberries (optional)

Blend ingredients together. A few sliced fresh strawberries (or drained frozen ones) may be added for color. Yield: 4 servings.

SEATING TIP

In planning your seating arrangement for a dinner party, remember the old Spanish proverb: "Two great talkers will not travel far together."

COFFEE TORTONI

2 eggs	2 tablespoons sugar
1/4 cup sugar	1 teaspoon vanilla extract
1/8 teaspoon salt	1/4 teaspoon almond extract
1 tablespoon powdered coffee	1/3 cup chopped toasted almonds
1 cup whipping cream	

Beat eggs, 1/4 cup sugar, and salt at high speed in small bowl of electric mixer. Beat until very light and fluffy; the mixture should more than half fill the bowl. Toward the end of beating add powdered coffee.

In another bowl beat whipping cream with 2 tablespoons sugar. When stiff, fold in vanilla and almond extracts. Fold into egg mixture, blending well. Stir in toasted almonds and pour into paper muffin cups or spoon into parfait glasses to freeze. A few more chopped nuts may be used to garnish top if desired. Yield: enough to fill 8 (4-ounce) paper cups. If it is to be served in parfait glasses, it will be enough for about 6, depending on size of glass. At any rate, it keeps beautifully in the freezer, so if you have some left, it will just be a windfall for someday when you're either too busy or too uninspired to prepare a dessert.

CAVIAR

Caviar bespeaks champagne — beverage and tastes. It is served to a connoisseur iced and on a wedge of crisp toast accompanied with a glass of champagne. But most people enjoy it many ways, with garnishes of lemon wedges, minced hard-cooked eggs, onions, avocados, or artichokes.

The prima donna of caviars comes from the sturgeon, the Beluga being the finest. In the price realm of permittable party splurges are the red salmon caviar, lumpfish and whitefish caviars dyed to the hues of the sturgeon caviar. Sturgeon caviar comes from Russian, Scandinavian, and Adriatic waters and is more liquid in consistency. Lumpfish caviar, from the Atlantic, has a crunchy texture. Whitefish caviar, from the Great Lakes, is tiny and tender. And large salmon caviar, from Alaska and the Pacific Northwest, is pungent.

To prepare these eggs, the roe is taken from the living fish (it does kill her) separated, salted, and kept in jars or under refrigeration. Although it is served chilled, often on a lump of ice, avoid freezing caviar or the eggs will burst.

Summertime Shrimp Luncheon

LUNCHEON FOR SIX

Shrimp Lutèce with Assorted Crackers

Italian Bread Sticks

Sherried Strawberries

Mocha Parfait with Cookies

Iced Tea   **Hot Coffee**

SHRIMP LUTÈCE

6 heads Bibb lettuce (1 small head
   per serving)

1 (1-pound) can artichoke hearts,
   drained and halved

2 avocados, sliced

2 pounds large raw shrimp in the
   shell, cooked

4 hard-cooked eggs, quartered

Wash and dry lettuce; gently separate leaves. Combine with other
ingredients and toss lightly.

Dressing

3/4 teaspoon salt
   Pinch salt
1/2 teaspoon prepared yellow mustard
1/2 clove garlic, crushed
1/4 cup tarragon vinegar

1 small egg yolk
1 cup salad oil
1/4 teaspoon sugar
1 tablespoon Worcestershire sauce
1/4 cup chili sauce

Make a paste of salt, pepper, mustard, garlic, and small amount vinegar.
Blend in egg yolk until smooth. Start adding oil very slowly until dressing is
consistency of mayonnaise. (Blender or rotary beater or fork may be used.)
Continue adding oil alternately with remaining vinegar. Beat in sugar and
Worcestershire sauce; fold in chili sauce and chill thoroughly. Yield: 6 servings.

ITALIAN BREAD STICKS
(may be prepared ahead of time)

1 package dry yeast	1/4 cup vegetable shortening
2/3 cup very warm water	1 egg
1 teaspoon salt	1 tablespoon water
1-1/2 teaspoons sugar	Sesame, poppy, or caraway seed
2 cups all-purpose flour, sifted	

Dissolve yeast in very warm water in bowl. Add salt, sugar, 1 cup of the flour, and shortening. Beat until smooth. Blend in remaining flour and knead on floured board until smooth, about 5 minutes. Place in large greased bowl, lightly grease top of dough, cover with light cloth and let rise in warm spot until double in bulk, about 1 hour.

Heat oven to 375°. Pinch off pieces of dough slightly smaller than a walnut; roll on board or between hands until strips are 8 inches long. Place 1 inch apart on greased baking sheet. Beat egg with water, brush on sticks, sprinkle with seed. Bake for 18 minutes, or until golden. Bread sticks keep well in a covered tin; they also freeze well. To reheat, place in slow oven for about 10 minutes. Yield: about 28 sticks.

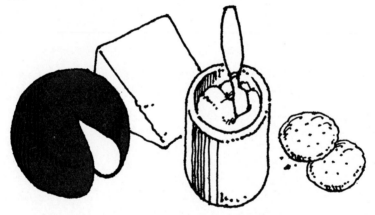

SHERRIED STRAWBERRIES

1 quart fresh strawberries	2 tablespoons sugar
3 tablespoons sherry wine	2 teaspoons freshly squeezed lemon juice
1 teaspoon grated orange rind	1 (10-ounce) package frozen
1/2 teaspoon grated lemon rind	raspberries, thawed
2 tablespoons orange juice	Rich vanilla ice cream

Wash and hull strawberries and slice lengthwise, or leave them whole. Combine with sherry, orange and lemon rinds, orange juice, sugar, and lemon juice. Cover and chill for an hour or more.

Put raspberries through a sieve to remove seed; chill. Just before serving, combine strawberries with raspberry sauce; spoon over firm vanilla ice cream in individual chilled dessert bowls. Yield: 6 servings.

MOCHA PARFAIT

Make parfaits by spooning coffee ice cream into parfait glasses and lacing with Sherried Chocolate Sauce.

Sherried Chocolate Sauce

6 ounces unsweetened chocolate	1 tablespoon dark corn syrup
1-1/4 cups boiling water	2 teaspoons vanilla extract
1-1/4 cups milk	2 tablespoons medium-dry sherry
2-1/3 cups sugar	

Mix chocolate and water to a smooth paste. Heat milk and sugar together in a saucepan and add to chocolate. Return to saucepan, add syrup and cook until thick, stirring occasionally. Remove from heat, cool to lukewarm, stir in vanilla and sherry and cool thoroughly. This sauce is excellent whenever a chocolate sauce is required. Yield: about 5 cups.

CHAFING DISHES

A chafing dish may be elaborated or improvised and used to flambé desserts at the dinner table or to keep a casserole warm on the buffet table. Possibilities for use are numerous as are the choice of units and fuels they use.

An omelet pan, a heavy, wide, shallow pan placed over direct heat, is used to sauté and flambé meats, fish, eggs, and fruit. If you plan to cook at the table, try the recipe on your family first. The process should appear effortless to the guests. Arrange a tray with all necessary ingredients, measured and ready, extra fuel and a small towel. To flambé with success, have food warmed and liqueur or brandy (have a higher alcohol content) at room temperature. Add the liqueur, tilt the pan and touch the match to the edge. Stir constantly until alcohol has burned out. Beware of adding more liqueur to a flaming pan as flames may jump.

The blazer pan with a *bain Marie* is used like a double boiler. The blazer or top pan may be used over direct heat for foods requiring higher cooking temperatures.

Fondue pots were designed for Swiss Fondue but may be used to serve and keep warm casseroles, stews, and soups.

Heatproof casseroles made of pyroceram may be placed over direct heat for warming.

Fuel for various vessels may be alcohol (denatured gives a hot cooking flame, rubbing alcohol may be used for keeping hot dishes warm), canned-heat, or candles for warming.

Gazpacho Luncheon

LUNCHEON FOR FOUR TO SIX

Antipasto

Gazpacho

Hot Cheese Toast

Milk-Chocolate Toffee

Iced Tea   **Coffee**

A Silk Purse Menu — Looks and tastes expensive, but isn't.

ANTIPASTO

12 very thin slices salami
    Canned anchovies, well drained
24 ripe olives
    Celery hearts, cut in 2-inch pieces

24 cherry tomatoes
6 radish roses
6 deviled eggs
    Salad greens (optional)

Roll salami slices in cornucopias and fasten with wooden picks. Place two or three on each small plate. Arrange other foods on the plate and garnish with wedges of lemon and salad greens if desired. Yield: 6 servings.

Note: As a main dish for luncheons, use luncheon plates and add tuna chunks, drained and marinated artichoke hearts, scallions, etc.

GAZPACHO

1 tablespoon oil
2 tablespoons freshly squeezed
    lemon juice
2 small cloves garlic, minced
2 tablespoons minced fresh dill, or
    1 teaspoon dill weed
1 slice day-old bread, crumbled
    (preferably rye or French)
5 large ripe peeled tomatoes, seeded
    and chopped

1 green pepper, chopped
4 or 5 scallions or green
    onions, chopped
1 medium cucumber, chopped
1-1/2 teaspoons salt
    Coarse black pepper
1 teaspoon sugar
1 (10-1/2-ounce) can chicken broth,
    skimmed of fat

The easiest and fastest method of making Gazpacho is to use an electric blender. If you don't have one, use a large mixing bowl, then puree the mixture through a fine sieve. Blender method follows:

Blend together oil, lemon juice, garlic, dill, and crumbled bread. Add remaining ingredients. Be cautious in using cucumber; too much can overpower the other flavors. Blend well, taste, and correct seasonings if required. Chill at least 4 to 5 hours. Yield: 6 servings.

Note: To serve Gazpacho in the traditional Spanish manner, serve the ice-cold soup in chilled bowls and pass separate bowls of chopped cucumber, chopped green pepper, chopped tomatoes, minced green onions, and crisp croutons. Guests may accept any or all of these condiments to add to their soup bowls. This is a great summertime main course; try it at least once!

HOT CHEESE TOAST
(see Index)

MILK-CHOCOLATE TOFFEE
(may be prepared the day before)

Crust

1/3 pound vanilla wafers, crumbled   1/2 cup chopped pecans

Mix and spread half in well buttered 10- x 6-inch dish.

Filling

1/2 cup butter or margarine   3 eggs, separated
1 cup powdered sugar   1/2 teaspoon vanilla extract
1-1/2 ounces unsweetened   1/2 teaspoon almond extract
   chocolate, melted

Cream butter and sugar thoroughly; add melted chocolate. Stir in egg yolks, then extracts. Beat egg whites until stiff and fold in. Spread on wafer crust; sprinkle remaining crumb-nut mixture over top and chill several hours before serving. (Overnight is better.) Cut into squares. Yield: 6 servings.

Chicken with Dried Beef Luncheon

LUNCHEON FOR SIX

Chicken with Dried Beef

My Favorite Tomato Aspic with Vegetables

Lemon Cream Dressing

Angel Biscuits   **Butter**

Strawberry Jam

Date-Nut Meringue Squares

Coffee   **Iced Tea**

CHICKEN WITH DRIED BEEF

This is an excellent luncheon dish, especially for the hostess who must do her own work.

6 chicken breasts, boned
3/4 pound dry chipped beef
6 strips lean bacon

1 (10-1/2-ounce) can condensed cream of mushroom soup

Arrange dried beef in bottom of shallow casserole. Wrap a strip of bacon around each chicken breast; arrange over beef. Spread undiluted soup over chicken, cover with aluminum foil and bake at 300° for 2 hours; increase heat to 350° and bake for another 20 to 30 minutes, basting several times. Yield: 6 servings.

Note: There is no seasoning stipulated; you may want to add a little black pepper. The beef and bacon, which dissolve completely in the cooking, season the chicken adequately. A little sherry may be added to the sauce for the last few bastings before serving. And for beauty's sake, some mushrooms may be added if desired.

MY FAVORITE TOMATO ASPIC

The world abounds with short-cut aspic recipes and I have found many good ones. However, the following is the one I learned on. And though I stray from it now and then, when I want one that suits me exactly, I return to my old love. Here it is. — C. M.

2 envelopes unflavored gelatin
1/4 cup cold water
1/2 cup boiling water
4 cups tomato juice
1 tablespoon minced onion
1 teaspoon sugar
1/2 teaspoon celery seed, or several minced celery tops

1 teaspoon seasoned salt
2 bay leaves
1 teaspoon Worcestershire sauce
2 whole cloves
1 teaspoon salt
Juice of 1 lemon

Soak gelatin in cold water for 5 minutes; dissolve in boiling water. In a large saucepan simmer all other ingredients except lemon juice for 15 minutes. Strain; add lemon juice and dissolved gelatin. Turn into a large 10-inch ring mold or six individual molds and chill until set. (To fill a larger mold, double the recipe but use 5 tablespoons gelatin instead of 4.)

Variations: Any chopped vegetables may be added when aspic is partially set; also shrimp, crabmeat, lobster, etc. Sometimes for party luncheons, I like to use the aspic plain, filling center of ring mold with salmon in sour cream. — C. M.

LEMON CREAM DRESSING
(may be prepared ahead of time)

1 whole egg
2 tablespoons grated Parmesan cheese
1 clove garlic, crushed
1-1/2 teaspoons Dijon mustard

Salt and pepper to taste
1/2 cup salad oil
1/3 cup freshly squeezed lemon juice

In blender container (or bowl, using rotary beater) put egg, cheese, garlic, mustard, salt, and pepper. Blend a few seconds, then alternately add oil and lemon juice. Chill thoroughly before using. Yield: about 1 cup.

Note: This is good for spinach or any vegetable salad; does not separate on standing; may be made the day before using — or before that.

ANGEL BISCUITS
(see Index)

DATE-NUT MERINGUE SQUARES

4 egg whites
1/8 teaspoon salt
1 cup sugar
1 cup chopped dates

1 cup chopped pecans
1/2 teaspoon vanilla extract
1/2 teaspoon almond extract
1 cup heavy cream, whipped

Beat egg whites with salt until stiff, gradually adding sugar after eggs are frothy. When sugar seems completely absorbed, fold in dates, pecans, and flavorings. Turn into well greased 8-inch square pan and bake at 350° for about 45 minutes. Let cool and cut into squares. Serve topped with whipped cream. Yield: 6 to 8 servings.

Seafood Stew Luncheon

LUNCHEON FOR SIX

Cioppino with Fluffy Rice

Spinach Salad with Croutons

Hot French Bread   **Butter Curls**

Frozen Lemon Cream with Orange-Walnut Cookies

Coffee   **Iced Tea**

CIOPPINO

4 tablespoons olive oil
1 green pepper, chopped
1 medium onion, chopped
4 tablespoons chopped fresh parsley
2 cloves garlic, minced
2 (1-pound) cans tomatoes
1 (6-ounce) can tomato paste
1/4 teaspoon dried basil, crushed
1 large bay leaf

1/2 teaspoon grated lemon rind
1 teaspoon salt
Dash black pepper
1 pound fish filets, cut in 2-inch pieces (haddock, bass, pike, etc.)
1 pound fresh raw shrimp, boiled, shelled, and cleaned
1/2 pound canned or frozen crabmeat
Hot cooked rice

Heat oil in large saucepan and sauté green pepper, onion, parsley, and garlic until tender, but not brown. Stir in tomatoes, tomato paste, basil, bay leaf, lemon rind, salt, and pepper. Cover and simmer for 30 minutes. Add fish filets and cook slowly for 15 minutes. Do not overcook; fish pieces should remain whole and not cook to shreds. Add shrimp and crabmeat and simmer for 10 minutes, stirring gently now and then. Serve Cioppino in large soup plate with mound of rice in center if desired. Yield: 6 servings.

CROUTONS

Remove crusts from six slices of white bread. Cut bread into small cubes and sauté in butter until delicately browned. Drain well on paper towels and put in a paper bag. Add some minced fresh parsley and grated Parmesan cheese and shake thoroughly. Store in covered container until ready to use. These are good over salad, squash, string beans, spinach, and a myriad of other dishes that need a touch of crispness.

SPINACH SALAD WITH CROUTONS

1-1/2 to 2 pounds fresh spinach
8 slices lean bacon, diced
2 cups small firm bread cubes
1/4 teaspoon garlic powder
Salt and freshly ground black pepper

1/2 teaspoon Dijon mustard
3 tablespoons freshly squeezed lemon juice
9 tablespoons oil (olive or peanut or mixed)

Wash spinach and discard any tough stems. Drain leaves and pat dry with clean towels. Wrap in a clean towel and refrigerate at least an hour.

Fry bacon until crisp, remove with slotted spoon and drain on paper towels. Drain off all except 4 tablespoons drippings; sprinkle bread cubes with garlic powder and sauté in drippings until lightly browned, stirring constantly. Remove and drain on paper towels.

Prepare dressing by stirring salt, pepper, and mustard into lemon juice. Gradually beat in the oil until blended. At serving time lightly toss bite-size pieces of spinach with bacon bits, bread cubes, and dressing. Yield: 6 to 8 servings.

FRENCH BREAD
(may be prepared ahead of time)

1 cake compressed yeast or 1 package dry yeast
1 tablespoon salt
1 tablespoon sugar
2 cups lukewarm water (very warm for dry yeast)

About 6 cups all-purpose flour
About 2 tablespoons cornmeal
Melted butter

Dissolve yeast, salt, and sugar in lukewarm (very warm for dry yeast) water in large bowl. Gradually stir in flour, adding only enough until mixture refuses to absorb more. (You may need no more than 5-1/2 cups.) Knead dough on floured board until slightly elastic, 3 to 4 minutes. Transfer to greased bowl, brush top lightly with a little oil or melted butter, and cover with damp cloth. Place in warm spot to rise until double in bulk.

Butter a baking sheet and sprinkle with cornmeal, shaking off excess. Punch dough down, turn onto floured dough board and divide into thirds. Shape into long, narrow loaves; place on prepared baking sheet and with sharp knife make several shallow diagonal cuts across tops. Brush lightly with melted butter, allow to rise about 45 minutes and bake at 450° for 5 minutes, then at 350° for 30 minutes more. Freezes beautifully. To serve after freezing, thaw completely; place in 275° oven to heat until crisp, about 20 minutes.

Note: Bake bread on rack in middle of oven. Before placing loaves in oven, place a shallow pan of hot water on floor of oven, or on the lowest rack. Allow it to remain there for entire baking period.

FROZEN LEMON CREAM

(may be prepared ahead of time)

1 cup milk	Pinch salt
1 cup sugar	Grated rind and juice of 2 lemons
1 cup heavy cream, unwhipped	1/2 teaspoon lemon extract

Put milk, sugar, cream, and salt in saucepan and heat just until sugar is dissolved. Be careful and don't let mixture boil. Pour into freezing tray and freeze until firm. Spoon into large bowl of electric mixer and beat just a few minutes, until mixture is smooth and creamy, adding lemon rind, lemon juice, and lemon extract as you beat. Return to freezer and when mushy, beat (in the tray) with a fork until quite smooth. Continue freezing until firm. Yield: 6 servings.

Note: An attractive way to serve this dessert is to cut oranges in half, scoop out the pulp, fill with the lemon cream and freeze in the cups. A twisted lemon slice perched on top of the dessert is a nice touch.

ORANGE-WALNUT COOKIES

1/4 pound butter or margarine	1/2 teaspoon vanilla extract
1/3 cup sugar	1 tablespoon grated orange rind
1 egg, separated	1 tablespoon lemon rind
1 cup all-purpose flour, sifted	2 cups chopped walnuts
Pinch salt	

Cream together butter, sugar, and egg yolk in large bowl of electric mixer. Blend in flour, salt, and vanilla. Add orange and lemon rinds. Form into small balls (about 1 teaspoon dough for each); roll in unbeaten egg white, then in chopped nuts. Place on well greased baking sheet; press down to flatten slightly and bake at 350° for about 12 minutes. Yield: 2 to 3 dozen.

THE GUEST BATH

Sparkling and shiny clean with touches of "you were expected" is how the bath should appear to guests. Give the bathroom a last minute once over just prior to party time. See that hand towels are fresh and individual guest soap is out in a clean, dry dish, and give a quick swipe to the sink and toilet bowl.

As an extra gesture of hospitality, set out a small toilette tray with a clean comb, extra hairpins, tissues, hand cream, and cologne and any other touch-up aid. For a festive air in the bath, fill a decorative (empty) cologne bottle with fresh flowers.

Salad Nicoise Luncheon

INFORMAL LUNCHEON FOR FOUR

Salad Nicoise

Crunchy Commercial French Bread

or　　　　　　　　　　　　　　　　　**Butter**

Hot Italian Bread

Fudge Pie with Vanilla Ice Cream or Whipped Cream

Coffee　　　　　　　　　　　**Iced Tea**

SALAD NICOISE

1 head firm lettuce, or about 3 cups combination of greens

2 (7-ounce) cans solid-pack white tuna, drained

2 tomatoes, cut in eighths; or 1/4 cup chopped pimientos

1/2 cup pitted ripe olives, quartered

1 small sweet onion, thinly sliced

2 tablespoons capers, drained

4 canned artichoke hearts, halved (optional)

1 small cucumber, peeled and thinly sliced

1 (2-ounce) can anchovy filets, drained and cut in half

1 green pepper, cut in strips
French dressing

Break greens into bite-size pieces in a large salad bowl. Add chunks of tuna, then all other ingredients. Salad may be assembled ahead of time, covered with waxed paper and refrigerated until serving time. Just before serving, toss lightly with dressing. Yield: 4 servings.

Note: There are many versions of Salad Nicoise. Some include sliced boiled potatoes, others cooked green beans, etc. But this is my favorite. — C. M.

ITALIAN BREAD

2 cups warm water (very warm for
  dry yeast)
1 cake compressed yeast or 1 package
  dry yeast
2-1/2 teaspoons salt

2 eggs, lightly beaten
2 tablespoons melted shortening
  About 7 cups all-purpose flour
1 tablespoon water
1 egg white

Pour water into large bowl; stir in yeast with wooden spoon until dissolved. Add salt, eggs, and shortening, then start adding flour. Begin with 5 cups, beating well. Continue until you've used about 6-1/2 cups. This should yield a dough you can manage. Turn onto floured surface and knead for about 15 minutes, turning dough and using small amount of flour as needed. When dough is smooth, elastic, and shiny, it's ready. Place in large greased bowl; turn so all sides are greased; cover with towel which has been wrung out in hot water, and allow to rise until double in bulk.

Punch dough down, cover and allow to rise again until double. Turn onto floured surface and shape as desired.

Place loaves on greased baking sheet sprinkled with cornmeal. With sharp knife mark several diagonal shallow slits across top. Mix 1 tablespoon water with slightly beaten egg whites; brush top and sides of loaves. Allow to rise until almost double, then bake at 375° for about 55 minutes. Before baking, place large shallow pan filled with hot water on lowest rack of oven; allow to remain during baking. Yield: 3 medium-size loaves or 2 long loaves.

Note: To make hard rolls, follow recipe, increasing melted shortening to 1/2 cup. Follow same rising procedure, shape crescents or squares, using cornmeal on board for rolling, and sprinkling more cornmeal over rolls before baking. Bake rolls for 20 to 25 minutes.

FUDGE PIE
(may be prepared ahead of time)

1/2 cup butter
  2 squares unsweetened chocolate
  2 eggs

1 cup sugar
1/4 cup all-purpose flour
  Pinch salt

Melt butter and unsweetened chocolate together over warm water. Beat eggs in a bowl; gradually blend in sugar. Add flour and a pinch of salt, then combine with chocolate mixture. Pour into ungreased 8-inch pieplate and bake at 350° for 20 to 25 minutes. Cool, then freeze. This pie does not require thawing before serving. Yield: 6 servings.

Note: Freezes beautifully; no hostess should be without one in the freezer at all times.

Party Shrimp Luncheon

LUNCHEON FOR FOUR

Party Shrimp in Shells

My Favorite Tomato Aspic

Crusty Commercial Rolls   **Butter Curls**

Stuffed Pineapple

or

Rum'd Apples with Whipped Cream

Iced Tea   **Coffee**

PARTY SHRIMP IN SHELLS

1-1/2 **pounds uncooked shrimp in the shell**
2 **tablespoons butter or margarine**
1 **(4-ounce) can sliced mushrooms, drained; or 1 pint fresh mushrooms**
1 **tablespoon all-purpose flour**
1 **(10-ounce) can condensed cream of shrimp soup, thawed**

1 **cup commercial sour cream**
1 **tablespoon finely minced parsley**
1-1/2 **tablespoons minced chives, or 2 tablespoons chopped green onion**
Dash pepper
Buttered breadcrumbs

Boil, shell, and clean shrimp. Heat butter in skillet and sauté canned mushrooms a few minutes. (If using fresh mushrooms, sauté as follows: Chop stems, put in skillet with hot butter, and sauté for about 3 minutes; then add sliced mushroom caps and sauté about 2 minutes.) Stir in flour, blend in soup, stirring constantly until smooth and thick. Blend in sour cream, parsley, and chives and when smooth again, add shrimp. Add pepper and taste to check seasonings. Turn into four large shells or ramekins, sprinkle with buttered crumbs and bake at 375° for 15 to 20 minutes. Do not overbake. Yield: 4 generous servings.

MY FAVORITE TOMATO ASPIC
(see Index)

STUFFED PINEAPPLE

1 large pineapple
1 banana, sliced
1 cup sliced fresh strawberries
2 oranges, sectioned

1/2 cup orange juice
1/4 cup honey
Juice of 1/2 lemon

Slice a large pineapple in half lengthwise, keeping leaves intact. Cut away the tough core with a sharp knife, remove pulp and dice fruit, reserving shells. Combine pineapple, sliced banana, sliced fresh strawberries, and sections of oranges in a bowl. Pour over fruit 1/2 cup orange juice mixed with 1/4 cup honey and juice of 1/2 lemon. Toss fruit gently and chill thoroughly. At serving time, arrange fruit in pineapple shells, bring to table on a tray and spoon into dessert dishes. Yield: 4 servings.

RUM'D APPLES

4 large firm tart apples
4 tablespoons peach or apricot preserves
Juice and grated rind of 1 orange
1/2 cup sugar

1/2 cup water
2 tablespoons rum (not rum flavoring)
Whipped cream

Peel, core, and cut apples in half horizontally. Place cut-side up in buttered 10- x 7-inch baking dish. Cook preserves, orange juice, rind, sugar, and water over low heat until thickened. Remove from heat, stir in rum and pour over apples. Cover loosely with aluminum foil and bake at 350° for 45 minutes to 1 hour, or until apples are tender, basting occasionally. Serve at room temperature or chilled with whipped cream. Yield: 4 servings.

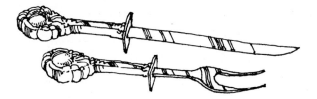

NOW, ABOUT THOSE MUSHROOMS

Fresh mushrooms are not available at all seasons and in all localities. Here's a guide for substituting canned ones:

1 (6- or 8-ounce) can is the equivalent of 1 pound fresh.

1 (3- or 4-ounce) can is the equivalent of 1/2 pound fresh.

If recipe calls for fresh mushrooms by measure instead of by weight, here's your guide:

For 1 quart (or 20 to 24 medium mushroom caps), substitute 1 (6- to 8-ounce) can.

For 1 pint (or 10 to 12 medium mushroom caps), substitute 1 (3- to 4-ounce) can.

Twelve-Boy Salad Luncheon

LUNCHEON FOR EIGHT

Twelve-Boy Salad

with

Mayonnaise Harvey, Wine French Dressing,

Anchovy Salad Dressing, Sour Cream-Roquefort Dressing

Hot Commercial French Bread   **Sweet Butter**

Superb Rum Cake with Fresh Strawberries

or

Chocolate Cheesecake

Iced Tea   **Iced Coffee**

TWELVE-BOY SALAD

Tremendous bowl of mixed salad greens tossed lightly with just enough oil to make them glisten, served with bowls of the following:

Chopped hard-cooked eggs	Julienne strips of cooked chicken or turkey
Drained chopped anchovies	Cubes of baked ham
Parmesan-Flavored Croutons*	Crisp crumbled bacon
Chopped green onions, including tops	Drained capers
Strips of Swiss cheese	Cherry tomatoes
Grated Parmesan cheese	Sliced unpeeled radishes

Arrange the buffet with greens first, then condiments in their separate bowls, then dressings last. Guests serve themselves greens on dinner plates, then as many condiments as they wish, then the dressing of their choice. All of the above may not be offered; they are merely suggestions — but certainly one meat and one cheese should be included.

*See Index for Parmesan-Flavored Croutons recipe.

MAYONNAISE HARVEY

1 whole egg	1/2 teaspoon commercial steak sauce
1-1/2 cups salad oil	1/2 teaspoon Worcestershire sauce
1-1/2 tablespoons freshly squeezed lemon juice	1 clove garlic, crushed
1/4 cup grated Parmesan cheese	3 drops Tabasco sauce
	Salt and pepper to taste

Beat egg thoroughly in small bowl of electric mixer. Add oil a teaspoon at a time until half has been added; beat in lemon juice, then remaining oil in several portions. Blend in all other ingredients and chill before serving. This is an exceptionally good dressing. Yield: 10 servings.

WINE FRENCH DRESSING
(prepare the day before)

1 teaspoon sugar	1/4 cup dry red wine
1 teaspoon salt	1 teaspoon scraped onion
1/2 teaspoon dry mustard	1/4 cup wine vinegar
1 teaspoon Worcestershire sauce	3/4 cup salad oil
1/3 cup catsup	

Combine all ingredients in jar with tight-fitting cover. Shake until thoroughly blended; chill. Best if made day before using. Yield: 8 servings.

ANCHOVY SALAD DRESSING

1 small onion, grated	1 (2-ounce) can anchovy filets, undrained
1 clove garlic, minced	1/3 cup wine vinegar
1/4 teaspoon dried basil	2/3 cup salad oil
1/4 teaspoon dried oregano	Generous dash Tabasco sauce
1/8 teaspoon dried leaf thyme	

If you have a mortar and pestle, mash first five ingredients together in it; otherwise, do the best you can with the back of a spoon; they must be well blended. Transfer to a bowl; add anchovies with their oil and blend until paste-like. Beat in vinegar, then oil and Tabasco; blend well and chill. Yield: 8 servings.

SOUR CREAM-ROQUEFORT DRESSING

1 cup commercial sour cream	2/3 cup crumbled Roquefort cheese
2 green onions, finely minced	Salt and pepper to taste
2 tablespoons mayonnaise	
2 to 3 tablespoons freshly squeezed lemon juice	

Stir all ingredients together by hand, blending thoroughly. Refrigerate several hours before serving. Yield: 8 to 10 servings.

SUPERB RUM CAKE
(may be prepared ahead of time)

1 cup butter (no substitute)	3 teaspoons baking powder
2 cups sugar	1/4 teaspoon salt
4 eggs	1 cup milk
3-1/2 cups all-purpose flour, measured after sifting	1 teaspoon rum extract

Beat butter and sugar thoroughly in large bowl of electric mixer. Add eggs one at a time, beating well after each addition. Sift flour, baking powder, and salt together three times. Add alternately with milk to first mixture, beginning and ending with dry ingredients and scraping the bowl constantly. Beat in flavoring; turn into well greased, lightly floured tube or kugelhupf pan. Bake at 325° for 1 hour and 20 to 30 minutes, until cake tests done when wire is inserted in center.

Rum Glaze

1 cup firmly packed brown sugar	1 cup water
1 cup granulated sugar	Pinch salt
2 tablespoons butter	2 tablespoons rum

In a saucepan, combine all ingredients except rum; boil for 3 to 4 minutes. Stir in rum; slowly pour half the glaze over hot cake while still in pan. Let cake almost cool, invert onto cakeplate and pour remaining glaze over it. This cake freezes well and is absolutely superb!

CHOCOLATE CHEESECAKE
(may be prepared ahead of time)

1 box thin chocolate wafer cookies, crushed	2 pounds cream cheese, softened
3/4 cup butter, melted	2 cups sugar
1/4 teaspoon ground cinnamon	4 eggs
1 (12-ounce) package semi-sweet chocolate bits	3 teaspoons cocoa
	2 teaspoons vanilla extract
	2 cups commercial sour cream

Combine crushed wafers with butter and cinnamon; press into bottom and sides of a 10-inch springform; chill.

Melt semi-sweet chocolate in top of double boiler over warm water. Beat softened cheese in large mixer bowl until fluffy and smooth. Gradually beat in sugar, then eggs one at a time, beating after each addition. Add melted chocolate, cocoa, and flavoring; blend thoroughly. Stir in sour cream and pour into chilled crust. Bake at 350° for 1 hour and 10 minutes. (The cake will be slightly runny but will become firm as it chills.) Cool at room temperature, then chill at least 5 hours before serving. Freezes well. Yield: 12 servings.

Crabmeat Thermidor Luncheon

LUNCHEON FOR SIX

Crabmeat Thermidor over Toasted Holland Rusk

Broccoli with Caper Sauce

Cranberry-Lime Salad with Sour Cream Topping

Lemon-Cheese Tarts

Coffee   **Iced Tea**

CRABMEAT THERMIDOR

1/2 cup chopped onion	1/2 cup shredded sharp Cheddar cheese
1/4 cup chopped green pepper	2 teaspoons freshly squeezed lemon juice
2 tablespoons butter or margarine	
1 (10-ounce) can frozen cream of potato soup, thawed	2 (6-ounce) packages frozen crabmeat; or 2 cans, drained
3/4 cup light cream	Minced parsley and paprika

Gently sauté onion and green pepper in butter until tender but not brown. Add soup, then cream; heat slowly, stirring constantly, until thoroughly heated but not boiling. Stir in cheese until melted. Remove from heat; add lemon juice and crabmeat; reheat.

Serve over toasted Holland Rusk, in patty shells or individual ramekins. Garnish with parsley and paprika. Yield: 6 servings.

Variations: Shrimp may be substituted for crabmeat; cream of shrimp soup may be substituted for potato soup. Two or three tablespoons sherry may be added. Mixed Swiss and Parmesan cheese may be substituted for Cheddar. Also, drained sliced water chestnuts and/or slivered blanched almonds may be added if desired.

BROCCOLI WITH CAPER SAUCE

Cook 2 pounds fresh broccoli in salted water until barely tender. Drain thoroughly. Place on heated serving dish and pour melted butter over it. Spoon bottled capers over broccoli, using both capers and juice as seasonings. Yield: 6 servings.

CRANBERRY-LIME SALAD

2 (3-ounce) packages lime-
  flavored gelatin
4 cups boiling water
1 (6-ounce) can frozen
  limeade concentrate

2 cups uncooked cranberries
2 cups diced celery
1 cup diced green pepper
  Lettuce
  Commercial sour cream

Dissolve gelatin in boiling water. Add frozen limeade and stir until dissolved. Refrigerate until syrupy. Cut cranberries into three pieces each. When gelatin has thickened, stir in cranberries, celery, and green pepper. Spoon into individual molds or a large mold and chill until set. Unmold on bed of lettuce and garnish with topping of plain sour cream. Yield: 12 (1/2-cup) servings.

LEMON-CHEESE TARTS
(may be prepared ahead of time)

3 eggs
1 cup sugar
1/2 cup freshly squeezed lemon juice
2 teaspoons grated lemon rind

1 (8-ounce) package cream
  cheese, softened
6 (4-inch) baked Pastry Tart Shells

Beat eggs in top of double boiler until thick and fluffy. Continue beating while gradually adding sugar, lemon juice, and rind. Place over hot water and cook, stirring constantly, until custard is thick and smooth; cool slightly. Gradually blend custard into softened cheese and when smooth, fill tart shells. Yield: 6 servings.

PASTRY TART SHELLS

1 cup all-purpose flour
1/2 teaspoon salt
1/3 cup vegetable shortening

Ice water
2 tablespoons soft butter or margarine

Sift flour and salt into bowl; cut in shortening with pastry blender; chill for 1 hour. When ready to make pastry, add ice water to dry mixture a little at a time, using as little as needed, mixing only until dough can be handled.

Roll out onto lightly floured board to about 1/4-inch thickness; spread with soft butter, fold dough into thirds (see Index); roll out again to 1/8-inch thickness; cut into rounds with a 4- or 5-inch cookie cutter. Fit and press rounds over back of muffin pans; prick entire surface with fork and bake at 425° for 12 to 15 minutes, or until golden brown. Remove from oven, cool, then carefully lift from pans. Yield: 6 shells.

Note: Muffin tins usually contain 12 cups. Since these tart shells freeze well, you may want to double this recipe to utilize a 12-cup muffin tin, use 6 for your lemon tarts and freeze the rest.

Chicken Salad Casserole Luncheon

LUNCHEON FOR SIX

Hot V-8 Cocktail

Hot Chicken Salad Casserole

Gingery Citrus Salad with Carrot Curls and Celery Fans

Beth Hardy's Rolls
or   **Butter**
Glorified Canned Biscuits

Strawberry Preserves

Coffee Charlotte

Coffee

A Silk Purse Menu — Looks and tastes expensive, but isn't.

HOT V-8 COCKTAIL

Use equal parts V-8 juice and undiluted canned beef bouillon. Add celery salt, Worcestershire sauce, and Tabasco sauce to taste. Heat thoroughly and serve as appetizer.

Note: If desired, vodka may be added. Should create quite a glow.

HOT CHICKEN SALAD CASSEROLE

2 cups diced cooked chicken	2 tablespoons freshly squeezed lemon juice
2 cups diced celery	1 cup commercial mayonnaise
1/2 cup slivered blanched almonds	1/2 cup shredded medium-sharp yellow cheese
1/2 teaspoon salt	2/3 cup broken potato chips
1/2 teaspoon grated onion	

Mix all ingredients except cheese and potato chips; turn into shallow buttered casserole. Combine cheese and potato chips and spread over top. Bake uncovered at 375° for 20 minutes. Yield: 6 servings.

GINGERY CITRUS SALAD

1 large grapefruit	1/4 teaspoon salt
1 or 2 oranges	3/4 cup orange juice
1-1/2 envelopes unflavored gelatin	1 (12-ounce) can ginger ale
1/4 cup freshly squeezed lemon juice	1/2 cup broken pecans
	Crisp greens
1/3 cup sugar	Commercial sour cream (optional)

Section grapefruit and oranges, removing all white membrane. Cut fruit into pieces. Soften gelatin in lemon juice, then dissolve over hot water.

Combine dissolved gelatin, sugar, salt, and orange juice in a bowl. Slowly pour ginger ale down side of bowl (to retain the bubbles). Mix gently with an up-and-down motion. Chill the mixture until syrupy; add diced fruit and nuts, again stirring with up-and-down motion. Pour into six individual molds and chill until firm. Unmold on crisp greens and spoon a generous tablespoon of sour cream over top if desired. Yield: 6 servings.

BETH HARDY'S YEAST ROLLS

2 envelopes dry yeast	1 cup plus 2 tablespoons lukewarm water
1/4 cup very warm water	3 eggs
5 tablespoons sugar	About 5 cups all-purpose flour
1/2 cup butter	1 teaspoon salt

Let yeast dissolve and foam in the 1/4 cup very warm water. Dissolve sugar and butter in boiled and cooled water, and combine with yeast mixture in large bowl of electric mixer. While beaters are running at low speed add 1 cup flour, then the eggs, one egg at a time, beating after each addition. Add remaining flour with salt and beat well, adding more flour if necessary, but the dough should remain moist. Turn out onto floured surface and let dough rest for 10 minutes, covered. Then knead thoroughly, turn into bowl, cover lightly and allow to rise in warm place until double in bulk.

Punch down, turn out onto floured surface and knead well. Divide dough in half and roll each portion into a circle about 1/3 inch thick. Spread with soft butter and cut into pie-shaped wedges. Starting with wide end of wedge, roll toward pointed end. Place, pointed-edge down, on lightly greased baking sheet; allow to rise until almost double in bulk. Bake at 375° for 15 minutes, or until rolls are nicely browned.

WHEN TO USE CANDLES

Candles should be used only after sundown or when the light dims outside, or on a dark, gloomy day. If they are on the table, always light them. Never use candles, not even in a decorative arrangement, without a charred wick.

GLORIFIED CANNED BISCUITS

Remove flaky baking powder biscuits from can and pull apart in the center to make each into two thin biscuits. Place on greased baking sheet, then with a fork punch each biscuit three times all the way through to the bottom. Brush with melted butter and bake at 450° until well browned, about 10 minutes. Serve immediately.

COFFEE CHARLOTTE
(prepare the day before)

12 **lady fingers**	3 **cups milk**
2 **tablespoons instant powdered coffee**	1/4 **cup cognac**
1/4 **teaspoon salt**	2 **cups heavy cream, whipped**
2/3 **cup sugar**	**Grated semi-sweet chocolate**
2 **envelopes unflavored gelatin**	

Split lady fingers in half and line bottom and sides of springform pan. Combine coffee, salt, sugar, and gelatin in saucepan. Add milk and stir over low heat until sugar and gelatin are dissolved. Remove from heat and stir in cognac. Chill until mixture mounds slightly. Fold in whipped cream and pour into prepared pan. Chill until firm. Remove sides of mold and garnish with grated semi-sweet chocolate. Yield: 8 generous servings.

TIP FOR GRATING CHOCOLATE

When you need a small amount of grated chocolate, a small hand grater (the kind with a rotating handle) is excellent for the purpose, because you may simply put semi-sweet chocolate bits or broken pieces of chocolate bars in grater, hold it over the dessert, and grind away.

Coquilles St. Jacques Luncheon

LUNCHEON FOR TEN

Coquilles St. Jacques

Chinese Salad

Hot Commercial Rolls
or
Riz Biscuits

Butter Curls

Easy Coffee Mousse
or
Baked Pears with Rum Sauce

Coffee

Tea

COQUILLES ST. JACQUES

2 pounds fresh or frozen scallops
1 (10-ounce) can chicken bouillon, undiluted
3 pounds raw shrimp in the shell, boiled and cleaned
5 tablespoons butter or margarine
1 cup chopped green onions
2 (3-ounce) cans mushrooms, drained, reserve liquid
4 tablespoons all-purpose flour
1/4 cup dry white wine
1 cup light cream
1/2 teaspoon seasoned salt
Generous dash white pepper
1/4 teaspoon paprika

Wash and drain scallops (if frozen, thaw); simmer in bouillon for 10 minutes. Drain, reserving cooking liquid. Cut large scallops in half; set aside with cooked shrimp.

Heat butter in saucepan; add onions and mushrooms; sauté for 3 minutes; remove and set aside. Stir flour into the pan and stir until smooth; gradually add reserved cooking liquid, cream, mushroom liquid, and wine. Cook slowly until thickened, stirring constantly. Add seasonings; return onion and mushrooms, then add scallops and shrimp. Let cook just a minute, then keep warm over hot water until ready to serve. Yield: 10 servings.

Note: Coquilles may be served in chafing dish or poured into a large casserole or individual ramekins or shells, topped with buttered breadcrumbs and baked at 350° for about 15 minutes, just to brown the crumbs. For this luncheon menu, use individual large shells or ramekins, as no accompaniments are suggested to fill the luncheon plate; the salad should be served in its own individual bowl.

CHINESE SALAD

2-1/2 to 3 quarts salad greens (several
   kinds of lettuce, torn into
   bite-size pieces)

About 2/3 cup sliced stuffed olives
Crisp Salad Topping
French Dressing*

Toss greens and olives with French Dressing until all greens are thoroughly coated. Add Crisp Salad Topping, toss briefly and serve immediately. If you must, toss the salad en route to the table. Yield: 10 servings.

*See Index for French Dressing recipe.

Crisp Salad Topping
(prepare ahead of time)

1 (3-ounce) can Chinese noodles
3 tablespoons melted butter or margarine
2 teaspoons Worcestershire sauce

1 teaspoon curry powder
1/2 teaspoon seasoned salt

Combine all ingredients in 12- x 8- x 2-inch baking pan and bake at 225° for about 1 hour or until crisp and toasted, stirring several times. Sprinkle over green salad at the very last moment; noodles must remain crisp.

RIZ BISCUITS
(see Index)

EASY COFFEE MOUSSE
(prepare ahead of time and freeze)

1 pint whipping cream
1/2 cup sugar
2 teaspoons instant powdered coffee

1/2 teaspoon vanilla extract
2 egg whites, stiffly beaten

Partially whip cream; add sugar, coffee, and vanilla and continue beating until cream holds its shape. Fold in stiffly beaten egg whites; turn into freezer tray and freeze, stirring once or twice. Yield: 8 to 10 servings.

Note: The mousse may be served in sherbet or ice cream dishes, or spooned into parfait glasses and placed in the freezer. If you like the combination of coffee and chocolate, lace the parfaits with chocolate syrup.

BAKED PEARS WITH RUM SAUCE

10 large, firm under-ripe pears
1/3 cup water
   Juice of 2 lemons

1-1/4 cups light brown sugar
1/2 cup light rum

Peel pears; cut in half and core. Place in shallow baking dish. Add water and sprinkle pears with lemon juice, then sugar. Slowly pour rum over the fruit, cover and bake at 250° for about 2 hours, or until pears are done, basting frequently with sauce in bottom of baking dish. Serve plain or garnished with vanilla ice cream. Yield: 10 servings.

Chicken Salad Luncheon

LUNCHEON FOR EIGHT

Molded Chicken Salad

with

Asparagus-Stuffed Eggs, Carrot Curls, Ripe Olives

Minted Fruit Salad

with

Minted Lime Dressing and Sour Cream Dressing

TVA Refrigerator Rolls

or   Butter

Flatbread Wafers

Cherry-Chocolate Refrigerator Pie

Ready-To-Drink Iced Tea

MOLDED CHICKEN SALAD

1 envelope unflavored gelatin
1/4 cup cold water
1 chicken bouillon cube dissolved in
   1 cup boiling water
1 cup commercial mayonnaise
1 teaspoon salt

Pepper to taste
3 cups cooked chicken or turkey, cut
   into small pieces
3 stalks celery, finely chopped
4 hard-cooked eggs, chopped
1/2 pound seedless white grapes

Soak gelatin in cold water for 5 minutes; dissolve in hot bouillon and cool. Stir slowly into mayonnaise until smooth; add other ingredients and turn into large fancy fluted mold or individual molds. Chill until set. If large mold with open center is used, pile carrot curls and ripe olives in the center. The contrast is lovely. Yield: 8 servings.

Note: This is a fine, delicately flavored salad; excellent for summer luncheons or buffet suppers.

READY-TO-DRINK ICED TEA

3 quarts medium-strength tea*
1/2 cup sugar

1 (12-ounce) can frozen
   lemonade concentrate
1 quart ginger ale

Combine tea, sugar, and concentrate. Just before serving, stir in ginger ale and pour over crushed ice in glasses. Yield: 10 servings.

*Steep 2 family-size tea bags in 3 quarts of water.

ASPARAGUS-STUFFED EGGS

8 hard-cooked eggs
3 to 4 tablespoons homemade
   mayonnaise
3 teaspoons grated lemon rind
1/2 teaspoon salt

1/2 teaspoon curry powder
1/4 teaspoon dry mustard
16 asparagus tips
   Pimiento strips

Cut eggs in half lengthwise. Scoop out and mash yolks. Add mayonnaise, lemon rind, salt, curry powder, and mustard; mix until creamy and thoroughly blended. Check taste, refill the egg whites with the mixture and place an asparagus tip across center of each egg half. Place a narrow pimiento strip across the asparagus tip. Yield: 8 servings.

MINTED FRUIT SALAD

1 (1-pound) can pineapple slices or
   spears, drained
3 cups fresh grapefruit sections
2 or 3 large oranges, peeled
   and sectioned

Salad Greens
Mint Leaves

Arrange pineapple, grapefruit, and orange slices on a bed of salad greens on individual serving plates or in a large salad bowl. Garnish generously with mint leaves. Serve with Minted Lime Dressing.

MINTED LIME DRESSING

3 tablespoons mint jelly*
2 tablespoons honey

Grated peel and juice of 1 lime
Juice of 1 lemon

In small bowl blend together mint jelly and honey until smooth. Add other ingredients. Chill before using. Yield: 8 servings.

Note: This is a beautiful salad with an unusual, lovely dressing which should be served in your best clear crystal bowl — that is, if you know your guests like mint flavor. For those who may not, you may offer two dressings to accompany the salad — the one above and another of plain sour cream to which has been added the grated rind and juice of 1 lemon.

*Mint jelly is commercial apple jelly flavored with mint.

TVA REFRIGERATOR ROLLS
(may be prepared ahead of time)

1 cup hot mashed potatoes
2/3 cup shortening
1/3 cup sugar
1 tablespoon salt
2 eggs

1 cake compressed yeast
1/2 cup lukewarm water (or water left
   from boiling potatoes)
1 cup scalded milk, cooled to lukewarm
6 to 8 cups all-purpose flour

Put hot potatoes in large mixer bowl. Mash; add shortening, sugar, salt, and eggs, beating well. Dissolve yeast in lukewarm water; add to lukewarm milk, then to potato mixture. Sift in enough flour to yield a stiff dough; turn onto floured surface and knead well. When fairly smooth, place in large greased bowl, cover with light cloth and let rise until double in bulk. Punch down, brush top of dough with melted butter, cover and refrigerate until ready to bake. Dough keeps well for several days.

About 1-1/2 hours before baking, pinch off dough, shape into rolls as desired, place in greased baking pan. Cover with light cloth and let rise until almost double in size. Bake at 400° for 15 to 20 minutes.

For Parker House rolls, roll dough to 1/3-inch thickness, cut with biscuit cutter, dip in melted butter or margarine on both sides and fold over. No need to grease baking sheets for these.

You may also make cloverleaf rolls by putting a ball of dough into a muffin cup, then cutting almost through to the bottom with scissors, making a deep crosscut.

These rolls freeze beautifully. You may bake them until barely colored, cool, and freeze. To reheat, thaw in their container, then bake at 350° for 8 to 10 minutes.

Note: If you have refrigerator space, the rolls may be prepared for baking the day before, then removed from refrigerator about 2-1/2 hours before baking.

FLATBREAD WAFERS
(see Index)

CHERRY-CHOCOLATE REFRIGERATOR PIE

Wafer Crust

Combine 2 cups finely crushed vanilla wafers with 1/3 cup melted butter. Reserve 2 tablespoons for top; press remainder in bottom of 1-quart refrigerator tray or dish.

Butter Layer

Thoroughly cream 1/2 cup butter with 1-1/2 cups sifted powdered sugar. Add 2 eggs, one at a time, beating well after each addition. Stir in 1/2 teaspoon vanilla extract and spread over bottom crust.

Chocolate Layer

Combine 1/4 cup sugar, 2 tablespoons cocoa, and 1 cup heavy cream. Whip until stiff. Fold in 1 cup chopped walnuts and 1/4 cup sliced maraschino cherries. Spread over butter layer. Sprinkle reserved crumbs over top. Chill 24 hours, or freeze. To serve, cut in squares. Yield: 9 to 12 servings.

Note: This is wickedly rich; serve sparingly!

THOSE LITTLE SQUARES OF MAGIC
(cooking with yeast)

The best kept secret of the twentieth century, I am convinced, is the ease of baking with yeast. Women are full of awe at the feat. Often you hear "She *even* bakes her own bread," the tribute equating it with making your husband's shirts or roofing the house yourself — projects a few women undertake in a spirit of defiance, just to prove they can, or, according to certain psychologists, to promote homemaking to the level of careerdom.

The plain truth is that some of us bake bread for the simple reason that we like homemade fresh bread — bread you can eat plain, without toasting or glamorizing.

I always chuckle inwardly at the delight of guests who walk into my house and, sniffing the aroma of baking bread, are impressed beyond belief, never suspecting what an easy operation it all is. (Somebody has passed up a good bet by not developing a household spray called "Mother's Homemade Rolls," though I have seen its first cousin, much to my surprise — a spray can labeled "Old-Fashioned Gingerbread.")

There must be some connection between the awe in which so many people hold yeast and a deep-rooted, subconscious suspicion of black magic. Perhaps it's because when the yeast works, you can't actually *see* what's happening unless you stand rooted to the spot to spy on the almost imperceptible escalation of the dough.

The important thing to remember in dealing with yeast is that you must show the dough who's boss. You mustn't be afraid of it, for actually you can take more liberties with yeast dough than with any other kind. It's just this simple: If the water in which you dissolve your yeast is somewhere near the proper temperature (stipulated on the package) and if your dough is placed in a fairly warm spot (around 75° to 80°) and if you turn your back and go about your business for a while, you'll return to find magic has indeed been wrought.

You don't have to make a science of baking with yeast. All you need is a clear, basic recipe — and some time. By time, I don't mean you must dedicate your whole day to the bread alone; but until you're a veteran at the business (that is, until you've done it twice!), it's a good idea to choose for your maiden voyage a day when you must be at home anyway, so you can look in on the rising dough now and then just to see what's going on.

Happy baking — with yeast! — C.M.

Cookouts

Succulent juices sizzle on hot coals, a rotisserie may drone a lulling tune, and wafts of charcoal tantalize the appetites. It's a cookout and it's fun because everyone gets into the act. Some help carry the salad and indoor provisions out, others take a turn basting the meat, and a few lucky ones may get a tasty pre-dinner bite. And everyone gathers round to cheer the chef as the steak sears or the fowl grows golden.

Cookouts are versatile. They'll pick up and go almost anywhere with cookout appliances that may be sophisticated or simple: a hibachi for a boat, an open fire for a campout, or a gas or electric grill for apartment or home patio or poolside.

Food is easily prepared and easily served. Dishes are few but plentiful enough to satisfy appetites that can't say no to seconds.

The secret to a successful cookout is the fire. Start the coals well in advance and allow the briquets to burn until they have a dusty white covering. To ensure an even heat, try to avoid adding charcoal after the fire has taken. A hot fire is needed for steaks and hamburgers, so begin with more coals and put the meat on the grill when coals reach their peak heat. A roast or any larger, longer cooking meat or fowl requires a slower, even-burning fire. So you may let the coals smolder a while longer or regulate the temperature by raising or lowering the grill.

When using gas or electric grills, experiment before entertaining. The gas or electric fire is usually hotter than charcoal fires, so cooking time may vary.

Grilled Steak Cookout

COOKOUT FOR SIX

Grilled Steak

Foil-Baked Tomatoes   **Suffern Inn Salad**

Grilled Garlic Bread

Herbed Cheese with Fresh Fruit Tray

or

Watermelon

Iced Tea   **Coffee**

GRILLED STEAK

2 tablespoons soy sauce
6 tablespoons good olive oil
1 tablespoon seasoned salt
1/4 teaspoon pepper

1/8 teaspoon garlic salt
6 thick individual steaks (filets, sirloin, small T-bone)

Combine first five ingredients; rub into the steaks by hand, on both sides, and allow to marinate at room temperature at least 2 hours before cooking. Turn steaks often. Grill over charcoal to stage desired — but these are best served medium-rare. Yield: 6 servings.

FOILED-BAKED TOMATOES

Cut three large tomatoes in half crosswise; brush with melted butter; sprinkle with salt, pepper, and curry powder or crushed dried basil. Wrap in aluminum foil and bake at edge of hot grill about 10 minutes, or until tender. Yield: 6 servings.

SUFFERN INN SALAD
(prepare ahead of time)

6 tablespoons mayonnaise
Juice of 1 lemon
1 small onion, finely minced; or 2 tablespoons minced chives
2 cups frozen peas (do not thaw)

1 cup Swiss or Cheddar cheese strips
Salt and pepper to taste
2 cups lettuce torn into bite-size pieces
8 slices crisp crumbled bacon

Twenty-four hours before serving, combine the mayonnaise, lemon juice, onion, frozen peas, and cheese strips in a bowl. Stir well, add salt and pepper to taste; cover and refrigerate.

Before serving, add lettuce and bacon, toss well and taste again. Yield: 6 servings.

Note: This salad must be prepared 24 hours before serving. It is most unusual and thoroughly delightful. Please follow directions carefully.

GRILLED GARLIC BREAD

1/2 cup butter or margarine, softened	1/4 teaspoon oregano
1 clove garlic, minced	1/4 teaspoon dried dill, crushed
1 teaspoon dried parsley flakes	1 loaf French bread

Combine butter, garlic, parsley flakes, oregano, and dill. (Flavor is better if mixture is prepared several days before using.) Put in covered container and refrigerate. Remove for 1 hour to soften before spreading on bread. Cut bread into 3/4-inch slices, but not quite through the bottom crust. Spread butter mixture generously between slices. Wrap loosely in aluminum foil and heat on grill for 15 minutes. Yield: 6 servings.

HERBED CHEESE

1/4 pound Jack or white Cheddar cheese, shredded	1/2 teaspoon dried marjoram, crushed
1 (8-ounce) package cream cheese, softened	1/4 teaspoon dried tarragon, crushed
	1 teaspoon grated lemon rind
1/4 cup grated Parmesan cheese	Juice of 1/2 lemon
1-1/2 tablespoons soft butter	1/3 cup Chablis (or other dry white wine)

Blend cheeses with butter in large bowl of electric mixer until creamy and smooth. (You may have to add a little of the wine to loosen the mixture so it will beat more easily.) Mix marjoram, tarragon, and lemon rind in small bowl; add to cheese mixture, then gradually beat in lemon juice and wine. Turn into bowl or small, lightly oiled mold and chill thoroughly. Serve with unsalted crackers and fresh fruit.

EASY STEAK BUTTER

1/4 pound butter or margarine, softened	1/4 teaspoon freshly ground black pepper
1 teaspoon minced green onion or chives	1/2 teaspoon seasoned salt
1 teaspoon dill weed	1/2 teaspoon paprika
1 teaspoon freshly squeezed lemon juice	2 teaspoons minced fresh parsley

Blend all ingredients together well and store in refrigerator until needed. Use on broiled steaks; as a topping for green vegetables; as a spread for French bread.

Beef Kabobs Cookout

COOKOUT FOR SIX

Beef Kabobs

or

Lamb Shish Kabobs

Bacon-Stuffed Potatoes   **New Orleans Corn Pudding**

Simple Green Salad with Clear French Dressing

French Bread   **Butter**

Toffee Cake

or

Honeydew Melon with Lime Wedges

Iced Tea   **Coffee**

BEEF KABOBS

    Juice of 1-1/2 lemons
3 tablespoons salad oil
1 medium onion, grated
1 teaspoon salt
    Several grinds black pepper
1/4 teaspoon ground ginger
2 teaspoons Worcestershire sauce
1 bay leaf

1 clove garlic, crushed
1/2 teaspoon prepared yellow mustard
3 pounds sirloin steak
    Whole fresh mushrooms
    Green pepper chunks
    Fresh tomato quarters
    Sweet onion chunks

Combine the first 10 ingredients in a shallow bowl to form a marinade. Cut steak into 1-1/2-inch cubes, and add with whole fresh mushrooms (stems removed, lightly rinsed, and dried) to marinade. Refrigerate at least 4 hours, turning meat and mushrooms occasionally.

On metal skewers alternate beef cubes with mushroom caps, green pepper chunks, fresh unpeeled tomato quarters, and chunks of sweet onion. Grill over glowing coals for about 20 minutes, turning frequently and brushing with marinade. Yield: 6 servings.

LAMB SHISH KABOBS

Cut 3 pounds of tender lamb (from the leg, preferably) into 1-1/2-inch cubes. Marinate in the refrigerator for 2 hours in the Marinade.

Marinade

Juice of 2 large lemons
4 tablespoons olive or vegetable oil
2 tablespoons grated onion
1 tablespoon ground chili powder

1 teaspoon ground ginger
1 teaspoon curry powder
2 teaspoons salt
1 clove garlic, crushed

On metal skewers alternate meat with similarly sized chunks of tomato, onion, green pepper, and mushroom caps. Broil on charcoal grill, turning frequently and brushing with Marinade. Yield: 6 servings.

BACON-STUFFED POTATOES
(may be prepared ahead of time)

8 large baking potatoes
1/4 cup butter or margarine
1 cup commercial sour cream
1 egg

1 teaspoon salt
1/8 teaspoon pepper
9 crisp bacon slices, crumbled fine
Paprika

Scrub potatoes and dry. Rub with a little butter or oil and bake directly on oven rack at 400° for about 1 hour, or until fork tender. Cut a long oval slice from one side of potato and scoop out into a bowl. Add butter, sour cream, egg, salt, and pepper. Beat well; stir in crisp, crumbled bacon. Pile back into six potato shells, mounding the potatoes high (that's why you baked two extra potatoes). Sprinkle with paprika. Allow to cool, then wrap each potato individually and freeze.

To serve: It is unnecessary to thaw potatoes; simply heat oven to 400°; unwrap frozen potatoes; place on oven rack and bake until heated through — 45 minutes to 1 hour. Yield: 6 servings.

SIMPLE GREEN SALAD WITH CLEAR FRENCH DRESSING
(see Index)

Salad with this menu is optional, remember, the skewers will contain vegetables.

FRENCH BREAD
(see Index)

NEW ORLEANS CORN PUDDING

6 ears fresh corn, or 2 (12-ounce) cans
whole-kernel yellow or white corn,
drained well
6 tablespoons butter or margarine
2 tablespoons sugar
2 tablespoons all-purpose flour (scant)
1/2 cup light cream

4 eggs, well beaten
1-1/2 teaspoons baking powder
2 tablespoons butter or
margarine, melted
2 tablespoons brown sugar
1/4 teaspoon ground cinnamon

Cut corn from ears (about 4 cups) and set aside. Heat butter with sugar in saucepan until butter is melted. Stir in flour until well blended; remove from heat. Gradually stir in cream; add eggs, then baking powder; mix well. Stir into corn and pour into buttered 1-1/2-quart casserole or soufflé dish. Bake at 350° for about 45 minutes, or until knife inserted in center comes out clean. Spread top with melted butter and sprinkle with brown sugar and cinnamon which have been combined. Return to oven for about 5 minutes. Yield: 6 to 8 servings.

TOFFEE CAKE

1 cup granulated sugar
1 cup brown sugar, firmly packed
2 cups all-purpose flour, sifted
1 teaspoon soda
1/2 teaspoon salt
1/2 cup butter or margarine

1 cup buttermilk
1 egg
1/2 teaspoon vanilla extract
5 ounces chocolate-covered toffee
bars, chopped
1/2 cup chopped pecans

Put sugars in large bowl of electric mixer. Sift in dry ingredients; stir to mix. Cut in butter with pastry blender, as for piecrust. Remove a half cup of the mixture and set aside. To remainder add buttermilk, egg, and vanilla. Beat thoroughly and turn into greased 13- x 9- x 2-inch pan. Combine reserved dry mixture with chopped candy and nuts; sprinkle over batter. Bake at 350° for 30 to 35 minutes (325° for glass pan). Serve from baking pan. Freezes beautifully. Yield: 12 servings.

HONEYDEW MELON WITH LIME WEDGES
(or similar fruit in season)

PAPER DOILIES

In making out your shopping list, don't forget to include paper doilies for all trays you plan to use. About the only serving piece which requires no doily is a ceramic or pottery platter used for raw vegetables. Use white paper doilies only — never plastic.

Roast Beef Cookout

COOKOUT FOR SIX

Rotisserie Roast Beef with Barbecue Sauce

Potato Puff Casserole   **Tomato Stacks**

Cucumber Salad

Commercial Hard Rolls   **Butter**

Frozen Bisque

Iced Tea   **Coffee**

ROTISSERIE ROAST BEEF

1 (4- to 5-pound) rolled rump, or sirloin
   tip roast (about 4 inches in diameter)
2 cloves garlic

Salt and pepper
Barbecue Sauce

With point of sharp knife make several deep gashes in fat of the roast. Cut garlic cloves into thin slivers and insert into gashes. Place roast on rotisserie spit; center it and fasten prongs on each end. Cook over low heat for 2 to 3 hours for rare; 2-1/2 to 3-1/2 hours for medium, or 3 to 4 hours for well done. Baste frequently with Barbecue Sauce. Yield: 6 servings.

Barbecue Sauce

6 tablespoons Worcestershire sauce
3 tablespoons commercial steak sauce
2 tablespoons vinegar

1/2 cup butter or margarine
Juice of 2 lemons
Several dashes Tabasco sauce

Melt butter and stir in all other ingredients. Serve with chicken, beef, or spareribs.

Note: This sauce contains neither sugar nor tomatoes; they tend to scorch and char during prolonged cooking.

MEAT TIP

When choosing meat for the grill, allow about 3/4 to 1 pound per serving for cuts with bone in, or 1/3 to 1/2 pound per serving for boneless cuts.

POTATO PUFF CASSEROLE

1 (8-ounce) package cream
  cheese, softened
5 cups hot mashed potatoes
1 egg, beaten
1/2 teaspoon salt
  Dash white pepper

Dash cayenne pepper
1/2 teaspoon paprika
2 tablespoons minced chives (frozen
  will do), or 1/2 teaspoon
  instant onion flakes

Combine softened cheese and hot potatoes, mixing until well blended. Add remaining ingredients, beat thoroughly and turn into buttered 1-1/2-quart casserole. Brush top with melted butter and bake uncovered at 350° for 40 minutes. This potato dish is excellent served with any beef. Yield: 6 servings.

TOMATO STACKS
(see Index)

CUCUMBER SALAD

1 large cucumber
4 or 5 green onions, minced
1/4 cup dry white wine
  Juice of 1/2 lemon
3 tablespoons oil

Salt and pepper
1 teaspoon dried basil, crushed
1 large head iceberg lettuce, or other
  salad greens

Peel and slice cucumber thinly; place in bowl with onions and add the wine and lemon juice. Allow to marinate for 1 hour in the refrigerator or at room temperature. When ready to serve, blend oil, salt, pepper, and basil, in large bowl. Add chunks of greens, toss thoroughly until all are coated. Add cucumber-onion mixture with its marinade, toss briefly. Yield: 6 servings.

FROZEN BISQUE
(may be prepared ahead of time)

6 graham crackers
1 pint whipping cream
3 eggs, separated
3/4 cup powdered sugar

2/3 cup shredded coconut
1/4 cup almond-flavored sweet sherry
1 teaspoon vanilla extract

Crush graham crackers with rolling pin; set aside. Whip cream; set aside. Beat egg yolks until light and fluffy; gradually add sugar and mix well. Fold into whipped cream, then fold graham cracker crumbs, coconut, sherry, and vanilla. Beat egg whites until stiff and fold into the mixture. Turn into 2-inch paper muffin cups and freeze. Excellent ahead-of-time dessert. Yield: 16 (2-ounce) servings.

Note: These may be served in two ways. They may be turned out into meringue shells and topped with frozen strawberries or raspberries, or turned into dessert dishes and wine-flavored strawberries or raspberries served separately. Almond flavoring or a little kirsch may be used for flavoring berries if desired.

Barbecued Spareribs Cookout

COOKOUT FOR SIX

Mexican Barbecued Spareribs

Rice-Sour Cream Casserole   **Fresh Corn Wrapped in Foil**

Green Salad with Olive Dressing

Commercial Hard Rolls   **Butter**

Fresh Peach Ice Cream

Iced Tea   Lemonade   Beer

MEXICAN BARBECUED SPARERIBS

1 (14-ounce) bottle catsup	2 tablespoons brown sugar
1/4 cup water	1/4 cup vinegar
2 teaspoons dry mustard	1/4 teaspoon Tabasco sauce
1/2 teaspoon chili powder	2 tablespoons Worcestershire sauce
1 teaspoon celery salt	1 tablespoon grated onion
1/2 teaspoon ground cumin	6 pounds spareribs
1/4 teaspoon ground cloves	

Combine first 12 ingredients to make sauce. Beat thoroughly. Cover ribs with sauce and marinate in refrigerator for 24 hours. Drain ribs; bake uncovered at 300° for 1 hour; drain off fat. Grill outdoors using marinade to baste during cooking. Turn ribs often to cook evenly. Yield: 6 servings.

RICE-SOUR CREAM CASSEROLE

3/4 pound sharp Cheddar cheese	1 (4-ounce) can sweet red peppers, drained and chopped; or 1 small jar pimiento strips, drained
2 cups commercial sour cream	
1 (4-ounce) can green chile peppers, drained and chopped	4-1/2 cups cooked rice
	Salt and pepper

Reserve a piece of the cheese to shred for topping; the size depends on size of casserole; cut remainder into strips. Combine sour cream with green and red peppers. Season the rice with salt and pepper. In a buttered shallow 1-1/2-quart casserole arrange layers of rice, sour cream mixture, and cheese strips, ending with rice as top layer. Sprinkle with the reserved cheese which has been shredded; bake uncovered at 350° for about 30 minutes or until lightly browned. Yield: 6 to 8 servings.

DROSTEN PLAIN BOILED RICE

Fill a 3-quart kettle, which has a tight lid, three-fourths full of water. Add a tablespoon salt and bring to a boil. Slowly add 1-1/2 cups long-grain white rice. (I use converted rice; no need to wash it before cooking.) When water boils again, set timer for 18 minutes and cook uncovered at a brisk boil. When done, drain into colander or strainer but do not rinse. Return at once to the still-hot kettle and place a double thickness of paper towels over top of pan before covering with tight-fitting lid. Return to stove and keep warm over lowest heat possible until serving time. (The heat may be turned off if you plan to serve the rice within 20 minutes.) If desired, a tablespoon or two of butter may be stirred in just before serving. Yield: 5 or 6 servings.

Note: The rice is dry and fluffy, each grain standing apart from its neighbor. When you remove the paper towels to serve, you'll see where all the moisture went. Latin Americans add a teaspoon of oil to the boiling water to prevent boiling over. I prefer to rub a small piece of butter around inside rim of pot, which accomplishes the same purpose. — C. M.

FRESH CORN WRAPPED IN FOIL
(see Index)

OLIVE DRESSING

1/2 cup salad oil	1/4 teaspoon paprika
3 tablespoons cider vinegar	1 tablespoon minced fresh parsley
1 teaspoon salt	1 tablespoon minced chives
1/8 teaspoon white pepper	3 tablespoons minced stuffed olives

Place all ingredients in a jar with tight-fitting cover and shake vigorously until dressing is blended. Cover and store in refrigerator until ready to use; shake again before pouring over salad. This is very quick, very easy — and best of all — very good! Yield: 3/4 cup.

FRESH PEACH ICE CREAM

8 very ripe unpeeled peaches	3/4 cup sugar
1 teaspoon almond flavoring	1 pint whipping cream
Dash freshly squeezed lemon juice	

Mash peaches, including skins and juices, with a fork or use a blender. Add almond flavoring and lemon juice. Add sugar to taste. Whip cream and blend thoroughly with peach mixture. Pour in ice tray and freeze. Remove from tray and cut into squares. Yield: 6 servings.

LEMONADE
(see Index)

Barbecued Chicken Cookout

COOKOUT FOR EIGHT

Barbecued Chicken

Fresh Corn Wrapped in Foil

or

Barbecued Corn-on-the-Cob

Betty's Coleslaw   **Cold Herbed Tomatoes**

Garlic French Bread   **Butter**

Fresh Fruit Platter

Iced Tea   **Lemonade**

BARBECUED CHICKEN

4 (2-pound) broilers

Marinade

3 cups vinegar
3-1/2 teaspoons salt
1-1/2 tablespoons prepared yellow mustard
4-1/2 tablespoons catsup

9 tablespoons freshly squeezed lemon juice
Black pepper

Browning Sauce

6 tablespoons sugar
1-1/2 teaspoons salt
9 tablespoons butter or margarine

3-1/2 tablespoons prepared yellow mustard
3-1/2 teaspoons Worcestershire sauce
1/4 teaspoon black pepper

Cut chickens in half; arrange in single layer in large pan (about 15 x 10 inches) and marinate overnight in marinade, piercing chicken with a fork so sauce can penetrate.

To cook, place chicken on grill (bony-side down) and baste with the marinade for first half of cooking time, then with Browning Sauce for last half of cooking time. Any remaining Browning Sauce may be heated and served with the chicken.

If your grill won't hold eight chicken halves, prepare four ahead of time and keep warm in oven set at low heat.

Cooked chicken freezes well. If you have some of the Browning Sauce left, some may be spooned into the rib cage of chicken before freezing. Be sure to reheat slowly. Yield: 8 servings.

FRESH CORN WRAPPED IN FOIL

1 **cup butter or margarine, softened**
2 **teaspoons salt**

8 **ears corn, husks and silk removed**
8 **(9- x 12-inch) pieces aluminum foil**

Mix softened butter and salt. Place corn in center of foil and coat generously with butter mixture. Wrap each ear separately in the foil. Bring long sides of foil together. Fold edges over three times, about 1/4 inch each time. Fold ends securely. Do not wrap tightly; the corn needs room for expansion. Bake wrapped corn at 450° for 20 to 25 minutes. Serve the corn in their wrappers; they should be opened just when ready to eat. Roll ear of corn in the butter in foil as it's eaten. Yield: 8 servings.

Note: If grill is large enough, you may want to roast the corn outdoors instead of inside. The corn may be prepared in the same manner described above and placed on the grill, allowing about 30 minutes (or more, depending on age of corn), turning often to cook uniformly.

BARBECUED CORN-ON-THE-COB

Use unhusked ears of corn. Lay back husks enough to remove silk. Return husks to their original position and wire into place (using any fine wire handy) at center and near tip of cob. Be sure kernels aren't exposed.

Roast on barbecue grill, turning three or four times so all sides are exposed to heat. Allow at least 30 minutes for roasting (depends on age of corn and proximity of heat). When done, snip wire with wire cutters, husk the ears (with gloves!) and serve with plan or seasoned butter.

BETTY'S COLESLAW

4 **cups grated cabbage**
1-1/2 **teaspoons salt**
1/2 **teaspoon dry mustard**
Pinch sugar

3 **tablespoons vinegar (or more if needed)**
2 **tablespoons commercial sour cream**
2 **tablespoons mayonnaise**

Grate cabbage. Add salt and mix thoroughly. Mix mustard, sugar, and vinegar together and add to cabbage. Combine sour cream and mayonnaise and other ingredients. Check seasonings and chill thoroughly. Yield: 8 servings.

TIP FOR GRILLING CHICKEN

In grilling chicken outdoors, place bony or rib-cage side of chicken down next to heat first. The bones act as an insulator and keep chicken from browning too fast.

HERBED TOMATOES

8 ripe tomatoes	1/3 cup minced fresh parsley
1-1/4 teaspoons salt	1/3 cup minced chives
1/4 teaspoon pepper	3/4 cup salad oil
3/4 teaspoon dried leaf thyme	1/3 cup tarragon vinegar

Peel tomatoes and place in bowl. Sprinkle with seasonings and herbs. Combine oil and vinegar and pour over. Cover and chill for 2 hours, occasionally spooning dressing over tomatoes. At serving time, drain tomatoes and serve dressing separately if desired. Sprinkle additional parsley over tomatoes before serving. Yield: 8 servings.

Note: These tomatoes are attractive served in pyramid fashion in a compote-type serving dish.

GARLIC FRENCH BREAD
(see Index)

LEMONADE

1-1/4 to 1-1/2 cups sugar	Ice
2-1/3 cups freshly squeezed lemon juice	Lemon slices
10 cups water	Sprigs of mint

Combine sugar and juice with 2 cups water. Boil for 5 minutes or until sugar is completely dissolved. Remove from heat. Add remaining water and cool. Just before serving, add ice. Garnish with lemon slices and mint. Yield: 12 servings.

Old-Fashioned Picnic

COOKOUT FOR TWELVE

Home-on-the-Range Burgers

or

Oyster Roast

Sidney's Potato Salad   **Janie May's Baked Beans**

Mrs. R.'s Coleslaw

or

Subgum Salad

Watermelon

Lemonade   **Beer**

HOME-ON-THE-RANGE BURGERS

3 pounds ground lean beef
2 cloves garlic, minced
2 small onions, minced
2 tablespoons chili sauce
2 tablespoons prepared yellow mustard
2 tablespoons Worcestershire sauce
3 teaspoons seasoned salt
4 eggs

12 sesame seed hamburger buns
Yellow mustard
Mayonnaise
Commercial barbecue sauce
Dill pickles
Sliced sweet onions
Sliced ripe tomatoes

Put beef into large bowl, add garlic, onions, seasonings, and eggs. Blend mixture well with fork and, handling lightly, form into 12 large hamburgers. Cook patties on greased grill over charcoal fire 3 to 5 inches from hot coals for 3 to 6 minutes per side. Serve on sesame seed hamburger buns with yellow mustard, mayonnaise, commercial barbecue sauce, dill pickles, sliced sweet onions, and sliced ripe tomatoes. Yield: 12 large hamburgers.

With the great expanse of sandy beaches in the Southland, the oyster roast is a popular way to cook out.

OYSTER ROAST

1-1/2 pecks oysters in shells
3/4 pound butter

Juice and grated peel of 1-1/2 lemons
Dash commercial hot sauce

Dig hole in ground deep enough to line with flat rocks. Build fire on rocks and keep burning until the rocks are sizzling hot. Remove wood and ashes. Cover the rocks with seaweed, then add the oysters. Cover with canvas, placing stones around the edge. Cook oysters for about 1-1/2 hours, then check for doneness. Melt the butter in a saucepan; add the lemon juice, lemon peel, and hot sauce. Mix together. Serve with oysters. Yield: 12 servings.

SIDNEY'S POTATO SALAD

About 12 medium boiling potatoes
2 bunches green onions, chopped
(about 12 onions)
1 green pepper, chopped
Pinch dried basil, crushed
Pinch bouquet garni* (optional)

Salt and pepper to taste
Garlic salt
Seasoned salt
2 parts mayonnaise to 1 part
salad dressing

Boil potatoes in their jackets; peel and cool to room temperature. Slice or cut into cubes. Combine remaining ingredients and mix well. Pour over potatoes, toss thoroughly but not violently, check seasonings and serve. Yield: 12 servings.

Note: The secret of this salad is the method of seasoning. By combining several small amounts of seasoning in the dressing before pouring over potatoes, the seasoning is more thoroughly incorporated into each piece of potato. You'll have to experiment a little to determine the amount of mayonnaise required; I would suggest starting with 2/3 cup. — C. M.

*See Index for Bouquet Garni recipe.

JANIE MAY'S BAKED BEANS

These are my favorite baked beans. Sorry, but neither Janie May nor I can supply proportions, but I suspect anything you do to this dish will be right. To serve 20, I have used 3 (32-ounce) cans of beans and 2 pounds sausage. — C. M.

To canned baked beans in tomato sauce add dry mustard, prepared yellow mustard, brown sugar, salt, pepper, molasses, and minced onion.

Lightly fry patties of pork sausage (the hot kind); drain thoroughly. Crumble with fork and stir into beans; cover and bake at 350° for at least 1 hour.

MRS. R'S COLESLAW

"Mrs. R" was a very ancient, beloved Southern lady who lived in Gadsden, Alabama. She was included in many family gatherings, whether she was related or not, and could always be depended on to bring a bowl of her famous coleslaw. People don't seem to make slaw like this any more, but all Southerners and ex-Southerners whose taste buds have good memories will recognize this pioneer version of coleslaw. — C. M.

1 head firm white cabbage	2 tablespoons prepared yellow mustard
1 stalk celery	1 cup homemade mayonnaise
2 green peppers	1/4 cup vinegar
2 sweet red peppers	Salt and pepper to taste
1 onion	

Shred cabbage and finely chop other vegetables; combine in bowl and add other ingredients. Let stand for an hour. When ready to serve, as "Mrs. R" used to say, "Stir well and you have something good." Yield: 8 servings as a vegetable or salad; 12 servings as a condiment.

SUBGUM SALAD

1/2 pound spinach	1 (5-ounce) can water chestnuts, drained and sliced
2 large green peppers	1 hard-cooked egg, chopped
1 large head lettuce	
1 (1-pound) can bean sprouts, drained	

Wash spinach; remove tough stems and pat dry. Tear into bite-size pieces. Slice peppers into thin slivers. Tear lettuce into bite-size pieces. Combine spinach, peppers, lettuce, bean sprouts, water chestnuts, and egg and refrigerate until just before serving at home or leaving for a picnic.

Dressing

1/4 cup oil	1/2 teaspoon ground ginger
2 tablespoons soy sauce	1 teaspoon sugar
2 tablespoons cider vinegar	1/4 teaspoon ground black pepper
2 tablespoons catsup	1 small clove garlic, crushed

Combine all dressing ingredients in jar with tight-fitting cover; shake well and refrigerate. Pour over salad just before serving. Yield: 12 servings.

Note: For serving at home, use chopped egg as a garnish after tossing the salad, instead of as one of the ingredients.

Lemon-Barbecue Chicken Cookout

COOKOUT FOR EIGHT

Lemon-Barbecue Chicken

Potatoes Gruyere   **Janie May's Baked Beans**

Western Slaw

Hot Garlic French Bread   **Butter**

Chocolate Icebox Cake

Iced Tea   **Lemonade**   **Hot Coffee**

LEMON-BARBECUE CHICKEN

2 (2-1/2- to 3- pound) broilers
1 cup salad oil
1/2 cup freshly squeezed lemon juice
1 tablespoon salt
1 teaspoon paprika

2 teaspoons crushed basil
2 teaspoons onion powder
1/2 teaspoon leaf thyme, crushed
1 clove garlic, crushed

Split chickens in halves or quarters; place in shallow baking pans. Combine other ingredients in a jar and shake well to blend. Pour sauce over chicken; cover tightly and marinate in refrigerator for 6 to 8 hours or overnight, turning chicken occasionally.

Remove chicken from refrigerator about an hour before grilling. Place chicken on grill, skin-side up, and cook about 20 to 25 minutes, brushing often with sauce. Turn chicken and cook an additional 20 minutes.

Chicken may be cooked in oven. Place 8 inches from broiler; brush often with sauce. Yield: 4 to 8 servings, depending on size of broilers. If they're small, allow half a broiler per person.

POTATOES GRUYERE

8 to 10 boiling potatoes
Butter
Salt and pepper

Beef or chicken broth*
1 cup shredded Gruyere or Swiss cheese

Generously butter a casserole. Peel and slice potatoes into 1/8-inch slices. Place a layer of potatoes in the dish, sprinkle with salt and pepper, and

The shady spot in your backyard is just the right one to set the stage for a cookout.

continue layering and seasoning. About every third layer, dot potatoes with bits of butter. Pour in enough broth to cover potatoes well; the broth should come almost to the top of the casserole. Bake uncovered at 350° for about 45 minutes. Check for doneness, using a small sharp knife. If too much liquid is left, drain it off. Sprinkle with cheese and return to oven until the cheese browns to a lovely golden color. Yield: 8 servings.

*Use beef broth if potatoes are to accompany beef; chicken broth for fowl.

JANIE MAY'S BAKED BEANS
(see Index)

WESTERN SLAW

About 4 cups finely shredded cabbage	Pinch sugar
1/2 cup ripe olives, chopped	2 tablespoons vinegar
1/4 cup minced onion	1 tablespoon salad oil
1 teaspoon caraway seed	Salt and pepper to taste
1/2 cup commercial sour cream	Tomato wedges
1 teaspoon seasoned salt	

Combine cabbage, olives, onion, and caraway seed in large bowl. Blend sour cream, seasoned salt, sugar, vinegar, oil, salt, and pepper together; pour over cabbage and toss. Check seasonings; more salt may be needed. Cover and chill before serving. Garnish bowl with tomato wedges or cherry tomatoes; it needs the color contrast. Yield: 8 servings.

GARLIC FRENCH BREAD
(see Index)

CHOCOLATE ICEBOX CAKE
(may be prepared ahead of time)

1/2 pound butter	1/2 teaspoon almond extract
3 cups powdered sugar	2 dozen lady fingers, split
6 eggs, separated	1 cup slivered blanched almonds
3 squares unsweetened chocolate, melted	Whipped cream
1 teaspoon vanilla extract	Toasted almond slivers (optional)

Cream butter and sugar thoroughly in large bowl of electric mixer. Add egg yolks one at a time, beating well after each addition. Blend in melted chocolate and flavorings. Beat egg whites until stiff and carefully fold in by hand.

Line a buttered springform pan with lady fingers; spoon in some of the chocolate mixture, almonds, and lady fingers to form a layer. Continue layering until all ingredients are used. Refrigerate overnight (or freeze for later use). Before serving, unmold and frost with whipped cream; sprinkle with toasted almond slivers if desired. Obviously, this is a rich dessert and small servings would be appropriate — with seconds available!

Shrimp Supreme Cookout

COOKOUT FOR SIX

Patio Shrimp Supreme

Herbed Hamburgers

Double-Boiler Rice   **Mediterranean Salad**

Cornmeal Crisps

Cantaloupe Halves with Lime Sherbet

Iced Tea   **Hot Coffee**

PATIO SHRIMP SUPREME

3 pounds shrimp, fresh or frozen
2 (4-ounce) cans sliced
   mushrooms, drained
2/3 cup butter or margarine, melted
1/4 cup chopped onion
2 tablespoons chili sauce
1/2 teaspoon garlic salt

Dash Tabasco sauce
1/2 cup chopped parsley
2 tablespoons freshly squeezed
   lemon juice
1 teaspoon salt
Dash Worcestershire sauce

Thaw frozen shrimp. Peel shrimp and remove sand veins. Wash and drain
on paper towels. Cut six (12-inch) squares of heavy-duty aluminum foil. Divide
shrimp into six portions. Place each portion of shrimp on half of each square
of foil. Place mushrooms on top of shrimp. Combine remaining ingredients
to make a sauce; pour over shrimp, using approximately 3 tablespoons for each
portion. Fold other half of foil over shrimp and seal edges making double folds
in the foil. Place packages of shrimp on a barbecue grill about 4 inches
from moderately hot coals. Cook for 20 minutes or until shrimp is tender. To
serve, cut a big cross in the top of each package and fold the foil back. Yield:
6 servings.

HERBED HAMBURGERS

2 pounds ground beef
1/2 cup minced onion
1/2 cup herb-flavored stuffing
    Dash ground nutmeg
1-1/2 teaspoons salt

1/2 teaspoon pepper
2 tablespoons Worcestershire sauce
2 tablespoons chopped parsley
2 eggs

Combine all ingredients and mix well. Shape into six oval-shaped patties. Place each patty on a square of aluminum foil and cook on grill for about 20 minutes, turning once. Yield: 6 servings.

DOUBLE-BOILER RICE

3-1/2 cups chicken broth (or 4 bouillon
    cubes dissolved in 3-1/2 cups hot
    water)*
1-1/2 tablespoons freshly squeezed
    lemon juice
1/2 teaspoon salt
    Dash pepper

1 bay leaf
3 tablespoons butter or margarine
1-1/4 cups uncooked long-grain white rice
1 (4-ounce) can mushroom slices,
    drained, reserve liquid
2/3 cup commercial sour cream
    Chopped chives or parsley

Place chicken broth, lemon juice, salt, pepper, bay leaf, and 1-1/2 tablespoons of the butter in top of double boiler over direct heat. When mixture starts to simmer, add rice. Cover and cook over boiling water for about 30 minutes, or until rice is tender and all liquid is absorbed. Remove bay leaf.

Sauté mushrooms lightly in the remaining 1-1/2 tablespoons butter and stir into rice with sour cream. Heat thoroughly and when ready to serve, sprinkle with chives or parsley. Yield: 6 servings.

Note: This rice has good staying qualities if dinner is delayed; just keep it warm in the top of double boiler.

*Liquid drained from mushrooms may be used as part of chicken broth.

MEDITERRANEAN SALAD

1 (1-pound) can artichoke hearts, drained
1/3 cup olive oil
1/3 cup freshly squeezed lemon juice
1 head romaine or other lettuce
2 tablespoons crushed dried mint

4 green onions, chopped
1 cup pitted Greek black olives
2 ripe tomatoes, peeled and cut in wedges
    Salt to taste

Marinate artichoke hearts for 2 to 3 hours in olive oil and lemon juice. Tear lettuce into bite-size pieces and combine with remaining ingredients in large salad bowl; add artichoke hearts with their marinade; toss lightly. Yield: 6 servings.

CORNMEAL CRISPS
(see Index)

Dinner Parties

A seated dinner party provides an evening to relax and relish each course and to enjoy the surrounding company, carefully chosen for compatibility. From six to eight is a perfect number, large enough for interest, small enough for intimacy. Among friends, a foursome can be perfection.

Table settings and arrangements will enhance an evening, whether a formal damask covers the table or a monk's cloth, for a Mexican meal. And the soft glimmer of candles creates a pleasant atmosphere, bathing guests and food in a becoming light.

The hostess, even without help, should effortlessly serve her meal. If three courses present a problem, it is better to omit the first course or serve it as an hors d'oeuvre beforehand. (Hors d'oeuvre suggestions for each menu are given on pages 413-416.) And in planning a menu, keep in mind the need for a balance of texture, color, and variety of flavors. The menus which follow may be used as they are or interchanged to suit your taste, but do substitute a vegetable for a vegetable and a starch for a starch.

Cornish Hen Dinner

DINNER FOR EIGHT

Madrilene with Clams

Baked Cornish Hens

Green Beans Espagnole　　　　　**Rice Mingle**

Oak Ridge Hot Baked Fruit

Cassata alla Siciliana

or

Sherbet

Coffee　　　　　　　　　　　**Tea**

No bread suggested because of rice, but a bread of your choice could be added if desired.

MADRILENE WITH CLAMS

2 (10-ounce) cans Madrilene
(jellied consommé)
1 pint commercial sour cream
1 teaspoon salt
1/2 teaspoon freshly ground black pepper

1 tablespoon minced chives
2 tablespoons freshly squeezed lemon
or lime juice
2 (8-ounce) cans clams, drained

Whip sour cream into consommé with rotary beater until mixture resembles strawberry mousse. Fold in seasonings, chives, lemon juice, and drained clams. Check seasonings and chill until serving time. Garnish with more minced chives. Yield: 8 servings.

Alternate garnish: An attractive topping for this delightful summertime first course is a tablespoon of sour cream topped with half a teaspoon of red caviar.

BAKED CORNISH HENS

8 Cornish hens
Salt and pepper
8 whole medium onions

3/4 cup butter or margarine
1/4 cup Kitchen Bouquet
1 (8-ounce) jar orange marmalade

Clean and dry hens. Season inside and out with salt and pepper; refrigerate overnight. When ready to bake, insert a whole onion in cavity of each hen and place in open roasting pan, leaving space between them.

In small saucepan put butter, Kitchen Bouquet, and orange marmalade; heat together until butter has melted and mixture is blended. Spoon over the hens and bake at 350° until hens are tender, about 1-1/2 hours, basting often. If sauce cooks down before hens are done, add a little hot water to the pan to assure having some of the delicious sauce left to accompany the hens. If hens appear to be getting dry during the baking, place a piece of foil loosely over the pan to retard the browning. Yield: 8 servings.

Note: For entertaining, onions should be removed from hens before serving; but for family enjoyment, leave them there!

GREEN BEANS ESPAGNOLE

3 (10-ounce) packages frozen French-style green beans
4 tablespoons butter or margarine
3 tablespoons minced chives or green onions

2 tablespoons minced green pepper
Juice of 1 small lemon
Pinch salt
Dash black pepper

Cook beans in boiling salted water until barely tender; drain. In large skillet heat butter, add chives and green pepper and sauté 2 or 3 minutes. Stir in lemon juice and seasonings, then add beans to the skillet and heat only until thoroughly heated. Yield: 8 servings.

RICE MINGLE

1 cup wild rice
2 cups boiling water
1 teaspoon salt
1 medium onion, chopped
1/2 cup butter

2 (10-ounce) cans beef consommé, undiluted
1 soup can water
1-1/2 cups regular long-grain white rice
1/2 teaspoon salt
1 tablespoon butter

Wash wild rice and add to 2 cups salted boiling water. Cover, reduce heat, and cook until tender, stirring occasionally. (This may take as long as 1-1/2 hours; start checking after 1 hour.)

Sauté onion in butter; stir in consommé and soup can of water. Bring to a boil and add white rice and 1/2 teaspoon salt. Bring back to a rolling boil, cover, reduce heat and cook for 20 to 25 minutes.

Drain wild rice, add 1 tablespoon butter, then mix and fluff with white rice. Yield: 8 servings.

OAK RIDGE HOT BAKED FRUIT
(may be prepared ahead of time)

1 (1-pound) package pitted prunes	1 (1-pound) can cherry pie filling
1/2 (11-ounce) package dried apricots	1-1/2 cups water
1 (13-ounce) can pineapple chunks, undrained	1/4 cup dry sherry
	1/3 cup slivered toasted almonds

Put prunes, apricots, and pineapple in a deep 9-inch round casserole. Combine cherries, water, and sherry and pour over fruit, mixing well. Stir in almonds, cover and bake at 350° for 1-1/2 hours. This casserole freezes beautifully — and refreezes, if necessary! Yield: 8 servings.

CASSATA ALLA SICILIANA
(Sicilian Cream Cheese Cake)
(may be prepared ahead of time)

This is a famous Sicilian specialty, usually served at Christmas or Easter. There are numerous versions, but the two ingredients common to all are the ricotta cheese and the chopped candied fruits used in the filling. Whichever version is served, and for whatever occasion, the cake is a lovely, rich wind-up for any dinner party.

Many recipes for this cake suggest using lady fingers or sliced sponge cake to line the mold. I prefer using an 11- x 7-inch cake, following the recipe for Hot Milk Cake. — C. M.

Filling

1 pound ricotta cheese (a rich, creamy cottage cheese, sieved, might be substituted)	2 tablespoons cream
	2 tablespoons honey
	2 ounces semi-sweet chocolate, grated
4 tablespoons sugar	4 or 5 tablespoons finely chopped candied fruit*
1 teaspoon almond extract	Powdered sugar (optional)
1 teaspoon vanilla extract	
3 tablespoons crème de cacao	

In large bowl of electric mixer put cheese and sugar and beat until smooth. Add flavorings, crème de cacao, cream, and honey and beat thoroughly. Fold in chocolate and chopped fruit.

Slice a sponge cake (or similar plain cake; pound cake will do, too) into 1/3-inch slices, about 4 inches long. Using a 1-1/2-quart soufflé dish, line the sides and bottom with cake. Pour in half the Filling; add more cake slices, then remaining Filling. Top with cake slices. Refrigerate until firm, preferably overnight. Unmold onto cakeplate, frost if desired or sift powdered sugar over the cake, and serve in small wedges. Freezes well. Yield: 8 to 10 servings.

*I use cherries and pineapple, but any candied mixed fruit which includes cherries may be used. — C. M.

For an elegant dinner on any occasion, serve Baked Cornish Hens with Rice Mingle and Green Beans Espagnole (page 181).

Frosting
(optional)

2 to 3 cups powdered sugar
1 egg white
1-1/2 teaspoons almond extract

2 tablespoons freshly squeezed lemon juice

In small bowl of electric mixer put 2 cups of the sugar, the egg white, flavoring, and lemon juice. Beat until of spreading consistency. If frosting seems thin, add a little more sugar; if too thick, add a little more lemon juice. Frost the Cassata and decorate as desired — red and green cherries for Christmas, candied orange peel, etc.

HOT MILK CAKE

4 eggs
2 cups sugar
2 cups all-purpose flour
1 cup milk
1/4 cup butter or margarine

2 teaspoons baking powder
1 tablespoon all-purpose flour
1/2 teaspoon salt
1 teaspoon vanilla extract
1/2 teaspoon almond extract

Beat eggs thoroughly in large bowl of electric mixer. Gradually add sugar and beat until light and fluffy. Sift the 2 cups flour three times and add to batter, beating again thoroughly.

Meanwhile, place milk and butter in small saucepan; let come to a boil and immediately pour into the first mixture all at one time. Beat until the batter is cool. (This may take about 8 to 10 minutes.) Sift in baking powder mixed with flour and salt; add flavorings, and beat a minute more. The batter will be quite thin; that's as it should be.

Grease and line two 8-inch square pans with waxed paper; pour in batter and bake at 350° for about 30 minutes, until cakes test done. (This amount of batter may also be used for two 11- x 7-inch cakes, but cakes will be slightly thinner.)

Fill and frost as desired, or leave plain. Butterscotch or caramel frosting is especially good for this light, delicate cake.

DRINK GLASSES ON THE BUFFET TABLE

Keep a watchful eye (or get a friend to), to make sure guests don't absent-mindedly leave drink glasses on the buffet table. They don't intend to clutter up the serving area, but some people become preoccupied or interrupted while filling their plates and wander off, leaving half-filled glasses on the buffet table.

Beef Bourguignon Dinner

DINNER FOR TEN TO TWELVE

Tomato Soup

Beef Bourguignon

Baked Rice with Almonds

Mixed Green Salad with Dijon Dressing

Dilly Bread   Butter Mounds

Ice Cream Bombe with Small Meringues

or

Fresh Fruit in Season

Coffee   Tea

CLEAR TOMATO SOUP

2 (46-ounce) cans tomato juice	6 peppercorns
1 beef bouillon cube for each 2 cups liquid	2 thick slices onion
	Parsley
4 stalks celery with leaves, chopped	Commercial sour cream
2 bay leaves	Chopped chives

Combine all ingredients except sour cream and chives in large soup kettle. Cover and simmer for 2 hours over low heat. Strain; check seasonings and serve with a dollop of sour cream combined with chives. Yield: 10 to 12 servings.

BEEF BOURGUIGNON, AMERICAN STYLE

4 slices bacon	2 cloves garlic, minced
3 pounds lean boneless beef, cut in 1-inch cubes (as tender as your purse permits)	2 to 3 cups good dry red wine
	12 small boiling onions
1/2 (10-1/2-ounce) can beef bouillon	1/2 pound fresh mushrooms, chopped; or 1 (4-ounce) can mushrooms, drained, reserve liquid
1 tablespoon tomato paste	
1/2 teaspoon leaf thyme	
1 teaspoon salt	Butter
Freshly ground black pepper	Minced parsley
1 bay leaf	

Simmer bacon in water for 10 minutes; drain; dry well. (This eliminates the smokey flavor.) Cut in 1/2-inch pieces. Place in heavy skillet and fry until

crisp; transfer bits to heavy flameproof casserole. To fat left in skillet, add a little oil if needed; heat, then brown beef on all sides. Do this in a single layer if possible, or use two skillets if necessary, as the meat should not be crowded and should brown thoroughly. Transfer meat to casserole; deglaze skillet with a little wine ("swish" it around, to save all the small crusty bits); pour that into casserole.

Now add the beef bouillon, tomato paste (remainder may be put in container and frozen for later use), thyme, salt, pepper, bay leaf, and garlic. Pour in enough wine to almost cover meat. Place casserole over direct heat, bring up to a simmer; cover and bake at 300° for 3 to 4 hours, or until meat is tender, basting occasionally. If liquid cooks down, add more wine, bouillon, or liquid from the canned mushrooms.

While meat cooks, prepare vegetables: Peel onions (cut a small cross in stem end to prevent their coming apart in the cooking) and simmer in a little beef broth (a bouillon cube and hot water will do) until tender, about 20 minutes. (If fresh onions are not available, use canned ones; rinse them well; then sauté a minute or two in a little butter.) Reserve cooking liquid from onions.

Sauté fresh mushrooms in a tablespoon or two of butter for 3 or 4 minutes. (If using canned mushrooms, drain, reserving the liquid, and sauté mushrooms in butter for about 2 minutes.)

When meat is done, drain off gravy into a saucepan. To this gravy, add liquid from cooking onions and any leftover mushroom liquid. If fat appears on surface, skim it off; then boil the gravy down for about 5 minutes. Thicken with a paste made by creaming 1 tablespoon butter with 1 tablespoon flour; gradually blend a little of the hot liquid into the paste, then pour that back into the gravy. Check seasonings.

Combine meat with onions and mushrooms; pour gravy over all, heat thoroughly about 5 minutes. Sprinkle minced parsley over top. Yield: 6 servings; make this recipe twice to serve 12. Do not try to bake all in one casserole.

BAKED RICE WITH ALMONDS

2 cups regular long-grain white rice	2 (10-1/2-ounce) cans beef consommé
6 tablespoons butter or margarine	2 soup cans water
1/3 cup slivered blanched almonds, toasted	Salt and pepper to taste

Melt butter in heavy skillet over low heat. Add rice and cook until lightly browned, stirring constantly. Toast almonds until just golden (about 15 minutes in a 275° oven). Add to rice, stir well and turn into deep casserole. Add liquids and seasonings if desired; cover and bake at 300° for 1-1/2 to 2 hours. Stir several times during baking. (After 1 hour, if liquid does not seem to be absorbing fast enough, remove cover and allow to finish baking uncovered.)

If casserole must wait after it is done, reduce oven temperature as low as possible to keep it warm, but avoid further cooking. Yield: 10 to 12 servings.

Beef Bourguignon may also be served with a green salad, a good wine, French bread, and cheese and fresh fruit for dessert.

MIXED GREEN SALAD

I like this salad best with Bibb lettuce and cherry tomatoes. However, if they are not available, any mixture of greens may be used, as the dressing makes the salad. Use a head of Bibb lettuce for each guest, or the equivalent in other greens. — C. M.

Prepare salad ingredients in large bowl. Be sure they are thoroughly dry. Keep refrigerated until a few minutes before serving, then thoroughly but gently toss with the Dijon Dressing.

DIJON DRESSING
(may be prepared ahead of time)

1-1/2 teaspoons Dijon mustard
9 tablespoons salad oil
5 tablespoons freshly squeezed lemon juice

3 tablespoons minced fresh parsley
Salt and freshly ground black pepper to taste

Put mustard in bowl; blend in oil, stirring constantly. Gradually add lemon juice until mixture is smooth. Season with salt and pepper to taste, then stir in parsley. May be made ahead of time and kept several hours at room temperature. Yield: 6 salad portions; double this recipe to serve 12.

DILLY BREAD
(may be prepared ahead of time)

1/4 cup warm water (very warm for dry yeast)
1 cake compressed yeast or 1 package active dry yeast
1 tablespoon soft butter
1 cup cottage cheese
1 tablespoon sugar

2 teaspoons dill seed
1 tablespoon dehydrated onion flakes
1/4 teaspoon soda
1 teaspoon salt
1 egg, unbeaten
2-1/4 cups all-purpose flour

Warm large bowl by allowing hot water to stand in it a few minutes. Empty it; now pour in 1/4 cup warm water; add yeast and stir with wooden spoon until dissolved. Blend in butter. Warm cheese slightly in top of double boiler over warm (not hot) water. Add to yeast mixture; then beat in sugar, dill seed, onion flakes, soda, and salt. Add egg and beat again. Add flour and stir until all flour is moistened.

Keeping the sticky dough in the bowl, knead until it appears slightly smooth, adding as little flour as possible. Grease top of dough with a bit of oil, cover with cloth and let rise until almost double in bulk, about 1 hour. Punch down; divide into six portions; pat each into a well greased miniature loafpan. Allow to rise about 40 minutes, or until dough has risen at least to top of pan. Bake at 350° for 35 to 40 minutes. When done, brush with melted butter and sprinkle immediately with coarse (kosher) salt. Freezes well. Yield: 6 miniature loaves; make this recipe twice to serve 12.

Note: I like to serve these small loaves whole, one to each guest, with a small sharp knife, individual cutting boards, and a mound of whipped butter in a tiny dish. — C. M.

ICE CREAM BOMBE
(may be prepared ahead of time)

This is a versatile, accommodating dessert. It may be prepared days, even weeks, ahead of time. Though easy to do, it is most impressive when garnished attractively and served at the table.

Line a large melon mold (or fluted cakepan) with vanilla ice cream, about 1 inch thick. (A wooden spoon and your hands are the best implements here.) Smooth another layer of Neapolitan or any other flavor of ice cream over the vanilla, also about a scant inch thick. If convenient, mold may be placed in freezer between steps of preparation.

To form the filling: Soak about 8 lady fingers (or broken almond macaroons) in sweet sherry for about 10 minutes. Tear into pieces with fork; combine with 1 cup chopped toasted almonds and 1/2 cup cut maraschino cherries. Stir this into orange sherbet or vanilla ice cream and spoon into cavity of mold. Try to bring this filling out to ends so those being served end cuts won't be short-changed. Now fill mold with vanilla ice cream, or any other flavor. Cover and freeze.

To serve, dip mold quickly into warm water, invert onto oval serving platter, and garnish with fresh fruit, meringues, coconut, or anything available. During the peach season, I pile slices of luscious fruit around base of mold — or if you're wallowing in luxury, whole marrons in brandy (the jarred kind) may be used. Yield: 12 servings.

Variations: Infinite! Any combination of ice cream may be used — coffee, chocolate, and buttered almond; strawberry, raspberry, and vanilla; or vanilla, and orange or pineapple sherbet. The outer layer should be ice cream rather than sherbet; it holds up better.

OVERNIGHT MERINGUES

2 egg whites, at room temperature	1/4 teaspoon orange extract
Pinch salt	1/2 teaspoon vanilla extract
2/3 cup sugar	1 cup coarsely chopped walnuts
1/4 teaspoon almond extract	

Beat egg whites with salt until foamy. Gradually add sugar; beat until stiff. By hand, fold in the flavorings, then nuts. Place plain white or brown paper on baking sheet and drop meringues onto paper by teaspoonfuls. (It is unnecessary to allow room for spreading; they don't.) Place pan in 350° oven and immediately cut off heat. Allow to remain in oven overnight. (*Do not open oven door, no matter how curious you get!*) Yield: 36 meringues.

Royal Seafood Casserole Dinner

BUFFET DINNER FOR EIGHT TO TEN

Royal Seafood Casserole

Squash Florentine

Hal's Salad with Cherry Tomatoes

Hot Commercial Crescents

or   **Butter**

Angel Biscuits

Lemon Custard Cake

or

Lemon-Butter Tarts

Coffee   **Tea**

ROYAL SEAFOOD CASSEROLE
(may be prepared ahead of time)

2 (10-1/2-ounce) cans condensed
cream of shrimp soup

1/2 cup mayonnaise

1 small onion, grated

3/4 cup milk

Salt, white pepper, seasoned salt,
ground nutmeg, and cayenne pepper

3 pounds raw shrimp, cooked
and cleaned

1 (7-1/2-ounce) can crabmeat, drained

1 (5-ounce) can water chestnuts,
drained and sliced

1-1/2 cups diced celery

3 tablespoons minced fresh parsley

1-1/3 cups uncooked white long-grain rice,
cooked until dry and fluffy

Paprika

Slivered almonds

Blend soup into mayonnaise in a large bowl. Stir until smooth. Add onion, then milk. Now begin seasoning; use a heavy hand because the rice is bland and so is the seafood. When mixture is well seasoned, combine with other ingredients except paprika and almonds. Check seasonings; add a few tablespoons milk if mixture seems dry; it should be moist. Turn into large, shallow buttered casserole, sprinkle with paprika and scatter almonds generously over top. Bake uncovered at 350° for about 30 minutes, or until hot and bubbly. Freezes well. Yield: 10 servings.

SQUASH FLORENTINE
(see Index)

HAL'S SALAD

Mixed salad greens (enough to
serve eight)
1 (6-ounce) jar marinated artichoke
hearts, undrained

1 (2-ounce) can anchovy filets, undrained
1/2 cup halved small stuffed olives
1/2 cup wine vinegar

Tear greens into bite-size pieces. Cut artichoke hearts into three or four
pieces. Combine with greens and other ingredients in large salad bowl; toss well.
Yield: 8 servings.

Note: Also good as accompaniment to any pasta.

ANGEL BISCUITS
(may be prepared ahead of time)

1 cake compressed yeast, or 1 package
active dry yeast
2 tablespoons lukewarm water (very
warm for dry yeast)
5 cups all-purpose flour
1 teaspoon soda

3 teaspoons baking powder
2 tablespoons sugar
1-1/2 teaspoons salt
1 cup vegetable shortening
2 cups buttermilk

Dissolve yeast in warm water. Sift all dry ingredients into a large bowl. Cut
in shortening with pastry blender. Add buttermilk, then yeast mixture. Stir until
thoroughly moistened, turn onto floured board and knead a minute or two. (No
rising is required.) Roll out to desired thickness (I like 1/2 inch) and cut into
rounds. Brush with melted butter and bake on ungreased pan at 400° for 12 to
15 minutes, or until lightly browned. Baked biscuits freeze beautifully.

Note: After mixing, dough may be refrigerated in plastic bag or covered
bowl until ready to use; it keeps well for several days. If using a plastic bag,
leave a little "head room" for dough to expand slightly. These may be readied
for baking the day before and kept refrigerated until an hour before baking,
allowing them time to attain room temperature.

LEMON CUSTARD CAKE

6 egg yolks	6 egg whites
3/4 cup sugar	3/4 cup sugar
3/4 cup freshly squeezed lemon juice	1 large commercial angelfood cake
1-1/2 teaspoons grated lemon rind	Whipped cream
1 envelope unflavored gelatin	Marschino cherries
1/4 cup cold water	

In small bowl of electric mixer, beat egg yolks with 3/4 cup of the sugar until thick and lemon colored. Blend in lemon juice; stir in rind. Transfer to top of double boiler and cook over hot (not boiling) water until mixture coats a spoon; remove from heat. Sprinkle gelatin over cold water, allow to soak for 5 minutes, then stir into hot mixture until dissolved. Cool custard at room temperature.

Beat egg whites until soft peaks form. Gradually add 3/4 cup sugar and beat until stiff. Fold into cooled custard. Oil a large tubepan; tear cake into bite-size pieces and arrange in pan in alternate layers with custard. Chill until firm. Unmold, fill center with whipped cream and decorate top with maraschino cherries. Or, entire cake may be iced with whipped cream and garnished as desired. Yield: 10 to 12 servings.

LEMON-BUTTER TARTS

3 whole eggs	1/2 cup freshly squeezed lemon juice (about 3 lemons)
3 egg yolks	1/4 cup butter, melted
1-1/4 cups sugar	1 teaspoon grated lemon rind
1/8 teaspoon salt	Baked Tart Shells*
Dash ground nutmeg	Whipped cream (optional)

Beat eggs, egg yolks, and sugar in small bowl of electric mixer until thick and pale yellow. Beat in salt and nutmeg. Gradually add lemon juice, then melted butter. Stir in rind and pour into top of double boiler. Cook over simmering water, stirring constantly, until mixture thickens, about 12 to 15 minutes. Cool and pour into Baked Tart Shells. Serve at room temperature or chilled. If desired, top with whipped cream, flavored or plain. (A bit of orange liqueur added to slightly sweetened whipped cream is delightful.) Yield: filling for 9 (2-1/2-inch) tart shells or 1 (10-inch) pie shell.

*See Index for Baked Tart Shells recipe.

SHRIMP TIP

To make a modest amount of shrimp go further in a casserole or creamed dish, split large, fat shrimp horizontally. This is especially effective in a layered dish when you want the whole shape of the shrimp to show. Also, the shrimp flavor permeates the mixture more thoroughly when you slice it as described.

Roast Brisket Dinner

DINNER FOR EIGHT

Tapenade

Roast Brisket with Gravy

Potatoes Dauphinois   **Sesame Spinach**

Italian Marinated Vegetables

Commercial French Bread   **Butter**

Apple Crisp Pie with Brandied Hard Sauce

or

Cheese Tray with Assorted Crackers

Coffee   **Tea**

TAPENADE
(may be prepared the day before)

1 (4-1/2-ounce) can slivered ripe olives	1 tablespoon Dijon mustard
1/4 cup drained capers	Juice of 1/2 lemon
1 (2-ounce) can anchovy filets (with their oil)	Freshly ground black pepper
	3 tablespoons minced fresh parsley
1 (7-ounce) can solid-pack tuna, drained	3 to 4 tablespoons mayonnaise
	Lettuce
1 large clove garlic, crushed	Hard-cooked eggs
1/2 teaspoon leaf thyme, crushed	Fresh tomatoes

Chop olives, capers, anchovies, and tuna in bowl, using a vegetable chopper, until finely minced. Add all other ingredients, except lettuce, hard-cooked eggs, and tomatoes, blending thoroughly. Check seasonings and texture; add more seasonings if needed. Serve on crisp lettuce leaves garnished with wedges of hard-cooked egg and fresh tomatoes. Yield: 8 servings.

Note: In France, Tapenade is traditionally made with a large mortar and pestle, grinding until of puree consistency. I prefer the texture described here. This is an unusual, excellent appetizer, but be sparing; don't serve too much; a little goes a long way. — C. M.

ROAST BEEF BRISKET

Select a 4- to 6-pound beef brisket and have butcher trim off most of the fat but not all, since you need a little to provide automatic basting during cooking.

Use a baking pan as near the size of your roast as possible. (If baking pan is too large for meat, the natural gravy will spread, and both pan and roast will dry out!) Season meat the night before cooking as follows:

Place meat in pan lean-side up. Sprinkle generously with Worcestershire sauce, smoothing it over surface with back of spoon. Now sprinkle Les's Seasoned Salt*, black pepper, and cayenne pepper over moistened surface. Turn roast over, fat-side up. Repeat seasoning process, cover tightly and refrigerate overnight.

Remove from refrigerator an hour or two before cooking to remove the chill, then place in a 300° oven and roast uncovered for about 3 to 4 hours, or until fork tender, basting occasionally with liquid that forms in bottom of pan. Add no water. When meat is about half-done, check juices, and if they seem to be cooking away, place a piece of aluminum foil loosely over meat.

The natural gravy from this roast is quite strong and may be too highly seasoned for some tastes. It may be diluted with a little water and thickened, if desired.

Brisket roast must be sliced across the grain. If grain is not readily discernible, turn meat upside-down and direction of the grain will then be obvious. Slice very thin. Yield: 8 servings.

*See Index for Les's Seasoned Salt recipe.

POTATOES DAUPHINOIS
(may be prepared for baking the day before)

3 cups milk	6 medium baking potatoes
4 tablespoons butter	2 cloves garlic, minced
Salt and white pepper to taste	1 cup shredded Swiss cheese

Combine milk, butter, salt, and pepper in a large saucepan. Bring slowly to a boil while you peel potatoes. (Do not soak the potatoes; you need their starch.) Slice 1/8 inch thick, dropping slices into hot milk. Add garlic, partially cover, and simmer for about 15 minutes or until potatoes feel almost, but not quite, done when tested with the point of a small sharp knife.

Pour potatoes with their liquid into a buttered casserole. Sprinkle with cheese and bake at 325° until sauce has thickened and cheese has melted to a lovely golden color, about 45 minutes. May be prepared up to the baking point the day before. Yield: 8 servings.

Note: Sometimes the casserole bubbles over onto the oven floor, creating quite a mess. To avoid this, place a large shallow pan of water or sheet of foil on lower rack of oven during the cooking.

SESAME SPINACH

3 (10-ounce) packages chopped frozen spinach; or 2-1/2 pounds fresh, cooked and chopped spinach
Boiling salted water
1-1/2 (10-1/2-ounce) cans cream of mushroom soup

Salt, pepper, and garlic salt
Generous dash ground nutmeg
3 tablespoons toasted sesame seed
1/3 cup slivered blanched almonds

Cook frozen spinach in boiling salted water until just tender, about 5 minutes. Drain thoroughly. Blend in soup, seasonings, sesame seed, and half the nuts. Turn into buttered baking dish, sprinkle remaining nuts over top and bake at 350° for 20 minutes. Yield: 8 servings.

Note: To toast sesame seed, put in shallow pan in 275° oven for 15 to 20 minutes.

ITALIAN MARINATED VEGETABLES
(may be used as appetizer or salad)

1 (8-ounce) can button mushrooms, drained
1 green pepper, cut in 1/2-inch strips
1 carrot, cut lengthwise into eighths
2 cups uncooked cauliflower flowerets
1 (1-pound) can artichoke hearts, drained and cut in half
12 small raw white onions, or 6 green onions including an inch of the green tops

1/2 cup stuffed olives
1-1/2 cups wine vinegar
1 teaspoon sugar
1-1/2 teaspoons salt
1/2 teaspoon black pepper
2 teaspoons oregano, crushed
1/2 cup salad oil
1/2 cup olive oil
Cherry tomatoes and minced parsley

Combine all vegetables except tomatoes and parsley in large bowl. Heat vinegar; stir in seasonings. Cool slightly, combine with oil, pour over vegetables and mix well. Cover and refrigerate for 24 hours before serving, stirring occasionally.

To serve: Drain vegetables and arrange in attractive lettuce-lined bowl. Garnish with cherry tomatoes, sprinkle with minced parsley and provide cocktail picks for spearing. Yield: 8 servings.

Note: A friend of mine reports a windfall as a result, literally, of a snowstorm! She had prepared this appetizer for an openhouse on Christmas Day. The day arrived, and so did an unexpected snowstorm, and the guests were unable to come. Result: a bowlful of vegetables growing stronger by the minute. She drained them, put the vegetables through the coarsest blade of the food grinder, added some of the drained-off marinade, and presto, she had an excellent relish! — C. M.

HOW MANY ICE CUBES

If you make your ice cubes ahead of time and store them in plastic bags in the freezer, count on about 350 cubes for 50 people.

PREPARING COMMERCIALLY BAKED FRENCH BREAD

With a serrated-edge bread knife, cut bread at a slight angle into slices 1/2 to 2/3 inch thick, but do not cut all the way through bottom crust — cut only about two-thirds the way through the loaf.

Melt 1/2 cup butter or margarine over low heat; stir in a crushed clove of garlic, or other seasonings of choice. Brush butter between slices, and if any is left, brush over entire surface of loaf. Wrap in aluminum foil until ready to heat.

The loaf should be heated for about 20 minutes at 375° — but if you're baking something else in the oven at 350° or even 400°, that's all right, too. To ensure the loaf's being crusty, turn back the foil from top of loaf.

FRENCH BREAD WITH AN ITALIAN ACCENT ·

Melt 4 tablespoons butter over low heat; stir in 1/4 cup Italian-style dressing and 1 teaspoon crushed oregano. Brush between slices of partially cut-through French bread, forcing butter well down between slices. Heat for about 20 minutes in a 375° oven. Bread may be prepared early in the day, wrapped in foil and heated for 20 minutes before serving.

APPLE CRISP PIE

8 large firm apples	3/4 cup chopped pecans
1-1/2 cups light or dark brown sugar	1/2 cup butter
1 cup all-purpose flour	Whipped cream or Brandied
1/4 teaspoon salt	Hard Sauce

Peel, core, and cube apples. Place in shallow rectangular baking dish; spread with half the sugar. Combine remaining sugar, flour, salt, and pecans; cut butter into mixture with pastry blender until crumbly. Spread over apples, pressing down around edges so topping completely covers the apples. Bake at 350° for 1 hour. Serve warm with sweetened and flavored whipped cream or with Brandied Hard Sauce. Yield: 8 servings.

BRANDIED HARD SAUCE

Cream 1/2 cup real butter in small bowl of electric mixer. Gradually beat in 1-1/2 cups powdered sugar until blended. Stir in 2 tablespoons brandy (or sherry) and chill several hours before serving over warm pie.

Veal Vaduz Dinner

DINNER FOR EIGHT

Lettuce and Tomato Salad with California French Dressing

Veal Vaduz

Noodles with Poppy Seed   **Asparagus with Lemon Crumbs**

Commercial Hard Rolls   **Butter**

Pears Punjab
or
Almond Stuffed Peaches

Coffee   **Tea**

VEAL VADUZ

  3 tablespoons butter
  1 (1-pound) can small whole onions
  1 large onion, coarsely chopped
  3 pounds veal, cut in 1- x 2-1/2-
    inch strips
1/2 teaspoon salt
  3 tablespoons minced fresh parsley
1-1/2 tablespoons paprika

  3 tablespoons dry white wine
3/4 to 1 cup chicken broth (bouillon cube
    may be used)
  3 tablespoons capers (with their juice)
  1 small dill pickle, cut in strips 1/2
    inch long and 1/3 inch thick
  1 cup commercial sour cream

Drain and rinse onions well. Melt butter in large heavy skillet; add whole onions and sauté gently, turning constantly so all sides are evenly browned. Remove and set aside.

In butter remaining in skillet, lightly sauté chopped onion; push to one side and add veal. Brown quickly, stirring constantly. Add salt, parsley, paprika, wine, and about 1/3 cup broth. Cover and cook 45 minutes, or until veal is tender, stirring occasionally and adding small amounts of broth as necessary. When meat is done, stir in capers with their juice, pickle strips, sour cream, and sautéed whole onions. Heat thoroughly over low heat but do not boil. Yield: 8 servings.

CALIFORNIA FRENCH DRESSING

1 teaspoon Dijon mustard
1-1/2 teaspoons seasoned salt
1 teaspoon Worcestershire sauce
1 teaspoon paprika
2 teaspoons grated onion
2 teaspoons minced fresh parsley
1/2 teaspoon sugar

1/2 teaspoon freshly ground black pepper
1/4 cup wine vinegar
1/4 cup tomato juice
1/4 cup olive oil
3/4 cup salad oil

Combine all ingredients in a jar and shake well, or use electric blender. Allow to stand at least a few hours to blend flavors before using. Yield: 1-3/4 cups.

NOODLES WITH POPPY SEED

10 ounces 1/2-inch noodles
1/3 cup blanched almonds, coarsely ground
7 tablespoons butter or margarine

1-1/2 teaspoons salt
Dash white pepper
3 teaspoons poppy seed

Sauté almonds in 3 tablespoons of the butter; set aside. Cook noodles, drain, rinse under hot water and turn into top of double boiler. Melt 4 tablespoons butter and stir it in along with the salt, pepper, poppy seed, and almonds. Stir well, cover and keep hot over simmering water or in chafing dish until serving time. Yield: 8 servings.

ASPARAGUS WITH LEMON CRUMBS

3 (10-ounce) packages frozen asparagus spears
1 cup coarse dry breadcrumbs

4 tablespoons butter
Grated rind of 1 lemon (yellow part only)
Salt and pepper to taste

Cook asparagus according to package directions; drain. Sauté breadcrumbs in butter; stir in lemon rind, salt, and pepper. Just before serving, pour over hot, well drained asparagus. (Crumbs may be prepared well ahead of time and stored, or frozen.) Yield: 8 to 10 servings.

PEARS PUNJAB
(must be prepared ahead of time)

Canned Bartlett pear halves (enough for 1/2 pear per serving)
Grated rind and juice of 1 lemon
Grated rind and juice of 1 orange

1/2 cup sugar
Vanilla ice cream
Whipped cream
Semi-sweet chocolate, grated

Drain pears into saucepan; to the liquid add rinds and other fruit juices. Stir in sugar and boil for 15 minutes. Cool slightly; pour over pear halves, cover and refrigerate overnight (or at least 10 hours).

Put a pear half in a sherbet dish with about 3 tablespoons or more of th
syrup. Top with a scoop of ice cream, then a generous teaspoon whipped cre
Sprinkle with grated chocolate. (This is delicious and easy, and the main part of
it must be prepared the day before or well ahead of time.)

Note: The above proportions are for 7 servings but the fruit rinds, juice,
and sugar will be enough for 8 servings.

ALMOND-STUFFED PEACHES

8 large firm fresh peaches, or 16
  canned halves
3 ounces finely ground blanched
  almonds, lightly toasted
4 tablespoons powdered sugar

1 teaspoon grated orange rind
2/3 cup cream (sweet) sherry
  Whipped cream
  Almond extract

Peel and halve fresh peaches (or drain canned ones thoroughly). Place
cavity-side up in buttered baking dish. Combine almonds with sugar and orange
rind. Pile into peach cavities, sprinkle with a little more powdered sugar, then
slowly pour sherry over all. Bake uncovered at 350° for about 30 minutes (20
minutes for canned fruit), basting several times with sherry in bottom of dish.
Serve barely warm, garnished with slightly sweetened whipped cream flavored
with 1/2 teaspoon almond extract. A magnificent dessert when fresh peaches
are at their best. Yield: 8 servings.

Note: To toast almonds, bake at 275° for about 15 minutes.

HIGHBALL GLASSES

Even if you have cocktail parties infrequently, renting highball glasses is a
nuisance — and could be more expensive in the long run. Plain tall highball
glasses can be bought inexpensively at the dime store, then stored for your
next party.

For a party of about 50, you might find it practical to invest in about 3 dozen
highball glasses and about 3 dozen old-fashioneds. And don't forget — lots and
lots of cocktail napkins; never serve a drink without one.

Empty liquor cartons are a great way of storing seldom used highball
glasses. Your friendly liquor dealer will be happy to oblige.

Rolled Marinated Rib Roast Dinner

DINNER FOR TEN TO TWELVE

Spinach Salad

Marinated Rolled Rib Roast

Green Beans with Water Chestnuts   **Potato Casserole Supreme**

Garlic French Bread   **Butter**

Cappucino Parfait with Butter Crisps

Coffee   **Tea**

SPINACH SALAD

1-1/2 pounds fresh spinach
   6 green onions including tops, sliced
    Dash pepper

5 hard-cooked eggs, coarsely cut
8 slices bacon, cooked crisp and crumbled

Wash spinach thoroughly; dry well. Remove stems and break leaves into bite-size pieces. Toss with other ingredients; cover and refrigerate for about 2 hours. Before serving, toss with Dressing.

Dressing

1 clove garlic, quartered
1/2 cup olive or salad oil
1 teaspoon salt
   Dash pepper

3 tablespoons freshly squeezed lemon juice
1/4 cup cider vinegar

Marinate garlic in oil for an hour or two; discard garlic. Combine oil, salt, and pepper in a small bowl. Combine lemon juice with vinegar; gradually blend into oil, beating well with rotary beater. The dressing will thicken somewhat. Yield: 10 servings.

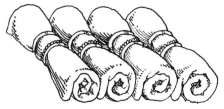

MARINATED ROLLED RIB ROAST

Have butcher remove bones and most of fat, but not the outside fat, from roast before he rolls it. For an 8- to 10-pound roast (before boning), prepare the following marinade:

2 cloves garlic, crushed	3 teaspoons grated lemon rind
1 teaspoon coarse black pepper	4 to 6 dashes Tabasco sauce
4 tablespoons minced fresh parsley	4 tablespoons olive oil
1 teaspoon leaf thyme	4 tablespoons red wine vinegar
2 teaspoons seasoned salt	

If you have a mortar and pestle, place all ingredients except oil and vinegar in the bowl and mash thoroughly. Start adding oil, a small amount at a time, blending well. When mixture is blended to a smooth paste, stir in vinegar.

With sharp pointed knife, make V-shaped slashes all over meat. Pour marinade into the slashes. Wrap meat in foil and refrigerate for 8 to 24 hours.

Place on rack in shallow roasting pan and use a meat thermometer. Insert the thermometer about half way through roast. Place roast in preheated 450° oven for 30 minutes. Reduce heat to 325° and cook to desired doneness. It will take about 20 minutes per pound to cook to the medium-done stage. Allow roast to rest in warm spot 20 to 30 minutes before carving.

There will be very little natural gravy resulting from this procedure. Therefore, at the beginning of roasting, make up a cup of beef broth and use it to baste roast during cooking. Any drippings may be poured off into a small saucepan and the fat skimmed from the top. This small amount of natural gravy will be very good; use it. Check it for seasoning and add beef broth if required for volume. To thicken gravy, put 1/2 teaspoon arrowroot or cornstarch into a small bowl, add a little hot gravy, then pour mixture into gravy and cook, stirring constantly, until thickened. Yield: 10 to 12 servings.

GREEN BEANS WITH WATER CHESTNUTS

3 (10-ounce) packages frozen French-style green beans	Salt and pepper to taste
1/2 cup butter or margarine	3 tablespoons freshly squeezed lemon juice
2 (5-ounce) cans water chestnuts, drained and sliced	1 tablespoon soy sauce

Cook beans according to package directions, until barely tender. Drain thoroughly. Meanwhile, in a large heavy skillet, heat butter and sauté water chestnuts a minute or two; stir in all seasonings. Add beans, heat thoroughly and serve immediately or turn into casserole and keep in warm oven until serving time. Yield: 10 servings.

Variation: When a creamy dish is desired, stir in 1/2 cup sour cream just before serving. However, for this menu this is not recommended.

POTATO CASSEROLE SUPREME
(may be prepared for baking ahead of time)

9 medium baking potatoes	2/3 cup warm milk
1/2 cup butter or margarine	1-1/2 cups shredded Cheddar cheese
1-1/2 teaspoons salt	1 cup heavy cream, whipped
1/4 teaspoon pepper	

Peel and boil potatoes until tender; drain and beat in large bowl of electric mixer until fluffy, adding butter, seasonings, and milk. Check seasonings; turn into buttered shallow casserole. Fold cheese into whipped cream and spread over potatoes. Bake at 350° for about 25 minutes, only until golden brown. Casserole may be prepared ahead of time, the topping added just before baking. Yield: 10 servings.

GARLIC FRENCH BREAD
(see Index)

CAPPUCINO PARFAIT
(may be prepared ahead of time)

Stir 1/2 teaspoon ground cinnamon and 1 teaspoon grated orange rind into 1-1/2 cups Minute Butterscotch Sauce. Alternate coffee ice cream and sauce in 10 to 12 parfait glasses. Freeze until serving time. Top with whipped cream and grated orange rind if desired. Yield: 10 to 12 servings.

Minute Butterscotch Sauce

1/2 cup butter	2 tablespoons corn syrup
1-1/2 cups light brown sugar	1/2 cup heavy cream
1/8 teaspoon salt	

Melt butter in saucepan; add light brown sugar, salt, and light or dark corn syrup. Bring to a boil and cook until sugar is dissolved. Gradually add 1/2 cup heavy cream, stirring constantly, and bring to boiling point again. Cool. Yield: 1-1/2 cups.

Variation: One-half cup chopped walnuts may be added to cooled sauce if you can stand the extra calories.

BUTTER CRISPS
(may be prepared ahead of time)

1 cup butter or margarine	1 egg, lightly beaten
1-1/2 cups powdered sugar	1 teaspoon vanilla extract
3 cups all-purpose flour	1 cup chopped pecans
1/4 teaspoon salt	

Cream butter and sugar thoroughly in large bowl of electric mixer. Sift flour with salt; add 1 cup to the creamed mixture and beat well. Blend in egg, then vanilla, scraping bottom and sides of bowl often. Beat in remaining flour; stir in nuts. Shape into two rolls about 2 inches in diameter; wrap in waxed paper; chill until ready to bake.

To bake: Slice refrigerator cookies about 1/8 inch thick, place on lightly greased baking sheet and bake at 350° for about 10 minutes. Cookies freeze well. Yield: 9 to 10 dozen.

Note: These cookies are done when *edges only* are brown. If you bake them until brown all over, you've ruined a good batch of otherwise delicious cookies! — C. M.

A MENU TO REMEMBER

When taste buds begin anticipating an evening at the mention of an invitation, then the hostess undoubtedly has the skill of serving memorable meals. A menu is a creation, a juxtaposition of individual dishes that work together for an unforgettable ensemble. Each dish should be perfection but one should never upstage but rather be a foil for the other. Dishes should contrast but complement.

Vary your dishes so that the flavor of each may be enjoyed to the fullest. Avoid repetition of colors, flavors, and textures in the same meal. Alternate piquante and bland, tart and sweet, creamy and chewy.

Add a spot of color where there was none: use a red onion in place of white; if potatoes and boiled onions *must* be in the same meal, join the onions with peas; and for slaw, have purple shreds among the green. Follow a robust roast with refreshing wine gelatin and angel cake. Save the smooth but rich chocolate mousse for after a luncheon of crunchy crisp chef's salad. Float crusty croutons on a creamy soup.

Make servings attractive. A loaded plate suffocates an appetite. Smaller, enticingly arranged servings tempt guests to seconds. Put ambrosia in orange baskets placed on an ivy leaf and serve with a madeleine.

To keep an appetite ready for more, have a balance between light and heavy. If an entree is heavy, let the sweetness be light like a slip-down soufflé — and vice versa.

Send taste buds on an adventure: Serve something that is unexpected — not shocking, just a little different — like eggplant ratatouille with lamb, and give the green peas a rest.

Tease the appetite with food that is appropriate to the season and the occasion. Lighter foods for warmer weather; elegant fare for formal dinners. Hearty stew hits the spot after a ball game but cold cucumber soup makes a cool summer appetizer. Consider the mood, elegantly dressed dinner guests are apt to take only token bites of corn-on-the-cob.

And always, always consider your guests. If you're aware of a guest's special diet or preference, do try to choose food they can enjoy.

Flemish Beef Ragout Dinner

BUFFET DINNER FOR SIX

Flemish Beef Ragout

Party Peas   **Fleutters**

Bean Salad

Garlic French Bread
or   **Butter**
Hot Commercial Hard Rolls

English Sherry Trifle

Coffee   **Tea**

A Silk Purse Menu — Looks and tastes expensive, but isn't.

FLEMISH BEEF RAGOUT

3 tablespoons butter or margarine	1 clove garlic, crushed
3 medium onions, chopped	1 tablespoon minced fresh parsley, or
2 to 2-1/2 pounds lean boneless beef, cut into 1-1/2-inch cubes	1 teaspoon dried parsley
1-1/2 tablespoons all-purpose flour	1 bay leaf
1/2 (10-1/2-ounce) can beef bouillon, undiluted	1/4 teaspoon thyme
1 cup beer	1/2 teaspoon paprika
1 tablespoon wine vinegar	1 teaspoon salt
	Black pepper to taste

Heat 2 tablespoons of the butter in heavy pot or Dutch oven; sauté onions until golden. Remove onions with slotted spoon and set aside. Add remaining butter to pot and brown meat well on all sides. Sift flour over meat; stir until it appears absorbed. Slowly stir in bouillon, then beer and all other ingredients. Return sautéed onions to the pot, cover tightly and simmer over low heat for 2-1/2 to 3 hours, stirring occasionally and adding more bouillon if gravy cooks down.

If preferred, the ragout may be transferred to an ovenproof casserole, baked at 300°, and served from the same casserole. The ragout may be garnished with clusters of fresh parsley. For an unusual touch which adds to the aroma and appearance of this dish, grate a little lemon rind over the ragout just before presenting it at the table. Yield: 6 servings.

PARTY PEAS

2 tablespoons butter or margarine	1 teaspoon salt
1 (10-ounce) package frozen peas	1/4 teaspoon black pepper
2 cups shredded crisp lettuce	Pinch dried sweet basil, tarragon,
1/4 cup chopped onion	or mint (optional)

Heat butter in large saucepan; add frozen peas, cover and cook slowly until peas are just defrosted. Do not add water. When peas are thawed completely, add lettuce, onion, and seasonings. Mix lightly, cover tightly and steam for 4 minutes — *no more!* Yield: 6 servings.

This is last-minute-y, I realize, but it's an excellent dish, too good to be ruled out because of timing. — C. M.

FLEUTTERS
(Potato Mounds)

This is an Alsatian dish, excellent with roast beef, and hot kraut dishes. May be prepared in the morning and refrigerated until baking time.

2 pounds boiling potatoes	1 clove garlic, crushed
2 tablespoons all-purpose flour	2 eggs
1/2 teaspoon salt	Melted butter
1/4 teaspoon pepper	Paprika
2 tablespoons minced parsley	

Peel and quarter potatoes; boil in salted water until done. Drain and mash thoroughly. Beat in flour, salt, pepper, parsley, garlic, and eggs. When smooth, form into 12 balls and place in buttered, shallow baking dish. Brush lightly with melted butter, sprinkle with paprika, and bake at 375° for about 25 minutes, or until puffed and lightly browned. Yield: 6 servings.

BEAN SALAD

1 (1-pound) can cut green beans	1 (1-pound) can black-eyed peas
1 (1-pound) can wax beans	1 (1-pound) can garbanzo peas
1 (1-pound) can kidney beans	1 (1-pound) can whole-kernel white corn

Drain and combine vegetables in a large bowl. Prepare Dressing.

Dressing

1/2 cup sugar	1 green pepper, sliced into thin rings, then in half
1 cup wine vinegar	
1/2 cup salad oil	1 medium onion, chopped
1/2 teaspoon dry mustard	Seasoned salt to taste

Mix all ingredients thoroughly, pour over beans, and chill before serving. If convenient, stir the salad several times during marinating. This recipe yields a large amount, but it's a versatile dish and may double as a relish or extra vegetable. Besides, it keeps beautifully.

GARLIC FRENCH BREAD
(see Index)

ENGLISH SHERRY TRIFLE
(may be prepared the day before)

1 jellyroll
About 1/4 cup cream (sweet) sherry
Boiled Custard
1 cup heavy cream, whipped

Maraschino cherries, drained and sliced
About 1/3 cup slivered, toasted, blanched almonds

Cut jellyroll into 1/2-inch slices. Place a layer in an attractive bowl; a crystal one is lovely for this purpose, as you will be serving it at the table. Sprinkle with sherry. Cover with Boiled Custard; add another layer of cake, then sherry, then more Custard. Chill thoroughly. Top with whipped cream; sprinkle cherries and almonds over top and chill again. This may all be done a day ahead; the trifle is actually better the second day. Yield: 8 servings.

Note: If you make your own jellyroll, fill it with strawberry jam, but a good bakery one works very well.

BOILED CUSTARD

2 cups milk
2 eggs
1/3 cup sugar

1 tablespoon all-purpose flour
1/2 teaspoon vanilla extract

First put milk in top of double boiler over simmering water; scald. Meanwhile, in small bowl of electric mixer, beat eggs until frothy; thoroughly beat in sugar mixed with flour. Very slowly blend hot milk into egg mixture. Return to double boiler and cook, stirring constantly, until custard barely coats a metal spoon. Remove from heat and stir in vanilla.

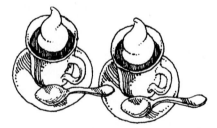

HOW TO ROLL PASTRY IN THIRDS

On lightly floured surface roll out pastry into a rectangle about 1/8 inch thick. Don't press down; roll with a light, quick motion. Spread with soft butter; fold top third (the one farthest from you) down toward bottom of dough (the edge near you). Fold bottom third up over folded part. Now fold right third to the left; fold left third over to the right, on top of folded dough, ending with a neat folded package. Dough is now ready to be chilled, then rolled out again.

Standing Rib Roast Dinner

DINNER FOR EIGHT

Quick Jellied Madrilene

Standing Rib Roast

Spinach with Lemon Crumb Topping   **Potato-Mushroom Casserole**

Thickly Sliced Tomatoes with Minced Fresh Parsley,

Chives, Radishes, Black Olives, and Celery Sticks

Commercial French Bread   **Butter**

Fresh Fruit and Cheese

or

Orange Macaroon Pie

Coffee   **Tea**

QUICK JELLIED MADRILENE

2 envelopes unflavored gelatin
1 cup cold water
2 beef bouillon cubes
2 chicken bouillon cubes
2 cups hot water

2 (8-ounce) cans tomato sauce
2 tablespoons freshly squeezed
  lemon juice
Lemon slices

Soften gelatin in cold water. Dissolve beef and chicken bouillon cubes in hot water; add to softened gelatin, and stir until dissolved. Stir in tomato sauce and lemon juice. Pour into shallow pan; chill until firm. To serve, cut into cubes, or spoon into soup cups. Float a slice of lemon on top of each cup. Yield: 8 servings.

THE GLASS FILLER-UPPER

Every hostess is occasionally faced with the guest who goes on filling his glass all during the evening; as long as the liquor lasts, he's yours to have and to hold! In the case of a dinner party where the food is substantial, the meal is leisurely, and ends with coffee, the bar may simply be closed during dinner and not reopened.

BEEF STANDING RIB ROAST

2- to 3-rib standing rib roast   Salt and pepper

Have chine bone removed to make carving easier. Season, and place fat-side up on rack in open roasting pan. Insert meat thermometer so the bulb reaches the center of the thickest part, but does not rest in fat or on bone. Do not add water or cover. Roast at 300° to desired doneness. The meat thermometer will register 140° for rare; 160° for medium; 170° for well done. Allow 23 to 25 minutes per pound for a rare roast; 27 to 30 minutes for medium; and 32 to 35 for well done.

Note: This roasting time applies to 7-inch rib roasts. Rolled beef rib roasts require approximately the same cooking time. For longer cut rib roasts, cooking time should be reduced approximately 5 minutes per pound.

SPINACH WITH LEMON CRUMB TOPPING
(may be prepared ahead of time)

3 (10-ounce) packages frozen   2 tablespoons all-purpose flour
  chopped spinach   1/4 teaspoon ground nutmeg
2 tablespoons butter   Salt and pepper

Cook spinach according to package directions; drain thoroughly. Melt butter in skillet, blend in flour and cook until lightly browned, stirring constantly. Add drained spinach and seasonings and cook a few minutes to blend flavors. (May be prepared ahead of time up to this point, then reheated later.)

Topping

3 tablespoons butter   Pinch salt
6 tablespoons coarsely ground   Pinch pepper
  dry breadcrumbs   1 teaspoon grated lemon rind

Melt butter in medium skillet; stir in coarsely ground dry breadcrumbs, and salt and pepper to taste. Stir over low heat until crisp. Add lemon rind, stir well and set aside to sprinkle over spinach just before serving. (Crumbs may be prepared the day before using, then reheated about 5 minutes in a slow oven.) Yield: 8 servings.

POTATO-MUSHROOM CASSEROLE
(may be prepared ahead of time)

8 or 9 medium boiling potatoes   Salt, pepper, and hot milk for
1/2 cup butter or margarine   mashing potatoes
2 medium onions, chopped   1 cup commercial sour cream
2 (3-ounce) cans mushroom slices,   Paprika
  drained, reserve liquid

Peel and boil potatoes. While they cook, prepare other ingredients. Heat butter in skillet; sauté onions slowly until yellow. Add drained mushrooms; sauté about 2 minutes. Remove onions and mushrooms with slotted spoon; set aside, leaving the butter in the skillet.

When potatoes are done, drain and whip lightly, adding the drained mushroom liquid, hot milk, and seasonings. Beat in the butter left in skillet. Spread a thin layer of potatoes in shallow baking dish, cover with a thin layer of sautéed onions and mushrooms, then a layer of sour cream. Repeat; top layer should be potatoes. You should now have three layers of potatoes and two layers of the vegetables and sour cream. Brush top with a little melted butter, sprinkle with paprika and bake at 350° for 20 to 30 minutes, until lightly browned. May be made ahead of time; any leftovers freeze beautifully. Yield: 8 to 10 servings.

ORANGE MACAROON PIE
(may be prepared ahead of time)

12 Almond Macaroons	2 tablespoons grated orange rind
1 cup orange juice	1-1/2 teaspoons almond extract
1/2 pound marshmallows	1/4 cup orange liqueur
2 cups heavy cream, whipped	Slivered toasted almonds

Toast about a dozen Almond Macaroons at 250° for about 30 minutes, or until dry. Crumble two-thirds of them over bottom of shallow casserole or deep pie dish.

In top of double boiler, over simmering water, heat orange juice and marshmallows until blended. Remove from heat and when mixture begins to jell, fold in whipped cream. Add grated orange rind, almond extract, and 1/4 cup orange liqueur. Pour over crumbled macaroons; sprinkle reserved crumbs and a handful of slivered toasted almonds over top. Chill thoroughly before serving. If preferred, the pie may be frozen, then removed from freezer and refrigerated for about 2 hours before serving. Yield: 8 servings.

ALMOND MACAROONS
(may be prepared ahead of time)

1 (8-ounce) can almond paste	1/4 cup all-purpose flour, sifted
3/4 cup sugar	Pinch salt
2 egg whites, unbeaten	

Put almond paste into large bowl of electric mixer. Beat to soften, then gradually beat in sugar and unbeaten egg whites. When thoroughly blended, add flour and salt. Mix well, then drop by teaspoonfuls onto lightly greased cookie sheet, 1 inch apart. Bake at 300° for 25 to 30 minutes. Remove from baking sheet immediately, using a sharp spatula. These freeze well in an airtight container, and are a windfall when you decide on the spur of the moment to bake a dessert calling for the usually hard-to-find macaroons. Yield: about 40 macaroons.

Beef Wellington Dinner

DINNER FOR EIGHT TO TEN

Vichyssoise

Beef Wellington

Lima Beans and Peas in Cream

Asparagus and Artichoke Heart Salad Rivermont

Commercial Hard Rolls   **Butter**

Chocolate Frosted Macaroon Mousse

Coffee   **Tea**

VICHYSSOISE

4 leeks or fresh green onions	1 quart chicken broth
1 small onion, thinly sliced	1/2 teaspoon salt
2 tablespoons butter	Pinch cayenne pepper
5 medium raw potatoes, peeled and sliced thin	3 cups light cream
	Minced chives

Cut leeks or green onions into fine strips; add onion and sauté lightly in butter. Stir in potatoes, broth, and seasonings. Cover and simmer gently for about 45 minutes. Put through blender or fine strainer, forcing as much vegetable pulp through as possible. Cool, stir in cream and correct seasonings.

Chill thoroughly and garnish individual servings with chives. Yield: 8 servings.

BEEF WELLINGTON
(prepare ahead of time)

Beef Wellington is a superb party dish, generally considered a difficult and time-consuming project, to be undertaken only by the most experienced and skillful of cooks. However, it is not really the villain it is popularly believed to be, and while not as simple as pot roast, it can be brought off beautifully by the novice in the kitchen.

A few methods are easier than the one I am describing — and several are considerably more trouble. I have studied many, and this one seems to me to combine the best features of them all. — C.M.

A 12-inch long tenderloin will serve eight people. When you buy your filet, ask the butcher to give you a large strip of beef suet. More about that later.

A good bit of the preparation may be done well ahead of time. The beef should be marinated for 24 hours before baking — and baked a day before serving! Two days before the party, place meat in a shallow dish and pour over it a mixture of about 1-1/2 cups dry red wine, about a tablespoon Worcestershire sauce; juice of 1 lemon, and several grinds of black pepper. Cover and refrigerate for 24 hours; turn occasionally.

To roast the beef: Remove meat from refrigerator the day before serving, drain off marinade and reserve. Dry meat. One end of the meat slopes off to a thin "tail." Fold that end down under meat and tie with twine, forming a uniformly thick strip about 12 inches long. Rub meat with oil or melted butter. Cut suet in half lengthwise. Into a shallow baking pan put one piece of suet, then the beef over it, then the other strip of suet over the beef. Bake at 425° for 30 minutes, turning meat once and replacing the suet over the top. Untie the meat, let cool, and refrigerate until the next day.

Make Madeira sauce the day before serving. After the meat has roasted, it will probably have drawn a small amount of pan juices. Skim off fat and discard. Put remaining juices in small saucepan; add about 1/2 cup each of canned beef consommé and Madeira wine, and salt and pepper to taste. Add a few tablespoons of the reserved marinade, allow to cook down for about 5 minutes. Taste for seasonings. Dissolve about 2 teaspoons arrowroot or cornstarch in a few tablespoons cold water and add to the sauce. Stir over low heat until slightly thickened. Refrigerate until time to reheat.

Make stuffing the day before serving. Heat 2 tablespoons butter in a skillet and sauté 1 to 1-1/2 pounds finely diced fresh mushrooms and 5 very finely minced shallots or green onions. Saute about 8 to 10 minutes, until mixture seems quite dry. Stir in about 1/2 cup Madeira wine; boil down until wine has practically evaporated. Season with salt and pepper, then blend in a 4- or 5-ounce can of pâté de foie gras. Cover and refrigerate.

Make pastry the day before serving. Put 3 cups all-purpose flour and 2 teaspoons salt into a bowl. Cut in 1-3/4 sticks chilled butter and 4 tablespoons vegetable shortening. Sprinkle in 3/4 cup iced water, a little at a time, tossing all the while, until dough holds together. Wrap in waxed paper and refrigerate.

To assemble: About 3 to 4 hours before serving, remove meat and stuffing from refrigerator and allow to attain room temperature. (Time your cooking schedule so beef will be ready no more than 30 minutes before serving.) Roll out pastry in a rectangle about 9 x 14 inches and 1/4 inch thick — large enough to envelop the meat. Stir the stuffing to soften it and spread over the pastry, leaving the borders uncovered. Place meat in center (with the side down that you want eventually to be up). Fold pastry over meat and seal seam and ends with water. Place, seam-side down, on a buttered cookie sheet and brush top and sides with an egg lightly beaten with a teaspoon of water. With a very sharp knife make hatch marks (in a herring-bone design) all over top of pastry. Prick with fork on sides. Place in 425° oven; after 15 minutes, decrease temperature to 375° and bake for 30 minutes more.

The beef should rest in a warm spot about 20 minutes before carving. When ready to carve, remove carefully with two spatulas to heated serving platter. (If it must wait to be served, it will hold for about 30 minutes in the oven set at its lowest temperature — about 120°, if possible.)

Slice in 1-1/2-inch slices. Serve with the reheated Madeira sauce. Yield: 8 servings.

LIMA BEANS AND PEAS IN CREAM

2 cups water	2 tablespoons butter
1 teaspoon salt	1/2 cup green onions, finely minced
1/4 teaspoon garlic salt	1-1/2 tablespoons all-purpose flour
1 teaspoon seasoned salt	3 tablespoons milk
2 (10-ounce) packages frozen baby lima beans	1 cup light cream
	1/4 teaspoon salt
2 (10-ounce) packages frozen green peas	Dash cayenne pepper
	Paprika

In a large saucepan bring water to a boil with 1 teaspoon salt, garlic salt, and 1/2 teaspoon of the seasoned salt. Add lima beans and cook until not quite done; add peas. Cook until both are just tender; drain and put in a 2-quart casserole.

In the meantime, heat butter in a skillet and sauté onions until yellow. Transfer with slotted spoon to the casserole. Stir flour into butter remaining in skillet; gradually add milk and cream, stirring over medium heat until slightly thickened. Add 1/4 teaspoon salt, remaining 1/2 teaspoon seasoned salt, cayenne pepper, and paprika. Pour over vegetables, mix gently, cover and bake at 325° for 30 minutes. Yield: 10 to 12 servings.

ASPARAGUS AND ARTICHOKE HEART SALAD RIVERMONT

Chill 2 (1-pound) cans artichoke hearts and 2 (1-pound) cans white or green asparagus spears; drain thoroughly. Prepare lettuce cups (one for each person); chill thoroughly. When ready to serve, arrange asparagus and halved artichoke hearts in lettuce cups, garnish with pimiento strips and serve the following Rivermont Dressing separately or spooned over salads. Yield: 8 servings.

Rivermont Dressing
(may be prepared ahead of time)

1 (1-ounce) can anchovy filets, undrained	7 tablespoons olive or salad oil
2 teaspoons prepared yellow mustard	7 tablespoons tarragon vinegar
2 tablespoons minced fresh parsley	6 green onions including tops, finely chopped
1/2 teaspoon salt	
1/4 teaspoon freshly ground black pepper	

Mash anchovies thoroughly in a small bowl. Gradually blend in seasonings, then oil. Pour into jar with tight cap; add vinegar and onions; shake well. Refrigerate until ready to use. Dressing may be made ahead of time; it does not separate on standing. Yield: 8 servings.

CHOCOLATE FROSTED MACAROON MOUSSE
(may be prepared ahead of time)

3 egg whites	1-1/2 cups chopped pecans
9 tablespoons powdered sugar, sifted	1 teaspoon vanilla extract
1-1/2 cups heavy cream, whipped	1 teaspoon almond extract
1-1/2 cups coarsely ground dry Almond Macaroons*	

Beat egg whites until stiff; continue beating while gradually adding powdered sugar. Combine with whipped cream; fold in ground macaroons, pecans, and flavorings. Turn into a large freezing tray and place in freezer.

Frosting

1 ounce unsweetened chocolate	4 tablespoons milk
1/2 cup granulated sugar	Vanilla and almond extracts
2 egg yolks	1 cup heavy cream, whipped

Melt unsweetened chocolate in top of double boiler over warm (not hot) water. Stir in sugar, egg yolks, then gradually add milk. Place over direct heat if desired, using low heat and stirring constantly to cook the mixture until thick and smooth. Remove from heat, add vanilla and almond extract, and cool. Whip 1 cup heavy cream and blend into cooled mixture. Spread evenly over bottom layer of mousse, return to freezer and freeze until firm. May be made days ahead of time. Yield: 12 (2-1/2-inch) squares.

Variation: In addition to other flavorings used, add 2 tablespoons rum to both bottom layer and top.

*See Index for Almond Macaroon recipe.

Herbed Pork Roast Dinner

DINNER FOR SIX TO EIGHT

Mixed Green Salad with Choice of Dressing

Herbed Pork Roast

Cranberry Beets
or
Carrots, Israeli Style

Barley Casserole

Peppered Pineapple Jelly

Commercial Hard Rolls

Butter

Baked Fruit in Wine

Coffee

Tea

MIXED GREEN SALAD
(see Index)

HERBED PORK ROAST
(may be prepared the day before)

1 (4- to 6-pound) loin of pork
2-1/2 teaspoons salt
1 teaspoon pepper

1 teaspoon leaf thyme
1/2 teaspoon ground nutmeg

Combine all seasonings and rub into meat. Place in 450° oven and roast uncovered for 30 minutes. Reduce temperature to 350° and add the following:

2 carrots, cut in small pieces
2 onions, coarsely chopped
2 large cloves garlic, minced
4 whole cloves

Few chopped celery leaves
Few sprigs parsley
3 bay leaves
1 (10-1/2-ounce) can chicken consommé

Cover and bake for about 3 hours or until meat is tender, basting often. Before serving, transfer meat to heated platter; skim fat from gravy, put pan juices and vegetables through a sieve or electric blender, removing cloves and bay leaves if you can capture them! Serve in sauceboat to accompany meat. This roast may be prepared a day ahead of time and reheated. Sliced cold, it makes excellent sandwiches. Yield: 8 to 10 servings.

CRANBERRY BEETS

1 (1-pound) can small whole
    beets, undrained
1 (8-ounce) can whole-berry
    cranberry sauce

1 tablespoon grated orange rind
1 tablespoon cornstarch
1 tablespoon cold water

Put beets and cranberry sauce into saucepan and heat until blended. Stir in orange rind, then cornstarch which has been dissolved in cold water. Cook over low heat, stirring constantly, until thickened. Fine with all pork dishes. Leftovers reheat well. Yield: 4 servings; double recipe to serve 6 to 8.

CARROTS, ISRAELI STYLE

1-1/2 pounds young carrots
   4 tablespoons butter or margarine
1/3 cup dry white wine

1/2 teaspoon ground nutmeg
2/3 cup white raisins
   3 tablespoons light brown sugar

Peel or scrape carrots and cut into 1/4-inch slices. (Diagonal slices are more attractive than round. If you have a corrugated cutter, use it to slice the carrots.) Put in saucepan with butter, wine, and nutmeg. Cover and cook over low heat until carrots are tender. Stir in raisins and sugar and continue cooking a few minutes longer, until raisins are plump and carrots are glazed. This is different and extraordinarily good. Yield: 6 servings.

BARLEY CASSEROLE
(may be prepared for baking ahead of time)

1/2 cup butter or margarine
  1 cup quick-cooking, fine pearl barley
  1 medium onion, chopped
1/2 cup slivered almonds
  1 (2-ounce) package dehydrated
    onion soup

2 cups chicken broth
1 (3-ounce) can drained mushroom
    slices, reserve liquid; or 3/4 to 1 cup
    fresh mushrooms
1 (5-ounce) can water chestnuts, drained
    and sliced

Heat butter in saucepan; add barley and onion and sauté only until a light golden color. Add almonds, dry onion soup, and chicken broth. Sauté mushrooms a few minutes in a little butter and add to barley along with water chestnuts and liquid drained from canned mushrooms. Stir well, turn into casserole, cover and bake at 350° for 1 hour, adding more liquid if necessary. (A little more chicken broth may be used if required.) This casserole may be prepared a day or two ahead of time and refrigerated before baking; leftovers freeze well. Yield: 6 servings.

ASHTRAY TIP

If you own large decorative ashtrays which aren't easily identifiable as ashtrays, before guests come take a puff or two of a cigarette, extinguish it and leave it on the tray.

PEPPERED PINEAPPLE JELLY

2-1/2 cups unsweetened pineapple juice
 3/4 cup cider vinegar
5-1/2 cups sugar

1 teaspoon crushed red pepper*
1 (6-ounce) bottle liquid pectin

Combine pineapple juice, vinegar, sugar, and pepper in large saucepan. Bring to a boil, stirring constantly. Stir in pectin at once and bring to a full rolling boil. Boil 1 minute; remove from heat. Skim with metal spoon, but try not to remove any bits of the red pepper. Pour quickly into sterilized glasses; cover with paraffin and seal.

*The crushed red pepper is not cayenne, it is actually chile peppers, crushed to a crumbly texture.

BAKED FRUIT IN WINE

12 Almond Macaroons, crumbled*
 4 cups canned drained fruit
1/2 cup slivered toasted almonds
1/4 cup brown sugar

1/4 cup melted butter
1/2 cup cream (sweet) sherry (an almond-flavored sherry is excellent)
Whipped cream (optional)

Butter a 2-1/2-quart casserole or large rectangular baking dish. Cover bottom with macaroon crumbs. Alternate fruit (use any combination you like — peaches, pears, apricots, pineapples, cherries, etc.) and crumbs in layers, ending with crumbs. Sprinkle with almonds and sugar; drizzle with melted butter, then pour sherry over all. Bake uncovered at 350° for about 25 minutes, basting once or twice during baking. Serve warm or at room temperature, topped with whipped cream if desired. Yield: 8 servings.

Note: This is an excellent buffet dish to serve with any fowl or pork dish.

*See Index for Almond Macaroon recipe.

HOW TO DETERMINE THE JELLY STAGE

Always use an unusually large pot for even a small amount of jelly because the syrup should boil furiously. The rapid boiling will decrease cooking time and also avoid jelly's spilling over and making a hideous mess!

Place ingredients in pot, bring to a boil, stirring, and boil hard, stirring often. (If you use a candy thermometer attached to edge of pot, the temperature should reach 220°.) This will probably take about 8 minutes.

To test, let jelly run off edge of large metal spoon. If the last several drops clinging to the spoon hesitate, then join forces and drop off together, the "jelly stage" has been reached.

Roast Leg of Lamb Dinner

DINNER FOR EIGHT

Asparachoke Salad with French Dressing Piquante

Roast Leg of Lamb

Crusty Baked Potatoes　　　**Mediterranean Tomatoes**

Commercial French Bread　　　**Herb Butter**

Orange Charlotte

Coffee　　　　　　**Tea**

ASPARACHOKE SALAD

1 (1-pound) can artichoke hearts, drained and cut in half

1 (1-pound) can asparagus spears, drained and chopped

3 cups mixed salad greens

1/2 cucumber, peeled and sliced very thin

Prepare the above and keep refrigerated in separate containers. Just before serving, place in a large salad bowl and toss gently with French Dressing Piquante. Yield: 8 servings.

FRENCH DRESSING PIQUANTE
(may be prepared ahead of time)

1 teaspoon dry mustard

1 teaspoon paprika

1 teaspoon sugar

2 teaspoons seasoned salt

1/4 teaspoon freshly ground black pepper

1/2 cup wine vinegar

1 clove garlic, crushed

2 tablespoons soy sauce

1 tablespoon chili sauce (optional)

1 teaspoon Worcestershire sauce

3/4 cup oil (preferably half olive and half salad)

First, mix all dry ingredients in small bowl. Put in electric blender (or jar with tight lid) with all other ingredients except the oil. Blend well, then add oil in several portions, blending after each addition. Chill before using. Dressing is better if made a day or two before using. Yield: about 1-1/2 cups.

ROAST LEG OF LAMB

1 (6-pound) leg of lamb	1/2 teaspoon dry mustard
1 teaspoon salt	1 teaspoon dried oregano
2 teaspoons seasoned salt	1 teaspoon black pepper
1 tablespoon paprika	Stuffed olives
1/2 teaspoon ground ginger	

Trim excess fat from lamb. Mix all other ingredients except olives and rub thoroughly into meat on all sides. Prepare Marinade.

Marinade

4 tablespoons freshly squeezed lime juice	1/2 teaspoon salt
	1/2 teaspoon dried marjoram
2 cloves garlic, crushed	3 or 4 dashes Tabasco sauce

Combine all ingredients and mix well. Gouge holes about 3/4 inch deep all over top of lamb by inserting sharp edge of paring knife and scooping out as if coring an apple. Into each hole pour a little of the Marinade and insert a stuffed olive, like a stopper. Cover meat and refrigerate overnight. Roast uncovered at 350° for 3 hours, or until tender, basting with remaining Marinade and adding small amounts of hot water if needed. Remove meat; skim off fat in pan; add enough hot water to make a rich gravy. Yield: 8 to 10 servings.

Variation: Season lamb as desired (with dry seasonings) and grate over the top a whole green apple and a whole onion. Bake slowly, basting with dry sherry during the cooking.

CRUSTY BAKED POTATOES

The following proportions are for 4 small to medium potatoes. Prepare a potato for each person (with about 2 extras for emergencies) and multiply recipe as required.

Wash and peel baking potatoes, leaving them whole; pat dry. Melt 4 tablespoons butter in small saucepan; roll potatoes in butter, then coat evenly with 1 cup fine dry breadcrumbs which have been mixed with 1 teaspoon salt and 1 teaspoon paprika.

Place potatoes in shallow buttered casserole, cover and bake at 350° for about 1 hour, or until tender. Any butter left from coating potatoes may be added to bottom of casserole. For the last 20 minutes remove cover and turn potatoes to brown evenly.

Note: The last time I prepared this dish, the potatoes were done at least 30 minutes before serving time. I reduced the oven temperature to 200° while dinner waited for the guests. The potatoes were lovely. — C. M.

MEDITERRANEAN TOMATOES

1 stick butter or margarine
8 large whole ripe tomatoes, peeled
2 teaspoons brown sugar
6 tablespoons minced chives

8 tablespoons minced celery
4 tablespoons minced parsley
1 teaspoon oregano, crushed
Salt and pepper to taste

Melt butter in skillet. Place whole tomatoes, stem-side down, into pan. Add sugar, cover and simmer gently for about 10 minutes over low heat. Carefully turn tomatoes; add other ingredients. Spoon butter in skillet over tomatoes, cover and again simmer for about 10 minutes. Serve immediately on heated platter with pan juices spooned over all. Yield: 8 servings.

HERB BUTTER
(prepare the day before)

1/2 pound butter
1 tablespoon freshly squeezed lemon juice
1 small clove garlic, crushed
2 teaspoons minced dried chives

2 tablespoons minced fresh parsley
1 teaspoon dried tarragon, crushed
1 teaspoon dill weed
Generous dash cayenne pepper

Cream the butter thoroughly in small bowl of electric mixer. Add all other ingredients and blend well. Turn into covered jar and refrigerate overnight before using. Use on French bread or as a topping for vegetables or broiled meat. Yield: 1 cup.

ORANGE CHARLOTTE

1/4 cup cold water
1 envelope unflavored gelatin
3/4 cup sugar
1/4 teaspoon salt
1/2 cup boiling water
2 tablespoons freshly squeezed lemon juice
1 cup orange juice

3 egg whites, beaten stiff
Lady fingers or slices of slightly stale sponge or pound cake
Whipped cream, slightly sweetened and flavored if desired
Fresh orange sections (optional)
Maraschino cherries (optional)

Pour cold water in bowl; sprinkle gelatin over it. Allow to soak for 5 minutes. Meanwhile, dissolve the sugar and salt in boiling water; stir in softened gelatin until dissolved. Add lemon juice, orange juice (if you use fresh orange juice, scrape some of the pulp into the juice; it gives a nicer texture), and cool. When mixture begins to jell, beat lightly, then thoroughly but gently fold in egg whites.

Rinse a 1-1/2-quart mold with cold water but do not wipe dry. Line bottom and sides with lady fingers (split in half, rounded edges on outside) and pour in orange mixture. Chill until firm, unmold onto attractive serving plate and mound top with whipped cream, or serve cream in separate bowl. Fresh orange sections and maraschino cherries surrounding the mold make an attractive garnish. Yield: 6 to 8 servings.

Gourmet Pot Roast Dinner

BUFFET DINNER FOR EIGHT

Gourmet Pot Roast

California Stuffed Potatoes   **Creamed Spinach with Crunchy Topping**

Sliced Dill Pickles and Relish Tray

Garlic French Bread   **Butter**

Creamy Orange Sherbet with Justine's Cookies

Coffee   **Tea**

A Silk Purse Menu — Looks and tastes expensive, but isn't.

GOURMET POT ROAST

1 (4- to 5-pound) beef pot roast
All-purpose flour seasoned with salt
and pepper
About 1-1/2 tablespoons cooking oil
2 onions, chopped
1/2 cup water
1/4 cup catsup
1/3 cup dry sherry
1 clove garlic, minced

1/4 teaspoon dry mustard
1/4 teaspoon marjoram
1/4 teaspoon rosemary
1/4 teaspoon thyme
1 small bay leaf
1 (8-ounce) can broiled sliced
mushrooms, undrained (or as large as
your purse permits)

Trim excess fat from meat and dredge in seasoned flour. Heat oil in heavy skillet or Dutch oven; add meat and brown slowly on all sides. When almost browned, add onions and cook in same fat for a minute or two. Stir in remaining ingredients except mushrooms. Cover and cook slowly on top of stove or bake at 300° for 2-1/2 to 3 hours. Add mushrooms with their liquid and cook for 30 minutes longer.

Remove meat to warm platter; skim fat from gravy. Blend 1-1/2 teaspoons cornstarch with 1/4 cup cold water; gradually stir into pan juices and cook until sauce thickens, stirring constantly. Yield: 8 servings.

CALIFORNIA STUFFED POTATOES
(may be prepared for baking the day before)

2 large baking potatoes
Salt and pepper
3 tablespoons cream

2 tablespoons milk
4 tablespoons grated Parmesan cheese

Bake potatoes at 400° for 1-1/2 hours. Cut off thin horizontal slice from top and scoop out potato. Mash with all other ingredients. Refill shells and allow to stand at room temperature for about 1 hour. Sprinkle with paprika and bake at 400° for about 20 minutes. These potatoes may be prepared the day before baking, refrigerated, then allowed to attain room temperature before baking. Yield: 2 servings; increase ingredients proportionately for number of servings desired.

CREAMED SPINACH WITH CRUNCHY TOPPING

3 (10-ounce) packages frozen chopped spinach

2 (3-ounce) packages cream cheese

4 tablespoons butter or margarine, divided

Salt and pepper

Generous dash ground nutmeg

Grated rind of 1 lemon (yellow part only)

1 cup packaged herb dressing

Cook spinach according to package directions. Drain thoroughly. Return to hot saucepan and immediately blend in cream cheese and half the butter. Season with salt, pepper, nutmeg, and lemon rind. Turn into buttered casserole, cover, and refrigerate until ready to bake. This may be done in the morning of the day it is to be served.

About 45 minutes before baking, remove from refrigerator, spread dry herb dressing over top and drizzle with remaining 2 tablespoons melted butter. Bake at 350° for about 25 minutes. Yield: 9 servings.

GARLIC FRENCH BREAD
(see Index)

CREAMY ORANGE SHERBET
(may be prepared ahead of time)

1 envelope unflavored gelatin

1/4 cup cold water

2 cups milk

1-1/4 cups sugar

1/4 teaspoon salt

Grated rind of 1 orange

1-1/2 cups orange juice

Juice of 2 lemons

2 tablespoons orange-flavored liqueur (optional)

Sprinkle gelatin over cold water and allow to stand for 5 minutes. Heat milk, add sugar and salt, stirring until dissolved. Remove from heat, add gelatin, and stir until dissolved. Combine grated rind, orange juice, and lemon juice in a bowl, then pour in the milk slowly. Stir in liqueur and pour into freezing tray. Stir every half hour until sherbet is frozen. Yield: 1 quart.

ORANGE TIP

Whenever a recipe calls for both orange juice and rind, wash and grate the orange before juicing.

JUSTINE'S COOKIES

1 cup butter or margarine	1/8 teaspoon salt
1 cup light brown sugar	1 teaspoon vanilla extract
2/3 cup sugar	1 cup uncooked oatmeal
1 egg, beaten	1 cup chopped dates
2-1/2 cups all-purpose flour	1 cup chopped pecans
2 teaspoons soda	Sugar

Cream butter and sugars together thoroughly in large bowl of electric mixer. Add egg and beat well. Sift flour with soda and salt and add to mixture. When blended, stir in oatmeal, dates, and nuts. Pinch off small amounts of dough, roll into balls about the size of a quarter, then roll in sugar. Place about 2 inches apart on greased cookie sheet and bake at 350° for 10 to 12 minutes. (Cookies will puff up, then seem to collapse, but don't worry; they're supposed to. They'll be crisp and crinkled on top, similar to macaroons.) Yield: about 7 dozen.

OUR SECRET — THE SILK PURSE MENUS

Let's conspire, you and I; let's engage in a little harmless conspiracy, secure in the belief that: "It takes much cleverness to know how to conceal cleverness."

This book doesn't claim that elegance can be produced from pennies or that you can make a silk purse of a menu from a sow's ear of provisions. This is an honest and realistic book; no evasions and no euphemisms, so let's face it. There are times when all of us must consider cost in planning our entertaining. The *silk purses* (menus that look and taste expensive, but aren't) are planned for just such times.

Remember, the successful party is one where food, important as it undoubtedly is, plays a secondary role to the general atmosphere created by the welcoming hostess. When such warmth and graciousness are present, then the choice of a menu may be governed by considerations of cost with no sacrifice of either good taste or pride. Certainly, the specter of an overdrawn bank account won't contribute to the serenity of a hostess. Agreed?

So for those times when we all look for menus planned with an eye toward "frugal elegance," we have designed the *silk purse* menus. They're scattered throughout the book, in most categories. Have fun with them. — C.M.

Roast Pork Dinner

DINNER FOR SIX TO EIGHT

Clear Tomato Soup

Roast Pork with Rosemary

Cinnamon Apple Rings   **Curried Lima Beans in Casserole**

Herbed Asparagus

Commercial Crisp Rolls   **Butter**

Fresh Peach Sherbet

or

Raspberry Ice Cream

Almond Butter Cookies

Coffee   **Tea**

CLEAR TOMATO SOUP
(see Index)

ROAST PORK WITH ROSEMARY

1 (4-or-more-pound) pork roast, fresh picnic shoulder, loin, rolled roast, Boston butt — any cut
3 cloves garlic

1 tablespoon dried rosemary, crushed
Salt, pepper, and seasoned salt
Dry white wine

Trim excess fat from pork. Cut garlic into slivers, moisten them with water and roll in the crushed rosemary. Cut small slashes on both sides of roast, using a small sharp knife, and insert garlic slivers into these holes. Sprinkle meat generously with salt, pepper, and seasoned salt. Wrap tightly in foil and refrigerate 24 hours before roasting.

Place meat in shallow roasting pan; pour enough wine over it to yield about 1/2 inch in bottom of pan. Sprinkle top of meat with more seasoned salt. Roast uncovered for about 45 minutes per pound, basting now and then and adding more wine or water as liquid cooks away. If meat appears excessively crusty and dry, cover lightly with foil and finish roasting. Yield: 6 to 8 servings.

Note: The small amount of gravy yielded will be quite fat. When roast is done, pour pan juices into a small saucepan, skim off the fat, add about a cup of chicken broth, check seasonings and if desired, thicken slightly. A good way to thicken the gravy (as with all gravies) is to make what the French call a "beurre manie" (fancy butter) — i.e., a tablespoon of flour blended into a tablespoon of butter then added to the hot gravy and stirred until sauce thickens.

CINNAMON APPLE RINGS
(may be prepared for baking ahead of time)

4 large, firm unpeeled apples	4 tablespoons sugar
4 tablespoons butter	1-1/2 teaspoons ground cinnamon

Core apples and cut in thirds, horizontally. Heat butter in heavy skillet. Add apple slices and allow them to brown over medium heat; carefully turn over to brown on other side. Do not allow apples to cook to pieces — cook only until fork tender.

Meanwhile, mix sugar and cinnamon and spread on large plate. When apple slices are brown, place them onto the sugar mixture and coat both sides heavily. Transfer to lightly buttered, shallow baking dish. (Apples may be prepared to this point hours ahead of time. Cover with waxed paper and keep at room temperature.) Before serving, bake apples at 375° until heated through, 5 to 10 minutes. Yield: 6 servings.

CURRIED LIMA BEANS IN CASSEROLE
(may be prepared for baking ahead of time)

2 (10-ounce) packages frozen baby lima beans	1 (10-1/2-ounce) can cream of mushroom soup
2 slices bacon, diced	1/2 cup commercial sour cream
1 medium onion, minced	2 tablespoons dry white wine, sherry, or milk
1 clove garlic, crushed	
1/2 teaspoon curry powder	1 (3-1/2-ounce) can French-fried onions

Cook beans according to package directions, until just tender. Drain. Fry bacon until crisp in a skillet; drain on paper towels. In the drippings remaining in the skillet, sauté onion, garlic, and curry powder for about 5 minutes. Blend soup, sour cream, and wine in a bowl until smooth. Add to skillet; heat to just under boiling point; stir in beans and bacon bits. Turn into 1-1/2-quart shallow casserole and top with slightly crushed French-fried onions. Bake at 325° for about 25 minutes. Yield: 6 to 8 servings.

HERBED ASPARAGUS

3 (10-ounce) packages frozen asparagus spears	1 tablespoon dehydrated onion flakes
1-1/2 cups chicken broth	1/2 teaspoon summer savory
1 clove garlic, split	1/2 teaspoon dried tarragon
	4 tablespoons butter or margarine

Put frozen asparagus in heavy skillet with tight-fitting cover. Combine chicken broth with all ingredients except butter and pour over asparagus. Cover, bring to a boil, remove cover and separate spears with a fork. Replace cover, reduce heat and simmer until asparagus is tender, about 10 minutes. *Do not overcook.* Stir in a little salt and pepper (it won't need much; the broth lends almost enough). Carefully remove spears from liquid to a heated serving dish, adding pieces of butter to each layer as spears are arranged. Yield: 8 to 10 servings.

Note: I'm sorry, but this is really a last-minute operation. It should be served immediately when done; asparagus behaves poorly if it must wait. Unless the rest of your menu requires you to be in the kitchen the last 10 minutes before serving, another green vegetable should be substituted. — C. M.

FRESH PEACH SHERBET
(may be prepared ahead of time)

1-1/2 cups sugar
1/2 cup water
3 cups fresh peaches
Juice of 2 oranges

1 teaspoon freshly squeezed lemon juice
2 egg whites, beaten stiff
1 cup heavy cream, whipped

Cook sugar and water together until syrup spins a thread. Let cool. Peel peaches and partially mash them; they should not be pureed. Combine with the cooked syrup, add lemon and orange juice and blend well. Turn into freezer tray and freeze until not quite firm. Remove to large bowl, beat well and fold in egg whites, then whipped cream. Return to freezer to harden. Stir several times during freezing. Yield: 8 servings.

RASPBERRY ICE CREAM
(may be prepared ahead of time)

1/2 gallon rich vanilla ice cream (French Vanilla if available)

2 (8-ounce) packages frozen raspberries, partially thawed

Soften ice cream slightly by allowing it to remain out of freezer a short time. Turn into large bowl and blend in raspberries with a wooden spoon. Return to freezer to harden. Yield: 8 servings.

ALMOND BUTTER COOKIES
(may be prepared ahead of time)

1 cup butter (no substitute)
2/3 cup granulated sugar
2-1/4 cups all-purpose flour
1 cup coarsely ground blanched almonds
Pinch salt

1/4 teaspoon vanilla extract
1/2 teaspoon almond extract
Blanched whole almonds or almond slices
Powdered sugar

Cream butter and granulated sugar thoroughly in large bowl of electric mixer. Blend in flour, ground almonds, salt, and flavorings. Chill for about 2 hours. Form into balls about the size of a quarter; place about 2 inches apart on greased cookie sheet; press down with a fork, dipping it in flour frequently to prevent sticking. (Press first in one direction, then in the other to create a checkerboard effect.) Insert an almond firmly in top of each cookie and bake at 350° for 12 to 15 minutes, only until light golden. Remove cookies and immediately sift powdered sugar lightly over tops. Freezes beautifully. Yield: about 5 dozen.

Blanquette of Veal Dinner

DINNER FOR SIX

Spinach and Mushroom Salad

Blanquette of Veal

Green Rice That Waits   Ginger Carrots

Crisp Commercial Hard Rolls   Butter

Peach-Raspberry Glow

or

Easy Biscuit Tortoni

Coffee   Tea

SPINACH AND MUSHROOM SALAD

1-1/2 pounds fresh spinach
1/2 pound fresh mushrooms
1 teaspoon salt
1 clove garlic
3/4 teaspoon dry mustard
Several dashes Tabasco sauce

3 tablespoons freshly squeezed lemon juice
1/2 cup olive oil
Freshly ground black pepper
Tomato wedges
3 hard-cooked eggs, cut into wedges

Remove stems from spinach; wash well and pat dry. Tear into bite-size pieces. Rinse mushrooms in cold water quickly; drain well and slice thin.

Put salt and garlic in bottom of large salad bowl. With wooden spoon, mash garlic into salt until all that remains of the garlic is a shred; discard it. Stir in mustard, Tabasco sauce, lemon juice, oil, and pepper, stirring until well blended. Add spinach and mushrooms to bowl and toss until all leaves are coated. Garnish bowl with tomato wedges and eggs. Yield: 6 servings.

BLANQUETTE OF VEAL

2-1/2 pounds veal, cut into 1-inch cubes
Salt, pepper, and all-purpose flour
6 tablespoons butter or margarine
3-1/2 tablespoons all-purpose flour
5 cups chicken broth
2 tablespoons dried parsley flakes
1/4 cup wine vinegar

1 teaspoon salt
1/4 teaspoon pepper
1/4 teaspoon thyme
1/4 teaspoon rosemary
1/8 teaspoon ground cloves
2 (1-pound) cans small white onions (about 24 onions)

Season veal with salt and pepper and coat lightly with flour. Heat butter in heavy skillet and brown meat; transfer to Dutch oven with slotted spoon. In butter left in pan, blend the 3-1/2 tablespoons flour until smooth. Slowly add broth, then all other ingredients except onions. Stir until smooth again, pour over veal in casserole, cover and simmer for 2 hours. Just before serving, add onions and reheat. Yield: 6 servings.

GREEN RICE THAT WAITS

4 tablespoons butter or margarine	3 cups chicken broth, or bouillon cubes and hot water
4 or 5 green onions including tops, finely chopped	1-1/2 cups regular long-grain rice
1/2 green pepper, finely chopped	1/4 teaspoon salt
1/3 cup minced fresh parsley	1/8 teaspoon pepper

Heat butter in saucepan; add onions, and green pepper and saute slowly until tender, 5 to 10 minutes. Stir in remaining ingredients; bring to a boil, reduce heat, check seasonings, cover and simmer about 20 minutes or until done.

Rice may be served as soon as tender, but if it must wait on the diners, turn into casserole with tight-fitting cover and place in warm oven until serving time. Yield: 6 servings.

GINGER CARROTS

3 to 4 cups diagonally sliced carrots	3/4 teaspoon ground ginger
1 cup orange juice	1-1/2 teaspoons grated lemon rind (important, don't omit)
1/2 cup chicken broth	
3 whole cloves	3 tablespoons sugar

Place all ingredients except sugar in saucepan and bring to a boil. Stir in sugar, cover and simmer for about 30 minutes or until carrots are tender. Yield: 6 servings.

PEACH-RASPBERRY GLOW

Peel 6 ripe, flavorful peaches; cut in half, remove pits and sprinkle with a little sugar. Pour over fruit about 1/4 cup sweet sherry (or if you have it, almond-flavored sherry). Let stand for 30 minutes, then place two peach halves in each of six sherbet dishes, cover with a large scoop of pistachio ice cream and spoon Raspberry Sauce over it. Yield: 6 servings.

RICE TIP

Cooked rice freezes well. It can be stored in refrigerator for a week; in the freezer for as long as 3 months.

Raspberry Sauce

2 (10-ounce) packages frozen raspberries
1 teaspoon cornstarch

2 tablespoons freshly squeezed lemon juice

Thaw raspberries; rub through a fine sieve or puree in blender; strain out seeds. Put the puree into saucepan and bring to a boil; add cornstarch dissolved in 2 tablespoons lemon juice. Cook until slightly thickened; cool and chill. Yield: 6 servings.

Note: This is a wonderful dessert to serve during the peach season. The combination of flavors is inspired! Incidentally, I have found pistachio ice cream easily available. However, if you can't find it, any butter-brickle or almond-flavored ice cream will do. — C. M.

EASY BISCUIT TORTONI

1-1/2 quarts vanilla ice cream, softened slightly
1/2 cup toasted ground blanched almonds

2-1/2 tablespoons cream (sweet) sherry
Ground almonds or ground almond macaroon crumbs
Maraschino or crystallized cherries

Into softened vanilla ice cream blend 1/2 cup almonds, then sherry. Spoon into six parfait glasses, sprinkle with extra ground almonds or macaroon crumbs and place in freezer. Before serving garnish with a cherry. Yield: 6 servings.

Note: If you prefer, ice cream may be spooned into 2-inch paper cups, which usually hold 4 ounces, and same procedure followed. In this case, the above proportions would fill 12 paper cups.

MAKE TWO LISTS

Here's a suggestion which may appear to be kindergarten stuff, but it is born of sad experience, for I have been known to get halfway through a company dinner before realizing that one of the courses was still waiting in the refrigerator.

When planning a party, however informal, make two schedules: a daily order of battle made simultaneously with selection of the menu; and an hourly plan written down early on the day of the party.

The first schedule lists those dishes that may be prepared ahead of time, and how far ahead, even the separate steps which, though minor, are pure nuisance — toasting breadcrumbs, chopping nuts, mincing parsley.

The second timetable is the real countdown. It stipulates the time to remove the appetizers from refrigerator or freezer; when to drain the celery sticks; the time to plug in the coffee pot. It's a good idea, too, that the time for each operation not be too critical for with gremlins lurking about, it's wise not to cut your cloth too fine.

Baked Ham Dinner

BUFFET DINNER FOR FIFTEEN

Baked Ham with Orange Glaze

Curried Shrimp and Rice Casserole   **Spinach with Artichokes**

Shanghai Salad

Cornmeal Crisps   **Melba Rye Sticks**

Fresh Fruit and Cheese   **Layered Apricot Squares**

Coffee   **Tea**

BAKED HAM WITH ORANGE GLAZE

Place a 10- to 14-pound smoked baked ham fat-side up on rack in open roasting pan. Insert meat thermometer so bulb reaches the center of the thickest part, but be careful that the bulb doesn't rest in fat or on bone. Do not add water; do not cover. Bake at 325° until thermometer registers 160° for a "cook-before-eating" ham and 130° for a "fully-cooked" ham.

If you do not use a thermometer, allow 20 minutes per pound for baking a "cook-before-eating" ham, and 15 minutes per pound for a "fully-cooked" ham.

About 30 minutes before ham is done, trim off skin and excess fat from top; spread with Orange Glaze and return to finish cooking.

Orange Glaze

1 cup brown sugar
1 tablespoon all-purpose flour
1 teaspoon dry mustard

1 tablespoon vinegar
3 tablespoons frozen concentrated orange juice

Combine ingredients; stir until smooth, and spread over ham.

Alternate Glaze: About half an hour before ham has finished baking, remove from oven, cut off any rind, score the fat (diamond-fashion), and place a whole clove in each diamond. Meanwhile, heat a jar of apricot jam, put it through a fine sieve, then spoon the puree over entire surface of ham. Return to oven for 30 minutes to finish baking.

CURRIED SHRIMP AND RICE CASSEROLE

1 tablespoon salt	1-1/2 cups regular long-grain white rice
1 thick slice unpeeled lemon	1 tablespoon salt
1 bay leaf	Sauce
4 pounds large raw shrimp	

Bring a large pot of water to a boil; add about a tablespoon salt, a thick slice of unpeeled lemon, and a bay leaf. Add shrimp to rapidly boiling water and after water returns to a boil, cook shrimp for 10 minutes; drain, shell and devein. Refrigerate until needed.

To boil rice: Bring water to a boil in a very large pot having a tight-fitting lid; add a tablespoon salt; stir in the rice and boil rapidly uncovered for 18 to 20 minutes. Start tasting at 18 minutes; it may be done at that point. It must not be mushy. Drain rice into a colander; return to the still-hot pot; cover with several paper towels, then place lid on tightly and return to the still-warm eye on the stove, but with the heat turned off. Allow to stand until ready to use. (The paper towels will absorb all the moisture and rice will be dry.)

Sauce

6 tablespoons butter or margarine	Dash white pepper
3 tablespoons grated onion	Generous dash ground nutmeg
5 tablespoons all-purpose flour	1/4 cup dry sherry
1 teaspoon curry powder	1 tablespoon finely minced parsley
3 cups warm milk or light cream	Paprika
1 teaspoon salt	

Heat butter in large saucepan and sauté onion until golden. Blend in flour and curry powder and cook for a few minutes, stirring constantly. Gradually add warm milk, very slowly, stirring constantly until thickened. Remove from heat; stir in salt, pepper, nutmeg, sherry, and parsley. Check seasonings, adding more if mixture is too bland.

Butter a large casserole and starting with rice, arrange rice and shrimp in layers, pouring some of the sauce over each layer. The top layer should be rice. Sprinkle with paprika, cover and bake at 350° for 30 to 40 minutes. Yield: 12 servings as the only main dish; 15 servings or more, if another main dish is provided.

Note: For added glamor, reserve about 8 shrimp, place over top of casserole and drizzle melted butter over them before baking the casserole.

SPINACH WITH ARTICHOKES

4 (10-ounce) packages chopped frozen spinach	Salt and pepper
	Seasoned salt
11 ounces cream cheese; 1 (8-ounce) and 1 (3-ounce) package	Several dashes ground nutmeg
5 tablespoons melted butter or margarine	2 (1-pound) cans artichoke hearts, drained thoroughly
Juice of 1 lemon	

Cook spinach according to package directions, only until completely thawed; drain thoroughly and set aside. Have cream cheese at room temperature; soften cheese well, then blend in the melted butter until smooth. Add lemon juice and combine with spinach. Stir in all seasonings, blend well and check seasonings.

Place artichoke hearts pointed-ends up in a large ovenproof baking dish (about 16 x 8 inches). Spoon spinach over artichokes, cover with aluminum foil, punch a few holes in the foil, and bake at 350° for 30 minutes. Yield: 15 servings.

Note: The dish may be put together ready for baking the morning of the party. Remove from refrigerator an hour or so before baking.

BAKED CANNED HAM

Stud ham with whole cloves over entire surface. Pat brown sugar thickly over surface. Wrap tightly in aluminum foil and bake at 450° for 30 minutes. Open foil, baste ham with syrup that has formed; pat more brown sugar on top. Reduce temperature to 350°, open foil and bake for 30 minutes more. The crust of the ham should be sugary and crisp, with some of the sugar remaining unmelted.

SHANGHAI SALAD

1 large head crisp lettuce, shredded	2 (5-ounce) cans water chestnuts, thinly sliced
2 (1-pound) cans bean sprouts, drained well	1/2 cup chopped toasted almonds (optional)
2 green peppers, coarsely chopped	

Place all ingredients, except almonds, in a very large bowl; just before serving, pour Dressing over all and toss well. Sprinkle almonds over top. Yield: 12 to 15 servings.

Dressing
(prepare the day before)

2/3 cup mayonnaise	5 tablespoons tarragon vinegar
1 teaspoon prepared mustard	1-1/2 teaspoons dried marjoram
1/2 teaspoon Tabasco sauce	1/2 teaspoon dried thyme
2 teaspoons chili powder	Several grinds black pepper
1 clove garlic, crushed	1 teaspoon salt
2 teaspoons grated onion	2 teaspoons soy sauce

Put mayonnaise in bowl and blend in all other ingredients. Transfer to jar with tight-fitting cover, shake vigorously, cover and refrigerate overnight. Yield: about 1 cup.

CORNMEAL CRISPS

2 cups plain, yellow or white cornmeal	5 dashes cayenne pepper
1/4 teaspoon salt	2-1/2 cups boiling water
1/8 teaspoon seasoned salt	3 to 4 teaspoons butter
Freshly ground black pepper	

Put cornmeal and seasonings in bowl; stir to blend. Pour the briskly boiling water over all and stir until there are no lumps present.

In the meantime, heat butter in large, heavy iron skillet. When melted, pour into the batter and stir well. Drop by tablespoonfuls into hot skillet. The circles should be 2-1/2 to 3 inches in diameter. The batter is fairly thin and, if the circles touch, it doesn't matter.

Place skillet in preheated oven and bake at 375° for 45 minutes. Turn the crisps, decrease temperature to 250°, and bake for 15 minutes longer. Turn heat off and allow crisps to dry out in the warm oven for another 15 minutes. Yield: about 20.

Note: These are versatile little corn pones, suitable as a bread for cocktail suppers, to accompany all seafood dishes, as a between-meal nibble, etc. — C. M.

MELBA RYE STICKS

1 loaf round rye bread, unsliced	2 cloves garlic, crushed
1/4 pound butter or margarine	Seasoned salt

For easier slicing, partially thaw loaf and slice into 1/8-inch slices. (If sliced rye bread is the only kind available, use directions given but allow longer to bake.)

Melt butter in small saucepan and stir in crushed garlic. Brush both sides of bread slices with butter and form a stack of the slices on a cutting board. Use a very sharp knife and cut all the way through the stack, cutting into strips 1 inch wide. You may remove the crusts if you desire. Separate strips and place on ungreased baking sheet. Bake at 250° until crisp, usually about 1-1/2 hours. Remove to paper towels to drain and store in airtight container.

Note: These bread strips make an excellent appetizer when brushed with butter and sprinkled with seasoned salt.

LAYERED APRICOT SQUARES
(may be prepared the day before)

1 cup all-purpose flour, sifted	1/2 cup butter
1/3 cup granulated sugar	

Sift flour with sugar into bowl; cut in butter with pastry blender (or fingers) until mixture is granular. Press into an ungreased 8-inch square baking dish and bake at 325° (350° for metal pan) for 30 minutes, or until lightly browned.

Topping

3/4 cup dried apricots, chopped	1/4 teaspoon salt
2 eggs	1/4 teaspoon almond extract
1 cup firmly packed light brown sugar	1/4 teaspoon vanilla extract
1/3 cup all-purpose flour	1/2 cup chopped walnuts
1/2 teaspoon baking powder	Powdered sugar

Cover apricots with water and simmer for 15 minutes in small saucepan. Drain, allow to cool, then cut into 1/4-inch pieces. (I find small sharp scissors best.)

Beat eggs in small bowl of electric mixer; gradually add sugar and beat until mixture is light. Sift flour with baking powder and salt and add to batter, then beat in flavorings. Fold in apricots and nuts. Spread over bottom layer and bake at 325° (350° for metal pan) for 30 to 35 minutes. Remove from oven and place on wire rack to cool. While still hot, sift powdered sugar over the squares. When cool, cut in 2-inch squares. These may be made the day before using and stored in an airtight container. Yield: 16; recipe should be doubled for this menu.

DOUBLE THE RECIPE

Throughout this book you will find recipes with proportions that will not serve the number of guests for which the menu is planned. At the end of these recipes you will see the suggestion "double the recipe," sometimes "triple the recipe."

In planning the section on serving a number of guests, I was tempted to increase the original recipes in order to agree with the number of guests. And then I remembered; not all kitchens are equipped to handle large quantities of food; the utensils and other equipment available are not always large enough to accommodate a doubled recipe; even when they are, and assuming your arm holds out, it is harder to blend flavors thoroughly, achieve desired texture, season subtly and fold in uniformly when you are handling a large volume of foods. I therefore resisted the temptation to tamper with what I knew to be manageable quantities for the average home kitchen, especially when the hostess must do the work herself.

You may find it practicable to double or triple a recipe with the utensils (and strength) you have. But in some cases you may find it easier to prepare the recipe several times in order to end up with an adequate amount to serve a sizeable group. Also, this will allow you to better control the seasoning. — C.M.

Lamb with Vermouth Dinner

DINNER FOR SIX TO EIGHT

Carrot Ambrosia

Lamb with Vermouth

Noodle-Rice Casserole

Mixed Green Salad with Parmesan Croutons

Dessert Squares à la Mode

Coffee　　　　　　　　　　　　　　　　　　　Tea

CARROT AMBROSIA

1 (1-pound) can pineapple chunks, drained	1 pound carrots
	1 (3-1/2-ounce) can flaked coconut

Peel and grate carrots, using large hole of grater. Cut each pineapple chunk into three or four smaller pieces. Combine with carrots and toss with flaked coconut. Yield: 8 servings.

LAMB WITH VERMOUTH

3 tablespoons butter or margarine	4 whole peppercorns
10 to 12 small white onions; or 2 medium onions, coarsely chopped	1 bay leaf
2 (3-ounce) cans button mushrooms, drained, reserve liquid	1-1/2 tablespoons all-purpose flour
	Equal parts dry vermouth and mushroom liquid
2 pounds lamb, cut into 1-inch pieces (shoulder or leg)	1/2 cup heavy cream
1 teaspoon salt	1/4 cup chopped fresh parsley

Heat butter in heavy skillet and sauté onions and mushrooms. Remove with slotted spoon to casserole. Add lamb to skillet and brown thoroughly in butter remaining in skillet; add to casserole. Stir in seasonings, sprinkle in flour, stir well, then add vermouth and mushroom liquid. Add small amount of water if necessary so liquid will almost cover meat. Cover and bake at 350° for 1 hour. Check seasonings; add more if desired, and cook 15 minutes longer or until lamb is tender. Stir in cream, sprinkle with parsley and serve. Yield: 6 servings.

NOODLE-RICE CASSEROLE

1 (4-ounce) package extremely fine noodles	About 1 cup chicken broth
1/2 cup butter	1 (10-1/2-ounce) can onion soup
1 cup regular uncooked long-grain rice	2 tablespoons soy sauce
	Sliced toasted almonds

Sauté raw noodles in butter in a saucepan until just golden. Add all other ingredients except almonds. Cover and simmer until rice is done, about 30 minutes, adding a little more broth if necessary to keep rice moist. Turn into buttered casserole, sprinkle with almonds and bake uncovered at 325° for 30 minutes. Yield: 6 to 8 servings.

MIXED GREEN SALAD

6 to 8 cups mixed salad greens, torn into bite-size pieces

2 peeled tomatoes, cut into wedges

3 slices crisp cooked bacon, finely crumbled

About 1 cup Parmesan-Flavored Croutons

About 1 cup Garlic-Flavored French Dressing*

Mix greens (Boston lettuce, iceberg lettuce, romaine, etc.) lightly in large salad bowl. Garnish with tomato wedges, sprinkle with bacon, and arrange croutons over top. Just before serving, pour salad dressing over all and toss lightly. Yield: 6 to 8 servings.

*See Index for Garlic-Flavored French Dressing recipe.

PARMESAN-FLAVORED CROUTONS

1/2 cup butter or margarine

1 (6-ounce) envelope Parmesan salad dressing mix

6 cups bread cubes, about 1/2 inch square

Divide butter in half and place in two shallow baking pans in a 350° oven. While butter melts, empty salad dressing mix into a paper bag; add bread cubes (made from commercial day-old sliced bread with crusts removed) and shake. Divide the cubes between the two pans, then stir to coat with butter. Bake at 350° for about 20 minutes, stirring occasionally to brown on all sides. Store croutons in covered jar in refrigerator.

DESSERT SQUARES
(may be prepared the day before)

4 egg whites

1/4 teaspoon salt

3/4 cup sugar

1 cup graham cracker crumbs

1/2 cup semi-sweet chocolate bits

1/2 cup coconut

1/2 cup chopped walnuts or pecans

1 teaspoon vanilla extract

1/2 teaspoon almond extract

1 teaspoon freshly squeezed lemon juice

9 whole graham crackers

Vanilla ice cream (optional)

Beat egg whites and salt till foamy. Gradually add sugar, beating until stiff peaks form. Fold in the crumbs, chocolate bits, coconut, nuts, flavorings, and lemon juice.

Line bottom of 8-inch square pan with whole graham crackers; spread with meringue mixture. Bake at 350° for 30 minutes. Cool and cut in squares. Excellent topped with vanilla ice cream. These cake squares keep well; may be made the day before serving. Freezes well. Yield: 9 servings.

Chicken Casserole Dinner

BUFFET DINNER FOR TWELVE

Chicken-Wild Rice Casserole

Carrots with Grapes   **Orange Beets**

Bibb Lettuce with Tarragon Dressing

Thin-Sliced Buttered Toast Triangles   **Pineapple-Lemon Conserve**

Berries Supreme

or

Filled Pastries and Chocolate Butterscotch Squares

Coffee   **Tea**

CHICKEN-WILD RICE CASSEROLE

(may be prepared ahead of time)

1 (1-3/8-ounce) package dehydrated onion soup

1 pint commercial sour cream

3 (2-1/2-pound) frying chickens, chopped

2 cups dry sherry

1 cup water

1 teaspoon salt

Dash pepper

1/2 teaspoon dried basil

Pinch thyme

1 teaspoon curry powder

6 tablespoons minced fresh parsley

1 (10-1/2-ounce) can cream of mushroom soup

1-1/2 cups uncooked wild rice

Blend dry onion soup into sour cream in a bowl and allow to stand for 2 hours. Place chicken in roasting pan; pour sherry and water over it; sprinkle with all seasonings and parsley; cover roaster tightly. (If lid doesn't fit securely, place a sheet of aluminum foil over pan before covering.) Bake at 300° for 1-1/2 hours, or until meat falls off bones. Remove chicken from roaster, cover loosely and set aside to cool.

Strain pan juices from roaster into saucepan and simmer until reduced to 1-1/2 cups. Blend in mushroom soup until smooth and heat together a few minutes. (This is better if you blend by pouring liquid into canned soup.) Slowly combine with sour cream mixture. The cream will not curdle if you blend slowly, pouring hot liquid into cream mixture a little at a time.

Cook rice according to package directions. Skin and bone cooled chicken; cut into bite-size pieces. Combine with rice and turn into buttered casserole. Pour sauce over and toss lightly. When ready to serve, heat uncovered at 250° for about 30 minutes. Excellent prepared ahead of time; freezes beautifully. Yield: 12 servings.

CARROTS WITH GRAPES

2 pounds fresh carrots
2 teaspoons dried basil
1/2 cup butter
1 teaspoon crushed chervil
1/8 teaspoon garlic powder

Pinch celery salt
3 cups seedless white grapes
2 tablespoons freshly squeezed lemon juice
Dash salt and white pepper

Scrape carrots; cut into julienne strips; place in saucepan with basil and enough water to cover and cook until just tender; drain. In the meantime, combine butter, chervil, garlic powder, and celery salt. A few minutes before serving, stir in grapes, lemon juice, salt, and pepper. Heat only until grapes are hot, and serve. Yield: 10 to 12 servings.

ORANGE BEETS
(may be prepared the day before)

3 (1-pound) cans small whole beets, drained, reserve liquid
2 tablespoons cornstarch
1-1/4 cups light brown sugar
1 (6-ounce) can frozen orange juice concentrate

6 ounces drained beet liquid
3/4 cup cider vinegar
1 tablespoon butter or margarine

Combine cornstarch and sugar in a saucepan. Blend in orange concentrate, then beet liquid, and vinegar. Cook, stirring constantly, until thick and clear. Add butter and beets, reheat and serve, or place in double boiler over simmering water to keep hot until serving time. May be prepared the day before, then reheated gently in double boiler. Yield: 12 servings.

TARRAGON DRESSING
(prepare the day before)

6 tablespoons salad oil
3 tablespoons tarragon vinegar
1-1/2 teaspoons dry white wine
1/2 teaspoon salt
1/4 teaspoon coarse black pepper

1-1/2 teaspoons paprika
1/2 teaspoon sugar
Generous pinch dried tarragon
1/2 teaspoon grated onion

Put all ingredients in jar and shake well. Prepare dressing the day before you plan to use it. This amount of dressing is sufficient for 4 servings of salad; adjust proportions to serve the number of guests invited.

TOAST TRIANGLES
(see Index)

PINEAPPLE-LEMON CONSERVE

1 (1-pound) can crushed pineapple
2 unpeeled lemons, very thinly sliced, and quartered

2 cups sugar
1 cup broken pecans or walnuts

Drain pineapple thoroughly. This is important! In a saucepan put drained pineapple liquid, lemon slices, and sugar. Cook over moderate heat, stirring occasionally, until syrup sheets from a spoon — the same test you would use for jelly. The jelly must reach this stage; otherwise the addition of the pineapple will dilute it. When jelly test is reached, stir in pineapple and nuts; pour into clean, hot jars. Let jelly cool, then pour melted paraffin over top to seal. Sealing is unnecessary if you plan to use the conserve within a few weeks.

BERRIES SUPREME

1-1/2 quarts fresh strawberries
Sugar
1 (10-ounce) package frozen raspberries

1 cup whipping cream
Liqueur (optional)

Wash and hull strawberries; arrange attractively in shallow serving bowl (berries are prettiest with pointed-ends up); sprinkle with sugar. Refrigerate. Partially thaw raspberries; put through electric blender or sieve to yield a thick puree; refrigerate until ready to serve, then spoon over strawberries. Serve accompanied by bowl of cream whipped with a little sugar and flavored with any liqueur you like (folded in after whipping) or a few drops of almond flavoring. This is as delicious as it is beautiful. Yield: 6 servings; double this recipe to serve 12.

FILLED PASTRIES
(may be prepared ahead of time)

2 cups all-purpose flour
3 tablespoons granulated sugar
1/2 teaspoon salt
2 (3-ounce) packages cream cheese
1/2 pound butter (no substitute)

6 tablespoons raspberry, cherry, or strawberry preserves
6 tablespoons cake crumbs or crumbled plain cookies
Sifted powdered sugar

Sift flour, granulated sugar, and salt into a bowl. Cut in cheese and butter with pastry blender until mixture may be formed into a ball with hands. Wrap in waxed paper and refrigerate overnight.

When ready to bake, roll out pastry on floured surface to 1/8-inch thickness. Cut into 3-inch squares. Combine preserves and crumbs; place a teaspoon on each pastry square. Fold to form a triangle; press edges together with fork. Prick top of pastry several times and place on ungreased baking sheet. Bake at 350° for about 20 minutes, or until pale golden in color. Remove from pan and while warm sift powdered sugar over pastries. Yield: about 36.

Note: These are also excellent filled with a mixture of canned almond pie filling and ground nuts. Pastries may be made ahead of time and frozen, thawed in their container, then heated at 275° for about 10 minutes, dusting with more powdered sugar while warm.

CHOCOLATE-BUTTERSCOTCH SQUARES

Bottom Layer

1/2 cup butter or margarine	1 tablespoon sugar
1 egg yolk	Dash salt
2 tablespoons water	1 teaspoon baking powder
1/2 teaspoon almond extract	6 ounces butterscotch bits
1-1/4 cups all-purpose flour	6 ounces semi-sweet chocolate bits

Beat butter, egg yolk, water, and almond extract in large bowl of electric mixer until well blended. Sift in flour, sugar, salt, and baking powder. Blend well; pat into greased 13- x 9- x 2-inch pan. Bake at 350° for 10 minutes; remove from oven and immediately scatter the butterscotch and chocolate bits over the top. Return to oven for about 4 or 5 minutes; remove and with small spatula smooth melted bits over pastry.

Top Layer

2 eggs	1 teaspoon vanilla extract
3/4 cup sugar	1/2 teaspoon almond extract
6 tablespoons melted butter or margarine	1 cup pecans or walnuts, finely ground

While first layer bakes, beat eggs; add sugar, melted butter, and flavorings. Pour over chocolate-butterscotch layer; sprinkle with nuts, return to oven and bake for 30 to 35 minutes longer. Cut into 1-1/2-inch squares. Yield: about 3 dozen.

Corned Beef Dinner

BUFFET DINNER FOR EIGHT TO TEN

Hot Homemade Corned Beef

or

Eight Pounds Commercial Corned Beef

Brown and Yellow Mustard   **Garlic Dill Pickles**

Spinach-Stuffed Tomatoes
or   **Mashed Potato Casserole**
Viennese Spinach

Fresh Rye Bread   **Butter**

Cranberry Parfait
or
Cheese and Fresh Fruit

Coffee   **Tea**

CORNED BEEF

2 (4-to 5-pound) beef briskets	1/3 cup salt
4 cloves garlic, minced	1 teaspoon saltpeter
3 tablespoons mixed pickling spices	About 2 cups warm water

Place meat in earthenware crock; sprinkle garlic and spices over and between the two pieces of meat. Dissolve salt and saltpeter in the water and pour into crock, against the side, not over the meat. Place a plate over meat and weight it down with a heavy object, pressing down firmly. Now add enough cold water to barely cover meat. Cover crock tightly with plastic to prevent odors from escaping, and refrigerate. Allow to remain 10 to 14 days, turning meat several times.

To cook: Remove meat from brine; rinse thoroughly in cold water. Place in shallow pan and sprinkle both sides generously with paprika and black pepper. No salt! Roast uncovered at 300° for 3 to 4 hours, until fork tender, basting with pan juices that form. If meat threatens to dry out, cover loosely with foil. Serve hot or cold, sliced thin across the grain.

Note: For 1 beef, use 2 or 3 cloves garlic, 1 tablespoon spices, scant 1/3 cup salt, scant teaspoon saltpeter, and 1 cup water.

When buying meat do not have butcher trim all fat from top of meat as the layer of fat automatically bastes the meat as it cooks.

If you do not have room for a crock in your refrigerator, a heavy plastic bag, securely tied, may be used.

GARLIC DILL PICKLES

1 peck small to medium firm
  cucumbers
1-1/2 to 2 ounces mixed pickling spices
  Fresh or dried dill

1 large ball garlic, cut in small pieces
  (this is the whole ball, the tight
  cluster of cloves)
  Salt and saltpeter

In a 3-gallon earthenware crock pack cucumbers (fresh, unwaxed, in-season, firm cucumbers; the small, rough, warty ones are best) in layers, adding pickling spices, several sprigs of dill, and pieces of garlic between layers. When all cucumbers have been packed, cover with brine made by adding 1/2 cup salt and a pinch of saltpeter to each gallon of water used (make up a gallon of brine at a time). Place a plate over cucumbers; weight the plate down with a heavy object; the brine must cover the cucumbers at all times.

Allow to stand at room temperature until done, about a week. If scum forms on surface of brine, skim it off — check it every day or so. When pickles are done to suit taste, refrigerate in their brine — in the same crock or in jars. If you transfer them to jars, be sure to pour in brine to completely cover the pickles.

SPINACH-STUFFED TOMATOES
(may be prepared for baking ahead of time)

8 medium, unpeeled ripe tomatoes
  Salt
8 slices bacon
2 (10-ounce) packages frozen chopped
  spinach
3/4 cup soft breadcrumbs

Salt and pepper
Pinch ground nutmeg
Pinch garlic powder
Melted butter
Commercial sour cream

With a sharp knife cut a thin slice from top of tomatoes; scoop out center pulp (you won't be needing this). Sprinkle inside of tomatoes with salt and turn upside down to drain for about an hour.

Cook bacon on wire rack over shallow pan in 350° oven for about 25 minutes, or until dry and crisp. Crumble and set aside.

Cook frozen spinach according to package directions, but only until just thawed. Drain thoroughly. Combine with breadcrumbs, seasonings, and finely crumbled bacon. Stuff tomatoes with this mixture; place in buttered baking dish. Drizzle a small amount of melted butter over tomatoes. All this may be done ahead of time and the dish refrigerated.

Bake uncovered at 350° for about 20 minutes, or until tomatoes are tender when pricked with a fork, but do not overbake; tomatoes must hold their shape. Before serving, top each tomato with a tablespoon of sour cream. Yield: 8 servings.

VIENNESE SPINACH

3 (10-ounce) packages frozen chopped spinach

3 tablespoons butter or margarine

6 teaspoons finely minced onion

3 tablespoons all-purpose flour

Generous dash ground nutmeg

Salt and pepper to taste

3 teaspoons freshly squeezed lemon juice

1-1/2 cups commercial sour cream

Cook spinach according to package directions; drain well. Heat butter in saucepan and sauté onion until golden. Stir in flour until smooth; add seasonings, lemon juice, then sour cream. When smooth, combine with spinach. Check seasonings and reheat. Yield: 8 to 10 servings.

Note: This is also good without the onion.

MASHED POTATO CASSEROLE

8 to 10 medium boiling potatoes

Salt and pepper to taste

1 (8-ounce) package cream cheese, softened

2 eggs, beaten lightly

2 tablespoons all-purpose flour

2 tablespoons minced fresh parsley

2 tablespoons minced chives, or 1 small onion, grated

1 (3-1/2-ounce) can French-fried onions

Peel and boil potatoes until tender; drain and put in large bowl of electric mixer. Beat until smooth; add salt and pepper, then cream cheese, and beat again. Blend in eggs, flour, parsley, and chives, and beat thoroughly. Check seasonings and turn into buttered casserole. Spread slightly crushed onions over top and bake uncovered at 325° for about 30 minutes, until puffy and golden. Casserole may be prepared in the morning and refrigerated until baking time, the onions added just before placing in oven. Yield: 8 servings.

CRANBERRY PARFAIT
(may be prepared ahead of time)

2 (1-pound) cans jellied cranberry sauce

4 tablespoons powdered sugar

2 egg whites, stiffly beaten

2 cups heavy cream, whipped

2 teaspoons almond extract

1 cup toasted blanched almonds, chopped

Using a fork, beat cranberry sauce and sugar together. Do not beat until mixture is smooth; allow small chunks to remain. Fold in beaten egg whites, whipped cream, and almond extract. Turn into freezing tray and freeze until mixture is almost firm. Beat with fork, return to freezer to finish freezing. Sprinkle parfait with toasted almonds before serving. This dessert keeps beautifully in the freezer and any leftover won't go begging. Yield: 10 to 12 servings.

SEATING TIP

In planning your seating arrangement for a dinner party, remember the old Spanish proverb: "Two great talkers will not travel far together."

Roast Duck Dinner

DINNER FOR EIGHT

Mushroom-Barley Soup

Roast Duck with Rum-Glazed Fruit

Dilled Green Beans   **Almond Rice**

Bernice Rosen's Cherry Tomatoes

Creamy Lemon Sherbet with Cinnamon Bars

Coffee   **Tea**

No bread suggested because of rice, but a bread of your choice could be added if desired.

MUSHROOM-BARLEY SOUP

1 ounce dried mushrooms	1/2 teaspoon salt
1-1/2 cups hot water	Few grinds coarse black pepper
2 tablespoons butter	2 small potatoes, peeled and diced
1 small onion, minced	1 bay leaf
1 small carrot, minced	Commercial sour cream
1/4 cup fine barley	Dill weed
6 cups chicken stock (or bouillon cubes and water)	

Soak mushrooms in hot water for 20 to 30 minutes. Strain through fine sieve, reserving the liquid. Chop the mushrooms (I used a wooden bowl and chopping blade); set aside.

In a large saucepan sauté the onion in butter until soft; add chopped mushrooms, carrot, barley, reserved mushroom liquid, chicken stock, salt, and pepper. Cover and simmer for 1-1/2 hours. Add potatoes and bay leaf. Cover and simmer soup for 30 minutes. Discard the bay leaf and stir in sour cream. Reheat soup but do not let it boil; garnish with just a pinch of chopped dill. Yield: 8 (1-cup) servings.

Note: To add sour cream, stir a little of the hot soup into cream, then a little more, then stir all together. Otherwise, the cream "lumps" into white globules. Most unattractive.

ROAST DUCK

Because ducks are usually so fat, it is desirable to eliminate as much fat as possible before they are roasted. The following is the suggested method for 2 (4- to 5-pound) ducks. Same method may be used for a (7- to 8-pound) goose.

Clean and dry ducks thoroughly. Truss by pressing wings close to body of duck and tying twine around entire upper portion. Tuck neck skin under the twine. Tie legs together. Place in open roasting pan. Prick with a fork over the entire surface of the ducks, pricking every inch. Roast at 350° for 1 hour with a piece of foil loosely placed over ducks to prevent their becoming dry. Pour off fat that accumulates in pan twice during the cooking.

Meanwhile, in a small bowl combine the following:

1 tablespoon salt	1 teaspoon poultry seasoning
1/2 teaspoon pepper	1/2 teaspoon ground ginger
1 teaspoon seasoned salt	2 to 3 dashes cayenne pepper
1/2 teaspoon garlic powder	

When ducks are cool enough to be handled, rub seasoning mixture thoroughly inside and outside. Return to oven and roast for 25 minutes per pound, or until skin is very crisp but meat is moist and tender. Baste often, adding a small amount of hot water as needed if ducks seem to be sticking to pan.

The skin should be very, very crisp. If the meat is tender but the skin isn't crisp and dry, place under slow broiler for a few minutes.

When done, remove ducks from pan; pour off all excess fat, add 1/2 cup hot water to pan and bring to a boil. Scrape up all "crustlings" adhering to the pan and simmer for about 2 minutes. Add to Giblet Gravy. Serve the ducks quartered. Yield: 8 servings.

Giblet Gravy

Giblets and necks of ducks	1/2 teaspoon ground ginger
4 cups water	2 stalks celery, sliced
1 onion, coarsely chopped	1/2 teaspoon salt
1 clove garlic, minced	1/4 teaspoon pepper
1 bay leaf	2 teaspoons cornstarch
1 teaspoon seasoned salt	

Thoroughly clean the giblets and necks of ducks. Place in saucepan with other ingredients except cornstarch. Bring to a boil, cover and reduce heat. Simmer for about 3 hours, until gizzards are quite tender. Strain, thicken if desired; cut up giblets and pieces of neck meat, and return to gravy.

To thicken the gravy, stir about 2 teaspoons cornstarch into a tablespoon cold water, then blend with the gravy; cook, stirring constantly until slightly thickened. Combine with pan juices left from roasting ducks.

RUM-GLAZED ASSORTED FRUIT

Using canned fruit, allow a slice of pineapple, a peach half, and an apricot half per person. Arrange in single layer on large baking sheet, sprinkle lightly with brown sugar and rum and dot with butter. Put under broiler until fruit is a delicate gold. Serve as a garnish for roast fowl or game, or on a separate platter.

The fruit may be arranged around the fowl or game either in separate pieces or in stacks with pineapple on the bottom, then the peach half, then the apricot half — any way that looks attractive.

DILLED GREEN BEANS

2 pounds fresh green pole beans
2 teaspoons dill seed, crushed

3 tablespoons butter or margarine

Break beans into 1-inch pieces and cook uncovered in rapidly boiling salted water for 20 to 30 minutes, until they are tender. Drain and set aside.

Crush dill seed, using mortar and pestle if you have one; if not, use back of heavy spoon. Heat butter in large skillet, add dill seed and simmer for 3 minutes. Add beans and stir to coat thoroughly, making sure the beans are heated throughout. Yield: 8 servings.

ALMOND RICE

3 tablespoons butter
1/2 cup slivered blanched almonds
1-1/2 cups uncooked regular rice

4-1/2 cups water
Salt to taste

Heat butter in saucepan; add almonds and sauté a few minutes, until just golden. Add rice and stir until it is thoroughly coated. Add water and salt to taste; increase heat to bring mixture to a lively boil. Stir briefly; boil until water barely disappears from surface. Lower heat immediately, cover tightly and cook until rice is done and fluffy, about 20 to 30 minutes.

Check once after cooking about 20 minutes and quickly stir rice with a fork. If rice is not to be served immediately, it will wait nicely for 15 to 20 minutes over lowest heat on range top, or in a 200° oven. Yield: 8 servings.

BERNICE ROSEN'S CHERRY TOMATOES

2 pints cherry tomatoes
Boiling water
1/2 cup olive oil
2 tablespoons red wine vinegar

2 cloves garlic, finely minced
Freshly ground pepper
1 tablespoon finely minced
fresh parsley

Cover tomatoes with boiling water and let stand for 30 to 40 seconds. Drain, and as soon as cool enough to handle, peel; it's really quite easy. Combine remaining ingredients and pour over the tomatoes. Chill at least an hour before serving on bed of lettuce — or watercress if available. Yield: 8 servings.

CREAMY LEMON SHERBET
(may be prepared ahead of time)

1-1/2 cups sugar

3 cups warm milk

3/4 cup freshly squeezed
lemon juice

1 teaspoon grated lemon rind

1/4 teaspoon salt

2 envelopes unflavored gelatin

1 tablespoon cold water

Stir sugar into warmed milk until dissolved. Slowly add lemon juice, grated rind, and salt. Soak gelatin in the cold water for 5 minutes; place over boiling water and heat until gelatin is dissolved. Stir into first mixture. Pour into freezing tray and freeze until firm about 1 inch from edge of tray. Stir and whip with a fork until smooth; freeze until firm. Turn into large bowl of electric mixer and beat until smooth and creamy; return to freezer. Yield: 8 servings.

CINNAMON BARS

1 cup butter or margarine

1 cup sugar

1 egg, separated

2 cups all-purpose flour

4 teaspoons ground cinnamon

1 cup chopped pecans

Cream butter and sugar thoroughly in large bowl of electric mixer. Add egg yolk, then flour sifted with cinnamon. Pat into ungreased 15- x 10-inch pan; pour unbeaten egg white over surface; drain off excess. Sprinkle nuts over top, pressing them down lightly with flat of hand. Bake at 325° for 25 to 30 minutes; cut into bars while hot. These freeze well. Yield: about 3 dozen bars.

THE GUEST BATH

Sparkling and shiny clean with touches of "you were expected" is how the bath should appear to guests. Give the bathroom a last-minute once over just prior to party time. See that hand towels are fresh and individual guest soap is out in a clean, dry dish, and give a quick swipe to the sink and toilet bowl.

As an extra gesture of hospitality, set out a small toilette tray with a clean comb, extra hairpins, tissues, hand cream, and cologne and any other touch-up aid. For a festive air in the bath, fill a decorative (empty) cologne bottle with fresh flowers.

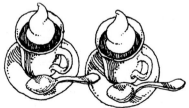

Chicken Tetrazzini Dinner

BUFFET DINNER FOR TWELVE

Chicken Tetrazzini

Orange Carrots   **Oriental Vegetables**

Bibb Lettuce and Grapefruit Sections with Lemon-Vermouth Dressing

Fresh Fruit and Cheese

Apricot Strudel and Shortbread Cookies

Coffee   **Tea**

No bread suggested because of spaghetti in the tetrazzini but a bread of your choice could be added if desired.

CHICKEN TETRAZZINI
(may be prepared for baking ahead of time)

1 (6-pound) hen
6 tablespoons butter or margarine
1 large onion, minced
1 large green pepper, minced
1/2 pound fresh mushrooms, coarsely chopped
1 (4-ounce) can pimientos, drained and chopped
5 tablespoons all-purpose flour

3-1/2 cups chicken broth (from stewing hen)
1 cup warm heavy cream
3 tablespoons dry sherry
1-1/2 cups shredded Swiss and Parmesan cheese, mixed
Salt and pepper, if needed
1 pound thin spaghetti

Cook hen until tender. Discard skin and bones; cut meat in small pieces, make broth. Measure 3-1/2 cups of the broth and set aside.

Make sauce: In a saucepan heat 2 tablespoons of the butter and sauté onion, green pepper, mushrooms, and pimiento until vegetables are tender, from 5 to 7 minutes. Set aside.

Heat remaining 4 tablespoons butter in saucepan and stir in flour. Gradually add the 3-1/2 cups reserved chicken broth and cook over low heat, stirring constantly, until sauce is thickened slightly. Add cream; cook another minute, then stir in sherry and about 3/4 cup of the mixed cheese. When cheese has melted, remove from heat and combine with sautéed vegetables.

Cook spaghetti in boiling broth made of hot water and bouillon cubes (1 cube to 1 pint hot water); cook until just tender; drain thoroughly. Divide sauce in half; mix half with the diced chicken and other half with spaghetti. (If spaghetti isn't moist enough, stir in about 1/2 cup chicken broth.) Put spaghetti into a large casserole, make a well in the center and pour in chicken mixture; sprinkle with remaining cheese. Bake uncovered at 350° for about 30 minutes until golden brown. Casserole may be prepared the day before baking; it may also be frozen before baking. Yield: 12 servings.

Note: The hen for this recipe may be prepared in any manner preferred. I bake mine in a covered roaster, breast-side up, resting on a bed of sautéed onion, celery, and chopped carrots. Add to the roaster 1 cup chicken broth made of bouillon cube and hot water. Brush hen with chicken fat or butter; sprinkle generously inside and out with salt and pepper. Bake at 350° for about 3 hours and when tender, remove skin and bones and cut meat in small pieces.

The broth is made by straining the pan liquids, adding a little hot water, then combining it with a broth you've made of the neck, wing tips, gizzard, etc. Refrigerate until fat congeals on top; discard fat. This is the liquid you will be using for the sauce in the Chicken Tetrazzini.

If you aren't ready to finish the dish when the chicken is done, pour a cup of broth over the chopped chicken (keeps it moist), cover and refrigerate overnight. — C.M.

ORANGE CARROTS

24 small young carrots	1/4 teaspoon ground nutmeg
6 tablespoons butter or margarine	1/4 teaspoon ground cinnamon
2/3 cup light brown sugar	4 slices unpeeled oranges
Juice of 4 oranges	

Wash and scrape or peel carrots, leaving them whole. Heat butter in large skillet or saucepan; add sugar, orange juice, and spices. Cook for 3 minutes, stirring constantly, then add carrots. Spoon syrup over them, cover with orange slices and cook, partially covered, until carrots are tender and liquid has almost cooked away. Baste frequently with liquid in pan. Yield: 12 servings.

Note: You may find it easier to cook these carrots in two portions or divide them into two large pans so they'll cook evenly with no stirring or bruising.

ORIENTAL VEGETABLES

6 tablespoons butter	1-1/3 cups chicken broth (use 1 bouillon cube and boiling water)
3 cups diagonally sliced celery	
2 (1-pound) cans bean sprouts, drained	2 tablespoons cornstarch
3 (10-ounce) packages frozen French-style beans	3 tablespoons soy sauce
	Salt to taste

Melt butter in saucepan; add celery and sauté until tender but still crisp. Cook beans according to package directions, just until barely tender. Combine cornstarch and soy sauce with chicken broth. Add beans and bean sprouts to celery, stir in sauce, and heat until sauce is slightly thickened. Check seasonings. Yield: 12 servings.

LEMON-VERMOUTH DRESSING

1 small onion, grated	1/2 cup freshly squeezed lemon juice (about 3 lemons)
3/4 teaspoon paprika	
1/4 teaspoon freshly ground black pepper	1-1/2 teaspoons Worcestershire sauce
	1/3 cup dry vermouth
1-1/2 teaspoons dry mustard	2/3 cup oil (half salad and half olive oil)
1 teaspoon salt	

Put onion, paprika, pepper, mustard, salt, and lemon juice into blender container. Blend thoroughly. Add Worcestershire sauce, vermouth, and oil. Blend again; chill before using over green salad; especially good over Bibb lettuce. Yield: 12 servings.

Note: This is an unusual, delicious dressing. Blender method is given here but dressing may be made by hand or with an electric mixer.

APRICOT STRUDEL
(may be prepared ahead of time)

2-1/2 cups all-purpose flour, sifted	2/3 cup softened butter
1/2 pound unsalted butter	Filling
2 egg yolks	Powdered sugar
1 cup commercial sour cream	

Cut the 1/2 pound butter into flour with pastry blender until granular. In a small bowl blend sour cream into egg yolks; add to flour mixture. Stir only until thoroughly moistened, cover and chill overnight. (Dough may be kept a week if necessary.)

When ready to bake, cut dough into four portions and follow these directions: Roll out first portion of dough onto lightly floured surface to 1/8-inch thickness; spread with softened butter; fold in thirds (see Index). Refrigerate and go on to second portion, spreading butter and folding in thirds, then refrigerating it. Continue until you have buttered and folded the fourth portion once and have refrigerated it. Now go back to the first portion and give it its second buttering and rolling and refrigerating, etc., until all four portions have been treated three times. This speeds up the operation without allowing the dough to become warm and unworkable.

Roll dough into rectangle about 16 x 8 inches. Spread one-fourth the Filling over pastry, spreading to edges. Roll up as tightly as possible; pinch ends to seal and quickly lift onto ungreased baking sheet. (Do not crowd the pan; if necessary use two pans for the four rolls.) Score lightly across top of rolled-up strip to indicate 1-inch slices.

Repeat with remaining three portions of pastry. Bake at 400° for 8 minutes; reduce temperature to 350° and bake for about 35 minutes longer, or until lightly browned. Loosen with spatula to prevent sticking to pan, sift powdered sugar over top, cool slightly, then with sharp knife carefully cut into slices.

(More sugar may be sifted over slices before serving if desired.) Strudel freezes well in airtight container. Allow to thaw in the container. (If preferred, cherry preserves may be substituted for the apricot.) Yield: about 55 slices.

Filling

2 cups shredded coconut	1-1/2 pounds apricot preserves
2 cups chopped pecans and walnuts, mixed	

Combine all ingredients and mix well.

SHORTBREAD COOKIES

2 cups all-purpose flour	1 cup butter or margarine
1/2 cup cornstarch	1/2 teaspoon vanilla extract
1/2 cup powdered sugar	1/2 teaspoon almond extract
1/2 teaspoon salt	

Sift flour with cornstarch, sugar, and salt three times. In large bowl of electric mixer beat butter until creamy. Gradually add flour mixture. Turn dough out onto lightly floured surface and pat or roll out to 1/2-inch thickness. Cut with small fancy cookie cutters and place on ungreased baking sheet. Bake at 325° for 20 to 25 minutes, just until slightly golden on the edges. Yield: about 4 dozen.

Note: This is a rich dough; you may find it easier to handle if you chill the dough about an hour before patting it out.

Fondue Parties

Fondue parties have become a popular type of entertainment, especially among the young marrieds. They're great ice breakers and suit spontaneous entertaining and casual settings where space and equipment are at a premium.

A simple, practically pre-prepared menu leaves the hostess free to mingle with the convivial gathering. Then when the time is come, guests gather around the pots (do borrow enough extras from friends), grab a fork, and the dipping begins: beef sizzled in hot oil, bread cubes swished in bubbly cheese, or fruit tidbits swirled in creamy chocolate.

The gaiety of the party is assured before the hostess buys her first pound of cheese or beef — for how can you avoid being friendly with others whose fondue forks are being stirred in unison with your own?

Beef Fondue Party

PARTY FOR SIX

Beef Fondue

with

Herbed Green Sauce	**Bernaise Sauce**
Barbecue Sauce	**Hot Mustard Sauce**

Green Salad with Cherry Tomatoes and Sherry French Dressing

Hot Garlic French Bread

Bavarian Cheesecake

or

Strawberry Soufflé

Coffee	**Tea**

BEEF FONDUE

3 **pounds filet of beef or boneless
    sirloin steak**
1/2 **pound butter (no substitute)**

3/4 **cup good grade olive oil**
Sauces for dipping

Carefully trim off any fat or connective tissue from meat. Cut into 3/4-inch cubes; refrigerate. About 20 minutes before serving, heat butter and oil together in saucepan. When mixture bubbles, pour into a 2-quart fondue dish. The hot fat should not be more than 2 inches deep.

Place the pot on the stand and light canned heat under it. When fat begins to bubble, invite each guest to spear a cube of meat with fondue fork or bamboo stick and lower it into the hot fat. Fry for 2 to 3 minutes, according to doneness preferred. Push meat off fork onto individual plates and spear another cube of meat to cook while you consume the one just finished.

Guests may be provided individual dishes of several kinds of dipping sauces, or a communal pot where all may dip into it. (The butter-oil mixture may be reused; keep refrigerated.) Yield: 6 servings.

BERNAISE SAUCE
(see Index)

HERBED GREEN SAUCE
(prepare ahead of time)

1 teaspoon dried tarragon	1/2 cup commercial sour cream
1 teaspoon dried chervil (optional)	1/2 cup mayonnaise
1 teaspoon dried basil	Lemon juice to taste
1/2 cup minced fresh parsley	Salt to taste
1/2 clove garlic, crushed	Dash ground nutmeg

Crush tarragon, chervil, basil, parsley, and garlic with mortar and pestle or in a bowl, using a wooden spoon. Stir into sour cream with mayonnaise; add lemon juice, salt, and nutmeg. Check seasonings; serve as sauce for fondue or as a salad topping. Should be prepared the day before using to allow flavors to blend. Yield: 1-1/2 cups.

BARBECUE SAUCE

1 clove garlic, crushed	1/4 teaspoon dried marjoram
1 medium onion, minced fine	1 (29-ounce) can tomatoes, put through blender or sieve
2 tablespoons salad oil	
2 teaspoons chili powder	1/4 cup vinegar
1 teaspoon dry mustard	1/2 teaspoon celery salt
1/2 teaspoon sugar	Dash Tabasco sauce (optional)
2 bay leaves	

Cook garlic and onion in the oil for about 5 minutes. Add other ingredients and simmer gently, stirring frequently, about 40 minutes, or until sauce is thick. Remove bay leaves, and store in refrigerator until needed. For fondue, the sauce should be heated and served warm. Yield: about 4 cups.

HOT MUSTARD SAUCE

3 tablespoons Dijon mustard	10 tablespoons butter
3 tablespoons Worcestershire sauce	

Combine mustard, Worcestershire sauce, and butter in a small saucepan. Stir over low heat until butter is melted and sauce is hot; do not boil. Should be served hot. Place over candle or other heating device. Yield: about 1-1/4 cups.

GREEN SALAD WITH CHERRY TOMATOES
(prepare greens the day before)

Thoroughly clean and dry 1-1/2 pounds mixed salad greens. Just before serving, toss lightly with about 1-1/2 cups cherry tomatoes, cut in half. Pour Sherry French Dressing over the salad; toss lightly and serve. Yield: 6 servings.

SHERRY FRENCH DRESSING
(prepare ahead of time)

1 small clove garlic
2 small white onions, chopped fine
1 teaspoon sugar
1 teaspoon salt
1/3 cup wine vinegar

1 to 2 tablespoons dry sherry
1/4 teaspoon freshly ground black pepper
3/4 cup olive or salad oil
Juice of 1/2 lemon

With mortar and pestle or wooden spoon mash garlic, onions, sugar and salt, blending until paste-like. Add vinegar, sherry, and pepper. Beat in 2 table-spoonfuls at a time, the oil, then lemon juice. Taste to check seasonings and pour over salad. Yield: 6 servings.

GARLIC FRENCH BREAD

1/2 cup butter, crushed
1 clove garlic, crushed

1 loaf French bread

Slowly heat butter and garlic in a small saucepan until butter is melted. In the meantime, cut bread in half, then in slices to within 1 inch of bottom crust. Spread butter between slices and over top and sides. Place on baking sheet and bake at 275° for about 20 minutes or until crisp and heated through. Yield: 6 servings.

Note: For an easy way to heat and serve this bread, see French Bread Tip.

BAVARIAN CHEESECAKE
(prepare the day before)

3 cups finely crushed vanilla wafers
1/2 cup butter or margarine, melted
3 tablespoons sugar

1-1/2 teaspoons ground cinnamon
3/4 teaspoon ground nutmeg

Combine all ingredients and blend thoroughly. Press firmly and evenly on bottom and sides of lightly greased 8-inch springform pan or two 8-inch cakepans. Chill for 30 minutes. Prepare the Filling.

Filling

1-1/2 pounds cream cheese, softened
1 cup sugar
3 eggs

1 tablespoon freshly squeezed lemon juice
1 teaspoon grated lemon rind
1/2 teaspoon vanilla extract

Beat cheese and sugar until light and fluffy. Add eggs one at a time, beating well after each addition. Blend in lemon juice, rind, and vanilla. Pour into chilled crust and bake at 375° for 45 minutes. Remove from oven and cool at room temperature for 30 minutes. (If using two cakepans bake only 30 minutes.)

Topping

2 cups commercial sour cream
3 tablespoons sugar

1 teaspoon vanilla extract

Blend together sour cream, sugar, and vanilla extract. Spread carefully over cooled cake; bake at 500° for 10 minutes. Cool; refrigerate overnight before serving. Yield: 12 to 16 servings.

STRAWBERRY SOUFFLÉ

1 (10-ounce) package frozen
   strawberries, thawed
1 envelope unflavored gelatin
1/4 cup cold water
3 eggs, separated
   Dash salt

1 tablespoon freshly squeezed
   lemon juice
1 teaspoon rum extract
1/2 cup sugar
1/2 cup heavy cream

Mash thawed berries with fork or put through blender. Soften gelatin in cold water. Beat egg yolks lightly; mix with salt and lemon juice in top of double boiler. Cook over hot water, stirring until slightly thickened. Add gelatin; mix well and remove from heat. When cooled slightly, add rum extract and berries. Beat egg whites until soft peaks form; gradually add sugar and beat until mixture is stiff. Whip cream until stiff, then fold egg whites and whipped cream into strawberry mixture, mixing gently until well blended. Pour into an 8-inch soufflé dish and chill about 2 hours, or until firm. Serve from the same dish. If desired, 1/2 cup of heavy cream may be whipped, sweetened and flavored, and swirled over top of soufflé before serving. Yield: 6 servings.

FRENCH BREAD TIP

This tip is for the hostess who has unhappily watched guests trying to break slices of French bread away from the bottom, uncut crust.

Prepare loaf in the usual manner. After buttering between slices, complete the slicing all the way through the bottom crust, holding the loaf into shape with your hands. Take a long skewer (the kind used for shish-kabobs) and ram it through the middle of the loaf, lengthwise, thus holding the loaf firmly in its original shape. Keep the skewer in the loaf throughout the heating process, and just at serving time, slide the slices off the skewer into a basket or onto a platter.

Cheese Fondue Party

PARTY FOR SIX

Cheese Fondue with French Bread

Kentucky Chef's Salad

Assorted Fresh Fruit

Cookies

Coffee   **Tea**

CHEESE FONDUE WITH FRENCH BREAD

1-1/2 pounds imported Swiss cheese, shredded
4 tablespoons all-purpose flour
3 cups dry white wine
Pinch white pepper

Dash ground nutmeg
2 tablespoons kirsch, brandy, or cognac
Bite-size pieces of French bread (cut so each will have a bit of crust on it)

Dredge cheese with flour. Set wine over low heat on stove. When air bubbles rise to surface (never let wine reach the boiling point) stir with silver fork. Add cheese little by little; keep stirring. Be sure each lot is melted before adding more. Keep stirring until mixture is bubbling lightly. Add seasonings and kirsch to cheese mixture; blend well; and pour into warmed fondue pot. Keep heat under pot very low; do not let fondue boil. Spear bread on fondue fork, securing points of fork in crust. Dunk with a stirring motion. Stir the fondue occasionally as you dunk. Yield: 6 to 8 servings.

KENTUCKY CHEF'S SALAD

1/2 head iceberg lettuce, shredded
3 heads Bibb lettuce (or about 1/2 head Boston lettuce)
About 1/2 cup French Dressing*

2 hard-cooked eggs, quartered
2 ripe tomatoes, peeled and quartered
3/4 cup julienne strips baked chicken
5 slices cooked crisp bacon, crumbled

Shred the iceberg lettuce into a large bowl and separate leaves of the Bibb lettuce. Toss with half the dressing until all greens are coated. Arrange egg quarters and tomato quarters around bowl and mound chicken in center. Sprinkle bacon over chicken, then dribble remaining dressing over all. Yield: 6 servings.

*See Index for French Dressing recipe.

Dessert Fondue Party

PARTY FOR SIX

Chocolate Sauce

Buttermilk Pound Cake   **Marshmallows**

Canned Pineapple Chunks   **Maraschino Cherries with Stems**

Canned Mandarin Orange Sections

Banana Chunks   **Other Fresh Fruit**

Coffee   **Tea**

BASIC CHOCOLATE FONDUE

2 (6-ounce) packages semi-sweet
  chocolate bits
1 cup light corn syrup

2 teaspoons vanilla extract
Dash salt

Combine ingredients over hot (not boiling) water; stir until chocolate melts and mixture is smooth. Mixture may now be transferred to chafing dish or fondue pot and kept warm for dipping marshmallows (on wooden picks), drained canned pineapple cubes, drained canned mandarin orange sections, banana chunks, fresh apple slices, cake squares, or dried fruit. Yield: about 2-1/2 cups.

DOUBLE CHOCOLATE FONDUE

1 (8 squares) package semi-
  sweet chocolate
1 (4-ounce) package sweet cooking
  chocolate, broken into pieces

3/4 cup milk
1/4 cup sugar
Dash ground cinnamon

Combine ingredients in top of double boiler. Place over warm water and stir until sauce is completely smooth. Pour into fondue pot or chafing dish. Keep warm while serving. If heated longer than 30 minutes, add additional milk for a proper consistency. Yield: about 2 cups.

BRANDIED CHOCOLATE FONDUE

2 (6-ounce) packages semi-sweet chocolate bits
2 tablespoons water
4 tablespoons heavy cream

4 tablespoons brandy
3 teaspoons instant coffee powder
Dash ground cinnamon

Combine chocolate bits and water in top of double boiler. Stir, over heat, until chocolate melts and mixture is smooth. Add remaining ingredients, stir until well blended and transfer to chafing dish or fondue pot. Keep warm while serving. Yield: about 2 cups.

BUTTERMILK POUND CAKE

1/2 cup butter (no substitute)
1/2 cup vegetable shortening
3 cups sugar
5 whole eggs
2 teaspoons vanilla extract

3 cups all-purpose flour
1/2 teaspoon salt
1 cup buttermilk
1/2 teaspoon soda
1 tablespoon boiling water

Cream butter, shortening, and sugar thoroughly in large bowl of electric mixer. Add eggs one at a time, beating well after each addition. Beat in vanilla. Combine flour with salt and add alternately with buttermilk, beginning and ending with flour. Dissolve soda in boiling water and beat into mixture. Pour into a greased and lightly floured tubepan and bake at 300° for about 1-1/2 hours, testing for doneness after 1-1/4 hours. Let rest 5 or 10 minutes before turning out.

To use small squares for dipping in chocolate sauce for fondue party, bake the cake in two 8-inch square pans at 325° for about 40 minutes. Cut in 1-inch cubes.

Dinners with A Foreign Flavor

For your next party, depart from the everyday and seek the pleasures of another land. A party featuring a foreign dinner adds adventure to an evening — new discoveries for some, for others, renewed delight in foods well liked but less frequently eaten.

The dinner becomes the entertainment, with each dish promising a different excitement. An ingenious hostess plays all possibilities to the fullest. To increase anticipation, she may send out invitations to correspond with the dinner, decorate the house and table in the same motif, and, if possible, offer as place cards a token remembrance from the country she has re-created.

This culinary sampling is but another rapprochement in a time when travel and cultural exchange diminish the distances between nations.

French Dinner

DINNER FOR SIX

Dry Red Dinner Wine

Chaussons au Champignons

Consommé Rouge

Steak au Poivre

Baked Fresh Asparagus

Parsley New Potatoes   or

Sautéed Green Beans

Salad Normande

Crusty French Bread   **Sweet Butter**

Strawberry Soufflé

Demitasse

CHAUSSONS AU CHAMPIGNONS
(Mushroom Pastries)

1/4 cup butter (no substitute)	1-1/2 tablespoons minced green onions
2 cups chopped fresh mushrooms	Salt and freshly ground pepper to taste
1 (4-1/2-ounce) can deviled ham, or 2/3 cup ground cooked ham	Nutmeg-Butter Pastry

Heat butter and sauté mushrooms until golden. Remove from heat; stir in ham. Add green onions and seasonings until well mixed; check seasonings. Place a heaping teaspoonful of the mushroom mixture into center of pastry circle. Fold over and pinch edges together firmly to seal. Place on lightly greased baking sheet; prick pastries with fork and bake at 425° for about 12 minutes, until golden brown. Serve warm. Yield: 6 servings.

Nutmeg-Butter Pastry

2 cups all-purpose flour	1/8 teaspoon ground nutmeg
1 cup butter	1/4 cup water
1/4 teaspoon salt	

Put flour, butter, salt, and nutmeg into large bowl. Cut in butter with pastry blender until mixture resembles small peas. Gradually add water until dough holds together. Roll out on floured surface to 1/8-inch thickness. Cut into 18 circles about 5 inches in diameter.

CONSOMMÉ ROUGE
(may be prepared ahead of time)

1 medium onion, cut in half and sliced paper-thin
2 small beets, peeled
1 teaspoon salt

1-1/2 teaspoons red wine
1 quart rich chicken stock (skimmed of all fat)

Cook sliced onion in large saucepan in water to cover until onion is soft. Pour off liquid; grate beets into the pot; add salt, wine, and chicken stock. Bring to a boil, reduce heat and simmer uncovered for about 25 minutes. Remove from heat and strain. Yield: 6 servings.

STEAK AU POIVRE
(Pepper Steak with Brandy Sauce)

4 tablespoons mixed black and white whole peppers
6 beef filets, at least 1 inch thick (or similar quality boneless steak)
2 tablespoons peanut oil

1 tablespoon butter (no substitute)
Salt
Sauce
Watercress (for garnish)

Crush peppercorns by grinding coarsely with pepper grinder. Press the pepper on both sides of meat with your hands. Cover with waxed paper and let stand from 1 to 3 hours, refrigerated.

Put oil and butter in heavy skillet (or two skillets if required) until butter foam begins to subside. Sauté steak on one side for 3 to 4 minutes; turn steak and sauté other side 3 to 4 minutes. This should yield a medium-rare steak; the most reliable test for medium-rare steak is to watch for the oozing of a little red juice on the surface of the meat. If you have any doubts, make a tiny incision into the meat to determine if it is too rare for your taste. Remove to a heated platter, season with salt, and keep warm while you complete the Sauce.

Sauce

2 tablespoons butter (no substitute)
4 tablespoons minced shallots or green onions
1 cup rich beef broth or canned beef bouillon

1/3 cup cognac
3 to 4 tablespoons softened butter

Pour fat from skillet; add 2 tablespoons butter and shallots or green onions; sauté gently for a minute. Add beef bouillon and boil down quickly over high heat while stirring and scraping up the brown bits from the skillet. Add cognac and boil rapidly for a minute or two more (this is to evaporate the alcohol). Remove from heat, swirl in the softened butter a half tablespoon at a time. Pour over steak and garnish platter with clusters of fresh watercress. Yield: 6 servings.

PARSLEY NEW POTATOES

2 dozen small new potatoes of
   uniform size

1/2 cup butter, melted (no substitute)
1/3 cup minced fresh parsley

Boil potatoes until done, peel and roll in melted butter, then in parsley.
Yield: 6 to 8 servings.

BAKED FRESH ASPARAGUS

2 pounds fresh asparagus
3 tablespoons minced fresh parsley
2 tablespoons olive oil

2 tablespoons melted butter (no substitute)
Salt and pepper to taste

Wash, drain, and break off tough white ends of asparagus spears. Arrange
in one layer in baking pan if possible. Sprinkle with parsley. Combine the oil
and melted butter and drizzle over the asparagus, then add salt and pepper.
Cover baking dish with aluminum foil and bake at 400° for 15 minutes — unless
you must arrange asparagus in two layers. In that case, increase time to 25
minutes. Yield: 6 servings.

Note: This is an excellent way to treat fresh asparagus; it emerges from the
oven tender but slightly firm to the bite — and all the inherent flavor of the
vegetable is intact. — C.M.

SAUTÉED GREEN BEANS

2 pounds fresh small young green
   beans, cut French style; or 2
   (10-ounce) packages frozen French-
   cut green beans
2 cups chicken broth (or bouillon
   cubes and boiling water)
1/2 teaspoon dried chervil

1-1/2 teaspoons salt
1/4 cup butter (no substitute)
1/4 cup sliced almonds
2 teaspoons freshly squeezed
   lemon juice

Put fresh beans, chicken broth, chervil, and salt in a saucepan. Cover and
bring to a boil. Reduce heat and simmer about 15 to 20 minutes, just until beans
are crisp tender. Drain thoroughly.

Heat butter in a large heavy skillet; add almonds and cook over low heat
until golden; stir in beans and lemon juice, mix well and serve as soon as heated
thoroughly. Yield: 6 servings.

Note: If you must use frozen beans, simmer in broth only about 6 to
8 minutes.

SALAD NORMANDE

2 quarts torn salad greens (use a mixture
   of romaine, escarole, head lettuce)
1/3 cup peanut or olive oil
3 tablespoons red wine vinegar

2 teaspoons seasoned salt
1/4 teaspoon tarragon
1 teaspoon chopped shallots

Put crisp greens into large salad bowl. Combine all remaining ingredients in a pint jar. Close lid tightly and shake well to blend. Pour over greens, toss well and serve immediately. Yield: 6 servings.

FRENCH BREAD
(see Index)

STRAWBERRY SOUFFLÉ
(may be prepared ahead of time)

2 envelopes unflavored gelatin	1/2 teaspoon vanilla extract
1-1/2 cups milk	2 cups crushed fresh strawberries
3/4 cup sugar	1/3 cup Grand Marnier
1/2 teaspoon salt	1 tablespoon freshly squeezed
4 eggs, separated	lemon juice
1/2 teaspoon grated orange rind	1/2 pint heavy cream, whipped
1/8 teaspoon ground nutmeg	Fresh Strawberry Sauce

Soften gelatin in milk; put in top of double boiler over hot water and heat until gelatin is dissolved; stir in sugar and salt; cook until hot and steaming. Beat egg yolks lightly, then beat in a little of the hot mixture; beat in a little more until about 2/3 cup has been added; return to double boiler. Add orange rind and nutmeg; cook until mixture thickens slightly, stirring constantly. Remove from heat; stir in vanilla and set aside to cool.

Meanwhile, combine strawberries, Grand Marnier, and lemon juice. When milk mixture is cool, blend in strawberry mixture. Allow to chill until mixture mounds on a spoon. Fold whipped cream into the mixture. Beat egg whites until stiff and gently fold them in until blended. Turn into a 1-1/2-quart soufflé dish with a collar, pushing the mixture gently up the sides. (To make the collar, cut a piece of aluminum foil or heavy paper 3 inches longer than circumference of soufflé dish and 3 inches wider than its height. Grease it well. Fit around outside of soufflé dish, pressing lightly so greased paper will stick to sides of dish. Press overlapping edges together firmly. Tie a string around the top of dish to hold paper collar firmly in place.)

Refrigerate 4 to 6 hours until firm. To serve, remove string; carefully remove paper, gently pulling it from soufflé edge. Serve at the table with Fresh Strawberry Sauce.

Fresh Strawberry Sauce

1/2 cup sweet sherry	1/8 teaspoon ground nutmeg
1/4 cup Grand Marnier	1 quart fresh strawberries
1/2 teaspoon grated orange rind	

Combine sherry, Grand Marnier, orange rind, and nutmeg. Wash and hull strawberries, leaving as many whole as possible. Add to sherry mixture in crystal bowl; chill at least 4 hours. Yield: 6 to 8 servings.

Chinese Dinner

DINNER FOR EIGHT

Wonton Soup

Chinese Barbecued Spareribs

Chinese Roast Pork

Rice

Chicken with Walnuts   **Broccoli with Mushrooms**

Egg Rolls

Hot Mustard Sauce   **Sweet-and-Sour Sauce**

Chinese Almond Cookies

Tea

Note: Recipe for Wonton Soup is included, to be used if practical for a buffet dinner. You might want to serve it as a first course, then invite guests to serve themselves at the buffet.

WONTON SOUP
(may be prepared ahead of time)

Wontons are small squares of noodle dough filled with a meat mixture, cooked in water and served in soup. Allow two to three per person and serve in a flavorful clear chicken soup. The wontons may be made ahead and frozen uncooked, then cooked while still frozen.

1-1/2 cups all-purpose sifted flour	About 3 tablespoons water
1 teaspoon salt	Cornstarch
1 egg	

Sift flour and salt into a bowl. Beat egg with fork, add 3 tablespoons water and add to flour. Work into a dough, adding a little more water if necessary. Turn out on a floured board and knead until smooth, about 5 minutes. Cover with a damp towel; let rest 30 minutes.

Filling

2 teaspoons soy sauce	1/2 pound lean cooked chicken or pork
1/4 teaspoon ground ginger	
1/4 teaspoon salt	8 water chestnuts
Dash pepper	2 green onions

Put chicken or pork, water chestnuts, and green onions in a chopping bowl and chop finely. Mix with rest of ingredients.

Roll out dough as thin as possible on board or cloth sprinkled with cornstarch. Cut into 2-1/2-inch squares. Place a wonton square in front of you with one point facing you. Put a teaspoon of filling on lower half of square; fold top half over, making a triangle. Moisten edges and press together, being sure you do not leave a pocket of air inside. Now cross the right and left points by bringing them together on the opposite side of the fold from the point toward you. Moisten and press together. Set aside on cornstarch-dusted surface.

Bring 3 quarts water to boil in large pot. Add all the wontons. Stir once, gently, so wontons won't stick to bottom. Bring to a boil and continue boiling until all wontons float to surface. Add 1 cup cold water. Bring to boil again. Remove wontons with slotted spoon and place in soup dishes. Pour hot soup over wontons. Yield: 36.

Note: If wontons are preferred as appetizers instead of soup, they may be made according to above directions and fried in deep oil at 375°.

CHINESE BARBECUED SPARERIBS

3 racks small spareribs
1 tablespoon monosodium glutamate
4 tablespoons catsup
4 tablespoons soy sauce
4 cloves garlic, crushed

4 tablespoons Hoisin sauce (optional)
4 tablespoons dry sherry
1 teaspoon powdered ginger
2 tablespoons honey

Cut spareribs into individual ribs and arrange on rack in baking pan. Sprinkle with monosodium glutamate and bake at 300° for 45 minutes.

Combine remaining ingredients and brush the ribs with the mixture. Bake 30 minutes longer and turn ribs; brush with sauce. Bake another 30 minutes or until ribs are browned and crisp, brushing again until all sauce has been used. Ribs may be kept warm in oven turned to its lowest heat. Yield: 8 servings, if other main dishes are served.

Note: I like to remove ribs to paper towels to dry and crisp; the towels may remain underneath while ribs wait in the warm oven. — C. M.

CHINESE-COOKING TIPS

Vegetables: For crispness when using canned bean sprouts, water chestnuts, or bamboo shoots, rinse well in cold water before adding to pan, heat just to serving temperature. Snow peas, a Chinese delicacy, are available fresh or frozen at some markets.

Ginger: To keep fresh ginger; peel, cover with sherry and store, covered, in refrigerator. If fresh ginger is unavailable, substitute 1/4 to 1/2 teaspoon ground ginger for two or three slices fresh ginger.

CHINESE ROAST PORK

This is an adaptation of an ancient Chinese cooking method. The meat is suspended from an oven rack set as high as possible with metal paper clips that have been twisted into "S" shapes. This roasting technique has the advantage of browning all sides of the meat evenly, sealing in juices and flavor.

5 strips boneless lean pork, each about 2 inches thick and 6 inches long, cut from the loin or butt	4 tablespoons canned Hoisin sauce (if unavailable, double the amount of soy sauce)
4 tablespoons granulated sugar	2 teaspoons salt
4 tablespoons dry sherry	2 teaspoons soy sauce
1/2 teaspoon pepper	2 tablespoons dehydrated minced onion
1/2 teaspoon ground ginger	5 large paper clips
1 clove garlic, crushed	

The day before cooking, combine all marinade ingredients in a shallow dish. Place pork strips into it in a single layer, turning them over and over a few times. Cover with foil and refrigerate overnight (or for two nights), turning strips occasionally.

To cook: Place top oven rack in its highest position. Place a double thickness of aluminum foil over a flat pan almost the same size as the oven rack and put it on the lowest rack of the oven. (This is to catch the drippings.)

Twist paper clip into shape of an "S;" push one curved end through end of pork strip, about an inch from the end. Hang other hook of the "S" on top oven rack, thus suspending the pork over the dripping pan. Start roasting meat in cold oven set at 425°. After 15 minutes, reduce heat to 325° and continue roasting about 1-3/4 hours, or until pork is tender.

When meat is done, remove strips from oven to cutting board. Using a sharp knife, cut meat diagonally into 1/8-inch slices. Yield: 8 or more.

Note: The marinade may be cooked down somewhat and used as an accompanying sweet-and-sour sauce if desired.

CHICKEN WITH WALNUTS

1 cup coarsely chopped walnuts	1 cup coarsely chopped celery
1 tablespoon butter or margarine	1 (7-ounce) can water chestnuts, drained and sliced
2 pounds chicken breasts (about 4), boned and cut into 1-inch cubes	3 tablespoons dry sherry
2 tablespoons cornstarch	1 teaspoon brown sugar
1/4 teaspoon salt	3/4 teaspoon ground ginger
5 tablespoons soy sauce	2/3 cup chicken broth
2 egg whites, unbeaten	Hot cooked rice
1/4 cup vegetable oil	
3 or 4 green onions including tops, chopped	

Boil walnuts in water to cover for 3 or 4 minutes; drain on paper towels. Put in shallow pan with butter and roast at 300° for about 15 minutes, shaking pan now and then. Set aside.

Combine 1 tablespoon of the cornstarch with salt, and 1 tablespoon of the soy sauce in a bowl; beat into egg whites with fork. Add chicken and stir until each piece is coated. Heat oil in skillet until quite hot (375°). Add chicken and cook about 10 minutes, or until tender, stirring to cook chicken cubes on all sides. Remove chicken and drain.

Add onions, celery, and water chestnuts to the skillet; cook, stirring constantly, 2 or 3 minutes only; the vegetables must remain crisp.

Combine remaining tablespoon cornstarch, remaining 4 tablespoons soy sauce, sherry, brown sugar, ginger, and chicken broth. Pour over vegetables and heat, stirring, until sauce has thickened. Stir in chicken and 2/3 cup of the walnuts; heat thoroughly and serve over hot rice. Use remaining 1/3 cup walnuts as a garnish. Yield: 5 to 6 servings.

Note: If chicken is prepared in the morning for evening serving, you can make a good broth for use in this recipe by boiling chicken skin and bones with a stalk of celery, an onion, and some seasoning for about 1-1/2 hours.

FRESH BROCCOLI WITH MUSHROOMS

1 bunch fresh broccoli	4 tablespoons salad oil
1/2 pound fresh mushrooms	1-1/2 teaspoons salt

Trim and discard tough ends from broccoli stems, then cut each stalk crosswise into two sections. Pare off tough outer covering from stems (I use a vegetable peeler); cut lower half of stem lengthwise into 1/4-inch strips; then cut rest of stalk, including flowerets, lengthwise into about six or eight strips. Rinse all in cold water.

Rinse mushrooms under cold running water; pat dry with paper towels, then cut into quarters.

Heat oil until very hot in large skillet. Add all the broccoli and mushrooms; sprinkle with salt. Stir-fry until oil coats vegetables. Cover skillet and cook 2 minutes over medium heat. Uncover and cook 3 to 5 minutes, or until broccoli is tender but still crisp, tossing often. Spoon onto heated platter and serve immediately. Yield: 8 servings.

EGG ROLLS

2 eggs	1/2 teaspoon salt
1 cup all-purpose flour, sifted	1 cup water

Beat eggs; stir in flour and salt alternately with the water to make a thin batter. Reserve about a tablespoon of the batter for use later.

Heat 1/2 teaspoon vegetable shortening (not butter) or oil over moderate heat in a small skillet (about 7-inch). Pour in enough batter (about 1-1/2 tablespoons) to make a thin pancake, tilting the skillet to cover the bottom thinly. Cook only on one side for about 1 minute; remove to a warm flat surface. Continue until all batter is used.

Filling

2 tablespoons shredded carrot
2 tablespoons shredded celery
1 tablespoon finely minced green onions
1/2 cup chopped water chestnuts
1/2 cup bean sprouts
1/2 cup ground or minced cooked pork,
    beef, or chicken

1 teaspoon salt
1/2 cup chopped cooked shrimp
    Dash pepper
1/2 teaspoon sugar

Cook carrot and celery in a little boiling water for about 4 minutes, drain, put in bowl to cool. Add all other ingredients and mix well. Put 1 generous tablespoon of filling in center of each cooled pancake (cooked side should be inside of egg roll). Roll pancakes, folding in the ends, seal them with the reserved batter and chill thoroughly.

Fry egg rolls in 2 inches of moderately hot oil (350° to 365°). Cook rolls to a golden brown on one side (about 15 minutes); turn to brown other side. Remove, drain on paper towels, cut in thick slices and serve with Hot Mustard Sauce and Sweet-and-Sour Sauce. Yield: about 18 to 20.

HOT MUSTARD SAUCE

Stir enough water or stale beer into dry mustard to make a thin paste. Allow to stand about 30 minutes before using.

SWEET-AND-SOUR SAUCE

1/2 cup vinegar
1/2 cup water
1/4 cup brown sugar
1/4 cup granulated sugar

1/4 cup cornstarch
1/2 cup pineapple juice (or half lemon
    and half pineapple)

Bring vinegar, water, and sugars to boil. Combine cornstarch and pineapple juice; add to hot mixture and cook until thickened. Yield: 2-1/4 cups.

CHINESE ALMOND COOKIES

1 cup butter or margarine
1 cup sugar
1 egg
1 teaspoon almond extract
2-1/2 cups all-purpose flour

1 teaspoon baking powder
1/2 teaspoon salt
1 tablespoon water
    Whole blanched almonds

Cream butter; gradually add sugar and beat until light and fluffy. Beat in egg and almond extract. Sift dry ingredients together and add alternately with water. Chill for about 2 hours. Form into balls 1 inch in diameter. Place on ungreased baking sheets and press down with bottom of small glass to 1/4-inch thickness. Press almond into center of each. Bake at 350° for 12 to 15 minutes. Remove to wire rack to cool. Yield: about 5 dozen.

Spanish Buffet Dinner

DINNER FOR EIGHT

Sangría

Sopa Rosita

or

Gazpacho

Inland Paella

Espárragos Con Salsa De Anchos

Cuban Water Bread

Amor Frío

or   Gelletas De Almendra

Bizcocho Borracho De Barcelona

Full-Bodied Red Wine

SANGRÍA
(see Index)

SOPA ROSITA
(Saffron Tomato Broth)

1 (46-ounce) can tomato juice
2 cups chicken broth (or bouillon cubes and hot water)
1/4 cup white dinner wine
1 teaspoon scraped onion
1/2 teaspoon dried basil, crushed

1/8 teaspoon ground nutmeg
1/2 clove garlic, crushed
Dash cayenne pepper
Pinch saffron
1 unpeeled lemon, thinly sliced

Combine tomato juice, chicken broth, and wine in a large saucepan. Stir in all other ingredients except lemon. Cover and simmer 25 to 30 minutes. Serve in small soup cups and garnish with lemon slices. Yield: 8 servings.

GAZPACHO
(see Index)

INLAND PAELLA

3 tablespoons olive oil
8 chicken breast halves and 8
  chicken thighs
4 medium onions, chopped
3 cloves garlic, crushed
2 cups uncooked rice
3 or 4 hot smoked link sausages, sliced
5 cups beef or chicken broth

Pinch saffron
Salt and pepper to taste
1 (7-ounce) can minced clams, undrained
1 pound raw shrimp, boiled and cleaned
1/2 (10-ounce) package frozen peas,
  cooked barely tender
1 (4-ounce) jar pimientos, drained

Heat oil in large skillet and brown chicken. Remove to a large, lightly greased casserole and set aside. Add more oil to skillet and sauté onions and garlic until onions are golden and tender. Add rice and sauté until golden. Add to the casserole.

Fry all grease out of the sausage slices; add them to casserole. Pour 4 cups of the bouillon in which saffron has been dissolved over the mixture. Add salt and pepper, cover and bake at 325° until chicken is done, about 1 hour.

During cooking, check to see if rice has absorbed all the bouillon; if it has, add remaining cup; continue adding bouillon if necessary; the rice should be cooked through but not mushy. It should also be yellow!

Just before paella is done, add clams and their juice, and the shrimp. When fully done, sprinkle top of casserole with cooked peas and pimientos cut in strips. Yield: 8 servings.

ESPÁRRAGOS CON SALSA DE ANCHOS
(Asparagus Spears in Anchovy Sauce)

2 (10-ounce) packages frozen
  asparagus tips
2/3 cup olive oil
1/4 cup freshly squeezed lemon juice
1 tablespoon anchovy paste

2 teaspoons seasoned salt
1 teaspoon scraped onion
1/2 clove garlic, crushed
1/2 teaspoon dried chervil
Crisp salad greens

Thaw asparagus; drain and arrange in layers in a deep bowl. Combine oil, lemon juice, anchovy paste, seasoned salt, onion, garlic, and chervil in container of an electric blender. Blend well, until completely mixed (or shake well in a pint jar). Pour over asparagus; cover and let stand 4 to 6 hours. Remove asparagus and arrange on crisp salad greens. Yield: 8 servings.

CUBAN WATER BREAD

Follow directions for making French Bread.* The difference between Cuban Water Bread and French Bread is in the manner of baking. Follow directions given for French Bread up to the point of putting bread in the oven. Then proceed as follows:

When loaves have risen and are almost, but not quite doubled, brush with cold water. Sprinkle with sesame seed if desired. Place in a cold oven. This is important. Set the oven at 400° and bake until bread is nicely browned, about 40 minutes. Brush loaves twice with cold water during last 20 minutes of baking. The loaves should be deliciously crisp.

*See Index for French Bread recipe.

AMOR FRÍO
(Strawberries in Spiced Malaga)

3 pounds fresh strawberries (about 1-1/2 quarts)	Dash ground nutmeg
	Pinch salt
1 cup sifted powdered sugar	1 pint whipping cream
1 cup Malaga wine*	1/4 cup granulated sugar
1 teaspoon grated lemon rind	Chopped crystallized ginger (optional)

Wash, hull, and halve strawberries. Sprinkle with powdered sugar. Combine Malaga wine, lemon rind, nutmeg, and salt. Pour slowly over berries and chill. Whip cream with 1/4 cup sugar until stiff. To serve, spoon berries into chilled sherbet glasses; top with sweetened whipped cream and sprinkle with chopped ginger. Yield: 8 servings.

*Any sweet dessert wine may be substituted.

BIZCOCHO BORRACHO DE BARCELONA
(Barcelona Drunken Sponge)

4 eggs, separated	3 tablespoons melted butter
3/4 cup granulated sugar	1-3/4 cups sifted all-purpose flour
1 tablespoon grated orange rind	1/2 teaspoon baking powder
1/2 cup plus 1 tablespoon freshly squeezed orange juice	1/2 teaspoon ground nutmeg
	1/4 teaspoon salt

Beat egg whites; gradually add 3/4 cup sugar, beating until stiff peaks form. Refrigerate. Beat egg yolks with remaining cup of sugar until light and fluffy. Beat in orange rind and juice, then butter. Sift together flour, baking powder, nutmeg, and salt. Fold into eggs by hand. Now fold beaten egg whites into batter. Turn into ungreased 9-inch tubepan and bake at 325° for 1 hour, or until cake tests done. Hang upside down to cool. Turn out onto serving plate. Carefully pour Brandy Sauce over top and allow to stand 2 to 3 hours. To serve, spread Nutmeg Whipped Cream over top and garnish with Sugar-Frosted Grapes.

Brandy Sauce

Boil 1/4 cup sugar and 1/4 cup water together for 6 minutes. Cool slightly; stir in 1/4 cup brandy. Pour over cake at once.

Nutmeg Whipped Cream

Whip 1/2 pint heavy cream with 1/2 teaspoon ground nutmeg and 1/4 cup sugar.

Sugar-Frosted Grapes

Dip small clusters of white grapes in water; shake well and dip into a bowl of granulated sugar. Set aside on a cookie sheet covered with waxed paper until dry.

GELLETAS DE ALMENDRA
(Almond Crackers)

1/2 cup blanched almonds	1/2 teaspoon grated lemon rind
3 egg whites	1/2 teaspoon cream of tartar
1 cup superfine sugar (very finely granulated)	1/2 teaspoon almond extract
	1/4 teaspoon salt

Grind almonds; place in ungreased pieplate and toast in a 300° oven for about 20 minutes, until golden. Cool.

Beat egg whites until very stiff peaks form. Slowly beat in sugar, lemon rind, and cream of tartar, being sure sugar is dissolved after each addition. Beat in almond extract and salt. Carefully fold in almonds; drop by teaspoonfuls onto a brown paper-lined baking sheet. Bake at 300° for 25 to 30 minutes, or until the cookies are barely golden. Remove at once to racks to cool. Yield: about 3 dozen cookies.

SANGRÍA

Spain's national beverage — Sangría — comes in for wide variations, with one region championing light dry wine poured over fresh fruit, another a full-bodied red wine; while some insist the only authentic Sangría is a blend of light red wine, cognac, and club soda poured over fresh peaches, strawberries, orange and lemon slices. Still others humph that the genuine Sangria must be flavored with spices (a cinnamon stick, usually), sweetened with sugar syrup and poured over sugared berries.

To which we say "to each his own'" — and suggest our favorite version of Sangría, which appears ritually at five o'clock throughout Spain, the version depending on where you are at the time, the refreshing beverage sipped until dinner time, and sometimes throughout.

Mexican Dinner

DINNER FOR EIGHT

Enchiladas	Tacos
Refried Beans	Guacamole Salad

Hot Tortillas

Flan

Coffee	Tea

ENCHILADAS
Enchilada Filling
(prepare ahead of time)

1-1/2 pounds coarsely ground beef
1 clove garlic, minced
1 medium onion, minced
2 tablespoons shortening

1/4 to 1/2 cup tomato puree
2 to 3 tablespoons chili powder
3/4 teaspoon salt
2-1/2 cups water

Cook beef, garlic, and onion in hot shortening until meat is white. Add tomato puree, chili powder, salt, and water and cook until almost all water has cooked out.

Enchilada Sauce
(prepare the day before)

1 large onion, minced
1 clove garlic, minced
3 tablespoons salad oil
3 cups tomato puree

4 to 6 tablespoons chili powder
1 teaspoon oregano
1 teaspoon cumin
1 teaspoon salt

Sauté onion and garlic in salad oil until yellow. Add tomato puree, chili powder, oregano, cumin, and salt. Cover and simmer for 30 minutes, stirring frequently. Strain through a sieve. Yield: about 4 cups.

To Make Enchiladas

16 tortillas
  Hot shortening
  Enchilada Sauce

Filling
2 cups shredded sharp Cheddar cheese

Use tongs to dip tortillas in medium-hot salad oil; fry just a few minutes or they will get crisp; cook only until they are limp. Dip tortilla in Enchilada Sauce and lay on flat surface. Fill with Enchilada Filling, and roll tortilla over filling. Place (with flap down) in a baking pan. Continue until all tortillas have been filled. Pour remaining Enchilada Sauce over rolled tortillas. Sprinkle shredded cheese over top and bake at 350° for 15 to 20 minutes or until done. Yield: 8 servings.

Note: Some people prefer to fill tortillas with chopped onion, cover with Enchilada Filling or homemade chili and shredded cheese and then bake.

TACOS

1 pound ground beef
1 medium onion, chopped
1 teaspoon ground cumin seed
1 teaspoon salt
1/2 teaspoon garlic powder
6 drops Tabasco sauce

1-1/2 cups cooked tomatoes, mashed
12 cornmeal tortillas
  Hot shortening
1 to 1-1/2 cups shredded
  Cheddar cheese
1-1/2 cups shredded lettuce

Lightly brown ground beef with onion. Drain fat from meat if necessary. Add cumin, salt, garlic powder, Tabasco, and tomatoes. Simmer, uncovered, about 30 minutes, stirring occasionally.

Place each tortilla in deep hot shortening, fold over quickly with tongs to form a taco shell. Fry until crisp. Watch carefully to make sure that they do not become too crisp or they will break. Drain on absorbent paper towels. Just before serving, fill each taco shell with hot meat filling, topped with cheese and shredded lettuce. Serve at once. Yield: 8 to 10 servings.

REFRIED BEANS

2 cups pinto beans
5 to 6 cups water

2 to 3 tablespoons shortening
  Salt to taste

Soak the beans overnight in water. The next morning, drain and add 5 cups water to the large saucepan in which you will cook beans. Bring to a boil and simmer until beans are tender, adding 1 extra cup of water if necessary.

Drain soft beans, reserving 1 cup of the liquid. Mash beans with a potato masher or put through a food mill. Heat shortening in heavy skillet and add the mashed beans. Add about 1/4 cup reserved liquid and stir beans as they cook. Do not add too much liquid for beans should not be soupy. Add salt to taste. Serve hot. Yield: 8 servings.

GUACAMOLE SALAD

2 large avocados
1 large tomato
1/4 cup chopped onion

1 tablespoon vinegar
Salt and pepper
Shredded lettuce

Peel and pit avocado. Put avocado, peeled tomato, and onion in blender and blend until smooth (or put through a food mill). Add vinegar, salt, and pepper, and mix until well blended. Serve as a topping for shredded lettuce. Yield: 8 servings.

FLAN
(Mexican Pudding)

1-3/4 cups sugar
8 eggs

2 (14-ounce) can evaporated milk
2 teaspoons vanilla extract

Put 1 cup sugar in heavy skillet and place over heat, stirring constantly, until sugar melts and turns golden. Pour immediately into eight custard cups. (This is difficult and must be done very quickly). Cool. Beat eggs, add milk, remaining 3/4 cup sugar, and vanilla. Mix well, then strain into custard cups. Place cups in a pan of hot water and bake at 325° for 45 minutes to 1 hour, or until knife inserted in center of custard comes out clear. When ready to serve, turn out on serving dish so caramelized sugar is on top. Flan should be thoroughly chilled before serving. Yield: 8 servings.

TORTILLAS

Tortillas are round, flat patties made from a corn mixture called masa. Dried corn is cooked in a lime solution until the husks can be rubbed off, then ground while still moist. Patties are then shaped by hand (the Mexican way) or by machine (the commercial way) and cooked on an ungreased griddle until dry and have slight freckle-colored spots. There are also tortillas made with wheat flour.

In some sections tortillas can be bought in sealed plastic bags or in cans. Because of their popularity, you should be able to find them in one of these forms. To serve tortillas as a bread, place a clean, thin dish towel in the bottom of a steam kettle (on a rack, of course) and steam them until warm, but not soggy. Wrap carefully and serve hot. To eat, spread lightly with butter, sprinkle with salt, and roll like a jellyroll, tucking in the bottom end to keep the butter from dripping.

Italian Dinner

DINNER FOR EIGHT

Chicken Cannelloni

Veal à la Marsala

Eggplant Salvia

Green Salad with Italian Dressing

Garlic French Bread   **Butter**

Fresh Fruit

or

Pears Zabaglione

Espresso

A dry wine would be suitable for this menu; white seems preferable, but choice to be made by the host.

CHICKEN CANNELLONI

1 (4- to 4-1/2-pound) hen	2 cups chicken broth
Salt	1 carrot, sliced
Pepper	1 stalk celery, sliced
Poultry seasoning	1/2 medium onion, coarsely chopped

Season hen inside and out with salt, pepper, and poultry seasoning. Place in deep heavy pot; add 2 cups chicken broth (made with chicken bouillon cubes and boiling water), sliced carrot, sliced celery, and chopped onion. Cover and simmer until chicken is tender, about 2 hours. Let cool in broth, then remove chicken and strain broth; set it aside. Remove and discard skin and bones of chicken. (This may be done the day before cooking the Cannelloni.)

Dough
(may be prepared the day before)

2 cups all-purpose flour, sifted	1-1/2 tablespoons water
2 large eggs	3/4 teaspoon salt

Place flour on pastry board, make a hole in the center and put the eggs, water, and salt in it. Beat eggs with fork, slowly mixing in half the flour. Mix in rest of flour by hand, then knead until dough is smooth and elastic, about 10 minutes. Cut dough in half and roll each piece on floured board until paper-thin. Cut into 4-inch squares. Cook six squares at a time for 5 minutes in 4 quarts of boiling salted water. Remove with slotted spoon one at a time and rinse immediately under running cold water. Arrange on a damp towel spread on a flat surface. Continue until all squares are cooked. Yield: about 2 dozen.

Mushroom Sauce
(may be prepared the day before)

1/2 cup butter (no substitute)
4 tablespoons chopped green onions
1/2 pound fresh mushrooms, finely chopped
8 tablespoons all-purpose flour
1-1/2 cups milk

1-1/2 cups chicken broth reserved from cooking chicken
2 cups heavy cream
2 cups grated Swiss and Parmesan cheese, mixed
Salt and pepper

Heat butter in heavy skillet; add green onions, and sauté a few minutes, stirring all the while. Add mushrooms and continue cooking until almost dry. Stir in flour, then gradually add milk and broth, stirring vigorously until smooth. Add cream and cook until thickened. Remove from heat; stir in cheese, salt, and pepper.

Filling
(may be prepared the day before)

Cooked meat of a 4- to 4-1/2-pound chicken
4 slices cooked ham, with fat removed (Italian prosciutto, preferably)

1/2 teaspoon ground nutmeg
1/2 cup finely chopped parsley
1 cup Mushroom Sauce

Grind chicken and ham using finest blade of food grinder; add nutmeg and parsley, then Mushroom Sauce. The mixture should be moist though not runny; add more sauce if needed. Check seasonings.

To Assemble the Dish

This must be done the day of serving. You will need about 1/2 cup grated Parmesan cheese. Spoon about 2 tablespoons of the Filling on each Cannelloni square along bottom edge, then roll as tightly as possible, leaving ends open.

Spoon about one-third of the sauce into bottom of baking dish; arrange filled Cannelloni in the dish in single layer and cover with remaining sauce. Sprinkle with Parmesan cheese; bake at 350° for about 30 minutes, or until golden brown. Yield: 8 servings.

GREEN SALAD WITH ITALIAN DRESSING
(see Index)

GARLIC FRENCH BREAD
(see Index)

VEAL `A LA MARSALA

2 pounds veal scallops
2/3 cup all-purpose flour
2/3 cup butter (no substitute)

1/2 cup dry Marsala
Salt and pepper to taste

If very thin scallops are not available, pound veal cutlets with edge of saucer until very thin, being careful not to tear the meat. Dip in flour and sauté in butter in a large heavy skillet, 2 or 3 minutes on each side. Sprinkle with salt and pepper; add Marsala and simmer 2 minutes more. Yield: 8 servings.

Note: If skillet will not accommodate all the scallops, remove to heated platter after sautéing until all meat has been cooked, then return all to skillet to simmer in the wine for the final 2 minutes before serving.

EGGPLANT SALVIA

2 small eggplants, peeled
2 medium onions
2 large ripe tomatoes, peeled

Salt, pepper, and ground sage
3 tablespoons freshly squeezed lemon juice
3 tablespoons olive oil

Slice eggplants, tomatoes, and onions into very thin slices, no thicker than 1/8 inch. Arrange in layers in a greased casserole, first the eggplants, then onions, then tomatoes, lightly seasoning with salt, pepper, and sage between each layer of eggplants and tomatoes. Repeat layering until all is used. Tomatoes should be on top. Combine lemon juice and oil and drizzle slowly over top. The dressing will penetrate even though it appears scanty. Bake uncovered at 350° until vegetables are done, about 40 to 50 minutes, basting occasionally with juices that form in the dish. Yield: 8 servings.

PEARS ZABAGLIONE

2 (29-ounce) cans pear halves
Grated rind and juice of 1 lemon

Grated rind and juice of 1 orange
1/2 cup brandy

Drain pears, pouring juice of 1 can into saucepan. Add to saucepan orange and lemon rinds and juice, bring to a boil and simmer, covered, for about 15 minutes. Now add drained pear halves to the saucepan and heat, spooning juice over fruit until heated throughout. Turn into shallow crystal bowl, pour brandy over fruit and bring to the table flaming. Serve with Zabaglione.

Zabaglione

8 egg yolks
1/8 teaspoon salt
1 cup sugar
Juice of 1/2 lemon

1 cup cream (sweet) sherry
2 teaspoons brandy
1 cup heavy cream, whipped

Beat egg yolks, salt, sugar, and lemon juice until light. Cook in top of double boiler over hot water, stirring constantly until thick. Gradually add sherry and brandy; cool, then fold in whipped cream. Yield: 6 to 8 servings.

Hawaiian Luau

LUAU FOR TWELVE

Hawaiian Cocktails

Shrimp and Vegetable Tempura

Shoyu Sauce   Apricot Sauce Honi

Chicken with Peanuts and Rice

Hawaiian Spinach Salad

Hawaiian Lemon Bread

Tropical Sundae

or

Fresh Coconut Cake

Hawaiian Party Punch

If you plan a luau for more than 12 guests, the menu may be expanded by the addition of Crisp Wonton and Almond-Sweet Potato Puffs.

HAWAIIAN COCKTAILS
(see Index)

SHRIMP TEMPURA

3 to 4 pounds large raw shrimp in the shell
1 cup cornstarch
1 cup all-purpose flour
1 teaspoon salt
1/2 teaspoon monosodium glutamate

2 eggs
1 cup water
  Vegetable oil
  Shoyu Sauce
  Apricot Sauce Honi

Shell and clean shrimp, leaving tails on. Split shrimp down back, cutting almost through. Open to butterfly shape.

Combine cornstarch, flour, salt, and monosodium glutamate in a bowl; add eggs and water and beat just until smooth — but do not overbeat. Using a deep-fat thermometer, heat oil to 375° in a deep saucepan or electric skillet. Holding shrimp by tail, dip in batter and drop gently, a few at a time, into the hot oil. When shrimp rise to surface, turn and cook until golden brown. Serve with sauces. Yield: 12 servings.

SHOYU SAUCE

1/8 teaspoon ground ginger	3/4 cup water
1/3 cup soy sauce	2 tablespoons dry sherry
1/2 teaspoon sugar	Pinch monosodium glutamate

Combine all ingredients in a bowl. Heat to lukewarm. Yield: 1-1/4 cups.

APRICOT SAUCE HONI
(Apricot Kiss Sauce)
(may be prepared ahead of time)

1/4 pound dried apricots	1/2 cup rum (optional)
1 cup water	1/3 cup vinegar
1/4 teaspoon salt	2 tablespoons honey
1/4 cup sugar	1 teaspoon paprika

Cook apricots in water in covered saucepan until soft, about 30 minutes. Most of the water should be absorbed; if not, drain. Puree apricots in electric blender or put through a fine sieve; add remaining ingredients and beat until smooth. Sauce will keep for months if properly refrigerated. Yield: about 1 pint.

VEGETABLE TEMPURA

Clean and cut 3 to 4 pounds of fresh vegetables into 2-inch lengths. Use green beans, eggplant, carrots, parsley clusters, yellow squash, asparagus, or any other fresh vegetable. If eggplant is used, peel, cut in half lengthwise, then into 1/4-inch thick strips. Use the same batter as for Shrimp Tempura and follow the same directions for cooking.

Note: In Hawaii, sauces are served in individual bowls, two small bowls for each diner. Bowls of freshly grated radishes (daikon), freshly grated horseradish, and freshly grated ginger root are provided. Each diner stirs as much of each of the three condiments as he chooses into his bowl of Shoyu Sauce. The hot tempura is dipped into his own sauce-condiment mixture, then eaten.

CHICKEN WITH PEANUTS AND RICE

4-1/2 tablespoons oil	1/2 teaspoon red hot pepper, dried or fresh
6 cups uncooked white meat of chicken, diced	4 tablespoons soy sauce
2 cloves garlic	1-1/2 cups chicken broth
1-1/2 cups shelled, roasted, unsalted peanuts	1 tablespoon cornstarch mixed with 3 tablespoons water
3 tablespoons scallions or green onions, chopped	1/2 teaspoon sugar
	3 tablespoons sherry
	Hot cooked rice

Heat 2 tablespoons of the oil in skillet. Add chicken and sauté for about 5 minutes, stirring constantly. Remove chicken and set aside.

Add remaining oil to pan with garlic into which wooden picks have been inserted (for easy removal later). Cook until garlic begins to brown, then discard it. Add peanuts, scallions, red pepper, partially cooked chicken, and soy sauce. Cook for 2 more minutes, stirring frequently. Stir in chicken broth and when it comes to a boil, add cornstarch paste and sherry. Cover and simmer for a few more minutes until sauce thickens. Serve with hot, fluffy rice. Yield: 12 servings.

Note: To prepare ahead, dice chicken in the morning, make broth (of neck, wings, etc.) and measure out ingredients. In the afternoon, cook chicken with scallions, red pepper, and soy sauce. Omit peanuts. Add chicken broth, set aside and cool. Before serving, bring chicken to a boil, add peanuts, cornstarch paste, sugar, and sherry. Cover and simmer until sauce thickens.

HAWAIIAN SPINACH SALAD

2 to 3 pounds fresh spinach	3 tablespoons vinegar
3 tablespoons soy sauce	1/2 teaspoon monosodium glutamate
3 tablespoons sesame oil	1 small clove garlic, minced
1-1/2 teaspoons sugar	3 tablespoons toasted sesame seed

Wash and dry spinach thoroughly. Remove tough stems and tear into 1-1/2-inch pieces. Chill until serving time. Combine rest of ingredients except sesame seed (but have them ready). Just before serving, toss spinach in large bowl with dressing and sprinkle with sesame seed. Yield: 12 servings.

Note: To toast sesame seed, place in shallow pan in 275° oven for about 20 to 25 minutes, until they give off a delightful nutty fragrance.

HAWAIIAN LEMON BREAD

1/4 cup butter or margarine	1 teaspoon salt
3/4 cup sugar	3/4 cup milk
2 eggs, beaten lightly	1/2 cup chopped walnuts
3 teaspoons grated lemon rind (about 1 lemon)	1 tablespoon freshly squeezed lemon juice
2 cups all-purpose flour, sifted	2 tablespoons sugar
2-1/2 teaspoons baking powder	

Cream together butter and 3/4 cup sugar until light and fluffy in large bowl of electric mixer. Add eggs and lemon rind; beat well. Sift together flour, baking powder, and salt; add to creamed mixture alternately with milk, beginning and ending with dry ingredients. Stir in walnuts by hand. Pour into greased 8-1/2- x 4-1/2- x 3-inch loafpan; spread batter toward sides of pan to prevent "humping" in center as bread rises. Bake at 350° (325° for glass pan) for 55 minutes to 1 hour, until bread tests done.

Combine lemon juice and 2 tablespoons sugar and spoon over hot bread immediately after removing from oven.

Note: This is an excellent cake-type bread for making dainty tea sandwiches. I like a filling of cream cheese beaten with honey and lemon juice, to taste. — C.M.

TROPICAL SUNDAE
(see Index)

FRESH COCONUT CAKE

1 large coconut (no substitute)	2 teaspoons baking powder
1/2 cup butter (no substitute)	2 eggs, separated
1 cup sugar	1/2 cup milk
1-1/2 cups all-purpose flour	1 teaspoon vanilla extract

Crack 1 large coconut, reserve the milk and grate the meat. Set aside. Cream butter and sugar thoroughly in large bowl of electric mixer. While mixture beats, sift flour and baking powder together three times. Add egg yolks to butter-sugar mixture; beat well, then alternately add sifted dry ingredients and milk, beginning and ending with dry ingredients. Beat in vanilla. Beat egg whites until stiff; vigorously stir a heaping tablespoon of this into the batter, then carefully fold in the remainder. Pour into large greased pan (at least 13- x 9- x 2 inches) and bake at 350° for about 30 minutes, or until cake tests done.

Frosting

1 cup sugar	1 egg white
Coconut milk	Grated coconut

In small saucepan, cook 1 cup sugar with reserved coconut milk until mixture spins a good thread. Pour into stiffly beaten egg white. Beat vigorously with wooden spoon and when mixture thickens, fold in about one-third of the grated coconut. Continue beating a few minutes, pour over cake, then quickly pat on remaining coconut. (The Frosting remains moist but the coconut holds it in place.) Cool and cut into small squares.

HAWAIIAN PARTY PUNCH

Juice of 6 lemons	Fifth of bourbon, vodka, or gin
24 ounces pineapple juice	1 (28-ounce) bottle club soda
4 teaspoons sugar	

Combine lemon juice, pineapple juice, sugar, and liquor. Just before serving, pour in the club soda. Punch may be served in hollowed-out watermelon or punch bowl. Yield: 25 (punch-cup) servings.

Note: If preferred, this punch may be poured over two ice cubes in punch cups, then garnished with a pineapple stick.

It is the spirit of the entertaining that assures the success of a luau. See page 279 for menu and recipes.

ALMOND-SWEET POTATO PUFFS

3 cups mashed cooked sweet potatoes
3 tablespoons melted butter
   or margarine
5 tablespoons orange marmalade

1 large egg or 2 small eggs
1/2 teaspoon salt
2/3 cup chopped almonds

Combine mashed potatoes with melted butter, marmalade, egg, and salt in mixing bowl. Beat until smooth; chill. Spread almonds on sheet of waxed paper; drop potato mixture by heaping tablespoonfuls onto almonds; roll to coat on all sides. Shape into 2-inch balls and place in greased shallow baking dish. Bake at 400° for about 15 minutes or until hot. Place a dollop of butter and a sprig of parsley, if you wish, on each puff before serving. Yield: about 12.

CRISP WONTON
(see Index)

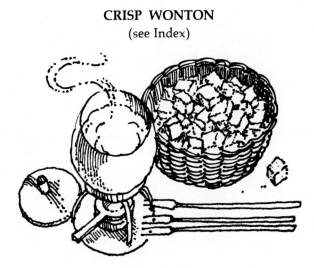

THE LUAU

Luau has two meanings. It is not only a feast but also the leaf of taro, a plant that contributes poi, a staple of the Hawaiian diet. Hence, many of the dishes included in an authentic Hawaiian luau (the feast) are made with luau (the leaf).

A traditional luau prepared in Hawaii would include a whole pig roasted in an "imu" or underground oven. Special imu stones, smooth and porous, sometimes kept within a family for generations, were heated and placed in the cavity of the pig. Then the pig was lowered into a pit heated with hot stones and lined with banana and ti leaves. Bananas, breadfruit, sweet potatoes, and other foods were buried with the pig and the whole steamed under a blanket of ti leaves and warm earth.

Whether one follows tradition rigidly or loosely, the luau as a social event has become so popular in Hawaii's 49 sister states that many versions have been adopted, according to available products. They all reflect the diversity of the real Hawaii — and to that degree they are authentic!

German Dinner

DINNER FOR EIGHT

Kartoffelsuppe

Wiener Schnitzel

Sauerkraut Mit Weissweine　　　　　　　**Grüne Bohnen**

Gurkensalat Mit Sauer Sahne

Commercial Rye Bread　　　　　　　**Butter**

Full-Bodied Rhine Wine

Mandeltorte

Coffee

In Germany this menu might be expanded — though it hardly requires it! — by the addition of Rollmops (rolled herring filets) as an appetizer, and browned new potatoes.

KARTOFFELSUPPE
(Bavarian Potato Soup)

1/2 cup butter	2 to 3 quarts chicken broth
1 carrot, diced	4 cups diced raw potatoes
1 leek, diced (optional)	Salt and white pepper to taste
4 medium onions, diced	Dash ground nutmeg
1/2 cup diced celery	Bouquet garni
2 cloves garlic, minced	1 cup light cream or evaporated milk
2 bay leaves	

Melt butter in heavy soup kettle; add carrot, leek, onions, celery, and garlic. Sauté about 5 minutes; do not allow vegetables to brown. Add bay leaves and chicken broth; simmer 10 to 15 minutes partially covered. Add potatoes, salt, pepper, nutmeg, and bouquet garni. Cover and simmer until potatoes are tender. Just before serving, remove bouquet garni and stir in milk or cream. Yield: 8 to 10 servings.

BOUGUET GARNI

A small cheesecloth bag containing 1 large bay leaf, 1/4 teaspoon leaf thyme, 1/4 teaspoon dried basil, about 8 sprigs fresh parsley, 1/4 teaspoon dried tarragon, 3 chopped green celery tops, 6 whole peppercorns, and a slashed clove of garlic.

WIENER SCHNITZEL
(Sautéed Veal Cutlets)

8 (6-ounce) boneless veal cutlets
All-purpose flour
2 eggs, well beaten
1-1/2 teaspoons salt
1/2 cup milk
1/2 cup dry white wine
1 teaspoon minced parsley

1/2 teaspoon freshly ground
black pepper
3/4 cup unsalted butter
1/4 cup freshly squeezd lemon juice
Minced parsley
8 lemon wedges

Pound veal cutlets with a wooden mallet or the edge of a saucer until very thin. Sprinkle lightly with flour and pound the flour into cutlets.

Combine eggs, salt, milk, wine, the teaspoon of parsley, and pepper. Dip cutlets into egg mixture, coating well. Heat 1/2 cup butter in large skillet and sauté cutlets until golden. Remove to a heated serving platter. Melt remaining butter in pan; stir in lemon juice until just blended. Pour over cutlets and garnish with parsley and lemon wedges. Yield: 8 servings.

SAUERKRAUT MIT WEISWEINE
(Sauerkraut in White Wine)

2 pounds sauerkraut, 2 (1-pound) cans
may be used
2 cups dry white wine
2 teaspoons seasoned salt
1 teaspoon caraway seed

5 whole allspice
1/4 cup butter
Commercial sour cream
1/2 cup crisp cooked bacon, crumbled

Drain sauerkraut well; combine with wine, seasoned salt, caraway seed, allspice, and butter. Cover and simmer 20 minutes to blend flavors. To serve, top with sour cream and crisp bacon bits. Yield: 8 servings.

GRÜNE BOHNEN
(Savory Green Beans)

2 pounds fresh or frozen green beans
1/4 teaspoon ground nutmeg
3 cups chicken broth (bouillon cubes
and hot water)
2 tablespoons butter
1-1/2 teaspoons all-purpose flour

1 tablespoon white wine vinegar
1/2 teaspoon dried summer savory
1 teaspoon minced parsley
1/2 teaspoon sugar
1-1/4 teaspoons salt

Clean fresh beans well; cut into bite-size pieces. Put in large saucepan with nutmeg, chicken broth, and butter. Cover and simmer for 20 minutes, or until crisp-tender. Blend flour into vinegar; add to beans along with savory, parsley, sugar, and salt. Cook, stirring constantly, until mixture thickens and boils. Remove from heat; cover and let sit about 5 minutes before serving. Yield: 8 servings.

A typical German dinner includes Kartoffelsuppe, Sauerkraut Mit Weissweine, Grüne Bohnen, Gurkensalat Mit Sauer Sahne, and Mandeltorte.

GURKENSALAT MIT SAUER SAHNE
(Sliced Cucumbers in Sour Cream)

5 large firm cucumbers	1/4 cup wine vinegar
2 tablespoons salt	1 teaspoon freshly ground black pepper
2 cups commercial sour cream	2 teaspoons minced chives

Wash and trim cucumbers and peel completely. Slice thinly; place in a china bowl; sprinkle with salt and let stand 30 minutes. Then add other ingredients and mix well. Cover and let stand at least an hour or possibly longer (the longer they sit the better they are) in refrigerator. Yield: 8 servings.

MANDELTORTE
(Almond Torte)

1 cup sifted all-purpose flour	5 tablespoons cold water
3/4 cup sugar	1/4 cup salad oil
1-1/2 teaspoons baking powder	1 teaspoon vanilla extract
1/2 teaspoon salt	1/4 teaspoon cream of tartar
1 teaspoon ground cinnamon	1 cup finely chopped toasted almonds
1 teaspoon grated orange rind	Chocolate Fluff Frosting
4 eggs	1/2 cup toasted slivered almonds

Sift together flour, sugar, baking powder, salt, and cinnamon into large bowl. Stir in orange rind. Make a well in the center. Separate eggs, reserving one yolk for frosting. Beat remaining 3 yolks well with water. Add oil, egg yolk mixture, and vanilla to the well in center of dry ingredients; beat by hand until smooth.

Beat all 4 egg whites with cream of tartar until stiff peaks are formed. Stir a big tablespoon of the whites vigorously into the batter, then gently fold in remaining whites. Fold in chopped almonds. Turn into an ungreased 9-inch tubepan and bake at 325° for 50 to 55 minutes, or until cake is golden and tests done. Turn cake upside down on pan legs or hang on a bottle until cool. Remove cake from pan, place on serving plate and frost completely with Chocolate Fluff Frosting. Sprinkle liberally with toasted slivered almonds for garnish. Yield: 10 servings.

Chocolate Fluff Frosting

2 (1-ounce) squares unsweetened baking chocolate	1 tablespoon powdered instant coffee
3 tablespoons unsalted butter	1 teaspoon grated orange rind
1 cup whipping cream	1 teaspoon vanilla extract
1/4 teaspoon salt	1 egg yolk (reserved when baking cake)
	3 cups sifted powdered sugar

Melt chocolate and butter together in top of double boiler over very low heat. Blend in 1/4 cup of the cream, salt, coffee, orange rind, and vanilla. Beat in the egg yolk you reserved from the cake, then sugar. Whip remaining cream until stiff and fold into chocolate mixture.

Traditional Holiday Dinners

Holidays are a time for groaning boards — tables resplendent in arrays of colorful dishes, where relatives and friends gather to share the joys of a season or particular day. Easter marks the promise of springtime; Thanksgiving is a moment to share one's blessings; and the Yule season brings out the cheer and comfort of Christmas and closes with New Year's, a harbinger of happiness to come.

When a holiday is at hand, the day, the mood, the party are all but planned for the lady who loves to entertain and give of herself.

New Year's Dinner

DINNER FOR FIFTEEN

Cassoulet

Mixed Green Salad with Anchovy Dressing

Hot Crusty French Bread   **Butter**

Sugarplum Cake with Brandied Whipped Cream

Coffee   **Tea**

This hearty menu demands a good dry red wine; select one from wine chart.

CASSOULET

It would be heresy to plan a New Year's dinner without including at least a "kissin' cousin" of black-eyed peas and hog jowl. The robust flavor of the following excellent recipe is in the same tradition, though its forebears originated in Western Europe, where many versions of Cassoulet abound.

2 **pounds dried white beans**	1 **teaspoon black pepper**
1 **bay leaf**	1 **medium onion, stuck with 3 whole cloves**
1 **stalk celery, chopped**	1 **ham shank, preferably with meat on it**
1 **tablespoon salt**	**Few sprigs fresh parsley**

Soak beans overnight in large kettle in water to cover (or cover with water, bring to a boil, simmer 2 minutes, remove from heat and let stand 1 hour). Add all other ingredients and more water if needed to cover the beans about 1/2 inch. Partially cover and simmer slowly until beans are almost but not quite done.

While beans cook, prepare the following:

4 **slices bacon, diced**	1/2 **teaspoon rosemary**
4 **medium onions, chopped**	**Salt, black pepper, and cayenne pepper to taste**
5 **cloves garlic, minced**	1 **cup dry red wine**
4 **to 5 pounds lean beef, cut into 1-inch cubes**	1-1/2 **pounds smoked link sausage (the fully cooked kind)**

Fry bacon slowly until crisp; remove to paper towels to drain. Sauté onions and garlic in fat remaining in skillet until tender but not brown. Remove with slotted spoon; place in large casserole. Brown meat cubes well on all sides (if necessary add small amount of fat to skillet). As meat browns, remove to casserole. Add seasonings and wine; stir in bacon. Cover tightly and bake at 300° for 2 to 3 hours or until meat is tender. Do not allow to dry out; add more wine or broth if required. When meat is tender, add beans with liquid and sausage links cut in 1/2-inch slices. Cover and bake for 1 hour. Freezes well. Yield: 15 servings.

ANCHOVY SALAD DRESSING

1 (2-ounce) can anchovies, mashed (include half the oil)

1 bunch green onions including about 1 inch of tops, chopped

1 tablespoon Worcestershire sauce

Black pepper to taste

1/2 to 2/3 (8-ounce) bottle Italian dressing

1/3 cup salad oil

1/3 cup tarragon or wine vinegar

Combine all ingredients and shake vigorously. Excellent on any tossed green salad; keeps well. Yield: about 1-1/2 cups.

SUGARPLUM CAKE

4 cups all-purpose flour, measured after sifting

1 (8-ounce) package dates, chopped

1 pound orange gelatin candy slices, chopped

1-1/2 cups shredded coconut

1 cup coarsely chopped pecans

1 cup coarsely chopped walnuts

1 cup butter or margarine

2 cups sugar

1 teaspoon soda

4 eggs

Pinch salt

1/2 cup buttermilk

1 tablespoon freshly squeezed lemon juice

1 teaspoon orange extract

Spread a large piece of waxed paper on table and sift onto it 1 cup of the flour. Add finely cut dates, candy, coconut, and nuts, dredging thoroughly. (I use scissors dipped repeatedly in a glass of hot water for cutting orange slices and dates; it works beautifully.)

Cream butter and sugar in large bowl of electric mixer. Add eggs one at a time, beating well after each addition. Sift remaining 3 cups flour with soda and salt and add alternately with buttermilk, beginning and ending with flour. Beat in lemon juice and flavoring, then by hand stir in flour-dredged mixture. (Batter will be stiff.) Turn into two greased and lightly floured deep loafpans, spreading batter evenly. Bake at 250° for 2-1/2 hours, or until cakes test done. (If preferred, cake may be baked in large tubepan.)

When cakes are done, immediately pour following mixture over them: 1 cup orange juice; 2 teaspoons grated orange rind; 2 cups sifted powdered sugar. (To hasten the absorbing, I punch holes with an ice pick down through cakes before pouring on the glaze.)

This is an extremely rich, moist cake and may be used in lieu of fruitcake. For this menu, thin cake slices may be topped with a dollop of whipped cream, sweetened and flavored with a little brandy. Freezes beautifully. Yield: 15 servings.

Calypso New Year's Dinner

DINNER FOR TEN

Green Salad with Savory Salad Dressing

Calypso Beef Roast

Roast Baking Potatoes　　　　**Broccoli with Piquante Sauce**

Black-Eyed Peas

or

Hopping John

Crunchy Hot French Bread　　　　**Butter**

Eggnog Cake

Coffee　　　　**Tea**

SAVORY SALAD DRESSING
(prepare ahead of time)

1/4 teaspoon chili powder	1/2 teaspoon dry mustard
1/8 teaspoon paprika	1/2 teaspoon salt
3 shakes cayenne pepper	1 teaspoon grated onion
1/8 teaspoon freshly ground black pepper	2/3 cup salad oil
1/4 teaspoon garlic powder	1/3 cup cider vinegar

Mix all dry ingredients in small bowl of electric mixer. Add grated onion, then gradually beat in oil. When well blended, add vinegar and beat again. Best if made several days before using. Yield: about 1-1/4 cups.

Alternate method: Place all ingredients in jar with tight-fitting cover; shake vigorously until blended.

CALYPSO BEEF ROAST

2 tablespoons oil	1 teaspoon ground ginger
1 (about 7-pound) boneless beef roast (preferably rump or round)	2 cloves garlic, crushed
All-purpose flour for dredging	2 medium onions, chopped
Salt, seasoned salt, and black pepper	1 (8-ounce) can tomato sauce
	1 cup dry red wine (Burgundy)

Heat oil in a skillet large enough to hold roast easily. Dredge meat lightly with flour, sifting it over all sides. Brown thoroughly, then transfer to Dutch oven or roaster with tight-fitting cover. Season generously, sprinkling all sides of meat with salt, seasoned salt, pepper, and ginger. Don't be sparing here; the seasonings have a long way to go.

Crush garlic into the pot (see that a little remains on top of the meat); add onion, then spread tomato sauce over top. Slowly pour wine over the roast so as not to disturb the seasonings and tomato sauce. Cover tightly and bake at 325° for about 3 hours, or until meat is tender, basting several times during cooking. Yield: 10 servings.

Note: The gravy resulting from this roast is thin; you may want to thicken it slightly with a little flour or cornstarch — but very slightly.

ROAST BAKING POTATOES

6 tablespoons butter or margarine	Seasoned salt
10 medium baking potatoes	About 1-1/2 cups chicken broth

Select a shallow pan just large enough to hold the potatoes in one layer easily. Melt butter in the pan in a 325° oven. Peel potatoes, round off edges nicely to give them a uniform shape. Roll in the melted butter until well coated. Sprinkle all over with seasoned salt. Bake uncovered for 1 to 1-1/2 hours. Remove pan from oven, turn potatoes and add chicken broth. Return to oven for about 45 minutes or until fork tender, basting several times. Yield: 10 servings.

BROCCOLI WITH PIQUANTE SAUCE
(may be prepared ahead of time)

Cook 3 (10-ounce) packages frozen broccoli spears until just tender; do not overcook. Drain thoroughly, put on heated platter and garnish with a sauce made of the following: mayonnaise, horseradish, mustard, vinegar, Worcestershire sauce, using quantities to taste. Yield: 10 servings.

BLACK-EYED PEAS

Soak 2-1/2 cups dried black-eyed peas in cold water overnight. In the early morning, place a ham bone or a piece of salt pork in a large kettle with about 4 cups water. Bring to a boil; add drained peas. Cover and cook slowly for several hours, until peas are tender. Season with salt and pepper when peas are half done. Stir gently with a fork once or twice to be sure peas are not burning. The peas absorb a great deal of water, so it may be necessary to add more from time to time. The peas should be tender but not mushy, so do not overcook. Yield: 10 servings.

HOPPING JOHN
(may be prepared ahead of time)

In the South it is said that without a dish of Hopping John on New Year's Day, a year of bad luck will follow. Naturally, we don't believe that. On the other hand, it's a mighty tasty dish and who wants to take a chance?

Some say the name "Hopping John" came from an old custom that children must hop once around the table before the dish is served (who knows why?); others believe it could have been the name of an especially lively waiter.

4 strips bacon
1/4 cup chopped onion
2 (10-ounce) packages frozen black-eyed peas, or 2 cups fresh peas

1/2 cup uncooked long-grained white rice
2 cups water
Salt and pepper to taste

Dice bacon into Dutch oven; add onion and fry over medium heat until bacon is almost crisp and onions are yellow. Add peas and rice, then water. Cover and simmer over very low heat about 20 minutes, or until rice is tender. Salt and pepper to taste. Yield: 10 servings.

FRENCH BREAD
(see Index)

EGGNOG CAKE
(may be prepared ahead of time)

1 large angelfood cake
1/2 pound sweet butter
1/2 pound powdered sugar (about 1-3/4 cups)
5 egg yolks, beaten
1 cup chopped almonds, lightly toasted
1/2 to 1/3 cup bourbon
2 to 3 tablespoons rum

1/2 teaspoon almond extract
1 dozen almond macaroons, toasted and ground*
1 cup heavy cream, whipped
2 tablespoons powdered sugar
1 tablespoon bourbon
1 tablespoon rum

Slice cake horizontally three times, yielding four layers. Cream butter and powdered sugar thoroughly; add egg yolks. Stir in 3/4 cup of the almonds, 1/2 to 1/3 cup bourbon, 2 to 3 tablespoons rum, almond extract, and ground macaroons. Spread filling between layers of cake; cover with plastic wrap and store overnight in refrigerator. Next morning whip cream, add 2 tablespoons powdered sugar, then slowly stir in 1 tablespoon bourbon and 1 tablespoon rum. Frost cake with cream mixture and garnish with remaining 1/2 cup almonds. Return to refrigerator until serving time. Leftovers freeze beautifully. Yield: 15 to 20 servings.

*See Index for Almond Macaroons recipe.

Nothing will add more elegance to your party dinner than a rolled rib roast. Recipe is on page 200.

Traditional
Thanksgiving Dinner

DINNER FOR TWELVE

Old-Fashioned Roast Turkey

Glazed Whole Apricots   **Cornbread Dressing**

Squash-Swiss Cheese Casserole (optional)   **Broccoli with Olive Butter**

Cranberry Salad

Hot Tea Room Rolls   **Butter Curls**

Tropical Sundae

or

Centerpiece of Fresh Fruit

Coffee   **Tea**

OLD-FASHIONED ROAST TURKEY

1 (14- to 16-pound) turkey	1 teaspoon garlic powder
Melted butter or margarine	1/2 teaspoon ground ginger
1 tablespoon salt	1 teaspoon paprika
1/2 teaspoon pepper	1/4 teaspoon cayenne pepper
2 teaspoons seasoned salt	1/4 teaspoon dried basil
1 teaspoon ground poultry seasoning	

Clean and dry turkey; reserve and set aside neck, giblets, and liver. Brush turkey with melted butter. Mix dry seasonings and rub thoroughly into inside and outside of bird. Truss and tie securely; place breast-side up in roaster. Add 1 cup water, cover and bake at 350° until tender, about 3 to 4 hours. If turkey is not evenly browned, remove cover for last 1/2 hour and lower temperature to 300°. Yield: 14 servings.

Note: Pan juices in roaster may be combined with giblet broth to make a delicious gravy.

Turkey Gravy

Put neck, giblets, and liver in saucepan. Add 4 cups chicken broth made of 4 chicken bouillon cubes and hot water. Add 1 stalk celery cut in chunks and 1 whole small onion. Cover and simmer slowly about 2 hours. When giblets are done, strain soup. Do not add seasonings; the chicken broth will have yielded enough. If desired, thicken gravy slightly by adding a little flour or cornstarch, stirred first into a small amount of the hot gravy, then the whole returned to the pot. Diced giblets may be stirred into the gravy before serving. Yield: about 3-1/2 cups.

GLAZED WHOLE APRICOTS

Drain a 1-pound can of whole apricots. Put apricots into a large skillet or saucepan with 1/2 cup of the apricot juice, 1 cup brown sugar, and 1/4 cup butter. Heat slowly at a simmer, turning apricots often until glazed all over. Drain, stick whole cloves in end and use to garnish poultry or pork.

CORNBREAD DRESSING

4 cups breadcrumbs (leftover biscuits or loaf bread)	Salt and pepper to taste
4 cups egg cornbread (use several eggs to make; use white meal)	1 teaspoon sage (optional)
1/2 cup chopped onion	3 cups chicken or turkey broth
1 cup chopped celery	1/3 cup butter or margarine
	1 cup milk

Toast bread for crumbs. Crumble in large bowl. Add onion, celery, and seasonings. Add hot broth to make soft mixture. Mix well. Add butter and milk. Mixture should be very soft to allow for loss of moisture during baking. Add more broth if necessary. Pour into greased pan and bake at 350° for about 1 hour, until well browned.

SQUASH-SWISS CHEESE CASSEROLE

The following casserole is so good that confirmed squash-haters have been known not only to go back for seconds but to refuse to accept the fact that it was squash they were eating, because, as one of my guests protested, "This can't be squash; I don't eat squash." — C. M.

3 to 4 pounds yellow squash	1 teaspoon seasoned salt
2 medium onions, minced	Several dashes ground nutmeg
2 bay leaves	Dash Worcestershire sauce
About 6 sprigs parsley	4 egg yolks, beaten
1/2 teaspoon leaf thyme	About 1-1/3 cups shredded Swiss cheese
6 tablespoons butter	Cayenne pepper
6 tablespoons all-purpose flour	Buttered breadcrumbs
3 cups milk	
Dash salt	

Cut squash into 1/3-inch slices. Place in large saucepan with onion, bay leaves, parsley, and thyme. Cover with boiling salted water and cook until

squash is barely tender. Drain, remove parsley and bay leaves and set aside.

While squash cooks, make cream sauce. In saucepan heat 6 tablespoons butter or margarine; blend in 6 tablespoons flour, then gradually add 3 cups milk and dash of salt. Cook, stirring constantly, until thickened.

To the sauce, add seasoned salt, nutmeg, and Worcestershire sauce. Remove from heat; gradually blend in egg yolks (by adding small amount of the hot sauce to yolks beaten in a small bowl, then adding a little more, etc., then returning all back to the saucepan). Stir in 1 cup of the cheese and add cayenne pepper.

Combine squash with sauce, stirring gently; turn into large buttered baking dish about 2 inches deep. Mix remaining cheese with equal amount (or more, if needed) buttered breadcrumbs. Sprinkle over squash and bake at 350° for about 35 minutes, or until top is bubbly and brown. Leftovers freeze well. Yield: 12 servings.

BROCCOLI WITH OLIVE BUTTER

2/3 cup butter or margarine	12 large stuffed olives, sliced
2 cloves garlic, crushed	4 (10-ounce) packages frozen broccoli
4 teaspoons freshly squeezed lemon juice	spears, cooked
Dash black pepper	Seasoned salt

Heat butter and garlic over low heat in small saucepan about 15 minutes. Add lemon juice, pepper, and olives; heat thoroughly but do not boil. Cook broccoli according to package directions; drain and arrange in heated serving dish. Sprinkle lightly with seasoned salt, then pour sauce over all. Yield: 12 to 14 servings.

CRANBERRY SALAD

2 oranges	1 cup sugar
2-1/2 cups fresh cranberries	Pinch salt
3 (3-ounce) packages orange-flavored gelatin	1-1/2 cups finely chopped celery
3 cups boiling water	1 cup crushed pineapple, undrained
2 tablespoons freshly squeezed lemon juice	1/2 cup chopped pecans (or more if desired)

Peel oranges; put peeling and cranberries through food grinder. Remove white membrane from oranges and section them, breaking each section into three or four pieces.

Dissolve gelatin in boiling water; add lemon juice, sugar, and salt. Stir until dissolved. Add orange pieces, the ground mixture, celery, pineapple, and nuts. Pour into molds and chill until set. This salad should be made at least 2 days before serving. Yield: 12 to 15 servings.

Bring out the finest crystal, silver, and china for your Thanksgiving dinner and serve your guests Old-Fashioned Roast Turkey, Cornbread Dressing, Squash-Swiss Cheese Casserole, Broccoli with Olive Butter, and Cranberry Salad.

TEA ROOM ROLLS

1/3 cup vegetable shortening
3 tablespoons sugar
1-1/2 teaspoons salt
1 cup boiling water
1 cake compressed yeast or 1 package dry yeast

1/4 cup lukewarm water (very warm water for dry yeast)
1 egg, beaten
About 4 cups all-purpose flour

Put shortening, sugar, and salt into a large bowl. Pour boiling water over; cool to lukewarm. Add yeast which has been dissolved in lukewarm water; beat egg. Now stir 2 cups of flour into the mixture and beat until smooth. Add remaining 2 cups flour and beat well. (I beat the mixture with a wooden spoon until blisters form on the dough; you'll recognize them when they appear. — C. M.) Grease top of dough, cover with a light cloth and allow to rise in a warm spot until double in bulk (about 1-1/2 hours). Stir the dough down and spoon into well greased muffin pans, filling them about two-thirds full. Allow to rise about 1 hour and bake at 400° about 20 minutes for large muffins; about 14 minutes for small ones. Yield: about 4 dozen.

Note: To make cloverleaf rolls, before second rising, use scissors to make two deep slashes in top of muffin, crosswise. Place a small bit of butter in the slash.

TROPICAL SUNDAE

This is a wonderful, rich, exotic finale to any festive dinner. To make it you should have coconut ice cream, which is not always available. To convert vanilla ice cream into coconut, follow these directions:

Empty 1/2 gallon vanilla ice cream into large bowl of electric mixer and allow it to soften slightly at room temperature. In another bowl stir 2 rounded tablespoons powdered sugar into 2 cups packaged or canned coconut. Add to ice cream and beat just a minute, adding 1 teaspoon coconut flavoring to the mixture as it softens slightly. Beat only until mixture is blended; pour into container (a plastic one is fine); cover and freeze.

To make the sundae: Allow 1 tablespoon each of pineapple preserves, apricot preserves, and good rum for each serving. Combine preserves and rum in a saucepan and warm over very low heat or place in a pan of boiling water until you are ready to serve the dessert. Turn sauce into chafing dish or sauceboat placed over a candle. Ignite sauce, allowing flames to burn down as you stir it.

Have large scoops of the ice cream ready in dessert dishes and when flames of the sauce have died down, spoon the warm sauce over the ice cream.

Thanksgiving Dinner

DINNER FOR EIGHT

Roast Capon with Water Chestnut Sauce

Peach Halves   Cranberry Conserve

Eastern Rice   Vegetables Mornay

Green Salad with Lemon French Dressing

Hot Rolls   Butter

Thanksgiving Rum Pie

Coffee   Tea

ROAST CAPON (OR HEN)

1 (7- to 9-pound) capon or 2 hens	1 small tart apple, unpeeled and cut in half
Salt	2 stalks celery, cut in chunks
Melted butter or margarine	Paprika
Seasoned salt	8 canned peach halves, drained
Poultry seasoning	Holiday Cranberry Conserve*

Clean capon well, wash and pat dry. Sprinkle inside generously with salt. Brush outside with butter and sprinkle with seasoned salt and poultry seasoning. Cut apple in half and place in cavity of capon, along with celery.

Place, breast-side up, on rack in roasting pan and cover lightly with aluminum foil. Roast at 350° for 25 minutes to the pound. When capon is about half done, sprinkle with salt and paprika. To serve, place capon on parsley bed on silver tray and garnish with drained canned peach halves, warmed about 15 minutes in a slow oven. Place peaches cavity-side up and spoon into the cavities a tablespoon of Holiday Cranberry Conserve.

*See Index for Holiday Cranberry Conserve recipe.

WATER CHESTNUT SAUCE

2 tablespoons fat from roasting pan	1/4 cup chopped green onions
1 (10-1/2-ounce) can chicken broth	2 tablespoons chopped pimiento
2 tablespoons soy sauce	1 tablespoon cornstarch
1/4 cup sherry	1/4 cup cold water
2 (5-ounce) cans water chestnuts, drained and sliced	

Drain excess fat from roasting pan, leaving about 2 tablespoons. Stir in chicken broth, scraping pan to loosen particles. Transfer to saucepan and bring to a boil. Add soy sauce, sherry, water chestnuts, chopped green onions, and pimiento. Check seasoning; if too salty, dilute with a little water. Simmer a few minutes; blend in 1 tablespoon cornstarch dissolved in 1/4 cup cold water. Cook, stirring constantly, until sauce thickens slightly. Serve in heated sauceboat. Yield: about 2-3/4 cups.

EASTERN RICE

1/3 cup butter or margarine	Black pepper to taste
1-1/2 cups long-grain white rice	3 cups chicken broth (bouillon cubes
1/3 cup chopped onion	and hot water)
1/4 teaspoon ground nutmeg	1/3 cup white raisins (optional)
1/4 teaspoon ground allspice	1/3 cup slivered almonds
1 teaspoon salt, or more to taste	

Melt butter in saucepan; add rice and onion and sauté until golden. Stir in remaining ingredients, cover and cook over low heat for 25 to 30 minutes, or until rice is tender and all liquid is absorbed. Do not overcook. Yield: 8 servings.

VEGETABLES MORNAY
(may be prepared the day before)

3 (10-ounce) packages frozen mixed vegetables	1/4 teaspoon seasoned salt
1-1/3 cups water	3 tablespoons butter or margarine
3/4 teaspoon salt	Sauce

Place vegetables, water, salt, seasoned salt, and butter in a saucepan. Cover and heat to boiling. Simmer for 5 minutes, drain vegetables and reserve cooking liquid. Pour vegetables into shallow casserole and prepare Sauce.

Sauce

1/3 cup butter or margarine	Cream or milk
4-1/2 tablespoons all-purpose flour	1/2 cup grated Parmesan and Swiss cheese, mixed
1/4 teaspoon ground nutmeg	Buttered breadcrumbs
1/4 teaspoon leaf thyme	
3/4 teaspoon salt	

Heat butter in saucepan. Blend in flour and seasonings and cook for about 2 minutes, stirring constantly. Remove from heat. Gradually stir in reserved vegetable liquid with enough cream or milk to make 3 cups. Return to heat and cook, stirring constantly, until thick and smooth. Stir in cheese and pour over vegetables. Cover with crumbs and bake at 350° for 30 minutes. Casserole may be assembled except for crumb topping the day before and refrigerated. Yield: 8 to 10 servings.

LEMON FRENCH DRESSING

2/3 cup salad oil
1/3 cup freshly squeezed lemon juice
1/2 teaspoon salt
1/8 teaspoon pepper

1/2 teaspoon dry mustard
1 teaspoon powdered sugar
1/2 teaspoon paprika

Combine all ingredients in blender or jar. Shake or blend well; chill before serving. This is good over fruit as well as green salads. Yield: about 1 cup.

HOT ROLLS
(see Index)

THANKSGIVING RUM PIE
(may be prepared the day before)

1 envelope unflavored gelatin
5 tablespoons cold water
3 cups hot milk
1/8 teaspoon salt
8 tablespoons sugar
3 eggs, separated
5 tablespoons rum

3/4 teaspoon almond extract
1 (9-inch) baked pie shell
1 cup heavy cream, whipped
1 tablespoon sugar
1 teaspoon rum
2 tablespoons grated semi-sweet
   chocolate

Sprinkle gelatin on cold water; allow to stand 5 minutes. Dissolve in hot milk; stir in salt and 4 tablespoons of the sugar. Beat egg yolks and add milk mixture; cook in double boiler over hot water, stirring constantly, until slightly thickened. Remove from heat; cool thoroughly. Stir in the 5 tablespoons rum and almond flavoring.

Beat egg whites until stiff, gradually adding remaining 4 tablespoons sugar. Fold into custard and turn into pie shell; chill thoroughly. When pie has set, spread with whipped cream to which the 1 tablespoon sugar and teaspoon rum have been added. Sprinkle with grated chocolate. Yield: 8 servings.

SAYING GRACE

In the household where the custom is to say grace before meals and where dinner is being served buffet style, it seems awkward for the first guest seated to wait until he gets a cue from the hostess that dinner may begin.

I have found this a practical way of solving the problem: Just after dinner is announced but before the first guest in line has served himself, ask for a moment of silence. A brief word of grace is then pronounced, and from that moment on, it is understood that one may begin eating as soon as he is seated, whether at a large dining table where the entire company will be gathered or at a small table set up elsewhere. — C.M.

Christmas Goose Dinner

DINNER FOR EIGHT TO TEN

Roast Goose

Casserole-Baked Tomatoes   **Pilaf of Lentils and Rice**

Ambrosia

Commercial Hard Rolls   **Butter**

Eggnog Cake

Coffee   **Tea**

ROAST GOOSE

About a 9-pound goose will serve 8 to 10 guests. Follow directions for roasting duck and making giblet gravy (see Index).

The following is a recipe for Wine Sauce to accompany roast goose, but if the goose is to be served with a vegetable containing wine, omit the wine in the sauce and increase the amount of broth by 1/2 cup.

Wine Sauce for Roast Goose

1/2 cup butter or margarine	1/2 cup dry red wine
4 tablespoons all-purpose flour	Salt and pepper to taste
4 cups broth (use all gravy from the goose plus as much of the giblet broth as required to make 4 cups)	1/4 cup minced fresh parsley (do not omit)

Melt butter in saucepan, stir in flour and blend well. Gradually add broth, stirring constantly until thickened. Add wine, salt, pepper, and parsley. Heat a moment longer and serve — or keep warm in sauceboat over candle or other heating device.

CASSEROLE-BAKED TOMATOES

2 (1-pound) cans solid-packed tomatoes	2 small onions, minced
2 tablespoons brown sugar	2 tablespoons chopped chives
2 teaspoons salt	4 grinds black pepper
1/2 teaspoon dried chervil	1/2 teaspoon dill weed
1/2 teaspoon seasoned salt	Coarse dry breadcrumbs

Put tomatoes in open casserole. Mix in all other ingredients except breadcrumbs. Scatter crumbs on top and bake at 250° for 2 hours. Yield: 8 to 10 servings.

PILAF OF LENTILS AND RICE

2 tablespoons olive or salad oil
1 large onion, chopped fine
3 or 4 tablespoons slivered blanched
  almonds
1 cup lentils

5 to 6 cups chicken broth
1 cup uncooked long-grain white rice
2-1/2 tablespoons soy sauce
Pepper to taste

Heat oil in saucepan and sauté onion until golden but not brown. Add nuts and sauté until crisp; remove with slotted spoon, allowing oil to remain in pan. Stir in lentils and enough broth to cover generously. Cover and simmer for 45 minutes to an hour, until lentils are almost soft.

Add rice and remaining soup broth, soy sauce, then half the onion-nut mixture. Check seasonings; add pepper to taste. Bring to a boil, cover and reduce heat. Cook slowly about 20 minutes, or until rice is done. Garnish with remaining onion-nut mixture. Freezes well. Yield: 8 servings.

HEAVENLY AMBROSIA

6 large and juicy oranges
4 ripe bananas
1 apple, diced

1/2 cup maraschino cherries, cut in halves
1/2 cup flaked coconut
Dash salt

Cut oranges first. When peeling orange, hold over bowl so all juice will remain in bowl. Be sure to cut sections deep enough to remove all membrane from orange. Remove sections by cutting along the side of each, dividing membrane from outside to center.

Peel bananas, and slice over oranges. Dice the apple in very small pieces and add to mixture. Add cherries, coconut, and salt. Toss lightly and garnish with additional coconut and a few chopped pecans. This is much better if made several hours ahead of time. Yield: 8 servings.

EGGNOG CAKE
(see Index)

CRUMB TOPPING FOR CASSEROLES

1/2 cup butter or margarine
1 clove garlic, crushed

1 cup dry breadcrumbs
1 cup chopped fresh parsley

Heat butter in large skillet with garlic. Add crumbs and stir over low heat until crisp. Add parsley, stir well, and spread over any casserole needing a crisp topping.

This mixture may be prepared, stored in freezer, and used as needed.

Christmas Dinner

DINNER FOR TWELVE TO FOURTEEN

Crown Roast of Pork with Lemon-Herb Stuffing
Fruit Garnish   **Holiday Cranberry Conserve**
Baked Lima Beans and Peas
Salad of Mixed Greens with Herbed French Dressing
Hot Commercial Hard Rolls   **Butter**

Baba Au Rhum

Coffee   **Tea**

CROWN ROAST OF PORK

Have butcher trim uncut pork ribs and form into a crown; the crown may consist of 14 to 22 ribs. A 20-rib roast will serve 15. Using a very sharp knife, trim away all excess fat. Salt and pepper roast on all sides; place in open roasting pan.

You may want to prepare your favorite poultry stuffing or use Lemon-Herb Stuffing. This is a good all-purpose dressing to use with any fowl.

LEMON-HERB STUFFING

1 (8-ounce) package seasoned bread stuffing
1 tablespoon grated lemon rind
1/4 cup finely chopped onion
1/2 teaspoon salt
3 tablespoons minced fresh parsley or
1 tablespoon dried parsley

1/2 cup melted butter or margarine
2 tablespoons freshly squeezed lemon juice
3/4 cup chicken bouillon
1/4 cup Sauterne (or more chicken bouillon)

Combine all ingredients, mix well. Stuff into center of roast; bake at 350° for 3-1/2 to 4 hours, or until fork inserted in thick part of roast indicates meat is well done. After roast has cooked about an hour, place a piece of aluminum foil loosely over roast so surface or stuffing will not cook dry. Baste several times during cooking with dry white wine if desired. Yield: 12 to 14 servings.

If you aren't ready to serve when roast is done, remove from oven and keep warm until serving time.

To make gravy: Drain off fat from roasting pan; pour pan juices into small saucepan; add about 1 cup chicken broth (bouillon cube and hot water), simmer about 5 minutes, then check and correct seasonings. Thicken by dissolving 1 teaspoon arrowroot powder or cornstarch in 3 tablespoons of the gravy, then stirring thickening into contents of saucepan. Cook a few minutes, stirring constantly until slightly thickened; pour into heated sauceboat.

Garnish roast with spiced crabapples or Fruit Garnish.

FRUIT GARNISH

1 (1-pound) can pineapple slices	Brown sugar
1 (1-pound) can peach halves	Butter or margarine
1 (1-pound) can apricot halves	Orange juice

Drain fruit; arrange individual mounds in a large ovenproof buttered baking dish as follows: first, the pineapple, then peach half (cavity-side up), then apricot half (cavity-side up). Sprinkle with light brown sugar, dot each serving with butter or margarine and bake at 325° about 30 minutes or until glazed, basting now and then with orange juice. Keep warm and arrange around roast.

HOLIDAY CRANBERRY CONSERVE

2 oranges, unpeeled	1 cup white raisins
2 cups hot water	1/4 teaspoon salt
4 cups fresh cranberries	1/2 cup coarsely chopped walnuts
2 cups sugar	

Grate orange rind, cut in half, remove seeds, and grind oranges. Place the grated rind and pulp in saucepan with hot water and cook covered for 20 minutes. Add cranberries, sugar, raisins, and salt; boil rapidly uncovered until mixture drops from spoon in a flake or sheet leaving the spoon clean. Stir in nuts and cook 5 minutes longer, stirring gently to avoid scorching. Chill. Serve in your prettiest crystal bowl. Yield: about 3 to 4 cups.

HERBED FRENCH DRESSING
(may be prepared ahead of time)

1 teaspoon salt	1/2 teaspoon sugar
1/8 teaspoon freshly ground black pepper	1 small clove garlic, crushed
1 teaspoon dried oregano	1/2 teaspoon powdered mustard
1 teaspoon dried basil	1 cup salad oil
1 teaspoon dried tarragon	1/4 cup cider vinegar
2 teaspoons scraped onion	Juice of 2 lemons

Combine all ingredients except vinegar and lemon juice. (If you have a mortar and pestle, grind all dry ingredients together first.) Allow to stand at least 1 hour. Pour into jar that has a tight-fitting cover, add vinegar and lemon juice, cap and shake vigorously. If preferred, mixture may be blended in an electric blender. Excellent over any green salad. May be made several days ahead of time. Yield: about 1-1/2 cups.

Note: For this menu, we suggest that you serve Herbed French Dressing over mixed greens, sliced raw mushrooms, artichoke hearts, and grapefruit sections.

BAKED LIMA BEANS AND PEAS

2 (10-ounce) packages frozen baby
    lima beans
2 (10-ounce) packages frozen peas
1 teaspoon dried sweet basil
1 teaspoon salt

4 green onions including tops, minced
4 tablespoons butter or margarine
3 tablespoons water
    Lettuce leaves

Thaw vegetables for several hours at room temperature or overnight in refrigerator. Place in greased 4-quart shallow casserole with tight-fitting cover. Stir in basil, salt, and green onions. Dot with butter and sprinkle with water. Place lettuce leaves (outer ones from head lettuce) over vegetables, cover and bake at 325° for about 45 minutes, or until vegetables are just tender. Yield: 12 to 14 servings.

BABA AU RHUM

1/3 cup butter
1/2 teaspoon salt
  3 tablespoons sugar
1/2 cup milk, scalded
  1 cake compressed yeast or 1 package
    dry yeast
1/4 cup warm water (very warm water
    for dry yeast)

2 eggs, slightly beaten
1 teaspoon grated orange rind
2-1/4 cups all-purpose flour, sifted
    Sauce
    Sugared strawberries
    Whipped cream (optional)

Sift butter, salt, and sugar into hot milk until dissolved; cool to lukewarm. Dissolve yeast in 1/4 cup warm water and stir into milk mixture. Add eggs, orange rind, and then flour. Beat well, cover with light cloth and let rise in warm spot until double in bulk. Punch dough down, beat a few minutes with wooden spoon. Fill greased muffin tins half full and allow to rise until double in bulk; bake at 350° for 20 minutes. Remove from muffin tin immediately and place in a shallow dish.

Dip babas into Sauce, then place in serving dishes. Spoon any remaining Sauce over babas and allow to stand at room temperature several hours before serving. Serve babas with sliced sugared strawberries, and, if you wish, a topping of whipped cream. More rum may be poured over babas before serving. They should be thoroughly rum-soaked. Yield: 12 babas.

While babas bake, prepare Sauce.

Sauce

1 cup apricot preserves
1 cup water

1/2 cup rum

Puree apricot preserves through a fine strainer into saucepan. Heat with 1 cup water until blended; stir in 1/2 cup good rum. Yield: 2-1/2 cups.

Easter Dinner with Roast Pork

DINNER FOR EIGHT

Grapefruit Salad with Poppy Seed Dressing

Roast Loin of Pork with Madeira Sauce or Caper Sauce

Party Green Beans　　　　　　**Beets with Pineapple**

Alabama Spoonbread　　　　　　**Butter**

Macaroon Pudding

Coffee　　　　　　**Tea**

POPPY SEED DRESSING
(may be prepared ahead of time)

1/2 cup finely chopped sweet onion	1 teaspoon salt
2 tablespoons salad oil	1 teaspoon dry mustard
2-1/2 tablespoons poppy seed	3/4 cup salad oil
3 teaspoons sugar	3/4 cup tarragon vinegar

Combine onion, 2 tablespoons oil, poppy seed, sugar, salt, and dry mustard in a bowl; beat thoroughly. Gradually add oil, then vinegar. Pour into jar with tight-fitting lid and refrigerate. Shake the jar vigorously before serving. Yield: almost 2 cups.

ROAST LOIN OF PORK

Have butcher bone and trim a 10-pound pork loin. Rub liberally with salt, freshly ground black pepper, 1 teaspoon sugar, and a pinch of cayenne pepper. Place in 450° oven for 10 minutes; reduce temperature to 300°. Sprinkle with rosemary, pour Chablis or Sauterne over meat, and roast 30 minutes to the pound, basting several times with more wine. Serve with Madeira or Caper Sauce.

There will be very little gravy resulting from this roast. However, the small amount should be carefully salvaged. Pour off all fat from pan; pour small amount (no more than 2 tablespoons) boiling water into pan; stir and scrape up all brown bits adhering to the pan. This may be added to the Madeira Sauce accompanying the pork. Yield: 8 servings.

MADEIRA SAUCE

2 tablespoons butter or margarine
2 tablespoons finely chopped green
  onions
1-1/2 cups gravy (with fat removed) from
  roasting meat

2 tablespoons freshly squeezed
  lemon juice
1/4 cup Madeira wine

Heat butter and sauté green onions until tender in a small saucepan. Add gravy, then lemon juice and bring to a boil. Stir in wine, reheat and serve in heated sauceboat. If desired, thicken slightly with a teaspoon arrowroot or cornstarch blended in at the end. Yield: 2 cups sauce.

CAPER SAUCE

1/4 cup minced onion
2 tablespoons wine vinegar
2/3 cup chicken broth
1/3 cup tomato puree

Salt and freshly ground black pepper
1/4 teaspoon cayenne pepper
3 tablespoons drained capers
2 tablespoons butter or margarine

Place onion and vinegar in small saucepan. Bring to a boil and simmer until much of the liquid evaporates. Add chicken broth and tomato puree and return to a boil. Add seasonings and continue cooking for about 5 minutes. Stir in capers, then butter, stirring just until butter melts. Serve in heated sauceboat to accompany pork.

Gravy salvaged from roasting pork (after fat is drained off completely) may be used as part of the 2/3 cup chicken broth. Yield: about 1-1/3 cups.

PARTY GREEN BEANS
(may be prepared ahead of time)

3 (10-ounce) packages frozen French-
  style green beans
1 (1-pound) can bean sprouts, drained
  and rinsed
2 (8-ounce) cans water chestnuts,
  drained and sliced
1/2 cup grated Parmesan and Swiss
  cheese, mixed

1/4 cup butter or margarine
2 tablespoons all-purpose flour
1-1/4 teaspoons salt
1/4 teaspoon pepper
  Dash cayenne pepper
1/2 teaspoon Worcestershire sauce
2 cups light cream
1 cup chopped almonds

Cook beans in boiling salted water for 5 minutes; drain. Turn into buttered shallow 2-quart casserole and alternate layers of beans, bean sprouts, water chestnuts, and cheese. Prepare cream sauce.

Melt 3 tablespoons of the butter in saucepan; blend in flour, salt, pepper, cayenne pepper, and Worcestershire sauce. Gradually add cream and cook until thickened, stirring constantly. Pour over vegetables, lifting mixture gently with a fork so sauce will penetrate, but do not stir.

Melt remaining butter in small saucepan; add almonds, and stir to coat well. Sprinkle over casserole and bake at 375° for about 20 minutes or until bubbly. Yield: 10 to 12 servings.

BEETS WITH PINEAPPLE

1 (1-pound) can tiny whole beets,
   drained, reserve liquid
1 (1-pound) can pineapple chunks,
   drained, reserve liquid
1 tablespoon cornstarch

1/3 cup sugar
1 tablespoon vinegar
   Salt and pepper to taste
2 tablespoons butter or margarine

Cook juice drained from beets and pineapple in small saucepan with cornstarch, sugar, and vinegar, stirring constantly until thickened. Add salt and pepper to taste, drained beets and pineapple, and butter. Cook slowly for 20 minutes and serve hot or cold. Yield: 8 servings.

ALABAMA SPOONBREAD

1 cup yellow cornmeal, sifted
2 cups boiling water
1 tablespoon butter or margarine
1-1/2 teaspoons salt
4 eggs, separated

1/2 cup milk
1/2 cup all-purpose flour, sifted
1 tablespoon sugar
2 teaspoons baking powder

Sprinkle cornmeal over boiling water. Add butter and salt, stirring until mixture is thick. Pour into large bowl; cook about 5 minutes. Combine egg yolks and milk; stir into batter. Sift flour, sugar, and baking powder together and add to batter, mixing well. Beat egg whites until stiff but not dry and fold in. Pour into large buttered baking dish (a soufflé dish is fine) and bake at 400° for 30 to 35 minutes, or until knife inserted in center comes out clean. Serve at once from baking dish with plenty of butter. Yield: 8 servings.

MACAROON PUDDING
(prepare the day before)

18 macaroons
1/2 cup sweet sherry
5 eggs, separated
1 cup sugar
   Pinch salt
3 cups milk
2 envelopes unflavored gelatin

2 tablespoons cold water
1 teaspoon vanilla extract
1 teaspoon almond extract
   Whipped cream
1/4 teaspoon vanilla extract
1/4 teaspoon almond extract

Line a deep pudding mold (or dish with straight sides) with macaroons; pour sherry over them. Beat egg yolks and sugar until light; add salt and milk and cook over hot water until slightly thickened. Soften gelatin in cold water, then stir into hot custard until dissolved. Remove from heat; add 1 teaspoon vanilla extract and 1 teaspoon almond extract and allow to cool slightly. Fold in stiffly beaten egg whites and flavorings. Pour over macaroons in mold and chill until firm.

To serve, unmold and garnish with slightly sweetened whipped cream flavored with 1/4 teaspoon each vanilla and almond extract. Yield: 8 servings.

Easter Dinner with Lamb

DINNER FOR EIGHT

Lamb in Pastry

Mixed Rice Dressing   **Squash Florentine**

Green Goddess Salad

Apricot Charlotte with Sauce Cointreau

Coffee   **Iced Tea**

No bread is suggested. If you feel it is needed, homemade hot rolls would be festive and appropriate.

LAMB IN PASTRY

Have butcher bone a 5-pound (or more) leg of lamb and tie it so it will be the shape of a shoulder lamb roast. Rub the roast with olive or salad oil, a little vinegar, a crushed clove of garlic, salt, and freshly ground black pepper. Put it in an uncovered roaster and bake at 350°. Turn occasionally and roast about 2 hours, or until lamb is crisp and brown. Pour off excess fat but do not discard any of the little brown particles or gravy.

Stir 1 tablespoon Worcestershire sauce and 1 teaspoon Kitchen Bouquet (browning sauce) into 2 cups hot water; pour into the roaster and add 1 chopped onion, salt, and pepper. Cover roaster and continue cooking for another hour or two, until the lamb is fork tender. Remove lamb and allow to cool. Reserve drippings for gravy. If butcher has used string to tie the roast into shape, remove it. Wrap roast in pastry. Seal edges well; cut a few small gashes in top of pastry; brush with melted butter, place on baking sheet and bake at 425° about 20 minutes, or until nicely browned. Yield: 8 servings.

Simple Puff Pastry

Make your favorite 2-cups-of-flour pastry or use a package of piecrust mix. Roll out to 1/8-inch thickness; dot with slightly softened butter. Fold in from each side to meet in center; fold remaining long ends to meet in center; pinch edges to seal. Wrap in waxed paper and chill until ready to use. Roll out to proper size and cover roast completely. (You may use the pastry trimmings to cut out interesting little designs — leaves, flower petals — to be applied to pastry with a little water.) Serve with gravy.

All the preparation for this lovely lamb may be done in advance with the exception of encasing lamb in pastry and baking it.

MIXED RICE DRESSING

1/2 cup butter	Poultry seasoning
2 (4-ounce) cans mushrooms, drained	Seasoned salt
1/2 cup chopped onion	Salt
1/3 cup chopped parsley	Freshly ground black pepper
1 cup chopped celery	Pinch thyme
1/4 cup chopped green pepper	Pinch rosemary
4 cups cooked long-grain and wild rice, mixed	1 cup chicken broth

Melt butter in skillet. Add mushrooms, onions, parsley, celery, and green pepper and sauté until onions are clear and celery and green pepper barely tender. Combine with rice cooked according to package directions; season with poultry seasoning, seasoned salt, salt, freshly ground black pepper, pinch thyme, pinch rosemary, and about 1 cup chicken broth or amount needed to moisten the mixture. Turn into baking dish, cover with aluminum foil; punch a few holes in the foil and bake at 350° for 30 minutes. Yield: 8 servings.

SQUASH FLORENTINE

Boil 8 whole medium yellow squash in salt water until barely tender. Remove small oval slice from long side of squash and carefully remove inside.

Stuffing

1 (10-ounce) package frozen chopped spinach	1/2 cup crushed round buttery crackers
	Pinch coriander
2 hard-cooked eggs, finely chopped	1/2 teaspoon Worcestershire sauce
1 teaspoon dried onion flakes	Salt and pepper to taste
4 tablespoons butter or margarine, melted	1/4 cup cracker crumbs
	1/4 cup shredded Cheddar cheese

Cook spinach according to package directions; drain thoroughly. Combine with all ingredients except 1/4 cup cracker crumbs and shredded cheese and stuff squash. Top with cracker crumbs mixed with shredded cheese. Place in shallow pan containing about 1/2 inch water; bake uncovered at 300° about 30 minutes. Yield: 8 servings.

GREEN GODDESS SALAD

2 heads iceberg lettuce	2 tablespoons tarragon vinegar
2 tablespoons anchovy paste	2 tablespoons garlic vinegar
1 cup mayonnaise	2 tablespoons wine vinegar
1 tablespoon freshly squeezed lemon juice	1/4 cup chopped onion
	1/3 cup chopped parsley
1/2 cup commercial sour cream	

Break lettuce into coarse chunks and set aside. Stir anchovy paste into mayonnaise. Add lemon juice to sour cream and mix well. Combine with mayonnaise mixture and other ingredients, mix well and refrigerate until ready to use. Pour over lettuce and toss briefly. Yield: 10 to 12 servings.

APRICOT CHARLOTTE WITH SAUCE COINTREAU
(may be prepared the day before)

6 egg yolks	2 tablespoons cream (sweet) sherry, or more to taste
1 cup sugar	
2 cups milk	2 cups heavy cream, whipped
2 envelopes unflavored gelatin	12 (double) lady fingers
1/2 cup cold milk	Canned peeled apricot halves, drained
1 teaspoon vanilla extract	Maraschino cherries
	Sauce

In top of double boiler over hot water, stir egg yolks, sugar, and 2 cups milk, using wooden spoon. Soak gelatin in cold milk for 5 minutes; add to hot custard and stir until dissolved. When custard thickens, remove from heat, cool and stir in vanilla and sherry. Fold in whipped cream and continue cooling until mixture is partially set.

Split lady fingers and line sides of mold, placing rounded side of cookies next to mold. (To anchor the lady fingers to the mold, make up a paste of about a tablespoon powdered sugar and a teaspoon water, spreading a dab on back of the cookies.) Pour in cooled custard and chill until set. When ready to serve, unmold and garnish with drained apricot halves and maraschino cherries. Top with whipped cream to further glamorize, and serve Sauce separately.

Sauce

2 (1-pound) cans peeled apricot halves	1/2 cup sugar
2 tablespoons all-purpose flour	Juice of 1 lemon
	Cointreau

Drain apricot halves; mash fruit through a sieve. Blend in flour, sugar, and lemon juice. Cook in double boiler over hot water until thick. Flavor to taste with Cointreau; serve Sauce warm over the cold Charlotte. (If prepared ahead, add Cointreau to Sauce after reheating.) Yield: 9 servings.

Dinners for Houseguests

An unhurried, unflustered hostess and unforgettable food go a long way to ensure a houseguest's comfort and welcome. A harried hostess who spends all day in the kitchen can only succeed in giving her guests a guilty feeling, even though the dinner is a masterpiece. After all, guests have not come primarily to eat, but to enjoy your company. So plan menus ahead, prepare in advance, and serve meals that taste delicious yet free you from the kitchen.

The first meal might be centered around a turkey, ham, or roast, so hopefully you will have leftovers enough for quick, easy-to-prepare sandwiches. Congealed salads, frozen desserts, and a well stocked refrigerator allow for flexible schedules and serving snacks or meals with equal ease.

As breakfast can be time-consuming and get your day off to a late start, some hostesses prefer to set out a partially prepared pick-up of juice, fruit, cereal or a pastry, coffee or tea. Then guests may rise and breakfast at their pleasure. Those who feel that a hot breakfast is a necessity find that bacon cooked in advance and frozen comes out crisp and tasty when warmed for a few moments under the broiler. Shortcuts can let you be a happy hostess without feeling that you have shortchanged your guests.

Beef Tips Dinner

DINNER FOR SIX TO EIGHT

Braised Sirloin Tips

Noodles au Tim

or

Rice with Almonds

Baked Carrots (optional)   **Green Peas, Chinese Style**

Brandy Peaches

Coffee   **Tea**

BRAISED SIRLOIN TIPS

3 tablespoons butter or margarine	2 tablespoons soy sauce
1-1/2 pounds fresh mushrooms, sliced	2 cloves garlic, minced
1 tablespoon salad oil	1/2 onion, grated
3 pounds sirloin steak or beef tenderloin tail, cut into 1-inch cubes	2 tablespoons cornstarch
3/4 cup beef bouillon	1/3 cup beef bouillon
3/4 cup Burgundy	1/2 (10-1/2-ounce) can cream of mushroom soup

Heat 1 tablespoon of the butter in skillet. Add fresh mushrooms and cook until they just begin to turn brown. Put into deep casserole. Add remaining 2 tablespoons butter and oil to skillet and heat. Brown meat on all sides; remove to the casserole where the mushrooms are waiting. Stir into skillet the 3/4 cup bouillon, wine, soy sauce, garlic, and onion. Heat, scraping bottom of skillet to salvage all the particles. Blend cornstarch with the 1/3 cup bouillon. Add to skillet, stirring constantly, and cook until mixture thickens. Pour into casserole, cover and cook at 275° for 1 hour. Stir in the mushroom soup until smooth, check for seasoning; it may need a little salt. Serve accompanied by noodles or rice. Yield: 8 servings.

NOODLES AU TIM

8 ounces 1/4-inch noodles	1 canned green chile, mashed (rest of can may be frozen)
2 cups cottage cheese	1 or 2 dashes Tabasco sauce
1-1/4 cups commercial sour cream	3 heaping tablespoons minced fresh parsley
1/4 cup melted butter or margarine	Salt and pepper to taste
1/4 cup minced onion	Paprika
1 clove garlic, crushed	
1 teaspoon Worcestershire sauce	

Cook noodles in boiling salted water for 8 to 10 minutes, or just until done. Drain and rinse thoroughly under cold water.

Combine all other ingredients in a large bowl except paprika. Add cooked noodles, check for seasoning, and turn into buttered casserole (I use a 12- x 8- x 2-inch baking dish). Sprinkle with paprika; cover with aluminum foil if casserole has no lid. Bake at 350° for 45 minutes. Yield: 8 to 10 servings.

RICE WITH ALMONDS
(see Index)

BAKED CARROTS

1-1/2 pounds carrots, scraped or peeled	3 tablespoons light brown sugar
3/4 teaspoon salt	3 tablespoons butter or margarine

Carrots may be left whole, cut in half or sliced. Arrange in casserole with tight-fitting cover; sprinkle with salt and sugar, and dot with butter. Bake at 325° for 1 hour if carrots are whole; for a shorter time if cut or sliced. Yield: 8 servings.

GREEN PEAS, CHINESE STYLE

1/4 cup olive oil	4 teaspoons cornstarch
1/4 cup salad oil	1 cup beef broth
3 (10-ounce) packages frozen peas	1 teaspoon soy sauce
3 medium onions, chopped	Salt to taste
1-1/2 cups coarsely chopped celery	
1 (5-ounce) can water chestnuts, drained and sliced	

Heat olive and salad oil in large skillet over high heat. Add all vegetables and when peas start sputtering, cover, turn heat low and cook for 10 to 15 minutes, stirring occasionally. *Do not allow vegetables to get overdone*; they must remain crisp. Dissolve cornstarch in 1/4 cup of the broth, then combine with remaining broth. Pour over vegetables and cook, stirring constantly, until slightly thickened and transparent. Add seasonings and cook 1 minute longer; serve at once or keep warm in slow oven. Yield: 10 servings.

BRANDY PEACHES
(may be prepared ahead of time)

Following are directions for 1 serving; multiply according to the number of servings required. Use the best grade of canned peaches in heavy syrup you can find. During peach season, fresh fruit may be used — but adjust baking time.

Place two peach halves in a shallow baking pan with some of the syrup, cavity-side up. Pour over peaches 1 tablespoon maple syrup and in the cavity put 1 tablespoon brown sugar and 1 teaspoon butter. Sprinkle with cinnamon and bake uncovered at 325° for about 20 minutes. (Bake fresh peaches about 40 minutes, or until done.) At this point, peaches may be refrigerated until needed (they'll keep at least a week). To serve, pour brandy over peaches and top with ice cream or whipped cream, as desired.

Ham-In-Claret Dinner

DINNER FOR SIX

Ham-in-Claret with Orange-Currant Sauce

Southern Green Beans
or
Green Beans with Bacon

Pineapple-Sweet Potatoes

Cranberry Waldorf Salad Ring
or
Relish Platter

Sour Cream Corn Pones   **Butter**

Elegant Pound Cake

Coffee   **Iced Tea**

Note: The inclusion of a sweet sauce in this menu is subject to question (my own, chiefly). However, it is the perfect accompaniment for baked ham, so despite the presence of other sweet dishes in this menu, I persuaded myself to let it come along.— C. M.

HAM-IN-CLARET

1 whole tenderized ham (preferably dry-cured, with no water added)
1 bottle (a fifth) Claret wine
4 whole cloves

6 very small whole onions
1 tablespoon brown sugar
1 small bay leaf
Madeira or dry sherry wine

Place ham in container large enough to allow cooking liquid to cover meat completely. Pour the wine over ham, then add enough water to cover the meat. Add cloves, onions, sugar, and bay leaf. Allow ham to come to a boil as slowly as possible; it will probably take 2 hours. Then let ham simmer quietly, until tender (about 20 minutes to the pound). Allow ham to cool in its cooking liquor, then refrigerate in the same liquor.

When almost ready to serve, remove ham from its bath of liquid and remove rind. Bake at 350° for 45 minutes, basting every 15 minutes with Madeira or dry sherry wine.

ORANGE-CURRANT SAUCE

2 teaspoons dry mustard
1 teaspoon paprika
1 teaspoon ground ginger
1/4 teaspoon salt

2 tablespoons freshly squeezed
  lemon juice
Juice and grated rind of 2 oranges
2 tablespoons water
1/2 cup currant jelly

Mix dry ingredients; add fruit juices, rind, and water. Allow to stand 1/2 hour; combine with jelly in saucepan and heat gently; do not boil. Sauce should be served just warm. Yield: about 1 cup.

SOUTHERN GREEN BEANS

3 slices bacon
4 cups water
2 pounds fresh green beans
1/2 teaspoon sugar

1 small dried red pepper
  pod or dash Tabasco sauce
Salt and pepper (optional)

Place bacon in large saucepan with water. Bring to boiling; reduce heat, cover and simmer for 30 minutes. Wash beans and trim ends; break into 1-inch pieces. Add beans, sugar, and red pepper to bacon. Cover and cook over very low heat for 3 hours. If necessary, from time to time add water just to keep beans from sticking. Taste during last hour of cooking and add salt and pepper if needed. Yield: 6 to 8 servings.

Note: No one ever cooked better green beans than my mother-in-law. She followed the above method, but about 15 minutes before serving, she would sift about a teaspoon of flour into the pot, stir it well into the juices in the bottom, then resume cooking the beans. This coated the beans ever so slightly and there was never one drop of clear, watery liquid to remain in a puddle in bottom of the cooking pot. — C. M.

GREEN BEANS WITH BACON

3 slices bacon, diced
1 medium onion, chopped

2 (10-ounce) packages frozen French-style
  green beans
Salt and pepper

Fry bacon in a skillet until almost crisp. Pour off excess fat, add onion and sauté until tender but not brown. Cook green beans according to package directions until barely tender. Drain and add to skillet. Stir well, season with salt and pepper; keep warm in covered dish until serving time. Yield: 6 servings.

PINEAPPLE-SWEET POTATOES

5 medium sweet potatoes
(preferably red yams)
3 tablespoons melted butter
1/4 teaspoon salt

1 (8-1/2-ounce) can crushed
pineapple, undrained
6 tablespoons chopped Brazil nuts
(pecans or walnuts may be
substituted)

Scrub and boil potatoes until tender. Peel and mash, adding butter, salt, and undrained pineapple. Beat with wooden spoon until smooth and light. Stir in 5 tablespoons chopped nuts and turn into buttered casserole. Bake covered at 375° for 20 minutes; remove cover, sprinkle with remaining nuts and continue baking for another 10 minutes, uncovered. Yield: 6 servings.

CRANBERRY WALDORF SALAD RING

2 envelopes unflavored gelatin
1 cup orange juice
2 (1-pound) cans whole-berry
cranberry sauce

1/2 cup chopped peeled apple
1/2 cup chopped celery
1/2 cup chopped walnuts
Crisp greens

Sprinkle gelatin on orange juice to soften; let soak for 5 minutes. Place over low heat; stir until gelatin is dissolved. Remove from heat and combine with cranberry sauce. Chill until partially set; fold in apple, celery, and walnuts. Pour into 1-1/2-quart ring mold; chill until firm. Unmold onto crisp greens. Yield: 8 to 10 servings.

SOUR CREAM CORN PONES

1 cup white cornmeal, unsifted
(preferably water-ground)
1/2 teaspoon salt
1/2 cup boiling water

1/4 teaspoon soda
1/4 cup commercial sour cream
1 tablespoon melted butter

Mix cornmeal and salt in a bowl; stir in boiling water. The mixture will resemble dry crumbs. Cover and refrigerate an hour, or until you're ready to bake pones.

About 45 minutes before serving, remove bowl from refrigerator. Stir soda into sour cream; mix with crumbs, then add melted butter. Mixture should be paste-like. Heat oven to 425°; on surface unit heat large heavy skillet containing 1 tablespoon butter. Form heaping tablespoons of batter into small cakes; pat them 1/2 inch thick; place in hot skillet and put in oven. Bake 25 to 30 minutes. If top of cakes are pale, turn and bake another 5 minutes. Serve piping hot with butter — and honey if you like it. Yield: about 10 small pones.

Variation: If preferred, sweet cream and 1 teaspoon baking powder may be substituted for sour cream and soda.

ELEGANT POUND CAKE
(may be prepared ahead of time)

8 eggs, separated
2-2/3 cups granulated sugar
1 pound butter (no substitute)

3-1/2 cups all-purpose flour, measured after sifting
1/2 cup light cream
1 teaspoon vanilla extract

Separate eggs. Measure sugar and set aside. Beat egg whites until soft peaks form; gradually add 6 tablespoons of the sugar while continuing to beat until stiff. Refrigerate until needed.

Cream butter in large mixer bowl until light; gradually beat in remaining sugar. Add well beaten egg yolks. Sift flour three times and add alternately with cream and vanilla, beginning and ending with flour. Beat until mixture is very light (about 10 minutes at low speed of mixer).

Now add egg whites, in this manner: Spoon out a heaping tablespoon of the whites and stir vigorously into the batter. Make no attempt to fold it in; it is to be stirred in thoroughly. (This loosens and lightens the texture of the batter and prepares it to receive the remaining whites.) Now fold in egg whites thoroughly. Pour into lightly greased 10-inch tubepan at least 4 inches deep. Bake at 300° for 1-3/4 hours. Invert onto wire rack and allow to cool. Loosen around edges with spatula and remove to serving plate. Requires no icing. Freezes well. Yield: 15 to 18 servings.

STOCKING THE BAR

For a large party, an experienced bartender should be hired. For a smaller group (20 or so), your co-host or a friend may be asked to tend bar for the first hour, after which time he may leave his post to join other guests, leaving bottles, ice, and mixers out so guests may help themselves to refills.

How much liquor to buy? There are seventeen 1-1/2-ounce drinks in a fifth of liquor; roughly 200 drinks to a case (12 bottles to a case). To be on the safe side, allow three drinks per guest. Some guests will have only one drink, but it's better to have too much than not enough.

If your party is a sizeable one you'll undoubtedly have some non-drinkers. For them, it's thoughtful to have a large pitcher of chilled fruit juice and another of chilled tomato or V-8 juice. Scotch, bourbon or rye, vodka, gin, plenty of mixers (tonic, ginger ale, club soda), and lots and lots of ice are necessary for stocking the bar.

You can start making ice a week before the party and store the cubes in plastic bags in the freezer. If you don't have a freezer, buy the ice during the afternoon of party-day and keep it in a tub out of sight.

And, oh yes, provide plenty of lemon wedges. And please provide a tray or table for used glasses!

Choucroute Garnie Dinner

DINNER FOR SIX

Choucroute Garnie

Stuffed Potatoes Lala

or

Buttered New Potatoes with Caraway Seed

Commercial Rye Bread   **Butter**

Apple Dumplings
or
Pecan Pie

Coffee   **Iced Tea**

Note: This is a lusty, flavorful menu recommended only if you know the tastes of your guests. — C. M.

CHOUCROUTE GARNIE

3 slices bacon, cut in thirds crosswise	10 juniper berries (optional)
1 carrot	12 (1/4-inch) slices baked ham
1 medium onion	1 (10-ounce) can chicken
1 (29-ounce) can shredded sauerkraut	bouillon, undiluted
1 (1-pound) can shredded sauerkraut	2/3 cup dry white wine
Coarse black pepper	12 link pork sausages

Arrange bacon slices like spokes of a wheel in bottom of heavy deep casserole. Between slices place carrot cut in long, thin slivers. Place whole onion in center.

Empty kraut into colander and run cold water over it quickly. Drain and press out liquid; now fluff it up with a fork so it is no longer packed.

Arrange a third of kraut in casserole over the bacon; sprinkle with pepper, then add 5 juniper berries. Cover with ham; repeat layering, then top with last third of kraut. Pour the bouillon, then wine over all; cover tightly. If casserole lid doesn't fit snugly, place a sheet of waxed paper over kraut before placing lid down firmly.

Bake at 300° for 2 hours, or if more convenient, several hours at 200°. About 30 minutes before serving, brown pork sausages slowly in skillet, drain off fat and keep warm. Just before serving, arrange over top of Choucroute. Yield: 6 servings.

STUFFED POTATOES LALA
(prepare ahead of time and freeze)

4 baking potatoes	2 tablespoons commercial sour cream
1 (3-ounce) package cream cheese with chives	1 egg
3 tablespoons butter or margarine	1/2 teaspoon salt
1/2 cup grated Parmesan cheese (or mixed Parmesan and grated Swiss)	Dash pepper

Scrub potatoes well; grease with shortening. Put into 400° oven and bake for 1 hour, or until fork tender. Split potatoes in half lengthwise and scoop out into large bowl of electric mixer. Add all other ingredients except egg and beat until well blended. Add egg and continue to beat until smooth and creamy. Fill six potato shell halves (discard the remaining shells); sprinkle top of each potato half with additional grated cheese and paprika. Bake at 375° for 20 minutes, or until puffed and lightly browned.

Potatoes may be frozen before second baking. If so, allow to thaw and add cheese and paprika topping just before baking. Yield: 6 servings.

Note: If cream cheese with chives is not available, use plain cream cheese and add a teaspoon of minced chives.

BUTTERED NEW POTATOES WITH CARAWAY SEED

Boil new potatoes in jackets until just tender, allowing three potatoes per serving. Drain and peel. Roll in melted butter; sprinkle with salt, paprika, and caraway seed. Serve immediately or keep warm in slow oven until serving time.

Variation: Wash potatoes thoroughly and using a vegetable peeler remove a thin strip of peeling around middle of each potato. Leave rest of peeling on.

APPLE DUMPLINGS

1-1/2 cups all-purpose flour	3 or 4 firm red apples
1/2 teaspoon baking powder	6 tablespoons sugar
1/2 teaspoon salt	1 teaspoon ground cinnamon
1/2 cup shortening	1/4 teaspoon ground nutmeg
1/4 cup ice water or orange juice	6 tablespoons butter

Sift flour, baking powder, and salt into a bowl. With pastry blender cut in 1/2 cup shortening. Gradually add about 1/4 cup ice water or orange juice until dough holds together. Form into a ball, wrap in waxed paper and chill until ready to use.

Wash and peel apples, reserving the peeling. Cut apples in small cubes; set aside. Combine 6 tablespoons sugar, 1 teaspoon ground cinnamon, and 1/4 teaspoon ground nutmeg; set aside.

Roll pastry 1/8 inch thick on floured surface; cut in 6-inch squares. In center of each place 1 tablespoon butter, then a generous 1-1/2 tablespoons cubed apple. Sprinkle with a tablespoon of the sugar mixture; gather up corners of pastry and pinch together in center and along cut edges. Place in greased baking dish with edges touching; bake at 375° for about 45 minutes, or until golden. Serve the dumplings warm with Sauce.

Sauce

Apple peelings	1 tablespoon all-purpose flour
1-1/2 cups water	1 cup sugar
1/4 cup butter	Juice of 1/2 lemon

In saucepan boil red peelings with 1-1/2 cups water until reduced to 3/4 cup; discard the peelings. In another saucepan melt 1/4 cup butter; blend in 1 tablespoon flour; gradually add peeling liquid. Stir in 1 scant cup sugar and juice of 1/2 lemon. Cook until thickened, stirring constantly. Serve warm over dumplings. Yield: 6 servings.

Variation: One cup cream, whipped, may be added to the cooled sauce. Either way, these dumplings are divine.

PECAN PIE

6 tablespoons butter (no substitute)	1 cup dark corn syrup
1/2 cup granulated sugar	1 cup broken pecans
3 eggs, beaten lightly	1 (9-inch) unbaked pastry shell
Dash salt	Unbroken pecan halves

Cream butter and sugar in bowl until blended but not fluffy. Add beaten eggs, salt, syrup, and broken pecans. Pour into unbaked pastry shell, top with unbroken pecan halves and bake at 325° for about 50 minutes, or until pie tests done when knife inserted in center comes out clean. Yield: 6 to 8 servings.

FOR THE CONVENIENCE OF GUESTS WHO SMOKE

Place several lighted candles around the room if you've invited guests who smoke. For some unkown reason they help to clear the air of smoke. Specially treated candles which do this little job even more effectively are available at most variety stores. They come in multicolored glass containers and also add to the overall decorative effect in the room. But most important, they ensure the comfort of non-smoking guests.

Set out your extra ashtrays the day before the party. There is nothing more discomforting to a smoker than a room without an ashtray, so always have plenty of them around. Be sure, too, that your ashtrays are large and comfortably spaced throughout the room.

Empty the ashtrays at regular intervals. It's easier to empty small ashtrays into one large one than it is to stack up several little ashrays for emptying. A thoughtful hostess always provides filter and non-filter cigarettes in several convenient places throughout the room.

Cantonese Turkey Dinner

DINNER FOR TEN TO TWELVE

Cantonese Turkey with Rice Dressing

Broccoli Amandine   **Cranberry Salad**

Hot Commercial Rolls   **Butter**

Butterscotch Parfait

or

Sherbet and Cookies

Coffee   **Tea**

CANTONESE TURKEY

1 (14-pound) turkey	1/3 cup soy sauce
1 teaspoon poultry seasoning	1/4 cup dry sherry
1 teaspoon seasoned salt	1/2 cup chopped green onions, or
1/2 teaspoon salt	1 medium onion, minced
1/2 teaspoon freshly ground black pepper	1/2 cup chopped celery
1 teaspoon ground ginger	1 cup water
3 cloves garlic, crushed	

Wash, clean, and dry turkey; reserve neck, giblets, and liver. Place turkey in roaster, breast-side up. Mix dry seasonings together and rub inside and outside of bird. Tie legs with string. Combine garlic, soy sauce, and sherry and pour slowly over turkey. Scatter onions and celery over and around bird; pour water into bottom of roaster. Cover and bake at 350° for about 3-1/2 hours, or until done, basting frequently.

When turkey is almost tender, remove cover and allow to finish baking uncovered, about 30 minutes. (If turkey has browned sufficiently, this is unnecessary.)

The liquid in bottom of roaster may be combined with giblet broth to make a delicious gravy. Yield: 12 servings.

Turkey Broth

Put neck, giblets, and liver into saucepan. Add 4 cups chicken broth made of 4 bouillon cubes and hot water. Add 1 stalk celery cut in chunks and 1 whole small onion. Cover and simmer slowly for about 2 hours. When giblets are done, strain the soup. Do not add seasonings; the chicken broth will have yielded enough. If desired, thicken gravy slightly by adding a little flour or cornstarch, stirred first into a small amount of the hot gravy, then return to the pot. If desired, dice giblets and stir into gravy.

RICE DRESSING
(prepare the day before)

2 cups regular long-grain rice	1/2 cup butter or margarine
3 large onions, minced	1 tablespoon salt
4 stalks celery, minced	1 tablespoon poultry seasoning
1 green pepper, minced	2 eggs
Fresh or canned mushrooms; reserve liquid (optional)	1 cup chopped pecans
Chopped cooked giblets from turkey	1/2 cup chopped parsley

Cook rice according to your favorite method. While it cooks, sauté onions, celery, pepper, canned or fresh sliced mushrooms, and giblets in the butter until vegetables are tender but not brown. Add seasonings and mix well. Combine with cooked rice and eggs which have been beaten until frothy. Add nuts and parsley; moisten with mushroom liquid (or chicken or turkey broth) if mixture seems dry. Turn into shallow greased baking dish and bake at 350° for about 30 minutes, or until brown and crusty. Yield: 12 servings.

BROCCOLI AMANDINE

3 (10-ounce) packages frozen broccoli spears	1/2 cup slivered blanched almonds
1/4 cup butter or margarine	1/4 cup freshly squeezed lemon juice

Cook broccoli according to directions on package, until just tender; do not overcook. Heat butter in a medium saucepan and sauté almonds for a few minutes; remove from heat; stir in lemon juice and just before serving pour over broccoli on a heated platter. Yield: 10 to 12 servings.

If good fresh broccoli is available, it would be preferable.

FRESH BROCCOLI

Follow directions precisely and you'll never drown or overcook another bunch of broccoli.

Cut away thin slice from tough bottom of broccoli stalks. Cut off each stalk at thick joint where flower-end begins, usually about 3 inches from the bottom. Peel lower stalk with vegetable peeler or small sharp paring knife; cut into 1/2-inch strips. Now peel lower stem-end of flowered stalk. Cut a shallow cross-slash in bottom of stem-ends to hasten cooking.

Put all into a bowl of cold water for a few minutes; swish the broccoli around, then rinse under cold running water.

To cook the vegetable you will need a huge pot for boiling and a wire salad basket or reasonable facsimile which will go into the pot. You can improvise here; I use the basket section of a deep fat fryer.

Put broccoli in the wire basket until time to cook. Bring salted water to a rolling boil in the big pot; plunge basket of broccoli into pot and boil uncovered for about 6 to 8 minutes. Taste to see if broccoli is done; it should be slightly crisp.

If broccoli is done before you're quite ready to serve, remove from cooking water and put in an ovenproof bowl in a warm oven until you're ready to serve it. The vegetable should not be allowed to remain in cooking water longer than necessary.

For fresh cauliflower: Trim off bottom and tough leaves. Separate flowerets (in fairly large clusters); cut a cross in stems as for broccoli, then follow same directions. Boil for around 8 to 10 minutes. Keep tasting; don't overcook.

CRANBERRY SALAD
(prepare the day before)

2 (3-ounce) packages lemon-flavored gelatin
2 cups boiling water
1 envelope unflavored gelatin
3 tablespoons cold water

2 cups sugar
4 red apples, cored but not peeled
4 cups fresh cranberries
1 whole orange, peeled (reserve peeling but remove white membranes)

Dissolve flavored gelatin in boiling water. Soften plain gelatin in cold water, then stir into hot mixture until completely dissolved. Add sugar, stir well and set aside.

Put apples, cranberries, orange rind, and orange pulp through food grinder. Combine with gelatin mixture; pour into 13- x 9- x 2-inch dish or into 12 individual molds. If preferred, mixture may be turned into a 10-inch mold. Chill until set. Yield: 12 servings.

BUTTERSCOTCH PARFAIT
(prepare ahead of time and freeze)

1-1/4 cups brown sugar
2 tablespoons butter (no substitute)
1/2 cup water
3 eggs, separated

1 teaspoon vanilla extract
1-1/2 cups heavy cream, whipped
1/2 cup chopped pecans

Put sugar and butter in small saucepan and heat to boiling; boil for 1 minute. Add water, stir until sugar is melted, then boil without stirring to 238° on a candy thermometer or until syrup forms a soft ball when a little is dropped into cold water. Cool slightly, about 10 minutes, then pour slowly into egg yolks which have been well beaten. Beat until cold and thick. Fold in stiffly beaten egg whites, vanilla, whipped cream, and nuts. Spoon into parfait glasses or freezing tray. A few additional chopped nuts may be sprinkled over top if desired. Yield: about 8 servings.

Chicken en Casserole Dinner

DINNER FOR EIGHT

Chicken en Casserole

Baked Fresh Tomatoes	
or	**Mushroom Spinach**
Winter Broiled Tomatoes	

Deep South Cucumber Salad (optional)

Corn Spoonbread

Apricot Brandy Pound Cake	**Ice Cream**
Coffee	**Tea**

CHICKEN EN CASSEROLE
(may be prepared the day before)

2 (2-1/2-pound) roasting or broiling chickens or 5 pounds breasts, thighs, and legs
Salt and pepper
3 tablespoons butter or margarine
1/3 cup small cubes of salt pork
1-1/2 cups dry white wine (Chablis is good)
1 can mushrooms (any size you can afford)
1 (1-pound) can small whole onions, drained
12 carrot pieces, cut about 1 inch long
Bouquet garni
1 cup commercial sour cream
Pinch dried tarragon

Season chicken pieces with salt and pepper. Heat butter and pork cubes in skillet. Add chicken and brown on all sides. Transfer all (including pork bits) to a large casserole. Stir in wine, undrained mushrooms, onions, carrot pieces, and bouquet garni. Cover casserole tightly (use foil if you have no perfectly fitting lid) and bake at 350° for 1 hour. Remove seasoning bag and stir in 1 cup sour cream flavored with a pinch of dried tarragon. Return to oven and bake another half hour. Yield: 8 servings.

BOUGUET GARNI

A small cheesecloth bag containing 1 large bay leaf, 1/4 teaspoon leaf thyme, 1/4 teaspoon dried basil, about 8 sprigs fresh parsley, 1/4 teaspoon dried tarragon, 3 chopped green celery tops, 6 whole peppercorns, and a slashed clove of garlic.

BAKED FRESH TOMATOES

4 large firm ripe tomatoes	1 clove garlic
3/4 teaspoon sugar	2 green onions, minced or 2 tablespoons minced chives
2 cups finely grated dry French breadcrumbs	1 teaspoon dried oregano, crushed
4 tablespoons melted butter or margarine	Salt and pepper to taste

Cut tomatoes in half. Salt each half lightly and sprinkle with a pinch of sugar. Combine breadcrumbs, melted butter, garlic, green onion, oregano, salt, and pepper. Mound over tomato halves, place under broiler just until golden on top, then bake at 350° for about 20 minutes — just until tomatoes are done but not collapsed. Yield: 8 servings.

WINTER BROILED TOMATOES

2 (1-pound) cans whole tomatoes	1/8 teaspoon dried basil (crushed as you sprinkle)
Salt and pepper	Chives
Sugar	
Garlic powder (optional)	1 to 2 teaspoons grated Parmesan cheese per tomato

Thoroughly drain tomatoes. If they are extra large, cut in half; otherwise leave whole. Arrange in shallow baking dish and sprinkle top of each tomato with above ingredients. Place under a slow broiler until tomatoes are heated through and cheese is lightly browned. Do not overcook or the cheese will be bitter. Broiling time is 5 to 10 minutes. Yield: 6 to 8 servings.

MUSHROOM SPINACH
(may be prepared the day before)

3 (10-ounce) packages frozen chopped spinach	1/2 teaspoon seasoned salt
2 tablespoons butter or margarine	1/2 teaspoon salt
2 tablespoons olive oil	Pepper to taste
1 small onion, grated	2 teaspoons soy sauce
2 (4-ounce) cans sliced mushrooms, reserve liquid	1/8 teaspoon ground nutmeg
	1 tablespoon all-purpose flour
1 clove garlic, crushed	1 cup commercial sour cream
	1 to 2 teaspoons grated lemon rind

Cook spinach according to package directions; drain thoroughly and set aside.

Heat butter and oil in heavy skillet; add onion and cook 1 minute. Stir in mushrooms and garlic; sauté 5 minutes, stirring constantly. Add spinach and all seasonings. Make a paste of flour and mushroom liquid; blend into sour cream; combine with spinach. Stir in lemon rind and heat through but do not boil. Keep warm until serving time. Yield: 8 to 10 servings.

DEEP SOUTH CUCUMBER SALAD
(prepare ahead of time)

2 cucumbers

1 cup commercial sour cream

1-1/2 teaspoons salt

Black pepper

1 (or more) large white onion, sliced

2 tablespoons vinegar

Peel and slice cucumbers very thin. Arrange in layers in large shallow dish; sprinkle each layer with salt and place a plate over dish. Weight the plate down with something heavy. Allow to stand at room temperature about 2 hours. Squeeze liquid from cucumbers with hands; combine with all other ingredients and chill several hours — or days — before serving. Yield: 8 servings.

CORN SPOONBREAD

1 cup white or yellow cornmeal

1 cup commercial sour cream

1 (1-pound) can cream-style corn

2 eggs

1-1/2 teaspoons salt

2 teaspoons baking powder

1/2 cup corn oil

Combine all ingredients except oil and mix only until blended. Heat oil in large casserole or skillet and when smoking, stir into batter. Turn into the still-hot casserole and bake at 375° for 30 to 40 minutes, or until bread tests done. Serve immediately. Yield: 8 servings.

Note: This recipe was given to me as cornbread. However, I find it serves beautifully as both bread and a starchy vegetable. With or without butter, it is excellent; very delicate with a fine texture. — C. M.

APRICOT BRANDY POUND CAKE
(may be prepared ahead of time)

1 cup butter (no substitute)

3 cups granulated sugar

6 eggs

3 cups all-purpose flour, measured
   after sifting

1/4 teaspoon soda

1/2 teaspoon salt

1 cup commercial sour cream

1/2 teaspoon rum flavoring

1 teaspoon orange extract

1/4 teaspoon almond extract

1/2 teaspoon lemon extract

1 teaspoon vanilla extract

1/2 cup apricot brandy

Grease and flour a large tube or bundt pan. In large bowl of an electric mixer cream butter and sugar thoroughly. Add eggs one at a time, beating well after each addition. Sift together flour, soda, and salt three times. Combine sour cream, flavorings, and brandy. Add dry ingredients alternately with cream mixture, beginning and ending with the dry. Pour into prepared pan and bake at 325° for 1 hour or until cake tests done. It usually requires 1 hour and 10 minutes. Freezes well. Yield: 15 servings.

Southern Fish Fry

DINNER FOR EIGHT

Manhattan Fish Chowder with Crackers

Fried Fish and Tartar Sauce

Mixed Salad Greens and Fresh Tomatoes with Oil and Vinegar Dressing

Hush Puppies

Iced Watermelon

or

Lemon Chiffon Bavarian

Coffee   **Iced Tea**

MANHATTAN CLAM CHOWDER
(prepare ahead of time and freeze)

3 slices bacon, diced	1 teaspoon salt
1 cup chopped onion	1/4 teaspoon freshly ground black pepper
1 cup chopped celery	1 bay leaf
1/2 green pepper, diced	1/2 teaspoon dried leaf thyme
1 (29-ounce) can tomatoes	3 cups diced raw potato
3 (7-1/2-ounce) cans minced clams	2 tablespoons minced fresh parsley
3 cups fish stock or water	2 tablespoons butter or margarine

In large Dutch oven or heavy kettle fry bacon until almost crisp. Add onion, celery, and green pepper; cook slowly for about 10 minutes stirring occasionally, until vegetables are tender and golden. Stir in tomatoes.

Drain clams, reserving the liquid; set clams aside. Add clam liquid to soup pot along with fish stock or water. Now add salt, pepper, bay leaf, and thyme. Bring to boiling point, reduce heat to a simmer, cover and cook slowly for about 1 hour. Add potatoes, continue cooking for about 30 minutes, until potatoes are quite tender. Now add reserved clams and cook uncovered for 15 minutes. Stir in parsley and butter before serving. Yield: about 3 quarts or 12 servings.

Note: I prefer to use fish stock instead of water, and if your fresh fish has been fileted, it's a waste not to make all those good bones and bits of fish meat into a stock. If you must use water, increase salt to 2 teaspoons.

FISH STOCK

This is the perfect way to use whole rough fish such as shad, buffalo, carp, or other fish you don't want to filet for frying.

2 tablespoons butter or margarine	2 bay leaves
3 to 4 pounds fish and bones (use fish, skin and bones left after fileting, plus about 2 whole fish; the exact amount doesn't matter, but you should have plenty)	2 cloves garlic, minced
	2 onions, coarsely chopped
	10 whole peppercorns
	1 carrot, coarsely chopped
3-1/2 quarts water	1 bunch celery, coarsely chopped
1/2 teaspoon dried leaf thyme	2 teaspoons salt

In the largest soup kettle you have, heat butter; when melted add fish and water. Stir well, add remaining ingredients, bring to a boil. Cover and simmer at least 1 hour; 2 is better. Strain stock, put in small containers and freeze. (I find it most practical to freeze the broth in 1-cup containers.)

Use this broth whenever a veloute sauce is required for preparing creamed seafood dishes.

FRIED FISH

Put 2 unbeaten egg whites in a shallow soup bowl. Put seasoned cornmeal (salt and a pinch of pepper) in another shallow bowl. Pat fish dry with paper towels. Dip in egg whites, then cornmeal, coating evenly though lightly on both sides. Fry in deep fat heated to 375°. Serve with lemon wedges and tartar sauce. Leftover fish may be frozen, and reheated in oven.

To keep fried fish hot and crisp, as you finish frying one batch, put on a platter in a warm oven, with the door wedged open. A little heat escapes into the kitchen, but it keeps the fish crisp.

TARTAR SAUCE PIQUANTE
(prepare ahead of time)

1 cup mayonnaise	2 teaspoons capers, drained
1 teaspoon minced sour pickle	1 tablespoon minced green olives
1 tablespoon minced chives or 1 teaspoon dried chives	2 tablespoons freshly squeezed lemon juice
2 teaspoons grated onion	Generous dash paprika
4 radishes, peeled and finely slivered	Black pepper and Tabasco sauce to taste

Combine all ingredients thoroughly and chill before serving. This is different from the routine tartar sauces and exceptionally good; it is better if made the day before using. Yield: about 2 cups.

MRS. CHANDLER'S POTATO SALAD
(see Index)

BASIC GREEN SALAD

This salad is like the little basic black dress; use as is, or dress it up.

The salad should be made in a large bowl. Ingredients should not fill the bowl as that makes thorough tossing difficult.

Place a scant teaspoon salt and 1 peeled clove garlic in bottom of bowl. With back of wooden spoon mash until garlic practically disappears. If there's a hair or two of it left, discard that. Now fill the large wooden spoon with oil and gradually work it into the salt. (A large wooden salad spoon usually holds about 2 measuring tablespoons.)

Tear a large firm head of rinsed, thoroughly dried lettuce (or any salad greens desired) into bite-size pieces, dropping them directly into the bowl. Don't toss it yet. This part may be done an hour ahead of serving, the bowl covered with a damp towel or waxed paper.

Just before serving, add several grinds black pepper; toss thoroughly until all greens are well coated with oil. Now add 3 or 4 ripe unpeeled tomatoes or any other vegetables you like; toss a few seconds. Taste for seasoning at this point.

Now pour the same large salad spoon full of lemon juice or wine vinegar and drizzle over salad; toss briefly and serve. This may seem to be scanty dressing, but it will be enough. Yield: 6 servings.

Variation: Follow same method of preparing salt and garlic as described. Add 2 drained anchovies; mash into salt. (Anchovy paste may be substituted.) Add a scant teaspoon Dijon or Dusseldorf mustard and a few grinds black pepper; continue to blend until paste-like. Pour salad oil into large spoon you're using and gradually work into a paste, using 2 large tablespoons in all. When well blended, gradually stir in 1 large tablespoon wine or tarragon vinegar. Add greens, toss well and serve.

HUSH PUPPIES

2 cups cornmeal	1 egg
1 tablespoon all-purpose flour	3 tablespoons minced onion
1/2 teaspoon soda	1 cup buttermilk
1 teaspoon baking powder	Hot shortening
1 teaspoon salt	

Mix in order listed and drop by spoonfuls into deep hot shortening. Fry until brown; drain on absorbent paper; serve piping hot with fish — or anything. Yield: 8 servings.

ASK A FRIEND TO HELP

If you're hostessing a party without help, ask a friend to keep you posted on when trays need replenishing. Better yet, ask her to refill them herself. I have never known a guest who wasn't pleased to be asked to help in this way.

LEMON CHIFFON BAVARIAN
(prepare the day before)

Crust

2 cups crushed vanilla wafers   1/2 cup melted butter
1/4 teaspoon ground cinnamon

Combine wafer crumbs, cinnamon, and butter; press onto sides and bottom of an 8- or 9-inch springform pan, reserving 1/4 cup of the crumbs mixture.

Filling

4 eggs, separated   1/4 cup cold water
1/2 cup sugar   1/4 cup hot water
Juice of 2 large lemons   1/2 cup sugar
Grated rind of 2 or 3 lemons   1 cup heavy cream, whipped
1 envelope unflavored gelatin

Beat egg yolks with 1/2 cup sugar in small bowl of electric mixer until thick and lemon colored. Add lemon juice and rind; transfer to top of double boiler and cook, stirring constantly until thickened. Soften gelatin in cold water; dissolve in hot water and add to custard. Stir well and cool until slightly congealed. (You may hasten the process by placing mixture in refrigerator but watch it closely as it congeals rapidly.)

Beat egg whites until soft peaks form; add the second 1/2 cup sugar a tablespoon at a time, until whites are stiff and glossy. Remove custard from refrigerator; fold in egg whites, then whipped cream. Pour into crust-lined pan, top with reserved crumbs and chill until firm.

To serve, remove rim of pan; place on paper doily on cakeplate. Yield: 8 servings.

Menus from Favorite Southern Restaurants

There's been a change in Southern restaurants in the past 25 years. Southerners have demanded more sophistication in their dining, and restaurants have responded.

In cities throughout the South, opportunities for excellent dining abound. Chefs, many of whom have received training abroad, have brought to the Southern states the delicate skill of making sauces and breathtaking desserts. And competent waiters match this elegance in their presentation of the food from chef to diner.

Though the background may differ, these restaurants maintain one common characteristic: their heritage of hospitality and pride in the art of preparing and serving a meal of perfection. It is a heritage that is nourished perhaps by the liaison between European and Southern traditions.

Favorite menus from several restaurants are included here in hopes that you may enjoy the specialties that add flavor and variety to the best of the South's cuisine.

Breakfast at Brennan's

BREAKFAST FOR TWO

Brennan Milk Punch

or

Bloody Mary

Grilled Grapefruit au Kirsch

Eggs Hussarde

Hot French Bread   **Butter**

Bananas Foster

Coffee

Piesporter Riesling

Take a trip to New Orleans, visit all the points of interest, and be sure that you include breakfast at Brennan's. Everyone does. In this city, noted for its fine restaurants, nobody seems surprised to find that Brennan's appears on all the preferred lists. Featured in *Southern Living* in August 1971.

BRENNAN MILK PUNCH

1-1/4 ounces bourbon or brandy
3 ounces breakfast cream or milk

1 teaspoon superfine powdered sugar
1 dash vanilla extract

Shake thoroughly and strain into an 8-ounce highball glass, and top with nutmeg. Yield: 1 serving; double the recipe to serve 2.

BLOODY MARY
(see Index)

GRILLED GRAPEFRUIT AU KIRSCH

1 large grapefruit, halved
About 4 tablespoons sugar
2 ounces Kirschwasser

Maraschino cherries
Mint sprigs

Prepare grapefruit by removing core and loosening meat from skin. Sprinkle top generously with sugar and then Kirschwasser. Broil for 2 to 3 minutes or until top starts to brown. Garnish with maraschino cherries and mint sprigs. Yield: 2 servings.

EGGS HUSSARDE

2 large thin slices ham, grilled
2 Holland rusks
1/4 cup Marchand de Vin Sauce
2 slices tomato, grilled

2 eggs, soft-poached
3/4 cup Hollandaise Sauce
Paprika

Lay a large slice ham across each rusk and cover with Marchand de Vin Sauce. Cover next with tomato and then egg. Top with Hollandaise Sauce. Garnish with sprinkling of paprika. Yield: 1 serving; double the recipe to serve 2.

Marchand de Vin Sauce

3/4 cup butter
1/3 cup finely chopped mushrooms
1/2 cup minced ham
1/3 cup finely chopped shallots
1/2 cup finely chopped onion
2 tablespoons garlic, minced

2 tablespoons all-purpose flour
1/2 teaspoon salt
1/8 teaspoon pepper
Dash cayenne pepper
3/4 cup beef stock
1/2 cup red wine

Melt butter in a 9-inch skillet and lightly sauté the mushrooms, ham, shallots, onion, and garlic. When the onion is golden brown, add the flour, salt, pepper, and cayenne. Brown well, about 7 to 10 minutes. Blend in the stock and the wine and simmer over low heat for 35 to 45 minutes. Yield: 2 cups.

Hollandaise Sauce

4 egg yolks
2 tablespoons freshly squeezed
lemon juice

1/2 pound butter, melted
1/4 teaspoon salt

Beat egg yolks in top half of double boiler, and stir in lemon juice. Cook very slowly in double boiler over low heat, never allowing water in bottom pan to come to a boil. Add butter a little at a time, stirring constantly with a wooden spoon. Add salt and pepper. Continue cooking slowly until thickened. Yield: 1 cup.

BANANAS FOSTER

2 tablespoons brown sugar
1 tablespoon butter
1 ripe banana, peeled and sliced
lengthwise

Dash cinnamon
1/2 ounce banana liqueur
1 ounce white rum
1 large scoop vanilla ice cream

Melt brown sugar and butter in flat chafing dish. Add banana and sauté until tender. Sprinkle with cinnamon. Pour banana liqueur and rum over all and flame. Baste with warm liquid until flame burns out. Serve immediately over ice cream. Yield: 1 serving; double the recipe to serve 2.

Dinner at Look's Restaurants

DINNER FOR TWO

Fresh Relishes on Crushed Ice

Romaine Salad

with

Avocado Dressing

Barbecued Shrimp

Baked Idaho Potato

Fresh Asparagus Spears

Rye Bread   **Butter**

Texas Tornado Cake

Coffee   **Tea**

Rose or White Wine

Prime beef and steak are the specialty of Look's Restaurants in Houston, but their seafood has won renowned recognition. The decor of the Sir-Loin House and Sir-Loin Inn is English Tudor with coats-of-arms, carvings, shields, and beautiful paintings of England's kings and queens. Look's Depot on Market Square was designed to bring back memories of the early railroad days with an authentic handcar and baggage cart as part of the decor.

FRESH RELISHES ON CRUSHED ICE

Slice fresh raw beets, turnips, and carrots and place them on bed of crushed ice along with Italian peppers, ripe and green olives, celery, and radishes.

ROMAINE SALAD

Use only the finest, fresh, crisp romaine lettuce. Tear into bite-size pieces, place on 9-inch salad plate. Garnish with fresh sliced ruby ripe tomato, Avocado Dressing, and fresh ground pepper.

AVOCADO DRESSING

1 egg
1/2 teaspoon dry mustard
4 ounces salad oil
1/4 teaspoon Tabasco sauce
Freshly squeezed juice of 2 large lemons
1 teaspoon Worcestershire sauce
1/2 teaspoon salt

1/2 teaspoon white pepper
2 medium avocados
3 fresh shallots, use tops only
Freshly ground garlic or garlic powder to taste
1 ounce anchovy filets
4 ounces mayonnaise
1/2 teaspoon saffron

Blend egg and mustard together, add oil and mix thoroughly. Add Tabasco, lemon juice, Worcestershire, salt, and pepper. Mix well.

Remove stones and peel avocados. Cut tops from shallots and peel garlic. Grind all together with the anchovies into a smooth paste. Blend gently but thoroughly with other ingredients. Add mayonnaise and saffron and mix thoroughly. Pour into container and chill for 2 hours. Serve as a dip or dressing for green salad. Yield: 1-1/2 pints.

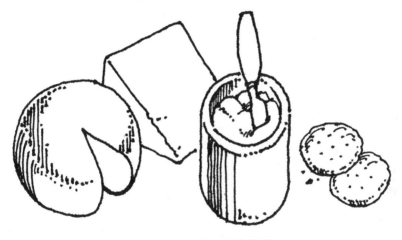

BARBECUED SHRIMP

12 jumbo-size shrimp
1 quart cooking oil
1 cup fine cracker crumbs
1/2 cup all-purpose flour

1 egg
1 cup milk
Salt and pepper to taste
1 pint Hickory House Smoke Sauce

Peel and devein shrimp leaving shell on tails. Wash and clean thoroughly. Dust shrimp with flour. Place well beaten egg in a bowl; add milk, salt, and pepper to taste. Dip shrimp in egg and milk mixture, then roll in fine ground cracker crumbs.

Heat oil in deep saucepan to 350°. Drop in shrimp and fry for 4 minutes to seal moisture in shrimp. Remove from pan and saturate in Hickory Smoke Sauce. Put in shallow pan and place under broiler or in oven for 5 minutes or until shell or tails become brown and crisp. Serve a mild, tasty barbecue sauce with shrimp.

BAKED IDAHO POTATO

Bake potato in foil. Before serving, cut the potato and slightly crumble meat — top with butter, sour cream, grated cheese, and chives.

FRESH ASPARAGUS SPEARS

Cook and season to taste.

RYE BREAD

2 packages dry yeast	2 tablespoons soft shortening
1-1/2 cups very warm water	1/3 cup molasses
1 tablespoon salt	3-1/4 to 3-3/4 cups all-purpose flour
1 tablespoon caraway seed	2-3/4 cups unsifted rye flour

Sprinkle yeast in very warm water; stir until dissolved, but let stand in warm place overnight.

Mix salt, caraway seed, shortening, molasses, rye flour, and half of all-purpose flour. Mix in more flour, a little at a time until dough is stiff and cleans side of bowl.

Turn dough onto lightly floured surface; knead for 5 minutes, or until smooth. Place dough in greased bowl, cover and let rise for 1 hour. Divide dough in half. Round each half into a round ball, place on a cornmeal sprinkled cookie sheet, cover with waxed paper, and let rise for 45 minutes.

Brush tops with cold water and bake at 375° for 35 to 45 minutes until brown. Cool on cake racks. Yield: 2 loaves.

TEXAS TORNADO CAKE

1-1/2 cups sugar	2 cups all-purpose flour
2 eggs	1/4 cup brown sugar
2 cups fruit cocktail, including liquid	1 cup chopped nuts
2 teaspoons soda	

Mix and cream together the first five ingredients. Pour into lightly greased and floured 13- x 9- x 2-inch cakepan. Mix the brown sugar and nuts together and sprinkle onto the batter. Place in oven and bake at 325° for 40 minutes. Spread Icing on cake while hot.

Icing

1 stick butter	1/2 cup evaporated milk
3/4 cup sugar	1 cup flaked coconut

Boil the butter, sugar, and milk for 2 minutes; add coconut. Spoon Icing over cake as soon as cake is removed from the oven. Cut into squares when cool and serve.

Dinner at LeRuth's

DINNER FOR FOUR

Baton du Bologna

Fromage

Carré d'Agneau Rôti Amandine

Pommes Dauphinoise

Truite Termereau

Sauce Beurre Neige

Ananas au Grand Marnier

Café

One of the best dinners you'll ever eat anywhere can be found at this new and popular New Orleans-area restaurant. LeRuth's is across the river from New Orleans in the town of Gretna. Patrons are charmed with the appearance of this elegant old house, with its long gallery, painted a pleasing charcoal gray. The hand-carved front door sets the mood for the elegant serving of the classic French cuisine to follow. Featured in *Southern Living* in January 1972.

BATON DU BOLOGNA

Wrap crisp bread sticks (5- to 6-inches in length) with very thinly sliced Martadella sausage. This is a type of bologna but has fat specks in it. Wrap at last minute so bread sticks will be crisp.

Wine: LeRuth's serves Tavel Cassis with this course (4 ounces chilled Tavel with 1 ounce cassis liqueur).

FROMAGE

Normally we try to select three cheeses (one mild, one medium, and one strong), for an example: Brie is mild; Port-Salut is medium; and Roquefort is strong.

CARRÉ D'AGNEAU RÔTI AMANDINE

Have butcher prepare lamb rack by removing blade and cover fat. Then cut in between rib bones 2 inches from the end to give French style. Salt and pepper and roast at 475° for 35 to 40 minutes to make pink inside. Remove fat from pan but save meat drippings. Add 1/4 cup white wine and 1/2 stick butter and bring to a good boil, washing brown specks from pan to give sauce a good taste. Place on platter, pour sauce over and cover freely with toasted almond slices.

Wine: LeRuth's serves Château Greysac 1966 or Gigandas 1969 with this course.

POMMES DAUPHINOISE

1 pint whipping cream	Pinch ground nutmeg
1 pint water	Salt and white pepper to taste
3 cloves garlic, finely chopped	3 large potatoes (bakers), thinly sliced

Boil all together until potatoes are slightly tender. Pour into a shallow, heavily buttered dish and bake at 425° until brown on top. Dot with butter.

TRUITE TERMEREAU

Roll a 5-ounce filet of speckled trout (no skin) around a 1- to 2-ounce lobster tail (a large shrimp can be substituted) and lay in a buttered pan. Brush with melted butter. Add about 3/4 cup white wine to cover pan bottom. Bake at 450° for 20 to 25 minutes basting two or three times. This method is called braised fish. Yield: 1 serving; make the recipe four times to serve 4.

Wine: LeRuth's serves Pouilly Fume La Docette 1970 with this dish.

SAUCE BEURRE NEIGE
(Butter Snow)

Place 4 egg whites in blender. Add 1 tablespoon lemon juice, 1 tablespoon tarragon vinegar, 1-1/2 tablespoons water, dash salt, white and red peppers. Start blender on medium speed. Slowly add 1 pound of boiling hot butter (fat and milk residue) as in making mayonnaise. Use rubber spatula to control mixing in blender. Sauce will stay homogenized for about 4 hours; do not heat.

ANANAS AU GRAND MARNIER
(Fresh Pineapple with Liqueur)

The French feel that fresh pineapple is excellent for digestion, aside from tasting wonderful. Try to ripen the pineapple until you can detect a sweet, pineapple aroma through the skin. Dice or cut into sticks. Marinate in several ounces of Grand Marnier. Use the pineapple shell for serving the sticks or dices.

Wine: LeRuth's serves extra dry champagne with this dish.

CAFÉ

Make it strong! 4 to 6 tablespoons per cup water.

Dinner at the Nations Room

DINNER FOR FOUR

Oysters Thomas

Golden Pheasant Salad

Pork Chops (Swedish Style)

Assorted Breads   **Sweet Butter**

Apples with Honey Flambé

White Bordeaux-Graves

Norfolk, Virginia, dating from 1688, is the oldest Naval facility in the United States, surrounded by beautiful beaches from Hampton Roads to North Carolina. A modern-day landmark in the lovely old city is the Nations Room, with its handsome decor, international cuisine, and old European service. The restaurant is located on the fifth floor of the Holiday Inn Scope Motor Hotel in downtown Norfolk.

OYSTERS THOMAS

16 to 24 oysters	1 sprig parsley
4 to 5 slices bread, toasted or French-fried	1/4 pound King crabmeat
2 spring onions	2 tablespoons butter, melted
	2 to 3 tablespoons Parmesan cheese

Shuck 4 to 6 oysters per guest and leave on the half shell. Finely chop toast, onions and top, parsley, and crabmeat and add butter; add Parmesan cheese, and mix well.

Place oysters on sheet pan and bake at 375° until slightly curled. Remove from oven and make a thin patty of crabmeat mixture and cover oysters.

Return to oven and let brown slightly or until hot through. Serve hot on rock salt or napkined plates. Yield: 4 to 6 servings.

WHEN TO USE CANDLES

Candles should be used only after sundown or when the light dims outside, or on a dark, gloomy day. If they are on the table, always light them. Never use candles, not even in a decorative arrangement, without a charred wick.

GOLDEN PHEASANT SALAD

1 clove garlic	Dash Worcestershire sauce
Pepper	Vinegar
Salt	1 head lettuce, broken in small bits
Oil	5 to 6 stemmed mushrooms, sliced
1/4 pound Roquefort cheese (blue cheese)	1 medium onion ring, 1/4 inch thick
Crushed red pepper	1/4 cup walnuts, chopped fine (optional)

Crush garlic in salad mixing bowl and rub into wood grain. Remove bulk, add fresh ground pepper, salt, and oil. Mix well. Add cheese and crush with fork and mix well with oil (leaving a lump or two of cheese). Add red pepper, Worcestershire sauce, and vinegar. Mix well. Add lettuce, mushrooms, and onions. Toss tenderly but well, sprinkle with nuts and serve on chilled plates. Yield: 3 servings.

PORK CHOPS (SWEDISH STYLE)

8 rib chops, 1/2-inch thick	1/2 pound prunes, or 1 small can (16)
1/2 teaspoon powdered ginger	1-1/2 cups water, if prunes are dry
2 tablespoons all-purpose flour	1 tablespoon Port wine
1/2 teaspoon white pepper	4 tablespoons heavy cream
1 teaspoon salt	2 tablespoons prune juice
3 tablespoons butter	

Trim most of fat from chops. Rub chops lightly with ginger and turn in mixture of flour, pepper, and salt. Melt butter in skillet and sauté chops over medium heat until brown and cooked thoroughly. Remove from skillet and keep warm. If dried prunes are used, cook in water until done. Drain and pit prunes and reserve liquor.

Add prunes and Port into skillet in which chops were cooked, stirring in any crumbs left from chops. Heat cream until lukewarm and add to pan, stirring steadily. Add prune juice and chops and cook over low heat for 5 minutes. Yield: 4 servings.

APPLES WITH HONEY FLAMBÉ

3 to 4 apples	2 dashes brandy
3 tablespoons butter	2 tablespoons honey
1 tablespoon ground cinnamon	Ice cream (1 scoop per serving)

Peel and core 3 to 4 firm apples and slice into thin slices. Add butter to skillet or crepe pan and cook apple slices until partly soft. Sprinkle with cinnamon; baste apples well with butter mixture. Add brandy and light. Add honey to snuff flame. Mix well. Serve over vanilla ice cream. (This can be served over a crisp biscuit also).

Dinner at Chalet Suzanne

DINNER FOR SIX
Baked Grapefruit
Chalet Suzanne Soup Romaine
Spinach Salad
Curried Shrimp with Orange Rice
Grilled Pineapple Ring
Rolls

Gateau Christina

Demitasse

Chalet Suzanne is nestled in the midst of citrus groves just 4 miles north of Lake Wales, Florida. The gourmet cuisine includes two specialties, romaine soup and baked grapefruit halves, which begin every meal served in the dining room. Menus are printed on glazed tiles and offer a tempting array of meats, fish, and fowl — served on one of the world's largest collections of tableware — German china, Italian pottery, and delicate Limonges. Featured in *Southern Living* in September 1971.

BAKED GRAPEFRUIT

Cut grapefruit in half, cut around sections and cut small hole in center. Fill center cavity until overflowing with honey and 1 teaspoon of butter. Sprinkle over entire top of fruit, a mixture of sugar and cinnamon. Put under broiler for a few moments until it turns a little brown. Garnish with a grilled chicken liver. Serve each guest a grapefruit half.

CHALET SUZANNE SOUP ROMAINE
(available at most food stores across the South)

SHRIMP TIP

To minimize odor of boiling shrimp, drop fresh celery leaves into the pot.

SPINACH SALAD

3 cups spinach, bite-size and scissor-cut
1/4 small Bermuda onion, sliced thin
1/2 cup diced celery
3 eggs, boiled and chopped
Salt and pepper to taste

1 clove garlic, crushed
1 cup commercial sour cream
1 package garlic cheese salad dressing mix
2 teaspoons freshly squeezed lemon juice

Combine spinach, onion, celery, eggs, salt, pepper, and garlic in a bowl, and put aside. Combine sour cream, dressing mix, and lemon juice in a second bowl. Mix together just before serving. Yield: 6 servings.

Variation: Add 1/2 cup of Mandarin orange sections at the last moment when mixing together.

CURRIED SHRIMP WITH ORANGE RICE

1/3 cup butter or margarine
3 tablespoons all-purpose flour
1 to 2 tablespoons curry powder
1/2 teaspoon salt
1/4 teaspoon paprika
Dash ground nutmeg
2 cups light cream or half-and-half
3 cups cleaned shrimp, cooked

1 tablespoon finely chopped candied ginger
1 tablespoon freshly squeezed lemon juice
1 teaspoon cooking sherry
1 teaspoon onion juice
Dash Worcestershire sauce
Salt to taste

Melt butter; blend in flour, curry powder, salt, paprika, and nutmeg. Gradually stir in cream; cook until mixture thickens, stirring constantly. Add remaining ingredients; heat through. Serve with Curry Condiments and Orange Rice.

ORANGE RICE

1 cup uncooked long-grain rice
1/2 cup orange juice

1 tablespoon fresh grated orange rind

Cook rice according to package directions. Do not overcook. Add orange juice and orange rind. Serve hot.

Curry Condiments

Any or all of the following may be used: chutney, chopped salted peanuts, chopped fresh parsley, crisp bacon bits, flaked coconut, and chopped orange rind.

GRILLED PINEAPPLE RINGS

Pineapple slices
Sugar

Butter

Dip pineapple slices in sugar and sauté in butter.

GATEAU CHRISTINA
(prepare ahead of time)

4 egg whites

1-1/2 cups sugar

1/3 cup finely ground almonds

Whip egg whites until stiff and gradually add the sugar and almonds. Cut out four rounds of paper about 8 inches in diameter. Spread each round of paper with meringue and bake on a baking sheet at 250° for about 15 minutes, or until the meringue is dry. Turn the layers over and continue to dry for about 5 minutes.

Filling

2 egg whites

1/2 cup sugar

2 tablespoons sweet cocoa

1 cup softened sweet butter

1/4 pound sweet chocolate, melted

Powdered sugar

Beat 2 egg whites until foamy in the top of a double boiler, over hot but not boiling water. Gradually beat in sugar, sweet cocoa, butter, and melted chocolate. Beat well and remove from the heat. When the filling is firm, spread it on three meringue layers and put them together, the fourth layer on top. Make a lattice-work of 1-inch wide strips of paper on top of the cake and dust heavily with powdered sugar. Remove the paper — the sugar will have etched an attractive design. This cake should ripen for 24 hours before serving.

PINEAPPLE TIP

How to select a pineapple? Pluck a leaf from the pineapple's crown. If it pulls out easily, the fruit is ready to eat.

Dinner at Bismarck Restaurant

DINNER FOR FOUR

Crepes St. Jacques

Hearts of Palm Vinaigrette

Filet Mignon Alfonse

Peach Melba

Gevrey Chambertine

The home of nickel beer in turn-of-the-century Houston is now the home of an elegant continental restaurant with an Old World flair, the Bismarck, in the downtown Old Market Square area. The Bismarck caters to businessmen at lunch and serves elegant candlelight dinners and after-theatre fare for patrons of the nearby Alley Theatre and the Jones Hall for Performing Arts. A strolling violinist and a concert pianist help set the mood for leisurely dining at night.

CREPES ST. JACQUES

Crepes

1/2 cup all-purpose flour	1/4 cup water
1 egg, beaten	1/2 teaspoon salad oil

Blend flour, egg, salt, and water until of pancake consistency. Melt salad oil in 6-inch frying pan. Pour batter to make very thin pancakes. Cook until done; keep hot while preparing Filling.

Filling

1 tablespoon butter	1 teaspoon all-purpose flour
2 tablespoons diced onion	1/2 cup Chablis wine
1 clove crushed garlic	1/2 cup heavy cream
1/2 cup crabmeat	Dash Worcestershire sauce
1/2 cup scallops	Freshly squeezed juice of 1/2 lemon
Salt and pepper to taste	Hollandaise Sauce or mushroom gravy

Melt butter in flat saucepan; simmer onion and garlic lightly. Add crabmeat and scallops, season to taste with salt and pepper, and sauté for 10 minutes. Add flour and mix well. Stir in wine, cream, Worcestershire sauce, and lemon juice. Distribute mixture evenly onto pancakes and roll them up. Put in 300° oven for a few minutes. Cover with Hollandaise Sauce or mushroom gravy and serve hot. Yield: about 4 servings.

HEARTS OF PALM VINAIGRETTE

8 hearts of palm
Shredded lettuce

Tomato wedges

Vinaigrette

1 hard-cooked egg, chopped
1/2 onion, finely chopped
1 clove crushed garlic
1 tablespoon chopped parsley

Olive oil
Wine vinegar
Salt and pepper to taste

Quarter hearts of palm and place on four individual salad plates. Garnish with tomato.

Combine all ingredients for Vinaigrette and pour over hearts of palm. Yield: 4 servings.

FILET MIGNON ALFONSE

4 (8-ounce) filet mignons, seasoned
1 tablespoon butter
1/4 cup diced bacon
1/4 cup diced onion
1-1/2 cups Pfifferlings (wild
   mushrooms), drained
4 artichoke bottoms

Salt and pepper
1/4 cup roast gravy
Dash of Burgundy
4 peach halves
4 maraschino cherries

Broil filet mignons to desired doneness. Melt butter in skillet; add bacon and onion and sauté for 5 minutes. Add pfifferlings and artichoke bottoms, and season with salt and pepper. Add gravy and wine and simmer for 10 minutes. Place filets on plates; put artichoke on top of filets, top with mushrooms, and garnish with peach halves and cherries. Yield: 4 servings.

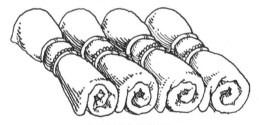

PEACH MELBA

4 scoops vanilla ice cream
4 peach halves
   Raspberry jelly thinned with cherry
   Suisse liquor or peach brandy

Whipped cream
Gaufrettes or other sweet crackers

Place a scoop of ice cream in four champagne glasses. Top with peach halves, and cover with sauce made from raspberry jelly thinned to pouring consistency. Garnish with whipped cream around edge of glass. Serve with gaufrettes or other sweet crackers. Yield: 4 servings.

Dinner at Perdita's

DINNER FOR SIX TO EIGHT

She Crab Soup
Low Country Shrimp Gumbo
Tossed Green Salad with Oil and Vinegar Dressing
Fresh Asparagus Hollandaise
Commercial Rolls   **Butter**

Grasshopper Pie

Coffee   **Tea**

Chassagne Montrachet

An enticing aroma pervades the Southern atmosphere as you stroll narrow, cobblestoned Exchange Street in Charleston, South Carolina, outside the black oak door of famous Perdita's Restaurant. A stone's throw from the harbor, the 180-year-old building, with its 2 feet thick brick walls and delicate grilled balcony, has been a landmark since Revolutionary days. Perdita's is one of the five American restaurants to receive the Counsel of Paris Medal of Honor and they are happy to share some of their recipes with you. Featured in *Southern Living* in March 1968.

SHE CRAB SOUP

3 quarts milk	1/2 tablespoon paprika
1/4 pound butter	1/4 tablespoon Accent
1/4 medium onion, finely chopped	3/4 cup all-purpose flour
8 ounces crabmeat	Salt and pepper to taste
3 ounces crab roe or yolks of 3 hard-cooked eggs, grated	1/4 cup sherry

Heat milk until hot, do not let it boil. Melt butter in double boiler, add onion and let simmer for a few minutes. Add crabmeat and crab roe. Stir. Add paprika and Accent, and stir. Fold in flour and simmer for a few minutes. Pour milk in double boiler, stir until blended; add salt and pepper to taste, then sherry. Keep on low heat for 25 to 30 minutes. Add a little sherry to each serving, if desired, at the table. Yield: 6 to 8 servings.

LOW COUNTRY SHRIMP GUMBO

1 small can mushrooms, drained	2 dashes Worcestershire sauce
2 small onions, finely chopped	2 dashes hot sauce
1/2 green pepper, finely chopped	Pinch pepper
2 tablespoons butter	2 teaspoons salt
3 medium tomatoes, peeled and chopped	1/2 cup dry sherry
2 tablespoons all-purpose flour	3 pounds shrimp, cooked and cleaned
1/2 cup half-and-half (milk and cream)	1/2 cup breadcrumbs

Sauté mushrooms, onions, and green pepper in butter until tender. Add tomatoes, and cook slowly for 8 to 10 minutes. Stir in flour and half-and-half. Put in seasoning, shrimp, and sherry. Simmer, then put in buttered casserole. Top with buttered crumbs. Bake at 375° to 400° for 10 minutes or until top is brown. Serve over rice or cornbread. Yield: 6 to 8 servings.

FRESH ASPARAGUS HOLLANDAISE

2 pounds fresh asparagus	Hollandaise Sauce*

Cut tender portion from woody base. Remove scales if sandy. Wash thoroughly; cut in pieces or leave whole. Cook covered in very small amount boiling salted water, or uncovered in boiling salted water to barely cover. Lower part of stalks may be cooked 5 minutes before adding tips. Serve Hollandaise Sauce over asparagus. Yield: 6 to 8 servings.

*See Index for Hollandaise Sauce recipe.

GRASSHOPPER PIE

1 cup chocolate wafer crumbs	2 tablespoons white crème de cacao
1/4 cup sugar	1/4 cup green crème de menthe
3 tablespoons melted butter	1 pint vanilla ice milk
1 cup heavy cream	Whipped cream, chocolate curls
2 tablespoons milk	or marshmallows
3-1/4 cups miniature marshmallows	

Combine chocolate wafer crumbs, sugar, and melted butter in medium bowl. Press mixture along sides and bottom of 9-inch pieplate; chill. Whip 1 cup heavy cream; chill. In top of double boiler, combine milk and miniature marshmallows. Heat over boiling water, stirring until marshmallows are melted. Remove from heat; cool completely, stirring occasionally. Add white crème de cacao and green crème de menthe; fold mixture into whipped cream. Spread vanilla ice milk, softened slightly, on piecrust to form an even layer. Pour marshmallow mixture over ice milk; freeze for 6 hours or overnight. If desired, garnish with whipped cream, chocolate curls, or strawberries. Yield: 1 (9-inch) pie.

Dinner at the Plantation Club

DINNER FOR EIGHT

Claret Cup

Brandied Shrimp Provencale

Roast Pheasant Alcantara

Wild Rice and Grapes

Plantation Club Salad

Bananas Foster

Coffee

It is somewhat rare to find good golf and good food in the same place. Sea Pines Plantation on Hilton Head Island, South Carolina, has an abundance of both. At the Plantation Club the preparation and serving of food should be described as superb and spectacular. Believing that the gourmet dines first with his eyes, the staff sees that food is served with drama and an artistic flair. Featured in *Southern Living* in January 1971.

CLARET CUP

1 bottle Bordeaux Claret
1/2 bottle Dubonnet Blonde

3 ounces Curacao

Serve over ice rocks, garnished with fresh mint and cut strawberries. Yield: 8 servings.

BRANDIED SHRIMP PROVENCALE

4 tablespoons butter
1 tablespoon finely chopped onion
1 clove garlic, chopped
48 shelled raw shrimp

2 ounces brandy
1 cup peeled and cubed fresh tomatoes
1 tablespoon chopped parsley
Salt and pepper to taste

Brown butter in sauté pan lightly; add onion, garlic, and shrimp and stir with fork rapidly for 2 minutes. Pour in brandy and light. Shake pan fast. Add tomatoes and parsley. Season to taste and serve. Yield: 8 servings.

ROAST PHEASANT ALCANTARA

2 (1-3/4-pound) pheasants	Salt and pepper
Chopped juniper berries	Cooked wild rice
2 cups cooking sherry	Seedless grapes

Soak pheasants in refrigerator in salt water (3 tablespoons salt to 2 quarts water) for 24 hours. Remove from water and sprinkle with chopped juniper berries and cooking sherry and cover with foil. Leave refrigerated overnight. Rub in salt, coarse pepper, and chopped juniper berries. Roast birds at 450° until golden brown, about 30 minutes. Remove from oven and rest for about 10 minutes before serving. Serve with sautéed wild rice and seedless grapes. Arrange sliced pheasant and wild rice on platter and glaze with brown sauce or brown sauce with Port wine flavor. Yield: 4 servings; make the recipe twice to serve 8.

THE PLANTATION CLUB SALAD WITH LEMON-MUSTARD DRESSING

1 teaspoon English mustard	1/2 cup olive oil
2 teaspoons brown mustard	1/2 cup salad oil
1/2 teaspoon white pepper	1/2 teaspoon mixed herbs (tarragon and sweet basil)
1-1/2 teaspoons salt	
2 teaspoons chopped chives	Tossed salad greens
1/2 cup freshly squeezed lemon juice	Hearts of artichokes
1 teaspoon Worcestershire sauce	Hearts of palms

Combine first ten ingredients and shake well in blender; refrigerate. Add salad dressing to tossed salad greens. Toss and serve well chilled. Top each serving with sliced heart of artichoke and heart of palm. Yield: 4 to 6 servings; double the recipe to serve 8.

BANANAS FOSTER

Slice bananas diagonally in six pieces, dust lightly with flour and sauté in skillet with butter; granulated and brown sugar will help flavor the bananas. Add fresh lemon juice from half of lemon and banana liqueur. Flame with rum and brandy; sprinkle cinnamon at end. Serve with small scoop vanilla ice cream and macaroons.

Dinner at Christiana Campbell's Tavern

DINNER FOR EIGHT

Captain Rasmussen's Clam Chowder

Colonial Game Pie

or

A Made Dish of Shrimp and Lobster

Wild Rice   **Spoonbread**

Mixed Green Salad with French Dressing

Corn Sticks   **Butter**

Tipsy Squire with Whipped Cream and Almonds

or

Rum Cream Pie with Chocolate Curls

Coffee   **Tea**

Christiana Campbell's Tavern is located in the restored area of Colonial Williamsburg and specializes in fresh seafood. It has a distinguished past and is known as where all the best people resort. George Washington and many of his friends were regular patrons. The tavern is simply furnished in a manner that was typical of the late 1700's. All the furnishings and decorative items are original 18th century antiques.

CAPTAIN RASMUSSEN'S CLAM CHOWDER

18 large clams	1 teaspoon paprika
1/2 cup butter	1 sachet bag (bouquet garni)
2 ribs celery, chopped medium	1/2 cup tomato puree
2 medium onions, chopped medium	3 medium potatoes, cubed
2 carrots, chopped medium	1/2 teaspoon salt
1 green pepper, chopped medium	1/2 teaspoon white pepper
1 clove garlic, minced fine	1 cup plum tomatoes, chopped

Scrub clams and boil in enough water to cover. Remove clams from shell, chop fine, and reserve. Strain liquid and add enough water to make 8 cups; reserve.

Melt butter, add celery, onions, carrots, and green pepper. Heat until onions are tender. Add garlic and paprika and sauté briefly.

Add reserved stock and sachet bag (which contains 1/4 teaspoon each of thyme, rosemary, and pickling spices tied in cheesecloth).

Add tomato puree, chopped clams, potatoes, salt, and pepper. Allow to simmer until potatoes and carrots are tender. Add plum tomatoes, cook for 10 minutes. Adjust seasonings. Yield: 8 servings.

COLONIAL GAME PIE

1 (4-1/2- to 5-pound) duck
2 pounds rabbit
2-1/2 pounds venison
1/2 cup vegetable oil
2 cups Port wine
1-1/2 quarts Basic Brown Sauce
1 tablespoon Worcestershire sauce
1 clove garlic, minced
1/2 teaspoon black pepper, crushed

1 cup currant jelly
1-1/2 pounds mushrooms, quartered
1/2 cup butter
1 pound slab bacon, cut into
   1/4-inch cubes
1 (15-1/2-ounce) can pearl onions
Pastry Crust Mix
2 eggs
1/4 cup milk

Preheat oven to 400°. Salt cavity of duck; place on rack in shallow roasting pan, breast-side up. Bake 30 minutes at 400°, reduce heat to 325° and bake until duck tests done.

Boil rabbit for 1 hour, or until tender.

Cut the venison in large cubes and sauté in the vegetable oil in a large skillet until well browned, stirring and turning as necessary. Remove venison and drain oil from the pan. Add Port wine to the pan and boil for 2 to 3 minutes, scraping down any brown particles. Return venison to pan and add Brown Sauce. Simmer for 45 to 60 minutes, or until venison is tender.

Cut the duck and rabbit into medium pieces, and place in the pan with the venison to keep warm. Season with Worcestershire sauce, garlic, pepper, and currant jelly. Sauté the mushrooms in butter until lightly browned.

Fry bacon until crisp; drain. Heat onions; drain. Divide mixture into individual casserole dishes and garnish the top of each with mushrooms, bacon, and onions. Cover with pastry crust, trim edges, and prick tops to allow steam to escape. Beat eggs lightly with milk to make an egg wash and brush the tops of the pastry with the mixture. Bake at 350° for 20 to 25 minutes or until crust is golden brown. Serve piping hot. Yield: 8 to 10 servings.

Pastry Crust Mix

3 cups all-purpose flour
1 teaspoon salt
2 teaspoons sugar

1 cup shortening
Ice water

Mix dry ingredients together. Blend in shortening with knives or pastry blender until mixture is of pebbly consistency. Store in covered container in refrigerator. Yield: 4-1/2 cups.

When needed, measure out these amounts:

	Single Crust	Double Crust
8-inch pie	1 to 1-1/4 cups	2 to 2-1/4 cups
9-inch pie	1-1/2 cups	2-1/2 cups
10-inch pie	1-3/4 cups	2-3/4 cups
12 tart shells	2-3/4 cups	

Moisten pastry mix with enough ice water to hold dough together when pushed lightly with a fork. Roll out on lightly floured board or pastry cloth.

Note: When recipe calls for prebaked shell or shells, line pan with dough, prick well with a fork, and bake at 425° for 12 to 15 minutes or until golden brown.

7 cups all-purpose flour
1 tablespoon salt
5 teaspoons sugar

1 pound shortening
Ice water

Follow instructions above. Yield: 9 cups.

Basic Brown Sauce

1/4 cup butter
1 cup all-purpose flour
1/2 cup tomato puree
2 quarts hot beef stock

1 tablespoon powdered beef bouillon
1 tablespoon bottled brown gravy sauce
Salt to taste
Caramel color (optional)

Melt butter in large heavy saucepan over low heat, and gradually add flour, stirring constantly, until mixture is chestnut brown. It may be necessary to turn off heat completely at intervals so that flour will not burn or become too dark. When desired color has been reached, add tomato puree and stir well.

Gradually add hot stock and powdered beef bouillon, using wire whisk to ensure smoothness. Bring mixture to a boil, then reduce heat to lowest degree possible. Simmer 2 hours or until sauce has been reduced to about 1-1/2 quarts. Add bottled brown gravy sauce, salt, and caramel color if desired. Remove from heat and strain through a fine sieve. Cool to room temperature and refrigerate. Yield: 1-1/2 quarts.

MADE DISH OF SHRIMP AND LOBSTER

3 green peppers, quartered
6 medium tomatoes
1 (6-ounce) package long-grain and wild rice
1 pound fresh mushrooms, quartered
1/2 pound butter, divided
1-1/2 pounds lobster, cooked and shelled
2 pounds shrimp, cooked and cleaned

2 (15-1/2-ounce) cans pearl onions
1-1/2 cups dry sherry
2 teaspoons freshly squeezed lemon juice
Worcestershire sauce to taste
Salt and white pepper to taste
Parsley

Partially cook green pepper in boiling water. Remove and cut quarters in half. Reserve. Scald tomatoes in boiling water for 60 seconds. Drain, remove skin, and cut in half. Squeeze out and discard the tomato juice, and cut each half into four pieces. Reserve.

Cook the rice according to package instructions. Sauté mushrooms quickly in a small amount of butter. Reserve. Cut lobster into bite-size pieces.

Melt remaining butter over medium heat and sauté lobster, shrimp, and onions. Add sherry, lemon juice, and seasonings. Add green pepper, tomato, and mushrooms and cook over low heat, stirring gently, until heated through. Arrange the seafood and vegetables in a heated serving dish with the rice. Sprinkle with a dash of sherry. Garnish with chopped parsley, if desired. Yield: 8 servings.

CAMPBELL'S TAVERN SPOONBREAD

1-1/3 teaspoons sugar	1-1/3 cups boiling water
1-1/2 teaspoons salt	3 eggs
1 cup cornmeal	1 tablespoon baking powder
4 tablespoons butter	1-1/3 cups hot milk

Preheat the oven to 350° and grease a 2-quart casserole. Mix sugar and salt with cornmeal and blend well. Add butter and pour in boiling water, stirring constantly. Allow to cool. Beat eggs with baking powder until very light and fluffy, then add to cornmeal mixture. Stir in milk and pour into prepared casserole.

Place casserole in shallow pan of hot water and bake at 350° for 35 to 40 minutes. Serve hot. Yield: 8 servings.

FRENCH DRESSING

1/2 teaspoon salt	3 tablespoons wine vinegar
1/4 teaspoon black pepper, freshly ground	6 tablespoons olive oil
3/4 teaspoon dry mustard	6 tablespoons vegetable oil

Mix dry ingredients in a jar. Add vinegar, cover, and allow to steep a few minutes. Beat with a small wire whisk or fork while gradually adding oils. Cover and use at room temperature. Yield: 1 cup.

INDIAN CORN STICKS

1 cup cornmeal	1 cup milk
1 cup all-purpose flour, sifted	2 eggs, beaten
1 teaspoon salt	2 tablespoons shortening, melted
2-1/2 teaspoons baking powder	

Preheat oven to 400°. Sift dry ingredients into mixing bowl. Combine milk with eggs and add to the dry ingredients. Add shortening and stir until blended. Pour into breadstick pans and bake at 400° for 20 minutes. Yield: 1 dozen.

TIPSY SQUIRE

1/2 cup shortening	1/2 teaspoon salt
1 cup sugar	3/4 cup milk
2 eggs	1 teaspoon vanilla extract
2-1/4 cups all-purpose flour, sifted	Whipped cream
3 teaspoons baking powder	Toasted slivered almonds

Preheat oven to 350°. Grease and lightly flour a 9- x 9- x 2-inch or 11-1/2- x 7-1/2- x 2-inch baking pan. Cream shortening and sugar. Add eggs and beat until lemon colored and fluffy. Add sifted dry ingredients alternately with milk, beating well after each addition. Add vanilla with last addition of milk. Pour into prepared cakepan. Bake at 350° for 35 to 40 minutes or until cake tests done. Cool on cake rack before cutting into portions. To serve, place portion of cake in a dessert bowl and pour Sherry Custard over it. Garnish with sweetened whipped cream and toasted almonds. Yield: 8 servings.

Sherry Custard

1 quart milk	3 egg yolks
3/4 cup sugar	1 egg
3 tablespoons cornstarch	1 teaspoon rum flavoring
1/8 teaspoon salt	1/2 cup cream sherry

Cook milk, sugar, cornstarch, and salt over medium heat, stirring constantly, until slightly thickened. Beat egg yolks and 1 whole egg. Add 1 cup hot milk mixture to beaten egg yolks, stir and return to hot milk. Continue cooking, stirring constantly, but do not boil, until of custard consistency. Add rum flavoring and sherry. Cool and serve over cake.

RUM CREAM PIE

1 envelope unflavored gelatin	1/3 cup dark rum
1/2 cup cold water	1-1/2 cups whipping cream
5 egg yolks	Unsweetened chocolate
1 cup sugar	Crumb Crust

Soften gelatin in cold water. Place over low heat and bring almost to a boil, stirring to dissolve. Beat egg yolks and sugar until very light. Stir gelatin into egg mixture; cool. Gradually add rum, beating constantly. Whip cream until it stands in soft peaks and fold into gelatin mixture. Cool until mixture begins to set, then spoon into Crumb Crust and chill until firm enough to cut. Grate unsweetened chocolate over top before serving.

Crumb Crust

2-1/4 cups graham cracker crumbs	2 tablespoons sugar
1/2 cup butter, melted	1/2 teaspoon ground cinnamon

Combine ingredients and press into 9-inch piepan; chill.

Dinner at Hugo's

DINNER FOR FOUR

Baby Frog Legs Meuniere

with

Whole Artichokes and Bearnaise Sauce

Lime Sherbet with Menthe

Grenadine of Beef, Dr. Schmitt

Asparagus with Mornay Sauce

Wild Rice   **Half Broiled Tomato**

Esquire Salad Hugo

Strawberries Jamaica

or

Paul's Coupé Regency

Hugo's is one of five restaurants located in one of the world's most spectacular buildings — Hyatt Regency Atlanta. This gourmet restaurant has a continental à la carte menu with imported wines. The atmosphere of teak and leather is quietly elegant. A popular luncheon spot at noon, Hugo's is a romantic candlelight retreat by night.

BABY FROG LEGS

16 baby frog legs	1 lemon
1 cup all-purpose flour	8 slices toasted bread, edges trimmed
1 stick salted butter	

Coat frog legs in flour and, using a large pan, sauté in salted butter until lightly brown. Squeeze the juice of a whole lemon on top and bake at 375° for 5 minutes. Remove from oven and place frog legs on slices of toast, after edges have been trimmed. Serve with lemon wedges.

MEUNIERE WITH WHOLE ARTICHOKES AND BEARNAISE SAUCE

4 artichokes, fresh	Salt
1 tablespoon freshly squeezed lemon juice	Bearnaise sauce

Add lemon juice and salt to boiling water and cook artichokes until tender. Drain well. Remove the heart and fill remainder of artichoke with Bearnaise sauce.

Wine: Hugo's serves Rhine or Mossell with this course.

LIME SHERBET WITH MENTHE

Lime sherbet
Crème de menthe

Melon balls, in season
Mint leaves

On flat glassware, place small scoop of lime sherbet. Top with a few drops crème de menthe and serve with melon balls on the side. Decorate with mint leaves.

GRENADINE OF BEEF, DR. SCHMITT

12 (2-1/2 to 3-ounce) slices filet of beef
   Ground pepper
   Salad oil
1 cup shallots
2 tablespoons Dijon mustard
1/2 pound sweet butter
1 pound sliced mushrooms, presautéed
   in butter

3 cups Sauce Periogourdine, or beef
   gravy with 1/2 cup
   Bordeaux wine added
4 tablespoons Sauce Robert
1 teaspoon Lea and Perrin Sauce
1/2 teaspoon salt
1 ounce Dry Sack Sherry

To prepare the beef, pound the ground pepper into the filet. In a large, hot frying pan, add only enough oil to cover the bottom. Add shallots and fry for 1 minute. Place meat in the pan and brown on both sides. Spread mustard on each piece of meat. Add butter and cook until brown, almost burned. Add all other ingredients listed above and simmer until the meat is cooked to preference.

Place slices of beef on plate and pour sauce over. Serve with wild rice, Asparagus with Mornay Sauce and half baked tomato. If desired, also serve with a slice of pâté de foie gras.

Venison may be substituted for beef in this recipe; however, the meat must be served rare as it will get tough if allowed to simmer very long.

Wine: Hugo's serves Bordeaux Rouge with this course.

ASPARAGUS WITH MORNAY SAUCE

Cook green asparagus in plain salted water until it cracks a little.

Mornay Sauce
3 tablespoons all-purpose flour
1/4 pound margarine, melted
1 cup milk

Salt and pepper
Dash ground nutmeg
1 egg yolk
4 tablespoons Parmesan cheese

Combine flour and margarine in a pan, mix until it is a roux. Add milk to mixture, add salt, pepper, nutmeg, and egg yolk. Do not let mixture boil. If roux is too thick, add more milk. If roux is too thin, add more flour.

Place asparagus in pan or ovenproof serving tray, pour Mornay Sauce over top. Sprinkle with Parmesan cheese, place in oven and broil until browned on top.

WILD RICE

1/4 pound wild rice
3 shallots, chopped very fine
2 ounces ham, finely diced
1 long scallion, diced

1 clove garlic, chopped very fine
Salt and pepper to taste
4 ounces butter

Combine shallots, ham, scallion, and garlic in a pan and sauté in butter until nicely browned. Add cooked rice.

HALF BROILED TOMATO

Cornflake crumbs
Butter
1 onion, finely chopped
2 cloves garlic, finely chopped

Parsley, chopped
Salt and pepper to taste
Pinch thyme

Sauté cornflake crumbs and onion in butter until golden brown. This will be paste-like. Add other ingredients, being careful not to burn the parsley. Spread on top of seasoned tomato, broil in oven until it looks crumbly.

Note: Prepare about 3 minutes before serving, or else it will be soggy.

ESQUIRE SALAD HUGO

4 hearts Limestone lettuce
1 dozen cherry tomatoes, halved
2 pounds mushrooms, thinly sliced
1 can hearts of palm, diced

1 cup crisp bacon bits, about 6 slices
1 cup pickled garbanza beans
1 cup small bay shrimp

Mix all the above ingredients, except shrimp, lightly. Add Dressing.

Hugo's Salad Dressing

1-1/2 cups oil
1/2 cup wine vinegar
Juice of 1/2 lemon
2 cloves garlic, minced
1/2 teaspoon Lea and Perrin Sauce

2 tablespoons tomato chili sauce
1 teaspoon prepared mustard
4 tablespoons Parmesan cheese
Dash of oregano
Salt and pepper to taste

Toss together lightly and decorate with shrimp.

THE TREND SETTERS

Sometimes guests are reluctant to be the first to help themselves to a spectacular edible table arrangement like grapefruit shells filled with strawberries, cantaloupe shells filled with green and pink melon balls, or other beautiful fruit. Conspire with a friend to wait until the crowd around the table is at its height, then have her casually spear a piece of the fruit with a cocktail pick. Once the trend is started, your fruit centerpiece will be enjoyed to the hilt.

STRAWBERRIES JAMAICA

1 cup brown sugar

2 ounces Jamaica Dark Rum

3 ounces Grand Marnier

4 cups commercial sour cream

3 dozen fresh strawberries, with stems

With stems up, set strawberries in large bowl of crushed ice.

In a bowl, mix brown sugar, rum, and Grand Marnier until sugar is dissolved. Add sour cream and whip until completely homogenized. Serve in sherbet glasses and dip strawberries in sauce.

Note: Finger bowls will be necessary.

Wine: Hugo's serves cognac with this course.

PAUL'S COUPÉ REGENCY

2 bananas

1 dozen fresh strawberries

1/2 ounce orange-flavored liqueur, Grand Marnier

1/2 ounce crème of banana liqueur

4 scoops French vanilla ice cream

3 cups whipped cream, divided

2 cups chocolate mousse or pudding

1/2 ounce cocoa or coffee liqueur, Tia Maria

2 halves preserved pears

Using four Normandy wine glasses or 18-ounce coupé glasses, slice layer of bananas in bottom. Add strawberries and flavor with orange liqueur and creme of banana.

In a bowl, whip ice cream until soft, but not runny. Add 2 cups whipped cream, stir, and top the fruit in the glasses.

In another bowl, whip mousse or pudding. When smooth, add 1 cup whipped cream and cocoa or coffee liqueur. Spoon mixture on top of ice cream in glasses.

Decorate with quarter of banana, small spoon of whipped cream, 1/2 preserved pear, and a strawberry in the middle.

HIGHBALL GLASSES

Even if you have cocktail parties infrequently, renting highball glasses is a nuisance — and could be more expensive in the long run. Plain tall highball glasses can be bought inexpensively at the dime store, then stored for your next party.

For a party of about 50, you might find it practical to invest in about 3 dozen highball glasses and about 3 dozen old-fashioneds. And don't forget — lots and lots of cocktail napkins; never serve a drink without one.

Empty liquor cartons are a great way of storing seldom used highball glasses. Your friendly liquor dealer will be happy to oblige.

Tampa's Columbia Restaurant is renowned for traditional Spanish cuisine.
See Columbia's menu on page 364.

Dinner at Columbia Restaurant

DINNER FOR FOUR

Spanish Black Bean Soup

Red Snapper Alicante

Chicken and Yellow Rice

1905 Salad

Cuban Water Bread   **Butter**

Spanish Custard

Coffee

Tampa, Florida, is proud of the restaurant that was acclaimed by the Spanish government in 1966 as being "the world's largest and finest Spanish restaurant." There's a light atmosphere and an air of gaiety about the service at the Columbia. Waiters sing out their orders to the chefs in the kitchen; Latin music is piped to all dining rooms; and floor shows featuring flamenco dancers, musicians, and singers delight dinner customers nightly. Featured in *Southern Living* in October 1968.

SPANISH BEAN SOUP

1/2 pound garbanzos	Pinch paprika
1 tablespoon salt	1 onion, finely chopped
1 beef bone	1 pound potatoes, quartered
1 ham bone	1 pinch saffron
2 quarts water	Salt to taste
4 ounces white bacon	1 chorizo (Spanish sausage)

Soak garbanzos overnight, with a tablespoon of salt, in sufficient water to cover beans. When ready to cook, drain the salted water from the beans and place them with the beef bone and ham bone in 2 quarts of water. Cook for 45 minutes over slow heat.

Fry the white bacon, paprika, and onion. Add to the beans along with the quartered potatoes, saffron, and salt to taste. When potatoes are done, remove from heat and add chorizo, which has been cut into thin slices. Yield: 4 servings.

RED SNAPPER ALICANTE

1 pound red snapper steaks	1/2 cup white wine
1 onion, sliced	12 almonds, grated
1/4 cup Spanish olive oil	3 green peppers, cut in rings
1/2 teaspoon salt	4 rings eggplant, breaded
Pinch white pepper	4 shrimp supreme
1/2 cup brown gravy	Parsley

Place the red snapper steaks on top of 3 slices of onion, spread over the bottom of a clay casserole. Over the fish, pour olive oil, salt, white pepper, brown gravy, white wine, grated almonds, and green pepper rings. Garnish with breaded eggplant rings and 4 shrimp supreme. Bake at 350° for 25 minutes. To serve, garnish with parsley. Yield: 2 servings; make the recipe twice to serve 4.

Wine: Columbia serves white Brilliante Spanish Sauterne or any good sauterne with the red snapper.

CHICKEN AND YELLOW RICE
(Valencia Style)

2-1/2 pound fryer	1 bay leaf
1/2 cup Spanish olive oil	Pinch yellow coloring
1 onion, chopped	1/4 pound Spanish Valencia rice
2 cloves garlic, chopped	1/2 cup small green peas
1 green pepper, chopped	Spanish pimiento
1/4 cup whole tomatoes	Parsley
1 quart water or broth	1 hard-cooked egg, sliced
1 tablespoon salt	4 asparagus tips
Pinch Spanish saffron	

Cut chicken into quarters, and simmer in olive oil in clay casserole until brown. Take out of the clay casserole and in the same olive oil braise the onion, garlic, green pepper, and tomatoes.

Place the browned chicken in the casserole, and add a quart of chicken broth or water. When it starts to boil, add salt, saffron, bay leaf, yellow coloring, and rice. When the rice begins to boil, cover casserole and bake at 350° for 20 minutes.

Garnish with small peas, pimiento, chopped parsley, hard-cooked egg, and asparagus tips. Yield: 4 servings.

Wine: Columbia serves Spanish Sangría with this dish.

TO CLARIFY CHICKEN OR BEEF STOCK

For each quart of stock you have, allow one egg. Separate eggs and reserve yolks for some other purpose. Beat whites slightly and crush the shells. Add whites and crushed shells to soup, bring to a boil, stirring constantly, and boil for 3 to 4 minutes. Reduce heat, cover, and simmer for 15 minutes. Remove from heat and let stand 10 minutes. Strain through several thicknesses of cheesecloth. The broth will be lovely and clear.

1905 SALAD

1/2 head of lettuce, chopped	2 slices onions
1 tomato, cut into 6 or 8 pieces	3 ounces olive oil
4 slices cucumbers	1/4 cup vinegar
6 slices green peppers	Juice of 1 lemon
10 ripe olives	1/4 cup Parmesan or Pecornino cheese
10 green olives	3 ounces Swiss cheese

Combine lettuce, tomatoes, cucumbers, green peppers, ripe and green olives, and onions for salad. Mix olive oil, vinegar, lemon juice, and cheeses. Pour over salt mixture and toss lightly. Yield: 2 servings; double the recipe to serve 4.

CUBAN WATER BREAD
(see Index)

SPANISH CUSTARD

3 cups sugar, divided	1 gram anisette
6 eggs	1 pinch salt
1 teaspoon vanilla extract	1 pint boiling milk

Boil a cup of sugar and 1/2 cup water until brown, then pour the caramel into six molds. Beat eggs, add sugar, vanilla, anisette, salt, and beat again; add boiling milk little by little, then strain through cloth or china colander. Pour mixture into molds, put molds into water-filled pan and bake at 350° for 30 minutes — don't let water boil, or custard will be filled with holes. Cool in refrigerator. When ready to serve, press edges of custard with spoon to break away from mold, then turn upside down. The caramel then tops the custard. Yield: 6 servings.

Cheese and Wine

For those who are discovering the delicacy of fine wines and for those who have long enjoyed them, a wine-tasting party is a particular delight. The perfect accompaniment to a *taste-vin* is a bite of cheese which removes any trace of the wine, refreshes the taste buds and leaves them ready to appreciate another wine flavor. In return, the wine brings alive the special subtlety or sharpness of a fine cheese. To savor the best of the cheese, serve with a bland bread, such as French, or water crackers.

To plan a wine-tasting party, refer to the cheese and wine charts in this chapter. Limit your variety of wines to eight or less. Though the wines should be different, do choose those with some common characteristic. Arrange the wines on a long table and provide at least two glasses per guest: one for red and one for white. Have several bowls of clean water nearby so guests may rinse their glass after each taste.

Open the tasting with the white wines, follow with the reds, rosé to deep burgundy. Always move from the light, brisk wines to the rich, full ones. Champagne may precede or follow the reds.

To get the best a wine offers, the temperature must be right. Reds should be brought from cellar to room temperature. Remove the cork an hour ahead of time. Chill white and sparkling wine in the refrigerator for a couple of hours.

Cheese Selection Guide

Cheese	Flavor and Texture	Used For	Goes With
Bel Paese (Italy)	Spongy, mild, creamy yellow interior	Dessert Use as is	Fresh fruit Crusty French bread
Brie (France)	Soft, *edible crust*, sharper than Camembert, creamy	Dessert Use as is	Fresh fruit
Blue (France)	Marbled, blue veined, creamy white, semi-soft, piquante, spicy	Dessert Use as is, in dips, salads, appetizers, cheese trays	Fresh fruit Bland crackers
Brick (United States)	Semi-soft, mild, cream colored to orange	Use as is, sandwiches, appetizers, cheese trays	Crackers and bread
Camembert (France)	*Edible crust*, creamy yellow, mild to pungent	Dessert Use as is	Especially good with tart apple slices
Cheddar (England) (American)	Mild to sharp, cream colored to orange	Dessert As an ingredient in cooking, sandwiches, salads, appetizers, cheese trays	Especially good with apples or pears
Cottage Cheese (United States)	Soft, moist, mild, white, large or small curd	Fruit salads, use as is, as an ingredient in cooking, appetizers	Canned or fresh fruit
Cream Cheese (United States)	White, soft, smooth, buttery, mild	Dessert Use as is, sandwiches, salads, as an ingredient in cooking	Jelly and crackers
Edam (Holland)	Firm, mild, red wax coated	Dessert Appetizer, cheese tray (cut off top and scoop out)	Fresh fruit
Feta (Greece)	Snow white, salty, crumbly, but sliceable	Use as is, as an ingredient in cooking	Usually Greek salad
Gorgonzola (Italy)	Semi-soft, blue veined, less moist than blue, piquante, spicy	Dessert Use as is, salads, appetizers, cheese trays	Fresh fruit or squares of crusty French bread
Gouda (Holland)	Softer than Edam, mild nut-like, with or without red wax coating	Dessert Use as is, appetizers, cheese tray	Fresh Fruit Crackers

Cheese	Flavor and Texture	Used For	Goes With
Gruyere (Switzerland)	Nutty blandness, similar to Swiss, firm, tiny holes	Dessert Use as is, appetizers, as an ingredient in fondue	Fresh fruit
Liederkranz (United States)	*Edible light orange crust*, texture of heavy honey, soft, robust	Dessert Use as is	Fresh fruit, matzo Pumpernickle, sour rye, thin slice onion
Limburger (Belgium)	Soft, smooth, robust, aromatic, creamy white	Dessert	Fresh fruit, dark bread, bland crackers
Mozzarella (Italy)	Semi-soft, delicate, mild, creamy white	As an ingredient in cooking Use as is in pizza	Italian foods
Muenster (Germany)	Semi-soft, mild to mellow	Use as is, sandwiches, cheese trays	Crackers and bread
Parmesan (Italy)	Hard, brittle body, light yellow, sharp, piquante	Use as is, grated as an ingredient in cooking, table use (use young cheese, not aged)	Italian foods Combine with Swiss for sauces
Pineapple Cheese (United States)	Pineapple-shaped, firm, sharp	Dessert (serve whole and scoop out) Appetizers, salads Use as is	Fresh fruit
Port Salut (France)	Fresh buttery flavor, semi-soft	Dessert Use as is, appetizers, cheese trays	Fresh fruit Crackers
Provolone (Italy)	Usually smoked, salty, hard, yellowish-white interior, mild to sharp	Appetizers, use as is, as an ingredient in cooking Dessert	Italian foods
Ricotta (Italy)	Soft, white and creamy, bland but semi-sweet	Use as is, as an ingredient in main dishes, filling for pastries	
Roquefort (France)	Semi-soft, pastry and sometimes crumbly, sharp, blue veined	Use as is in dips, salads, appetizers Dessert	Bland crackers Fresh fruit Demitasse
Stilton (England)	Semi-soft, blue veined, slightly more crumbly than blue	Use as is, dips, salads, Dessert Cheese trays	Fresh fruit Bland crackers
Swiss (Switzerland)	Sweetish, nut-like with large holes, light pale yellow	Use as is, as an ingredient in cooking, salads, sandwiches, appetizers Dessert Cheese trays	Fresh fruit Squares of crusty French bread

SERVING CHEESE

Cheese is a fruit of the soil and is most compatible with natural surroundings. When serving cheese you will find that crystal or china somehow seem inappropriate. The wood of a cheese board, adorned with only a few large leaves from the garden for the cheese to rest on, or a garnish of fresh watercress or parsley, provides the best setting. A slab of fine marble may also be used instead of wood, but most households already have breadboards or chopping boards and these can be used to serve the cheese.

Do not crowd too many cheeses on a board. Cheese shows to best advantage if not crowded and it's easier for guests to serve themselves from an uncluttered board.

Strong and mild cheeses both suffer if placed next to each other; place them apart or serve them on separate boards or trays. And if you're serving several cheeses, provide separate knives or slicers for each. The flavor of delicate cheese should be respected and not overpowered by strong beverages and highly flavored breads or crackers.

How to serve: When serving cheese for dessert, provide each person with a small plate and knife. Cheese may be eaten with the fingers, but in dignified or formal settings cheese is eaten with a fork. You may wish to provide both knife and fork.

Avoid cheese arrangements involving wooden picks, bits of cherry, pineapple, and other such embellishments. Don't gaily decorate cheese; a good cheese is beautiful in itself.

Serve all cheeses at room temperature except cottage cheese and cream cheese. Cheese should be removed from the refrigerator to allow time for attaining room temperature. This may be anywhere from 1/2 hour to 2 or 3 hours since soft cheeses like Camembert warm faster than hard cheeses.

Accompaniments: Cheese is delicious served with crusty chunks of French bread, lightly salted or bland crackers, or rye bread. The type of cheese determines the choice of bread or crackers. The important thing to remember is that the cheese should never be subordinated to other flavors.

If you serve cheese for dessert, fruits such as apples and pears are happiest as a foil. If you feel that some of your guests still yearn for just a bite of something sweet, place some mints on the table.

Affinities: Although wine is the classic accompaniment to cheese, all cheeses may be enjoyed with tea or coffee.

Cheese is not only versatile but is also harmonious with many kinds and combinations of food. As a last course it enhances any dinner or luncheon, with these exceptions: It does not fit well in a menu containing rich meat or poultry. It should be used sparingly, if at all, following a rich creamed or cheese dish. Avoid its use with dishes from those countries where little cheese is eaten. For example, cheese seems inappropriate following a Chinese or Japanese dinner, or a hot Indian curry.

From soup to nuts, cheese plays an important part in meal planning.

Cheese may be served at any time of day; serve with breakfast, as a snack, sprinkled over soup, as a luncheon dish, as an hors d'oeuvre, as part of a buffet, or as a dessert.

Will it freeze? With the exception of a few smooth-bodied cheeses such as blue, Camembert, and Limburger, freezing will affect the body and texture of most cheeses. They will still be suitable for cooking even though they may appear crumbly or mealy. Many people like to buy a fairly large wheel or wedge of Cheddar or Swiss cheese, shred it and freeze it for any recipes calling for shredded cheese.

Cream cheese which has been frozen should be used for cooking; during freezing it tends to become grainy and loses its usual smooth spreading consistency.

For best results cheese should be tightly wrapped for storing in refrigerator. Cheddar, Swiss, processed American cheese, and cream cheese may be stored, if properly wrapped, in the freezer for up to 3 months.

Buying cheese: In buying cheese packaged in clear plastic, examine the cheese to make sure it looks good. It may seem absurd to say this, but good cheese almost invariably looks good. Naturally, it should be tightly wrapped and refrigerated.

If it is not possible or practical for you to visit a cheese shop, you can make your own dessert and appetizer cheeses by combining readily available cheeses from your supermarket. You will find several recipes for both kinds in the Index.

Helpful Cheese Measurements

Cheddar
Swiss
Parmesan
Romano
} 1 pound — 4 cups, grated

Cream
Cottage
} 1 pound — 2 cups

SERVING WINE

The pleasure of serving wine is twofold: In the drinking and in the enhancement of good food. Wine, like music, can be as enjoyable to the blissfully ignorant as to the expert. The only danger in having a little knowledge is that one's pleasure may be lessened by worrying about one's lack of expertise!

Wine is an all-occasion drink. It can be served formally or informally; before, during, or after meals; as a pick up; when guests drop in and one's larder is empty of solid refreshments; for parties and picnics.

However, so much has been written about the serving of wine that it has caused confusion and needless concern about a subject which deserves to be regarded as pure pleasure. The opinion of many wine "experts" has made a complicated art of a simple practice. It all boils down to this: Select a wine you enjoy; then serve it.

Forget the fripperies, fetishes, frumperies, and snobberies about serving wine. While wine adds a festive touch to any occasion, it requires no more formality than the serving of coffee or tea, and the modern hostess values its compatibility and versatility.

While there are certain acknowledged customs regarding the serving of wine, there is no mysterious ritual. The few practical suggestions which follow tell you all you need to know to make the serving of wine in your home entertaining, easy, and comfortable.

Vintage: Vintage, the year in which the grapes are grown, or the age of the wine, should be no deterrent to your enjoyment of wine. Modern authorities tell us that vintage is important only in considering European wines made of grapes grown on lands subject to changeable weather.

The amenities: At home or in a restaurant the host usually samples the wine before guests are served. This is to make sure the wine is good. Another reason, a practical one, too, is that cork may have crumbled into the wine and the fragments will be poured into the first glass, this assures that guests will be served the clearest wine.

A bottle of inferior wine is just as easily spotted as a poor quality steak. One test of a good, sound wine is to break the cork after removal and smell it. If you detect a musty odor, the bottle of wine will not be good.

How much to serve: An average serving of dinner wine is 3-1/2 to 4 ounces, while an average serving of appetizer and after-dinner wines is 2 to 3 ounces.

A good all-purpose wine glass is clear, stemmed, shaped vaguely like a tulip, and has a 6- to 9-ounce capacity. The mouth should be slightly smaller than the widest part of the bowl. It should never be filled over half full.

In a table setting the wine glass should be placed to the right of the water goblet. It is perfectly proper in informal entertaining to place the wine bottle on the table, but a napkin should be wrapped around the bottle to avoid dripping as it is poured (usually by the host, who keeps a watchful eye on the glasses of his guests).

To store wine: Wine bottles sealed with corks should be stored on their side so the cork will remain moist. If the cork dries out, air may enter the bottle and thus spoil the wine. (Try the musty cork test here.) Exposure to air will hasten spoilage of wine; therefore, it is best to keep bottles closed even while on the table.

Buying wine: In buying wine, the best advice one can be given is to *read the label.* It will tell you if it is a sparkling wine like champagne or a still wine like sherry or rosé (although there are now some sparkling rosé wines on the market.)

Terminology: In the language of wine "dry" means not sweet. "Sec" is French for dry. "Demi-sec" means semi-dry. "Brut" is the French term usually applied to dry champagne, while the French word "doux" means sweet.

Cool (room temperature) means 65°. Chilled means 50°. Temperature for sparkling wines and champagne is 40°.

Interesting to know: Wine has certain basic enemies. A vinegary salad will turn the taste of wine to vinegar. Acid fruits such as grapefruit, orange, or lemon discourage the palate from tasting the wine. And oily fish makes wine taste rather metallic or steely, particularly red wine.

Wine Buying Guide

The following size bottles give you approximate servings based on 3- to 3-1/2-ounce servings for dinner wines and champagne; 2- to 2-1/2-ounce servings for appetizer and dessert wines.

Size	Ounces	Dinner Wines and Champagne	Appetizer and Dessert Wines
Fifth (4/5 qt.)	25.6	8 servings	8 to 12 servings
Tenth (4/5 pt.)	12.8	4 servings	4 to 6 servings
Split (2/5 pt.)	6.4	2 servings	2 servings
Quart	32.0	10 servings	10 to 14 servings
Pint	16.0	5 servings	5 to 7 servings
1/2 Gallon	64.0	20 servings	20 to 30 servings
Gallon	128.0	40 servings	40 to 60 servings
Magnum	52.0	16 servings	

How much champagne should be bought for a large gathering? One case of 12 (4/5-quart) bottles will yield about 100 glasses or will provide 4 to 5 servings for 20 to 25 guests. Five cases to 100 guests is the usual rule.

Just add cheese to a Plain Omelet (page 436), serve with a full-bodied red wine, and you have a guest-pleasing meal.

Wine Selection Guide

Type of Wine	Specific Wine	Serve With	Temperature	When To Serve
Appetizer	Sherry, dry Vermouth, dry Port	Appetizers Appetizers Nuts-Cheese	Chilled, room temperature, over ice	Before dinner
Table Wines (white)	Rhine, Chablis Sauterne, Light Muscat, Sauterne, Riesling, White Chianti	Fish, seafood Poultry, cheese, Lamb, veal, eggs Lighter foods, Pork (except ham)	Chilled	With dinner
Table Wines (red)	Rosé	Curry patio parties, Chinese food, any food	Slightly chilled	With dinner any time, with or without food
	Claret	Game, Italian food, beef Hawaiian food	Slightly chilled	With dinner
	Chianti Vino Rosso	Red meat, cheese Roasts, game Italian food	Slightly chilled	With dinner
	Burgundy	Cheese, Italian food, game, ham heartier foods, roasts, steaks	Slightly chilled	With dinner any time, with or without food
Sparkling Wines	Champagne, dry	Appetizers, fish, seafood, poultry main courses, desserts, cheese, any festive meal	Chilled	Any time with or without food
	Sparkling Burgundy	Appetizers, main courses, roasts, game, desserts	Chilled	Any time
Dessert Wines	Port; Muscatel, Tokay; Champagne (sweet); Sherry, (cream); Madeira, sweet; Sauterne; Marsala; Malaga	Desserts, fruit, nuts, cheeses, cakes, pastries	Cool room temperature	After dinner With dessert

Hors d'oeuvres

Hors d'oeuvres are those pleasantly tantalizing finger foods served with drinks before a meal. They may be quite light so as to whet rather than satisfy the appetite before a formal dinner or a buffet supper. Or, they may be abundant and varied if the evening is to be a demi-dinner revolving around a continual parade of hot and cold hors d'oeuvres with a dessert table for a finale.

Whichever, serve a variety of appetizers with a thought to eye as well as palate appeal. The recipes that follow are keyed to specific menus. They have been chosen for their compatibility with the other dishes in the menu to provide appropriate color, texture, lightness, and flavor.

ALBONDIGAS

1 pound ground lean beef
1/4 pound chorizo sausage, minced*
1 teaspoon salt
Dash ground nutmeg
1 tablespoon minced parsley

2 slices bread, soaked in water
1 egg
3 tablespoons olive oil
Sherry
Beef bouillon

Combine meat, salt, nutmeg, and parsley. Squeeze water from bread, add bread and egg to meat mixture and work to a paste. Form into small balls and sauté in olive oil. Serve hot this way or keep warm in sauce made of equal parts sherry and beef bouillon. Yield: about 3 dozen (appetizer-size) meatballs.

*If unavailable, use 1-1/2 pounds meat loaf mixture of beef, veal, and pork instead of sausage and the 1 pound of beef.

LILLIPUT MEATBALLS

1 pound ground beef
1/2 cup soft breadcrumbs
1 tablespoon finely chopped onion
1/4 cup milk
1 teaspoon salt

2 tablespoons butter or margarine
1/2 cup dry sherry or Burgundy
1/2 cup catsup
1/4 teaspoon dried oregano

Mix beef, breadcrumbs, onion, milk, and salt. Shape into little balls using 1 teaspoon per ball. Heat butter in a large, heavy skillet; brown balls nicely on all sides. Pour off most of fat from skillet. Combine wine, catsup, and oregano; pour over balls; check seasonings. Cover and simmer slowly for about 30 minutes, shaking pan gently from time to time to cook balls evenly. Serve in chafing dish or in flameproof casserole set over a candle warmer. Provide wooden picks for spearing balls. French rolls may be sliced crosswise, buttered and served as an accompaniment for those who like a bit of bread with their meat. Yield: about 60 tiny meatballs; double the recipe for a cocktail supper for about 20.

SWEDISH MEATBALLS

3 slices white bread
2 cups water
1-1/2 pounds ground beef
1/2 pound mild pork sausage
1 onion, minced
3 tablespoons butter or margarine

2 medium potatoes, boiled
    and mashed
1 teaspoon salt
1/8 teaspoon pepper
1 teaspoon seasoned salt
2 eggs
Gravy

Soak bread in water for a few minutes, then press to drain. Combine beef and sausage with bread. Saute onion in 1 tablespoon of the butter; add to meat along with mashed potatoes, all seasonings, and eggs. Beat together with electric

Speared and ready to go into the hot oil in the fondue pot are, from top to bottom: shrimp, teriyaki steak strips, chicken livers wrapped with bacon, ham and pineapple wedges, and wedges of sirloin steak. See page 250 for fondue menus and recipes.

mixer until light. Shape into 1-1/2-inch balls and brown in remaining butter, gently turning balls to brown evenly; remove carefully. When all are done, prepare Gravy using the same skillet and place meatballs in it. Cover and simmer for 40 minutes. Will freeze. Yield: 10 to 12 servings.

Gravy

3 tablespoons butter or margarine
3 tablespoons all-purpose flour
3 cups beef broth (bouillon cubes and water)

1 cup sweet cream
1/2 teaspoon seasoned salt
1 teaspoon Kitchen Bouquet
Pepper to taste

Heat butter in same skillet used for browning meatballs, add flour and stir until yellow. Gradually add beef broth and stir until smooth and thick. Add cream and seasoned salt, then Kitchen Bouquet and pepper.

OLIVE AND DRIED BEEF RAREBIT

1 cup medium white sauce*
1 cup shredded sharp Cheddar cheese
1/4 teaspoon dry mustard
1/2 teaspoon Worcestershire sauce

1/2 cup sliced ripe olives
1/4 cup finely shredded dried chipped beef

Put white sauce in top of double boiler over warm water; gradually add cheese, stirring until melted. Add seasonings and mix well; stir in olives and dried beef. Transfer to chafing dish and serve with corn chips. Yield: 6 servings.

*See Index for Sauce Preparation Guide.

OLD-FASHIONED CHICKEN SALAD

4 cups cooked chopped chicken
Chicken broth
1/2 cup heavy cream, whipped

1 cup homemade mayonnaise*
2 cups chopped celery
1 cup slivered blanched almonds

Chicken will be more moist if cut from bones the day before you make the salad, covered with broth in which it was cooked, then chilled until ready to use.

Remove chicken from broth; scrape away the jellied broth and use it for another purpose. Combine whipped cream with mayonnaise, then blend all ingredients together, adding more mayonnaise if needed. If desired, a few drops of fresh lemon juice may be added to spark up the flavor; taste it and see. Yield: 8 servings; double the recipe to serve 20.

*See Index for Mayonnaise recipe.

BACON-CHESTNUT APPETIZERS

15 slices bacon, cut lengthwise

2 (5-ounce) cans water chestnuts, drained (30 chestnuts)

Wind bacon slices around whole chestnuts; secure with wooden picks. Put on rack in 350° oven and bake for about 25 minutes, until bacon is well done and crisp, turning the chestnuts when half done if necessary. Drain on paper towels and keep warm until serving time. Yield: 30 appetizers.

BACON ROLL-UPS
(may be prepared ahead of time)

1/4 cup butter or margarine	1 egg, slightly beaten
1/2 cup water	1/4 pound hot or mild, bulk
1-1/2 cups packaged	pork sausage
herb-seasoned stuffing	1/2 to 2/3 pound sliced bacon

Melt butter in water in saucepan. Remove from heat; stir into stuffing, then add egg and sausage. Blend thoroughly. Chill for about an hour for easier handling, then shape into small oblongs about the size of pecans. Cut bacon strips into thirds, crosswise; wrap one piece around dressing mixture and fasten with wooden pick. Place on rack in shallow pan and bake at 375° for 35 minutes, or until brown and crisp, turning at halfway point in cooking. Drain on paper towels and serve hot. May be made the day before baking; also freezes well before baking. Yield: about 36 appetizers.

CURRIED BACON-BRAZIL NUTS

Moisten shelled Brazil nuts slightly by placing them in a colander and passing them quickly under cold running water. Sprinkle curry powder lightly over nuts; then wrap with a piece of bacon (1/4 of a strip or less cut crosswise) and fasten with a wooden pick, making sure the pick is inserted into the nut. Place on wire rack over a shallow pan and bake at 350° for about 25 minutes or until dry and crisp. Drain on paper towels and serve just warm.

ROAST PORK STRIPS

1/2 cup soy sauce	3 tablespoons honey
1/4 cup bourbon	1 clove garlic, crushed
1/2 teaspoon ground ginger	1 (3-pound) pork tenderloin

Combine soy sauce, bourbon, ginger, honey, and garlic. Place pork in shallow glass dish and pour marinade over it. Cover and refrigerate overnight, turning the meat occasionally.

Place meat on rack in open shallow pan and bake at 300° for about 1-1/2 hours, spooning marinade over it from time to time.

To serve as an appetizer, allow meat to cool, then cut into thin slices (about 1/8 inch thick). Cut slices into strips and spear each with a wooden pick. Arrange on a bed of lettuce or parsley — or insert picks into a grapefruit or apple or pineapple — or any other attractive contrivance you can come up with.

This pork is best served at room temperature. The flavor is subtle and the pork requires no dipping sauce to enhance it. Yield: 12 servings.

ASPARAGUS SPEARS ROLLED IN HAM
(may be prepared ahead of time)

18 canned asparagus spears	Freshly ground black pepper
3/4 cup salad oil	1/2 teaspoon dried basil
1/4 cup wine vinegar	9 slices thin boiled or baked ham
1/2 teaspoon salt	

Marinate asparagus in oil, vinegar, salt, pepper, and basil for 2 hours. Drain thoroughly. Cut ham in half crosswise and wrap around asparagus spear, securing with a wooden pick. Yield: 6 servings.

CHERRY TOMATOES WITH SMOKED OYSTERS

Wash but do not remove stems from cherry tomatoes. Cut down through each tomato to within about 1/2 inch of the base; spread apart just enough to slip a canned smoked oyster inside each. Serve either at room temperature or slightly chilled.

Note: A 3-ounce can of smoked oysters usually contains about 40 tiny oysters.

LOMI LOMI CHERRIES
(may be prepared ahead of time)

1 quart cherry tomatoes	1 onion, minced
1/4 pound smoked salmon, minced	1 green pepper, minced

Cut off and discard tops of cherry tomatoes. Scoop out seed and pulp with a small pointed spoon. Combine pulp with minced salmon, onion, and green pepper. Refill tomatoes with this mixture and chill before serving. Yield: 2 to 3 dozen.

MARINATED ANCHOVIES

3 (2-ounce) cans rolled anchovies, undrained	4 tablespoons wine vinegar
1 clove garlic, crushed	1 large onion, very finely minced
	6 tablespoons minced fresh parsley

Arrange anchovies and some of their liquid in shallow serving dish. Combine garlic and vinegar and pour over the anchovies. Mix onion and parsley; spread in a thick layer over anchovies. Carefully spoon the marinade in the dish over all to moisten, then place in refrigerator (well covered)! for at least 3 hours. Serve with small rounds of rye bread. Yield: 10 servings.

BACON-WRAPPED SHRIMP
(may be prepared ahead of time)

Marinate shelled, cleaned, but uncooked shrimp for 1 to 2 hours in the refrigerator in any good French dressing. Drain, wrap each shrimp in 1/4 slice of bacon, fasten with wooden pick. Broil, turning once, until bacon is crisp; or place on rack over shallow pan and bake at 350° for about 20 minutes, turning once, until bacon is dry and crisp. Drain on paper towels. May be used as an appetizer or garnish.

DEVILED SHRIMP
(prepare the day before)

2 pounds raw shrimp in the shell	1 tablespoon wine vinegar
1 lemon, thinly sliced	1 clove garlic, crushed
1 red onion, thinly sliced	1/2 bay leaf, broken
1/2 cup pitted ripe olives	1 tablespoon dry mustard
2 tablespoons chopped pimiento	1/4 teaspoon cayenne pepper
1/2 cup freshly squeezed lemon juice	Freshly ground black pepper
1/4 cup salad oil	1 teaspoon salt

Shell and devein raw shrimp. Bring water to a boil and add shrimp; cook for 3 minutes. Drain at once; combine with lemon and onion slices, olives, and pimiento.

Combine lemon juice, oil, vinegar, and seasonings in another bowl. Stir into shrimp mixture. Cover and refrigerate overnight, stirring once or twice. To serve, spoon from bowl onto small plates, or provide picks for spearing. Yield: 6 servings; triple the recipe for a cocktail party for about 20.

CURRIED SHRIMP IN CASSEROLE
(may be prepared ahead of time)

5 pounds raw shrimp in the shell	2-1/2 teaspoons curry powder
3 (10-ounce) cans cream of shrimp soup	1 medium onion, chopped fine
3 cups commercial sour cream	2 tablespoons butter or margarine

Boil shrimp, shell and devein. Combine thawed soup with sour cream, curry powder, and cooked shrimp. Sauté onion in butter and add to the mixture. Allow to stand for an hour or two before heating so flavors will be well blended. When ready to serve, turn into large casserole, cover and bake at 325° only until heated through, about 30 minutes. For buffet service, place casserole on an electric hot tray. This recipe serves 20 amply for luncheon or a buffet, served over hot rice. It may also be used to fill tiny pastry shells; in that case it will fill about 60. For a cocktail supper for about 50, double the recipe and garnish with Bacon-Wrapped Shrimp* or Water Chestnut-Pineapple Roll-Ups*. Serve with Toast Triangles*.

*See Index for recipes.

HAWAIIAN GRAB BAG
(may be prepared ahead of time)

Select at least five of the following: cherry tomatoes, peeled cucumber cubes, green pepper chunks, halved water chestnuts, avocado chunks, cold boiled and cleaned shrimp, Pickled Mushrooms*, or any other vegetable or solid-meat seafood you like.

Sauce

2 cups homemade mayonnaise	2 teaspoons ground mustard
1/2 cup commercial sour cream	1/2 teaspoon salt
2 tablespoons prepared horseradish, drained	1 tablespoon freshly squeezed lemon juice
1/2 teaspoon monosodium glutamate	

Combine all ingredients for sauce. Place in attractive serving bowl, lightly stir in vegetables and seafood, provide guests with wooden picks or bamboo skewers for spearing. This amount is sufficient for a pupu appetizer tray for 12, since other appetizers are provided.

*See Index for Pickled Mushrooms recipe.

MARINATED SHRIMP PORT GIBSON

5 pounds raw shrimp in shell, cooked and cleaned	4 tablespoons grated onion
1 cup salad oil	1 clove garlic, minced
1/2 cup vinegar	5 tablespoons minced fresh parsley
1-1/4 cups finely minced celery	3/4 cup horseradish mustard
2-1/2 tablespoons finely minced green pepper	1-1/2 teaspoons salt
	1/4 teaspoon pepper
	4 tablespoons paprika

Place shrimp in deep bowl. Mix other ingredients thoroughly and pour over shrimp. Cover and marinate in refrigerator for 24 hours before serving, stirring occasionally. This shrimp may be used as an appetizer, first course, or main dish salad. Yield: 10 to 12 servings. Because of the excellence of this shrimp, the recipe should be doubled for a cocktail party of 20.

PICKLED SHRIMP

3 to 4 pounds raw large shrimp in the shell	3-1/2 teaspoons salt
1/2 cup chopped celery tops	2 cups sliced onion
1/4 cup mixed pickling spices	7 or 8 bay leaves

Put shrimp in large pot; cover with boiling water. Add celery tops, pickling spices, and salt. Cover and simmer 5 minutes. Drain. Cool by immersing in cold water; peel and devein.

In shallow bowl alternate shrimp with 2 cups sliced onion and 7 or 8 bay leaves.

Marinade

1-1/4 cups salad oil	1-1/2 teaspoons celery seed
3/4 cup vinegar	1-1/2 teaspoons salt
1-1/2 tablespoons capers (with juice)	Dash Tabasco sauce

Combine marinade ingredients, mix well and pour over shrimp. Cover; chill at least 24 hours. Serve shrimp in bowl with marinade and provide picks and small plates. Pickled shrimp will keep at least a week in the refrigerator. Yield: 15 servings.

SEA ISLAND SHRIMP
(prepare the day before)

2 to 3 pounds raw shrimp	2/3 cup tarragon vinegar
2 unpeeled lemons, sliced paper-thin	Juice of 2 lemons
1 large onion, sliced paper-thin	2 teaspoons salt
1-1/3 cups olive oil	Freshly ground black pepper

Boil and devein shrimp; slice if desired. Place in bowl with lemon and onion slices. Place all other ingredients in jar with tight-fitting cover and shake vigorously; pour over shrimp. Cover and refrigerate overnight. Serve shrimp in their marinade with wooden picks for spearing. Yield: 8 to 10 servings.

DEVILED EGGS WITH SALTED ALMONDS

12 hard-cooked eggs	1 teaspoon salt
4 tablespoons mayonnaise	3 teaspoons Dijon mustard
4 tablespoons commercial sour cream	1/3 cup chopped salted almonds

Cut eggs in half and scoop out yolks. Mash with mayonnaise and sour cream; add salt and mustard and blend well. Taste for seasonings; add more if too bland; you may want to add a dash of cayenne pepper. Refill egg whites and sprinkle with chopped almonds. Yield: 12 servings.

DILLED GREEN OLIVES
(prepare ahead of time)

1 (8-ounce) jar unstuffed jumbo green olives	1 teaspoon dill seed
1 clove garlic, split	1/4 teaspoon black pepper
1 small whole dried red pepper*	2/3 cup salad oil
	1/3 cup cider vinegar

Drain olives and put in jar with tight lid. Add all other ingredients. Prepare several days ahead of serving and keep refrigerated, turning jar upside down several times to distribute the marinade. Yield: about 1-1/2 cups.

*Steal one from your mixed pickling spices.

GARLIC OLIVES
(prepare ahead of time)

2 (8-ounce) jars olives
1/3 cup olive oil

1 tablespoon minced garlic
1/2 teaspoon oregano, crushed

Use large green or black olives. Drain, reserving 1/2 cup of the liquid. Combine liquid with olive oil, garlic, and oregano. Pack olives into jars, cover with marinade and refrigerate at least 24 hours before serving.

SPICED RIPE OLIVES
(prepare ahead of time)

1 (1-pint) jar ripe olives
1 small dried chili pepper*
2 cloves crushed garlic

Few sprigs fresh dill, or about 1/2
teaspoon dried dill weed
3 tablespoons olive oil

Drain olives, reserving the liquid. To the jar add the above ingredients; then fill jar with reserved liquid. Let olives marinate 2 days before serving. Yield: 2 cups.

*Steal one from your mixed pickling spices.

MARINATED SPANISH OLIVES
(prepare ahead of time)

1 (8-ounce) jar unpitted green olives
1/4 cup vinegar
1/4 cup olive oil

2 tablespoons minced chives
1 clove garlic, slashed
1/4 teaspoon whole peppercorns

Drain olives, then add all ingredients to them. Fasten lid on jar tightly and let olives stand for 24 hours at room temperature, turning the jar upside down occasionally to distribute the marinade.

OLIVE QUICHE
(may be prepared the day before)

6 eggs
1 cup slivered ripe olives
1 pint commercial sour cream
1 teaspoon oregano
1-1/2 cups shredded Swiss cheese

2 tablespoons chives
3/4 teaspoon salt
Dash cayenne pepper
Pastry for double-crust pie (piecrust
mix is satisfactory)

Beat the eggs with a wooden spoon in large mixing bowl. Add all ingredients and mix well. Prepare pastry according to package directions; roll out to fit a 15- x 10- x 1-inch jellyroll pan, bringing pastry partially up sides of pan. Pour olive mixture over pastry and bake at 425° for 15 minutes. Reduce temperature to 375° and continue baking for about 25 minutes, or until filling is set (when a knife inserted in center comes out clean). Cool slightly and cut into bars about 1-1/2 x 2-1/2 inches. Serve warm. Yield: about 48 bars.

WATER CHESTNUT-PINEAPPLE ROLL-UPS
(may be prepared ahead of time)

Cut bacon slices in fourths crosswise; slice water chestnuts in half, and drain canned pineapple chunks. Wrap a bacon piece around a chunk of pineapple and a slice of water chestnut; secure with a wooden pick. Place on rack over a shallow pan; bake at 350° for about 20 minutes, or until crisp, turning once. Drain on paper towels. May be prepared ahead of time, then reheated at 350° for about 5 minutes. Use as an appetizer or garnish.

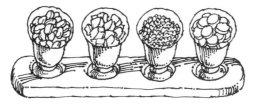

CHILI ALMONDS
(may be prepared ahead of time)

2 tablespoons butter or margarine
1 tablespoon chili powder
1 large clove garlic, crushed

2 cups unblanched almonds
Coarse salt

Put butter in a shallow pan in a 250° oven. When melted, stir in the chili powder and garlic. Add almonds and stir until all are coated. Return to oven and bake for about 1-1/2 hours, stirring every 15 minutes or so if convenient. While still hot, sprinkle generously with salt (salt salvaged from the pretzel box may be used) and when cool store in airtight jar. May be made weeks ahead of time and frozen. Yield: 10 servings; double the recipe for a cocktail party of about 20.

PARTY ALMONDS
(may be prepared ahead of time)

For each cup of almonds, use 1 teaspoon butter or salad oil. Put butter in a shallow pan in 300° oven; when melted, stir in almonds and bake for 20 to 25 minutes, stirring frequently. Remove and toss with garlic salt and a little cayenne pepper. These keep well in an airtight container. Prepare 2 cups to serve 6.

BARBECUE PEANUTS

1 tablespoon liquid smoke
1 teaspoon Worcestershire sauce
1/3 cup water

1-1/2 cups salted peanuts
1 tablespoon butter, melted
1/4 teaspoon garlic salt

Combine liquid smoke, Worcestershire sauce, and water in small saucepan; bring to a boil. Add peanuts; let stand 30 minutes. Drain off liquid; spread nuts in shallow baking pan and bake at 250° for 1 hour. Toss nuts with butter and drain on paper towels. Sprinkle with garlic salt.

COCKTAIL PECANS
(prepare ahead of time)

2 tablespoons butter or margarine
1/2 teaspoon seasoned salt
1 or 2 dashes Tabasco sauce

1 pound pecan halves
3 tablespoons Worcestershire sauce

Put butter, seasoned salt, and hot sauce in 12- x 8- x 2-inch baking dish. Place in 300° oven until butter melts. Add pecans, stirring until all are butter-coated. Bake for about 20 minutes, stirring occasionally. Sprinkle with Worcestershire sauce, stir again and continue baking another 15 minutes, or until crisp. Will freeze. Yield: about 20 servings.

CURRIED PEANUTS

1 pound salted peanuts

3 or 4 tablespoons curry powder

Put peanuts in shallow pan. Bake at 300° for 15 to 20 minutes, stirring occasionally to prevent burning. Remove and while still hot, stir in curry powder. Cool and place in airtight container.

ITALIAN ARTICHOKE HEARTS

1 (1-pound) can artichoke hearts, drained
3 tablespoons commercial Italian or
  French dressing

1/4 cup commercial mayonnaise
2 tablespoons capers, drained
  Paprika

Drain artichoke hearts and cut in half. Place in shallow dish, cut-side up. Blend dressing into mayonnaise, stir in capers. Pour over artichoke hearts and chill several hours. Before serving, sprinkle the dish with paprika and if desired scatter a few more drained capers over all. Serve with wooden picks. Provide small plates for these; they're apt to be drippy; but good. Yield: 6 servings.

MARINATED CARROT STICKS
(prepare the day before)

8 small carrots
3 tablespoons vinegar
3 tablespoons salad oil
1 small clove garlic, crushed

3/4 teaspoon seasoned salt
1/4 teaspoon salt
Minced fresh parsley

Peel and cut carrots into thin, short, 3-inch sticks. Place in shallow dish; mix other ingredients except parsley and pour over carrots, spooning marinade over the carrots so all will be coated. Cover tightly and refrigerate overnight, turning sticks occasionally if convenient. Drain off marinade, arrange carrot sticks attractively in serving dish and sprinkle with parsley. Yield: 6 to 8 servings when other appetizers are provided.

Variation: Young turnips may be treated in the same way as carrots; they may be substituted for the carrots or combined with them.

CAVIAR-STUFFED CELERY

Celery
Cream cheese, softened
Commercial sour cream
Grated onion

Freshly squeezed lemon juice
Salt and pepper
Red caviar

Select small inner stalks of celery with some of leaves showing. Beat cream cheese until soft and smooth, blending in a small amount of sour cream to thin the mixture slightly; do not allow filling to be runny. Add grated onion, lemon juice, salt, and pepper to taste. Stuff celery, then spoon caviar sparingly in a line down the center of the filled celery.

STUFFED CELERY DIABLE

4 to 5 stalks celery
2 ounces Roquefort or blue cheese
3 ounces cream cheese

Big pinch cayenne pepper
1/4 cup finely ground walnuts
Paprika

Peel and cut celery into 4-inch pieces. Combine Roquefort and cream cheese until smooth in small bowl of electric mixer. Beat in pepper, then stir in walnuts. Stuff celery; sprinkle with paprika. Yield: 4 servings.

CELERY STUFFED WITH LIPTAUER
(may be prepared the day before)

Using a vegetable peeler, remove every string from lower 7 or 8 inches of celery stalks. This may be done a day ahead of time, the stalks then kept in a pitcher of ice water in refrigerator until an hour before serving. Dry thoroughly; stuff with Liptauer Cheese Spread.

Liptauer Cheese Spread

1/2 cup butter, softened
1 (8-ounce) package cream
  cheese, softened
4 anchovy filets, mashed with about
  1 teaspoon of their oil
1 teaspoon dry mustard
1 teaspoon paprika

1 teaspoon finely minced fresh parsley
1 teaspoon finely minced onion
1 tablespoon drained capers
1 tablespoon chopped chives
1 teaspoon caraway seed, crushed
  or ground
Dash pepper

Cream butter and cheese in small bowl of electric mixer. Add remaining ingredients, blend well and chill. Use as a stuffing for celery or as a spread with melba toast rounds. May be made several days ahead of time; also freezes well. Yield: about 1-1/2 cups.

Note: By adding 1 cup sour cream this spread may be used as an excellent dip for raw vegetables.

MINCED MUSHROOMS IN CHAFING DISH

2 quarts fresh mushrooms, or
2 (6- to 8-ounce) cans, drained
4 tablespoons butter or margarine
2 medium onions, finely chopped

1/2 to 1 (10-1/2-ounce) can cream of
mushroom soup, undiluted
Salt to taste
Seasoned salt
1/4 cup dry sherry

Chop mushrooms coarsely. Heat butter and gently sauté onions until yellow; add mushrooms; continue sautéing for a few minutes. Gradually blend in soup. Add salt, seasoned salt, and sherry; heat gently until hot but not boiling. Transfer to chafing dish.

TOAST TRIANGLES

I like to serve this delicate appetizer with sliced white bread with crusts removed, then cut into triangles and toasted at 225° until golden. If desired, triangles may be spread with herb or plain butter before toasting. — C. M.

MUSHROOMS À LA GRECQUE

1 pound small whole button mushrooms
1 cup water
1 cup salad oil
Juice of 2 lemons, cut into chunks
after juicing
3 tablespoons wine vinegar
1 stalk celery, cut into chunks
1 clove garlic, minced

1/2 teaspoon dried rosemary
1/2 teaspoon ground sage
1/2 teaspoon dried leaf thyme
1 bay leaf
1 teaspoon ground coriander (optional)
8 whole peppercorns
1 teaspoon salt

Do not remove stems from mushrooms but trim off a thin slice from bottom. Rinse in cold water quickly. Combine all ingredients in a large saucepan and bring to a boil. Add mushrooms and simmer for 4 minutes, stirring several times. Pour into bowl, cover, and marinate overnight in refrigerator. Drain and serve on wooden picks as hors d'oeuvres or as a first course on a bed of lettuce.

PICKLED MUSHROOMS
(may be prepared ahead of time)

1 pound fresh mushrooms, or 2 (4-ounce)
cans button mushrooms, drained
1/2 cup vinegar
1/2 cup oil

1 teaspoon salt
1 clove garlic, minced
1 tablespoon chives
1 bay leaf

Wash mushrooms quickly in cold water and cut off thin slice from bottom of stems. Combine remaining ingredients and pour over mushrooms. Cover and marinate at least overnight, turning several times. Yield: about 12 servings.

MARINATED MUSHROOMS

Drain off and save liquid from an (8-ounce) can or jar of whole button mushrooms; use the liquid (you may freeze it) for soup, or some other wholesome purpose. Place mushrooms in a bowl and cover with a tart salad dressing in amount equal to the liquid drained off — or enough to cover mushrooms. Cover and refrigerate for 24 hours, until mushrooms are chilled and flavors are blended. Stir occasionally. Before serving, drain off dressing. The reserved dressing may be used for salads and meat marinades.

COCKTAIL CRUNCH
(may be prepared ahead of time)

1/2 cup butter or margarine	1 teaspoon seasoned salt
1 (6-ounce) package blue cheese, or garlic salad dressing mix	4 cups bite-size shredded wheat cereal
1 tablespoon Worcestershire sauce	2 cups bite-size rice cereal
	2 cups unblanched whole almonds

Melt butter in large shallow pan in 250° oven. Stir in salad dressing mix, Worcestershire sauce, and seasoned salt. Add cereals and almonds; stir well until all are coated. Return to oven and bake for 1 hour, stirring every 15 minutes. May be prepared the day before; also freezes well. Yield: 12 servings.

PARTY MIX
(may be prepared ahead of time)

1/2 cup butter or margarine	1 (7-1/2-ounce) box cheese crackers
1 (1-3/8-ounce) package dry onion soup mix	3 to 4 cups bite-size shredded rice cereal

Put butter in a 12- x 8- x 2-inch pan in a 250° oven. When melted, stir in dry soup mix and blend thoroughly. Add other ingredients, stir well to coat thoroughly and bake for about 1 hour, stirring three or four times. Will freeze. Yield: about 8 cups.

ASPARAGUS FOLD-OVERS
(may be prepared ahead of time)

Trim crusts from slices of whole-wheat bread; roll flat with rolling pin. Spread lightly with soft butter and sprinkle sparingly with grated Parmesan cheese. Thoroughly drain canned asparagus spears and pat dry with paper towels. Place a spear of asparagus diagonally across bread square, bring up two opposite points of bread and insert a wooden pick to fasten. Brush with melted butter; bake at 400° for about 12 minutes and serve hot. These fold-overs may be frozen after brushing with butter. Place, frozen, in hot oven and bake until lightly browned.

Variation: If you prefer a rolled sandwich, place asparagus spear along one edge of bread square and roll tightly, as for a jellyroll.

CARAWAY BISCUITS
(may be prepared ahead of time)

1 cup all-purpose flour, measured before sifting
1 teaspoon dry mustard
1 teaspoon salt
1/2 cup shredded Swiss cheese (or Swiss and Parmesan mixed)

1/2 teaspoon paprika
2 teaspoons caraway seed
1/3 cup butter or margarine
Several drops Tabasco sauce
1/2 teaspoon Worcestershire sauce
About 3 tablespoons cold water

Sift flour, mustard, and salt into bowl. Stir in cheese, paprika, and caraway seed. Cut in butter until particles are about the size of peas. Sprinkle with Tabasco, Worcestershire sauce, and cold water. Toss lightly with fork until dough holds together. Form into a ball and roll out on floured surface into a 13- x 9-inch rectangle. Using a pastry wheel cut into 1-inch squares. Place on ungreased baking sheet, sprinkle with a little paprika and bake at 425° until brown, just about 7 minutes. Do not overbake. Will freeze. Yield: about 8 dozen small squares.

CRUNCHY CHEESE BISCUITS

1/2 cup butter or margarine, softened
1 cup all-purpose flour, measured before sifting
1 cup shredded sharp Cheddar cheese, softened

1/2 teaspoon salt
Tabasco and Worcestershire sauce to taste
1 cup rice cereal bits

Blend all ingredients except cereal bits by hand in a bowl until thoroughly mixed. Work in cereal bits. Pinch off into tiny balls about the size of a nickel. Place on ungreased baking sheet, press down with fork, and bake at 325° for about 10 minutes, or until faintly colored. Yield: about 48 balls.

GENIE'S CHEESE BISCUITS
(may be prepared ahead of time)

1/2 pound butter or margarine
1/2 pound sharp Cheddar cheese, shredded
1 or 2 dashes cayenne pepper

1 egg
1 long white loaf commercial bread, thinly sliced

Place first four ingredients in small bowl of electric mixer and beat until fluffy.

Use 1 long loaf commercial bread. Stack three slices, remove crusts. Cut into quarters. Spread cheese-butter mixture generously between slices, then ice top and sides very thinly. Place on lightly greased baking sheet and bake at 350° for 12 to 15 minutes. Serve warm. Yield: 36 squares.

Note: Biscuits freeze beautifully and require no thawing before baking. To freeze, complete the icing, place biscuits on flat tray, place uncovered in freezer until firm, then store in freezer container with waxed paper between layers.

SESAME COCKTAIL BISCUITS
(may be prepared ahead of time)

1 (3-ounce) package cream
cheese, softened
1/2 cup butter or margarine, softened
1-1/4 cups all-purpose flour

1/2 teaspoon seasoned salt
1/3 cup toasted sesame seed
Coarse (kosher) salt or more
seasoned salt

Cream cheese and butter together in large bowl of electric mixer until blended. Add flour, 1/2 teaspoon seasoned salt, and sesame seed. Mix thoroughly. Flour hands lightly and form mixture into a long roll about 1 inch in diameter. Wrap in waxed paper and chill thoroughly.

To bake, slice into 1/4-inch rounds, place on greased baking sheet and bake at 350° for about 15 minutes, or until light golden. While still hot, sprinkle with a few grains of coarse salt or a little seasoned salt. Store in airtight container; biscuits may be frozen, then thawed in same container.

Note: To toast sesame seed, put in shallow pan in a 275° oven for about 25 minutes, shaking the pan a little from time to time.

CHEESE SNACK BREAD
(may be prepared ahead of time)

2 cakes compressed yeast or 2 packages
dry yeast
1 cup warm water (very warm water
for dry yeast)
4 cups all-purpose flour
1 (8-ounce) jar processed yellow
cheese spread

2 tablespoons sugar
2 tablespoons soft butter
3/4 teaspoon salt
1/2 cup soft butter
1 (2-ounce) package dehydrated onion
soup mix

Dissolve yeast in warm water in large mixer bowl. Add 2 cups flour, cheese spread, sugar, butter, and salt. Beat well, scraping bowl several times. When smooth, gradually add remaining flour and mix thoroughly. Cover with light cloth and let rise in warm place until doubled in size. While the dough rises, prepare filling. Combine 1/2 cup soft butter with onion soup mix; blend well.

Divide dough into thirds. Roll out each portion to about 12 x 7 inches; spread with one-third of filling. Roll up, jellyroll fashion; seal edges and ends and place seam-side down on greased baking sheet. Repeat with other two portions. Using sharp knife, make a lengthwise cut down center of each roll, halfway through loaf. (You'll see why after bread is baked.) Cover; let rise in warm place until not quite double in bulk, about 35 minutes. Bake at 350° for about 30 minutes. Serve in thick slices while hot. Yield: 3 loaves.

Note: This bread may be baked in advance, frozen, then reheated after thawing in a 350° oven for about 10 minutes.

TINY CHEESE BISCUITS
(may be prepared ahead of time)

1 pound sharp Cheddar
  cheese, shredded
1 pound butter or margarine, softened
4-1/2 cups all-purpose flour

1/2 teaspoon salt
1 teaspoon cayenne pepper (use less if
  you aren't a pepper fancier)

Working with hands or electric mixer, blend cheese and butter into sifted dry ingredients until smooth. Pat or roll out on floured surface to about 1/3-inch thickness. Cut with inside of doughnut cutter or other small cutter. (The cutter is stubborn about turning loose of the dough. To avoid this, dip cutter frequently into cold water.) Place about 1/8 inch apart on ungreased pan and bake at 325° for about 15 minutes. Do not allow the biscuits to brown; it's easy to overbake them. Store in airtight tin, placing waxed paper between layers. Freezes beautifully; thaw in closed tin. Yield: about 125.

CHEESE DREAMS
(may be prepared ahead of time)

1/2 cup milk
1 egg, beaten
1/4 teaspoon dry mustard
1/2 teaspoon salt

3/4 pound sharp Cheddar cheese, shredded
Melted butter
Paprika

Heat milk in top of double boiler over hot water. When scalded, add egg, mustard, salt, and cheese; cook for 15 minutes, stirring constantly. Remove from heat; cool, cover, and store in refrigerator.

When ready to use, spread cheese mixture on rounds of white bread, cover with another round in which you have cut a small hole in middle with inside of doughnut cutter. Brush with melted butter, sprinkle with paprika, and bake at 450° until nicely browned. Serve immediately. Yield: 15 servings.

TOASTED GARLIC-CHEESE ROUNDS

1/2 cup butter or margarine
2 cloves garlic, slashed
1 day-old loaf sliced white bread

About 1 cup grated Parmesan and
shredded Swiss cheese, mixed (or
mixed Parmesan and Gruyere)

Combine butter and garlic in a small saucepan and heat until butter bubbles. Remove from heat, let stand for about 3 hours, then discard the garlic.

Cut crusts from bread and with a cookie cutter cut into circles about 1-1/2 to 2 inches in diameter. Arrange on a baking sheet, brush with garlic butter and sprinkle generously with grated cheese. Bake at 275° to 300° until crisp.

Note: Parmesan cheese alone is satisfactory; however, I find a cheese mixture a little less acrid. — C.M.

FROZEN CHEESE CANAPE
(may be prepared for baking ahead of time)

1/2 pound sharp Cheddar cheese
6 slices bacon, cooked not quite crisp
1 small onion

1 teaspoon dry mustard
1/2 teaspoon Worcestershire sauce
2 teaspoons mayonnaise

Put cheese, bacon, and onion through food grinder. Add remaining ingredients, mix well and form into roll about 1-1/2 inches in diameter. Wrap securely and freeze. Keep frozen until ready to use, then cut into 1/4-inch slices, place on bread rounds or crackers (or on split English muffins if using to accompany a main dish or for a hot open-faced sandwich). Place under broiler until golden brown. These may also be served to accompany a salad for lunch.

HOT CHEESE SQUARES
(may be prepared for baking ahead of time)

1 loaf white bread, unsliced
1/2 cup butter or margarine
1 (3-ounce) package cream cheese

1/4 cup shredded sharp yellow cheese
2 egg whites

Trim crusts from bread; cut into 1-inch slices, then cut each slice into quarters. Melt butter, blend in cheeses. Beat egg whites until stiff; fold into cooled cheese mixture. Spread bread cubes on all sides; refrigerate at least overnight. If preferred, squares may be frozen at this point. Bake at 400° for about 15 minutes or until nicely browned; serve hot. Yield: about 60 squares.

PARMESAN CHEESE BITES
(may be prepared ahead of time)

1 cup all-purpose flour
1 or 2 dashes cayenne pepper
2/3 cup grated Parmesan cheese

1/2 cup butter or margarine, softened
Evaporated milk or cream

Sift flour into mixing bowl; stir in pepper and cheese. Cut in butter with pastry blender, then work dough with hands until it holds together. Roll out on floured surface to 1/3-inch thickness and cut into 1- or 1-1/2-inch squares. (A pastry wheel gives an attractive edge.) Transfer to ungreased baking sheet, brush tops with evaporated milk or cream and bake at 350° for 12 to 15 minutes. Do not overbake. Freezes well. Yield: about 30 appetizers.

Note: These are delicious appetizers and I have found it always advisable to double the recipe. They will keep well in an airtight container, if there are any left — which there won't be! — C.M.

HOW MANY ICE CUBES

If you make your ice cubes ahead of time and store them in plastic bags in the freezer, count on about 350 cubes for 50 people.

CHICKEN OR TURKEY STRUDEL
(may be prepared ahead of time)

1 (8-ounce) package cream
cheese, softened
1 cup butter or margarine, softened

2-1/4 cups all-purpose flour, measured
before sifting
1 teaspoon salt
1/4 teaspoon mixed herbs

In large bowl of electric mixer (or by hand), beat cheese and butter until smooth. Gradually add flour mixed with salt and herbs. When dough holds together, form into a ball, wrap in waxed paper and refrigerate overnight.

Filling

1 small onion, minced
1/4 cup butter
2 cups minced cooked chicken or turkey
1/2 cup minced fresh parsley
3 tablespoons minced celery
1 egg, lightly beaten

1/2 teaspoon salt
Few grinds coarse black pepper
Generous dash poultry seasoning
Small amount chicken broth or gravy
for moistening if needed (1 to 2
tablespoons are enough)

Heat butter in saucepan and sauté onion until tender but not brown. Stir in all other ingredients and mix well.

To bake the Strudel: Allow pastry to sit at room temperature for 30 minutes after removing from refrigerator. Cut into fourths, working with one portion at a time. Roll out on floured board to a rectangle about 4 x 18 inches, 1/8 inch thick. Place one-fourth of filling in center of strip, draw up long edges to meet and pinch together to seal, moistening the pastry with a little water to encourage it to hold together. Transfer filled strip to an ungreased baking sheet; repeat with other three portions of dough. Chill an hour or two, then with a sharp knife cut the rolls into 1-inch slices, separating the slices slightly. Brush with a lightly beaten egg mixed with 1 teaspoon water; bake at 325° for 25 to 30 minutes, or until lightly browned. May be frozen before baking, then baked from the frozen state, allowing at least 35 minutes. These are delicious served slightly warm. Yield: 4 to 5 dozen slices.

OLIVE AND CRABMEAT CANAPES

1/3 cup pitted ripe olives, well drained,
coarsely chopped
1 (7-3/4-ounce) can crabmeat, drained
and flaked
1 tablespoon minced green pepper

1/4 teaspoon grated lemon rind
Mayonnaise
Firm white bread
Softened butter
Minced parsley

Combine olives, crabmeat, green pepper, and lemon rind. Mix with just enough mayonnaise so mixture holds together. Cut bread into rounds with a large cookie cutter, butter and bake at 300° until lightly browned. Spread with the crab mixture and sprinkle with parsley. Makes about 18 canapes. Yield: 6 servings.

PIZZA BITES
(prepare ahead of time and freeze)

2 (12-count) packages refrigerator rolls
1-1/2 pounds hot bulk pork sausage
1-1/2 (6-ounce) cans tomato paste, or
1 (8-ounce) can pizza sauce
1 (29-ounce) can whole tomatoes, drained and chopped

1-1/2 teaspoons salt
3/4 teaspoon black pepper
2 small cloves garlic, crushed
1-1/2 teaspoons dried oregano
3/4 pound sharp Cheddar cheese, shredded

Separate rolls into fourths. Place on ungreased cookie sheet; prick each roll several times with fork. Bake at 300° for 10 minutes, or until slightly browned.

Put sausage into heavy dry skillet and fry slightly until crumbly; do not let it fry hard; remove to paper towels to drain; set aside.

In saucepan combine tomato paste, tomatoes, and all seasonings. Cover and simmer for 10 minutes; allow to cool to lukewarm. Place a teaspoon of this mixture on each biscuit; cover with a teaspoon of cooked sausage, then sprinkle with shredded cheese. Freeze until needed. To use, bake from frozen state at 350° for about 15 minutes, or just until bubbly. Yield: 96 small pizza pies.

Variation: These pizza pies are a windfall for Sunday night suppers for the family — or for a sudden onslaught of the young set. To use as a main course, do not separate rolls. Roll them out on a lightly floured board to about 5 inches in diameter. Place on baking sheet and proceed as above. If you don't want to freeze the pies, bake them as soon as assembled at 375° for about 10 minutes. Two or three are a generous portion. If preferred, other meat, olives, or mushrooms, etc., may be substituted for the pork sausage. — C. M.

FLATBREAD WAFERS

1-3/4 cups all-purpose flour
3/4 cup cornmeal
1/2 teaspoon salt

5 tablespoons butter or margarine
2/3 cup warm water

Sift flour, measure, then sift again with cornmeal and salt into bowl. Add butter and mix until granular. (Use fingers or pastry blender.) Stir in warm water only until dough is moistened, then chill thoroughly.

When ready to bake, form chilled dough into balls the size of a quarter. Roll out into paper-thin rounds about 4 inches in diameter. Place on ungreased baking sheet and bake at 350° for 5 to 7 minutes, or until very lightly browned. Cool. Store in tightly covered can.

Use as accompaniment to salad, soup, or as a nibble with cocktails. If desired, seasoned salt may be added to dough or sprinkled over top before baking. Yield: about 3 dozen.

Note: These wafers will be uneven around the edges, but this makes them all the more interesting.

SAUSAGE BALLS IN CHEESE PASTRY
(may be prepared ahead of time)

1 pound hot or mild pork sausage
3/4 cup dry breadcrumbs
About 1/3 cup chicken broth

1/8 teaspoon ground nutmeg
1/4 teaspoon poultry seasoning

Combine all ingredients. Form about a teaspoonful of mixture into small balls. Fry slowly in a dry skillet until done; drain on paper towels. (If you fry these at low heat, a hard crust should not form.)

Cheese Pastry

1-1/2 cups all-purpose flour
1/4 teaspoon salt
1 teaspoon paprika

1/2 pound Cheddar cheese, shredded
1/2 cup softened butter or margarine

Sift flour, salt, and paprika into a large bowl. Stir in sharp Cheddar cheese. Cut in 1/2 cup soft butter or margarine, then work with hands until you have a smooth dough. Pinch off small pieces of dough (about 1 tablespoon) and form smoothly around sausage ball. The balls may be baked at 375° for about 15 to 20 minutes at this point, or placed unbaked in freezer until ready to use. To serve, bake unthawed balls at 400° for about 20 to 25 minutes. Yield: about 45 balls.

SAUSAGE BISCUITS
(may be prepared ahead of time)

Heat together 1 pound shredded sharp Cheddar cheese and 1 pound uncooked hot or mild bulk pork sausage in large saucepan. Stir together with wooden spoon until cheese has melted. Stir in 3 cups dry biscuit mix until smooth. Cool, then chill for about an hour for easier handling. Form into balls about the size of a nickel or slightly larger; place on ungreased baking sheet and bake at 400° for 8 to 10 minutes. Remove, place on paper towels to drain. Serve warm. These sausage balls freeze beautifully after baking. Simply place in a slow oven to heat thoroughly before serving. Yield: at least 4 dozen.

3-B COCKTAIL CRACKERS
(may be prepared ahead of time)

1/2 cup butter
1/2 teaspoon dried sweet basil
1/2 teaspoon dried summer savory

2 tablespoons brandy
1 box whole wheat wafers

Melt butter in large shallow 15- x 10- x 1-inch jellyroll pan in a 250° oven. Crush basil and savory together, using a mortar and pestle if you have one;

otherwise with the back of spoon. Blend into butter; stir in brandy. Add the crackers, turning them to coat both sides well. Bake for 1 hour, turning crackers every 15 minutes. Crackers may be made ahead of time and frozen or stored in airtight container. However, before serving, they should be heated slowly and served warm and crisp. Unusual and good. Yield: about 2-1/2 dozen.

APPETIZER CRACKERS

2 to 3 tablespoons butter or margarine
1/2 teaspoon curry powder

1/4 teaspoon seasoned salt
Soda crackers or whole wheat wafers

Put butter in shallow pan in a 225° oven. When melted, add other ingredients and stir well. Place crackers in the seasoned butter, turn to coat other side and bake for about 1 hour, turning crackers every 15 minutes.

WELCOME COCKTAIL WAFERS

3/4 cup butter or margarine
2/3 cup shredded Cheddar cheese
1/2 cup blue cheese
1 small clove garlic, crushed

1 teaspoon minced fresh parsley
1 teaspoon minced chives
2 cups all-purpose flour

In large bowl of electric mixer beat butter with Cheddar and blue cheese until well blended. Add all other ingredients and beat again. Dust hands lightly with flour and shape into two rolls about 1-1/2 inches in diameter. Chill thoroughly. Slice 1/8 inch thick and bake at 375° for 8 to 10 minutes. Yield: about 70 wafers.

BUTTERCUP CHEESE STRAWS
(may be prepared ahead of time)

3-1/2 cups all-purpose flour
1/4 teaspoon salt
3/4 teaspoon cayenne pepper

3/4 pound butter or margarine
1 pound sharp Cheddar cheese, shredded (scant 4 cups)

Sift flour, salt, and pepper into large bowl. Cut butter into small pieces and blend into dry ingredients with fingers until mixture resembles coarse crumbs. Add cheese and continue blending until dough hangs together and is no longer crumbly.

Work with a fourth of the dough at a time. Roll out to a rectangle 1/3 inch thick; cut into strips 1/2 inch wide and about 4 inches long, using a pastry wheel if you have one. Place on ungreased baking sheet and bake at 375° for 10 to 12 minutes, only until very lightly browned. (Do not overbake, which is easy to do.) Remove, cool, and store in an airtight tin, placing waxed paper between layers. Freezes beautifully. Yield: about 125 strips.

TOASTED ONION STICKS

1 (2-ounce) package dehydrated onion
  soup mix
1/2 pound butter or margarine, softened

1 loaf sliced white bread
  (about 20 slices)

Blend onion soup mix into butter. Let stand at room temperature until you are ready to toast the sticks.

Trim crusts from bread. Spread with onion butter; cut each slice into three strips. Place on ungreased baking sheet and bake at 350° for about 10 minutes, or until golden. Yield: about 54 sticks.

KUMMELSTANGEN
(Caraway Crisps)

2 cups sifted all-purpose flour
1 teaspoon baking powder
1 teaspoon salt
1/2 cup butter or margarine
2 tablespoons cream cheese

1 egg, beaten
1 egg white, unbeaten (or milk)
  Caraway seed
  Coarse salt or kosher salt

Combine flour, baking powder, and salt in bowl. Cut in butter and cream cheese until granular. Add beaten egg and work with fingers to a smooth dough. Chill, then roll out between sheets of waxed paper or on pastry cloth to 1/4 inch thickness. Cut into strips 1 x 3 inches. Brush with egg white or milk; sprinkle with caraway seed and salt. Twist each strip and place on ungreased baking sheet. Bake at 400° about 15 minutes, or just until golden. Yield: about 36.

TINY TART SHELLS
(prepare ahead of time)

2 cups all-purpose flour, measured
  before sifting
1 teaspoon salt

1/3 cup butter or margarine
1/3 cup vegetable shortening
  Ice water

Sift flour and salt into bowl; cut in butter and shortening with a pastry blender until mixture resembles coarse meal. Add ice water sparingly while tossing with a fork, using only enough for dough to hold together.

Roll thin on floured board, cut in circles and press over bottom of tiny muffin tins. Prick all over with a fork; put the tin, pastry-side up, on a baking sheet and bake at 425° for 5 minutes. Now place a flat cookie sheet over top of pastry to keep bottoms flat; reduce heat to 350°, and bake until lightly browned. Allow to cool before removing from pans. Prepare this recipe ahead of time and freeze until needed.

ANCHOVY-CHEESE DIP
(may be prepared the day before)

2 (3-ounce) packages cream cheese
2 tablespoons soft butter or margarine
1/3 cup mayonnaise
1 tablespoon anchovy paste
1 teaspoon paprika

1 teaspoon Worcestershire sauce
1 tablespoon grated onion
1/2 teaspoon caraway seed
Salt, if required
1 or 2 dashes cayenne pepper

With wooden spoon blend cream cheese and softened butter together. Blend in mayonnaise gradually, then all other ingredients until of dipping consistency. (If you prefer a spread, reduce amount of mayonnaise.)

Note: This dip may be made a day ahead of time, but refrigeration makes the mixture stiff and buttery in consistency. It may be served that way, but it is also attractive to beat it with an electric mixer until fluffy. Serve with plain melba toast.

ARTICHOKE DIP

1 (1-pound) artichoke hearts, drained
About 1/3 cup mayonnaise
1 tablespoon chopped onion
Salt, pepper, and cayenne pepper to taste

3 or 4 slices bacon, cooked crisp and finely chopped
Juice of 1/2 lemon

Chop artichoke hearts to a pulp. Add other ingredients, stir well, check seasonings, and chill. Serve with corn chips for dipping.

AVOCADO DIP NO. 1
(may be prepared ahead of time)

1 avocado, mashed
1 (8-ounce) package cream cheese, softened
2 tablespoons freshly squeezed lemon juice

Dash Worcestershire sauce
1/3 cup minced green onion
3/4 teaspoon salt
2 green chiles, mashed

Blend avocado into cheese until smooth. Add other ingredients, blend well, cover, and chill. Serve with corn chips. Yield: 6 servings.

Note: This dip may be prepared ahead of time, even the day before serving. Spread a thin layer of mayonnaise over surface to prevent darkening; stir it in just before serving.

AVOCADO DIP NO. 2
(may be prepared the day before)

2 large avocados, mashed
1 tablespoon lime juice
1 canned green chile, minced; or 1/2
    teaspoon chili powder

1 small clove garlic, crushed
1/4 teaspoon salt
1/3 cup mayonnaise
4 strips bacon, cooked crisp and crumbled

Mash avocados and add lime juice, chile, garlic, and salt. Blend well and turn into small bowl; spread mayonnaise over top, covering the mixture completely. Chill at least an hour, although the dip may be prepared the day before. Before serving, stir mayonnaise into avocado mixture; check seasonings, add more if needed, and garnish with crumbled bacon. Use corn chips as dippers. Yield: about 2 cups.

CHILE CON QUESO

2 pounds processed yellow cheese
2 large onions, minced
1 (1-pound) can tomatoes, drained
    and chopped

2 small cloves garlic, minced
2 (4-ounce) cans green chile peppers,
    drained and mashed
2 tablespoons Worcestershire sauce

Melt cheese in top of double boiler over hot water. Blend in other ingredients and cook for 30 minutes, stirring occasionally. Serve in chafing dish with corn chips for dipping. (Glance at the dip occasionally during the party to make sure it isn't "skimming"; if it is, give it a stir with a wooden spoon.) Any leftover dip may be frozen successfully. To use again, allow to thaw at room temperature, then reheat in top of double boiler. Yield: about 6 cups.

HOT CLAM-CHEESE DIP
(may be prepared the day before)

1 small onion, finely minced
1/4 green or sweet red pepper,
    finely minced
3 tablespoons butter or margarine
1 (7-ounce) can clams, drained,
    reserve liquid

1 pound processed American cheese
2 tablespoons catsup
2 tablespoons Worcestershire sauce
2 tablespoons dry sherry
1/4 teaspoon cayenne pepper

Sauté onion and green pepper in butter until just tender. Add drained clams; set aside. Melt cheese in top of double boiler over simmering water; add catsup, Worcestershire sauce, sherry, and pepper. Combine with onion-clam mixture, using reserved clam liquid as needed for dipping consistency. Transfer to chafing dish. Keep warm; use corn chips as dippers. The flavor is improved if dip is prepared the day before it is to be used, then reheated. Yield: 8 servings.

CLAM-CREAM CHEESE DIP

6 (3-ounce) packages cream cheese
3 (7-ounce) cans clams, drained,
    reserve liquid

1 large onion, grated
    Freshly squeezed lemon juice

Soften cream cheese thoroughly. Add clams, onion, and lemon juice (start with juice of 1 lemon, adding more to taste) or use reserved clam juice to moisten the mixture. Turn into chafing dish and serve hot, with sturdy potato chips or crackers for dipping. This amount will serve a crowd, the size depending on number of other appetizers offered. Leftover mixture will freeze satisfactorily.

CRABMEAT MARYLAND

6 tablespoons butter or margarine	**Salt, pepper, and paprika**
3 tablespoons all-purpose flour	**1/4 cup dry sherry**
2 cups milk	**Freshly squeezed lemon juice (about**
1 pound crabmeat	**1/2 lemon)**
1/2 cup cream	

Melt 4 tablespoons butter in top of double boiler placed over direct low heat. Blend in flour; gradually add milk, stirring constantly until thick and smooth.

Place pan over hot water, cover, and cook for about 5 minutes. Add crabmeat (which has been carefully picked over), stirring gently to avoid breaking lumps. When heated through, carefully stir in cream and remaining 2 tablespoons butter. Season to taste with salt, pepper, and paprika. Add sherry and lemon juice to taste. Keep heat low until serving time; then transfer to chafing dish. May be served over toast points or with melba rounds for dipping. Yield: 8 servings; double the recipe for a cocktail supper for 20.

CURRIED CRABMEAT DIP
(prepare the day before)

1 (7-ounce) can crabmeat, drained	**Pepper to taste**
1/2 (8-ounce) package cream cheese	**1/4 teaspoon curry powder**
5 tablespoons commercial sour cream	**1 tablespoon minced chives**
1/4 teaspoon salt	**1 tablespoon capers, drained**

Shred crabmeat fine. Combine cheese with other ingredients except capers and beat until light. Fold in crabmeat and capers, chill and serve with potato chips or melba rounds for dipping. Yield: 6 to 8 servings when other appetizers are provided; double the recipe for a cocktail supper for about 16 to 20.

HOT CRABMEAT DIP

1 (8-ounce) package cream cheese	**2 tablespoons dry white wine**
3 tablespoons commercial mayonnaise	**1 (7-3/4-ounce) can crabmeat, drained**
1 teaspoon Dijon mustard	**and flaked**
1/4 teaspoon salt	

Combine cream cheese, mayonnaise, mustard, and salt in top of double boiler over simmering water. Stir until smooth and well blended. Add wine gradually, then crabmeat; check seasonings. Transfer to chafing dish and serve hot with melba rounds or toast triangles for dipping. Yield: about 2 cups.

CUCUMBER DIP

2 large unpeeled cucumbers	1/2 teaspoon garlic salt
1/2 cup vinegar	2 (8-ounce) packages cream cheese
2 teaspoons salt	3/4 cup homemade mayonnaise

Wash and grate unpeeled cucumbers, using grater with 1/2-inch holes. Add vinegar and salt; stir, cover, and allow to stand overnight in refrigerator. Next day, press out liquid. Blend garlic salt, cheese, and mayonnaise, then combine with cucumbers.

DILL DIP FOR RAW VEGETABLES

1 cup fresh homemade mayonnaise*	1 tablespoon minced parsley
2 cups commercial sour cream	Salt, if needed
2 tablespoons dried dill weed	Raw vegetables

Gently combine mayonnaise with sour cream and other ingredients. Serve in a bowl surrounded by crisp raw vegetables: cauliflower flowerets, celery curls, carrot sticks, tiny green onions, radishes, and raw mushrooms — rinsed, dried and rolled in lemon juice to retain their color.

*See Index for Mayonnaise recipe.

LIPTAUER DIP
(may be prepared the day before)

1 (8-ounce) package cream cheese, softened	1-1/2 tablespoons drained capers
1/4 pound butter or margarine, softened	1 teaspoon paprika
1-1/2 tablespoons anchovy paste, or 1 (3/4-ounce) can of anchovies, mashed with their liquid	1 teaspoon caraway seed
	1/2 teaspoon Dijon mustard
	1 cup commercial sour cream
	Juice of 1 lemon

Blend cream cheese and butter together thoroughly. Stir in all other ingredients until smooth. The flavor of this dip improves if allowed to mellow overnight in refrigerator. Excellent as a dip for raw vegetables, potato chips, or as a spread for melba toast.

MALLEY'S DIP FOR RAW VEGETABLES
(may be prepared ahead of time)

1 pint commercial mayonnaise	3 tablespoons grated onion
1 pint commercial sour cream	3 tablespoons dill weed
3 tablespoons minced fresh parsley, or 1 tablespoon dried parsley	1-1/2 tablespoons seasoned salt

Blend all ingredients together and chill before serving. May be made several days ahead of time. Yield: about 4-1/2 cups.

SHRIMP DIP

1 (8-ounce) package cream cheese
1/3 cup sweet or commercial sour cream
2 teaspoons freshly squeezed lemon juice
1/4 teaspoon onion juice

Dash Worcestershire sauce
1 cup chopped cooked shrimp
Paprika

Soften cheese and blend in cream and seasonings. Stir in shrimp and add paprika as desired for color. Serve with sturdy potato chips or other "dippers." Yield: 2-1/2 cups.

SMOKED OYSTER DIP

2 (8-ounce) packages cream
cheese, softened
1 teaspoon Worcestershire sauce
2 teaspoons freshly squeezed lemon juice

1 cup commercial sour cream
1 (3-2/3-ounce) can smoked
oysters, undrained

Blend cheese with Worcestershire sauce, lemon juice, and sour cream. Combine with undrained oysters. Serve with corn chips. Yield: 12 to 14 servings. One recipe is enough for a party of 20, when a variety of hors d'oeuvres are served.

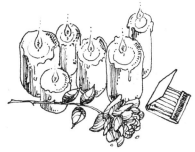

TAPENADE DIP
(may be prepared ahead of time)

1 (6-1/2-ounce) can white solid-pack
tuna fish, drained
2 anchovy filets
1 tablespoon anchovy oil
4 tablespoons chopped ripe olives
1/2 small onion, grated
1 clove garlic, crushed

1/4 cup chopped celery
1/4 cup cubed cooked potato
1/2 teaspoon Worcestershire sauce
Dash Tabasco sauce
Juice of 1 small lemon
Freshly ground black pepper
1/2 cup mayonnaise

Put all ingredients into container of electric blender and blend until smooth. Use as a dip for raw vegetables. Yield: 10 servings.

Note: The average home electric blender resists blending such solid matter as the above; you must use a rubber spatula to repeatedly push the mixture into the path of the blades. You might find it easier to do half the recipe at a time. This is an excellent, different hors d'oeuvre, well worth the trouble to prepare. Don't omit the potatoes; they contribute to the smooth texture.

WESTERN OLIVE DIP
(prepare the day before)

1 (8-ounce) package cream cheese
1 to 2 tablespoons commercial sour cream (sweet cream may be substituted)

1 teaspoon chili powder
1-1/2 teaspoons grated onion
1/2 cup chopped ripe olives

Beat cheese with other ingredients except olives in small bowl of electric mixer. When smooth and light, fold in olives. Chill thoroughly and serve with corn chips. Yield: about 1-1/2 cups.

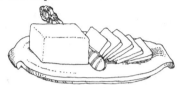

AMSTERDAM CHEESE MOLD

1 small Gouda cheese (about 8-ounces)
2 ounces crumbled blue cheese
1/2 cup commercial sour cream
4 tablespoons butter or margarine

2 tablespoons wine vinegar or cider vinegar
1 tablespoon grated onion
1/8 teaspoon cayenne pepper

Peel the rind from Gouda cheese and shred cheese into a saucepan. Add all other ingredients and heat slowly, stirring constantly with wooden spoon until cheeses melt completely and mixture is smooth. (If you have an electric blender, use it for a more velvety texture after cheeses are completely melted.) Lightly oil a 2-cup mold and pour in cheese. Cover and chill overnight. When ready to serve, unmold by running a sharp knife around mold and shaking it onto a serving plate. Garnish, if desired, with olive slices or plant a generous bunch of parsley atop the mound. Provide melba rounds to accompany. This is best served at room temperature, as the flavor is delicate and serving it ice-cold tends to detract from the subtlety.

ANCHOVY CHEESE

1 pound cottage cheese
4 drained anchovies, shredded fine
2 tablespoons chopped fresh parsley
2 tablespoons minced chives or onion
1 teaspoon poppy seed (do not omit)
Freshly ground black pepper

About 1 teaspoon freshly squeezed lemon juice
About 1/2 teaspoon of oil drained from anchovies
Salt to taste

Mix all ingredients except salt in a bowl, then taste and add salt if needed. (The anchovies lend a good bit of salt to the mixture.) Mound the cheese in center of a serving dish; surround with pumpernickel, melba toast, or dark rye bread rounds. Yield: 10 servings; double the recipe for a cocktail party for about 20.

MOLDED BLUE CHEESE SPREAD
(prepare ahead of time)

2/3 cup minced fresh parsley
2 (3-ounce) packages cream cheese
4 ounces blue cheese
1 teaspoon Worcestershire sauce

Dash cayenne pepper
1 tablespoon freshly squeezed lemon juice
4 tablespoons mayonnaise

Prepare small mold by generously oiling the inside. Press parsley around sides and bottom.

Thoroughly combine cream cheese, blue cheese, Worcestershire sauce, cayenne pepper, and lemon juice in small bowl of electric mixer. Stir in mayonnaise until blended. Spoon carefully into prepared mold, cover and chill. Unmold and serve with unsalted crackers or melba rounds. Yield: 12 servings.

CHEESE BALL
(may be prepared ahead of time)

1/2 pound sharp Cheddar cheese, shredded
1 (8-ounce) package cream cheese
1/4 pound Roquefort or blue cheese
1 clove garlic, crushed
2 teaspoons grated onion

Cayenne pepper to taste
1 teaspoon Worcestershire sauce
1 cup finely minced parsley
1 cup chopped pecans

Thoroughly mix all ingredients except parsley and pecans. Combine parsley and pecans and blend half of them into cheese mixture. Spread remaining parsley mixture on sheet of waxed paper. Form cheese into a ball and roll it in parsley mixture until well coated. Chill before serving. May be made long before serving. Freezes beautifully. Yield: about 3 pounds.

GARLIC CHEESE ROLL
(may be prepared ahead of time)

1 pound sharp Cheddar cheese, shredded
1 (8-ounce) package cream cheese
1/2 teaspoon salt
2 cloves garlic, crushed
3 dashes Tabasco sauce

1 tablespoon Worcestershire sauce
1 tablespoon mayonnaise
1/4 teaspoon dry mustard
2 tablespoons paprika
2 tablespoons chili powder

In large bowl of electric mixer blend the two cheeses. Add all other ingredients, except paprika and chili powder, mixing until smooth. Mix paprika and chili powder together and spread evenly on a piece of waxed paper placed on a flat surface. Dust hands lightly with flour and shape cheese mixture into two rolls about the diameter of a silver dollar. Roll in paprika and chili powder until completely covered. Flatten ends of roll and coat them also. Wrap in waxed paper and refrigerate 24 hours before using. This cheese freezes (and refreezes!) beautifully.

LONDON CHEESE ROLL
(may be prepared ahead of time)

11 ounces cream cheese (1 large and 1 small package)
4 ounces blue cheese

1 cup thinly sliced ripe olives
2 cups coarsely chopped walnuts or pecans

Have cheeses at room temperature. Blend thoroughly in large bowl of electric mixer. Stir in the olives and 1 cup of the nuts. Spread remaining nuts on a sheet of waxed paper. Flour hands lightly and shape mixture into one long or two short rolls about the size of a silver dollar. Roll back and forth in nuts until well coated; wrap in waxed paper and refrigerate overnight before using. Serve with crackers or melba rounds. This cheese freezes beautifully and may be made well in advance of serving.

BUTTERED PIMIENTO SPREAD
(may be prepared ahead of time)

1/4 pound butter or margarine, softened
1/4 pound pimiento cream cheese*
1 tablespoon grated onion
1/2 teaspoon Worcestershire sauce
1 teaspoon freshly squeezed lemon juice

1 tablespoon minced green pepper
1 teaspoon caraway seed
1 (2-ounce) can anchovies, drained
Several grinds coarse black pepper

Cream butter and cheese together in large bowl of electric mixer. Add remaining ingredients and blend well. Chill and serve with melba rounds.

*If pimiento cream cheese is not available, use 1/4 pound cream cheese into which a small jar of drained pimiento strips has been blended.

SESAME-CHEESE ROLL
(prepare ahead of time)

1/4 pound blue cheese
1 (8-ounce) package cream cheese
1/2 cup butter
1/3 cup chopped stuffed green olives
1 tablespoon minced chives

2 tablespoons minced fresh parsley
1 clove garlic, crushed
2 tablespoons good cognac
1/3 cup toasted sesame seed

If your sesame seed are not toasted, put them in a shallow pan in a 275° oven until golden brown, about 30 minutes, watching carefully to see that they do not scorch. Shake the pan occasionally.

Cream cheeses and butter in large mixer bowl. Add remaining ingredients except seed; blend well. Chill several hours for easier handling.

Remove cheese from refrigerator and divide into two parts. Spread seed on a sheet of waxed paper. Form cheese into two rolls about the size of a silver dollar; roll in seed until thoroughly coated. Wrap tightly in waxed paper and refrigerate overnight or freeze.

To use frozen cheese, allow to stand at room temperature about an hour. Serve surrounded with plain melba rounds for spreading.

CHOPPED CHICKEN LIVERS
(may be prepared the day before)

2 tablespoons butter or margarine
1 whole clove garlic
2 onions, finely minced
1 pound chicken livers
Salt and pepper

2 hard-cooked eggs
1/4 cup melted butter (or half cream and half butter)
1 tablespoon sherry (optional)

Heat the 2 tablespoons butter and the garlic, with a wooden pick in it, in skillet. Add onions and sauté until tender and yellow; do not brown. Discard the garlic; turn onions into a bowl. Add a bit more butter to skillet and sauté livers until done; do not overcook. Stir in seasonings, then put the mixture and eggs through the finest blade of meat grinder. Blend in melted butter and sherry, stirring until smooth. May be made a day ahead. Leftovers freeze well. Yield: 12 servings, if another appetizer is provided.

RUMAKI SPREAD
(prepare the day before)

1/2 pound chicken livers
1 tablespoon soy sauce
1/2 cup soft butter
1/2 teaspoon onion salt
1/2 teaspoon dry mustard
1/4 teaspoon ground nutmeg

Dash or two cayenne pepper
1 (5-ounce) can water chestnuts, drained and minced
6 slices crisp cooked bacon, crumbled
Thinly sliced green onions for garnish (optional)

Cook seasoned chicken livers in butter. When done place in blender with soy sauce, butter, onion salt, mustard, nutmeg, and cayenne pepper. Blend until mixture is smooth, stirring it down with rubber spatula as needed. Remove from blender; stir in chestnuts and bacon; garnish with onions. Serve with crisp crackers. Makes 1-1/2 cups. Yield: 6 servings.

Note: This spread should be prepared a day ahead of serving but should be removed from refrigerator and allowed to soften slightly at room temperature for 1 hour before serving.

SHERRIED CHICKEN LIVER PÂTÉ
(may be prepared ahead of time)

1 **pound chicken livers**
Flour seasoned with salt and pepper
2 **tablespoons butter or margarine**
1 **medium onion, finely chopped**
2 **tablespoons dry sherry**
Pinch rosemary

Pinch thyme
6 **tablespoons softened butter or margarine**
2 **tablespoons dry sherry**
2 **tablespoons cognac**
Salt, pepper, and seasoned salt to taste

Pat livers dry with paper towels. Sprinkle lightly with seasoned flour. Heat butter in skillet and sauté livers over medium heat for about 5 minutes. Add onion and continue cooking and stirring until onion is barely yellow, about 3 minutes. Stir in 2 tablespoons sherry, rosemary, and thyme and simmer for a minute. Add softened butter, remove from heat and puree in electric blender, blending one-third of the mixture at a time and pushing down from sides into path of blades. When all has been blended until smooth, stir in remaining 2 tablespoons sherry, cognac, salt, pepper, and seasoned salt to taste. Chill in container from which pâté is to be served. Garnish with clusters of fresh parsley and serve with melba rounds. Yield: 10 servings.

VELVET CHICKEN LIVER PÂTÉ
(may be prepared the day before)

1/2 **pound chicken livers**
2 **tablespoons butter**
1/3 **to 1/2 cup chicken broth**
2 **hard-cooked eggs**

6 **ounces cream cheese, softened**
Salt, pepper, and seasoned salt to taste
2 **tablespoons dry sherry**
Olives and parsley sprigs (optional)

Sauté livers in butter until just tender, or about 10 minutes. Stir in broth, swirl in pan a minute, then put livers, broth, and eggs through electric blender until smooth. (This won't be easy but the results make it worthwhile.) Blend seasonings into cheese, then combine with liver mixture. Add sherry, blend well, check seasonings, and chill before serving. Pâté may be turned into oiled mold or bowl, then turned out and garnished with olives and parsley sprigs. Yield: 8 servings.

LIVERWURST PÂTÉ

1 (8-ounce) package liverwurst
 sausage (Braunschweiger)
4 tablespoons soft butter or margarine
6 slices bacon, cooked crisp and crumbled

2 tablespoons minced green onion including
 some of the top
1 tablespoon sherry

Mash liverwurst with fork. Blend with soft butter until smooth. Pack into pottery container from which you plan to serve the spread and chill thoroughly. Serve with rye rounds. Yield: 8 to 10 servings, if other hors d'oeuvres are provided.

HOT CREAMED CRAB

1 (8-ounce) package cream cheese
1/2 cup commercial mayonnaise
1 tablespoon freshly squeezed lemon juice
1/2 teaspoon Worcestershire sauce
1 teaspoon all-purpose flour

Dash cayenne pepper
1 (7-1/2-ounce) can crabmeat, drained
 and shredded
1/3 cup slivered toasted almonds
Salt to taste

Beat cheese until smooth in small bowl of electric mixer. Add mayonnaise, lemon juice, Worcestershire sauce, flour, and pepper; beat again until smooth. Fold in crabmeat, almonds, and salt to taste. Turn into covered flameproof casserole and bake at 300° for 20 minutes. Place over heat (candle or other heating device), or turn into chafing dish and keep warm until serving time. This is a very delicately flavored mixture and should be served with unsalted crackers or plain melba toast. Yield: 2-1/2 cups.

ANCHOVY SAUCE FOR SEAFOOD

3 teaspoons anchovy paste
1 tablespoon paprika
 Pinch salt if needed

2 tablespoons tarragon vinegar
1 cup mayonnaise
1/2 cup heavy cream, whipped

Mix anchovy paste, paprika, salt, and vinegar. Blend into mayonnaise, mixing well after each addition. Fold in cream. If mixture is too thick, thin with a little cream. Yield: 2 cups.

COCKTAIL SAUCE FOR SHRIMP

2 cups catsup or chili sauce
1/2 cup Worcestershire sauce
1/2 cup minced celery
1/2 cup chopped fresh parsley
1/4 cup prepared horseradish

1/4 cup freshly squeezed lemon juice
 Dash Tabasco sauce
 Dash sugar
 Salt to taste

Combine all ingredients the day before using. This yields enough sauce for 5 pounds raw, boiled shrimp in the shell.

CURRY SAUCE FOR RAW VEGETABLES
(prepare the day before)

1/2 cup mayonnaise
1 cup commercial sour cream
2 tablespoons freshly squeezed
  lemon juice
Salt and pepper to taste
1 teaspoon curry powder
1/2 teaspoon paprika

2 tablespoons minced fresh parsley
1/2 teaspoon dried tarragon, crushed
2 tablespoons grated onion
2 teaspoons prepared mustard
1 tablespoon minced chives
Several dashes Tabasco sauce

Combine mayonnaise, sour cream, and lemon juice. Blend with all other ingredients. Check seasonings and chill overnight before serving. Use as a dip for an assortment of raw vegetables (cauliflower flowerets, sliced raw yellow squash, cucumber slices, celery sticks, carrot sticks, etc.)

RAW VEGETABLES WITH HERB SAUCE

The day before the party, drain 1 or 2 (1-pound) cans artichoke hearts. Cut artichokes in half and marinate overnight in homemade (or good commercial) French or Italian dressing.

Prepare an assortment of any or all of the following: carrot sticks, celery hearts, raw asparagus, young turnip sticks, green onions, radishes, green pepper strips, raw yellow squash slices, cauliflower flowerets, raw mushrooms, or any other crisp vegetables available. Drain artichoke hearts; arrange with all vegetables on a large tray around a bowl which contains the Herb Sauce for dipping.

Herb Sauce
(may be prepared the day before)

1 (8-ounce) package cream
  cheese, softened
1 cup commercial sour cream
1 tablespoon minced chives
1 tablespoon minced fresh parsley
2 teaspoons soy sauce

1 teaspoon minced fresh, or ground
  dried tarragon
1 teaspoon dill weed
1 teaspoon curry powder
Milk

Blend sour cream into softened cheese. Add all other ingredients, using enough milk to yield a dipping consistency. Blend thoroughly. May be prepared a day or so ahead of time.

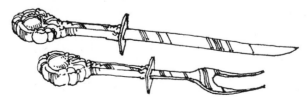

SELECTING HORS D'OEUVRES

To help you complement the menu you have chosen to serve your guests, we have compiled a list of suggested hors d'oeuvres. Since only party-type foods are served at teas, receptions, and coffees, those menus are not listed here. Below are listed in alphabetical order the menus that appear in this book followed by our suggestions for one or more appropriate hors d'oeuvres to be served with that menu. Check the Index for page numbers of hors d'oeuvre recipes.

Baked Ham Dinner
    Spiced Ripe Olives
    Marinated Spanish Olives
    Clam-Cream Cheese Dip

Barbecued Chicken Cookout
    Sausage Balls in Cheese Pastry
    Celery Sticks

Barbecued Spareribs Cookout
    Amsterdam Cheese Mold with
        Melba Rounds

Beef Bourguignon Dinner
    Buttercup Cheese Straws
    Celery Sticks with Les's
        Seasoned Salt

Beef Filet Cocktail Party
    Party Mix
    Molded Blue Cheese Spread with
        Melba Rounds
    Tiny Tart Shells Filled with
        Chicken Salad

Beef Fondue Party
    Shrimp with Anchovy Sauce
    Olive and Crabmeat Canapes
    Party Almonds

Beef Kabobs Cookout
    Cheese Snack Bread

Beef Tips Dinner
    Marinated Mushrooms
    Cheese Ball

Beef Wellington Dinner
    Cucumber Dip with Melba Rounds
    Bacon-Chestnut Appetizers

Blanquette of Veal Dinner
    Olives and Dried Beef Rarebit with
        Corn Chips
    Appetizer Crackers
    Salted Peanuts

Breakfast at Brennans
    No hors d'oeuvres suggested.

Calypso New Year's Dinner
    Pickled Shrimp
    Cheese Dreams

Cantonese Turkey Dinner
    Pickled Shrimp
    Salted Nuts

Celebration Brunch
    Buttercup Cheese Straws

Cheese Cloud Brunch
    No hors d'oeuvres suggested.

Cheese Fondue Party
    Asparagus Spears in Ham
    Rumaki Spread

Chicken Almondine Cocktail Supper
    Swedish Meatballs with
        Toast Points
    Curried Crabmeat Dip with
        Potato Chips
    Cocktail Pecans

Chicken Casserole Brunch
    No hors d'oeuvres suggested.

Chicken Casserole Dinner
    Peeled Cherry Tomatoes with
        Seasoned Salt
    Olives
    Cashew Nuts
    Hot Creamed Crab with
        Melba Rounds

Chicken en Casserole Dinner
    Cashew Nuts
    Dilled Green Olives

Chicken Salad Casserole Luncheon
    Toasted Onion Sticks

Chicken Salad Luncheon
    Toasted Garlic-Cheese Rounds

Chicken Tetrazzini Cocktail Supper
  Pizza Bites
  Smoked Oyster Dip with
    Corn Chips
  Olives
  Mixed Nuts

Chicken Tetrazzini Dinner
  Curried Bacon-Brazil Nuts
  Dilled Green Olives
  Hot Crabmeat Dip with Melba
    Rounds or Toast Triangles

Chicken with Dried Beef Luncheon
  Marinated Mushrooms
  Avocado Dip No. 1 with
    Corn Chips

Chinese Dinner
  Cheese Straws
  Commercial Macadamia Nuts

Choucrote Garnie Dinner
  Rumaki Spread
  Toasted Garlic-Cheese Rounds

Christmas Dinner
  Celery Sticks with Les's
    Seasoned Salt
  Salted Nuts
  Green and Black Olives
  Chopped Chicken Livers with
    Melba Rounds

Christmas Goose Dinner
  Marinated Anchovies
  Olives
  Mixed Nuts

Cocktail Party with Baked
Eye-of-Round
  Cold Deviled Shrimp
  Chile Con Queso with Corn Chips
  Chicken Strudel
  Salted Nuts

Coquilles St. Jacques Luncheon
  Caraway Biscuits
  Celery Hearts
  Nuts

Corned Beef Dinner
  Liverwurst Pâté with Rye Rounds
  Celery Sticks
  Marinated Carrot Sticks
  Welcome Cocktail Wafers

Cornish Hen Dinner
  Garlic Olives
  Celery Sticks with Les's
    Seasoned Salt
  Sesame Cocktail Biscuits
  Minced Mushrooms with Toast
    Triangles

Crab Casserole Brunch
  No hors d'oeuvres suggested.

Crabmeat Thermidor Luncheon
  Nuts

Deep South Cocktail Party
  Marinated Shrimp Port Gibson
  Chili Almonds
  Anchovy Cheese with
    Pumpernickel Slices or
    Melba Rounds

Dessert Fondue Party
  No hors d'oeuvres suggested.

Dinner at Chalet Suzanne
  Assorted Dry Roasted Nuts
  Garlic Olives
  Cheese Ball with Crackers

Dinner at Christiana Campbell's
Tavern
  Selected Cheeses
  French Bread

Dinner at Columbia Restaurant
  No hors d'oeuvres suggested.

Dinner at Hugo's
  Hors d'oeuvre recipes given
    with menu.

Dinner at LeRuth's
  Hors d'oeuvre recipes given
    with menu.

Dinner at Look's Restaurants
  Hors d'oeuvre recipe given
    with menu.

Dinner at Perdita's
  Selected Cheeses
  French Bread

Dinner at the Nations Room
  Selected Cheeses
  French Bread

Dinner at The Plantation Club
No hors d'oeuvres suggested.

Easter Dinner with Lamb
Sherried Chicken Liver Pâté with
Melba Rounds
Commercial Macadamia Nuts

Easter Dinner with Pork Roast
Tapenade Dip with Crisp Raw
Vegetables

Flemish Beef Ragout
Hot Clam-Cheese Dip with
Corn Chips
Marinated Carrot Sticks

French Dinner
Hors d'oeuvre recipe given
with menu.

Gazpacho Luncheon
Anchovy-Cheese Dip with
Melba Rounds
Salted Nuts

German Dinner
Kummelstangen (Caraway Crisps)

Gourmet Pot Roast Dinner
Mixed Nuts
Olive Quiche

Grilled Steak Cookout
Artichoke Dip with Corn Chips

Ham and Artichoke Casserole Brunch
No hors d'oeuvres suggested.

Ham-in-Claret Dinner
Molded Blue Cheese Spread with
Melba Rounds
Olives

Hawaiian Luau
Pupu Appetizer Tray of:
Lomi Lomi Cherries
Roast Pork Strips
Hawaiian Grab Bag

He-Man Brunch
No hors d'oeuvres suggested.

Herbed Pork Roast Dinner
Celery Stuffed with Liptauer
Avocado Dip No. 2 with
Corn Chips

Italian Dinner
Hors d'oeuvre recipe given
with menu.

Ladies Gala Brunch
No hors d'oeuvres suggested.

Lamb with Vermouth Dinner
Parmesan Cheese Bites
Raw Vegetables and Curry Sauce

Lemon-Barbecue Chicken Cookout
Liptauer Dip with Celery Sticks,
Cauliflower Flowerets, Cherry
Tomatoes, Carrot Sticks, and
Squash Slices
Barbecue Peanuts

Marinated Rolled Rib Roast Dinner
Cocktail Crunch
Raw Vegetables with Malley's Dip

Mexican Dinner
Chili Con Queso with Corn Chips

New Year's Dinner
Pickled Shrimp
Cheese Dreams

Old-Fashioned Hot Pot
Chopped Chicken Livers with
Party Rye Bread
Crisp Raw Vegetables with
Dill Dip

Old-Fashioned Picnic
No hors d'oeuvres suggested.

Party Meatballs Cocktail Party
Tiny Cheese Biscuits
Italian Marinated Vegetables

Party Shrimp Luncheon
Tiny Cheese Biscuits

Roast Beef Cookout
Garlic Cheese Roll and Crackers

Roast Brisket Dinner
Bacon Roll-Ups
Italian Marinated Vegetables

Roast Duck Dinner
Sea Island Shrimp
Sesame-Cheese Roll with
Melba Rounds

Roast Leg of Lamb Dinner
  Marinated Mushrooms
  Celery Sticks
  Pickled Okra
  Olives
  London Cheese Roll with
    Melba Rounds

Roast Pork Dinner
  Mushrooms a la Grecque
  Buttered Pimiento Spread with
    Melba Rounds

Royal Seafood Casserole Dinner
  3-B Cocktail Crackers
  Velvet Chicken Liver Pâté with
    Melba Rounds
  Celery Sticks with Les's
    Seasoned Salt

Salad Nicoise Luncheon
  Frozen Cheese Canape
  Stuffed Celery Diable

Sausage Balls Cocktail Supper
  Velvet Chicken Liver Pâté with
    Melba Rounds
  Curried Shrimp in Casserole
  Water Chestnut-Pineapple
    Roll-Ups
  Bacon-Wrapped Shrimp
  Toast Triangles
  Chile Con Queso with Corn Chips

Scrambled Eggs Brunch
  No hors d'oeuvres suggested.

Seafood Stew Luncheon
  Black and Green Olives
  Hot Cheese Squares

Shrimp Supreme Cookout
  Crunchy Cheese Biscuits
  Curried Peanuts

Southern Cocktail Supper
  Sausage Biscuits
  Crabmeat Maryland with
    Melba Rounds

Southern Fish Fry
  Western Olive Dip with
    Corn Chips
  Celery Sticks
  Marinated Carrot Sticks

Spanish Dinner
  Albondigas

Standing Rib Roast Dinner
  Genie's Cheese Biscuits
  Shrimp Dip with Crackers or
    Potato Chips

Summertime Bridge Luncheon
  No hors d'oeuvres suggested.

Summertime Luncheon
  Asparagus Fold-Overs
  Mixed Salted Nuts
  Olives

Thanksgiving Dinner
  Cocktail Crackers
  Italian Artichoke Hearts
  Caviar-Stuffed Celery

Traditional Cocktail Supper
  Lilliput Meatballs
  Buttercup Cheese Straws
  Cocktail Sauce for Shrimp

Traditional Thanksgiving Dinner
  Cherry Tomatoes with Smoked
    Oysters
  Stuffed Celery Diable
  Deviled Eggs with Salted Almonds

Twelve-Boy Salad Luncheon
  Olives
  Chili Almonds

Veal Vaduz Dinner
  Raw Vegetables with Herb Sauce
  Cheese Ball with Crackers

Mixed Drinks

When guests arrive, the offer of something to drink is a symbol of welcome and an invitation to rest and visit awhile. In the bourbon- and whiskey-producing South, these standbys are popular, but often a mixed drink, an apertif, wine, or punch can be a delightful refresher.

And do keep provisions on hand for those who prefer their fruit juice straight or tonic water with a lemon twist only.

Filling requests for drop-in guests is relatively easy, but when a large crowd is expected, a punch bowl of cheer can satisfy thirsts and eliminate bartending problems.

MANHATTAN

1 jigger bourbon
1/2 jigger (sweet) vermouth

Dash of bitters (optional)
Cherry

Combine ingredients. Stir in 1/2 cup cracked ice, strain into cocktail glass, and add cherry.

MINT JULEP

5 sprigs fresh mint
1 teaspoon sugar

Dash water
2 ounces bourbon

Crush 4 sprigs of mint and sugar in water in a tall, chilled glass. Pack glass with cracked ice. Pour in bourbon, and stir until glass is frosted. Insert straw and remaining sprig of mint.

OLD-FASHIONED

1/2 teaspoon sugar (optional)
Dash bitters
1/2 ounce water

1 jigger bourbon
Orange slice
Cherry

Stir sugar, bitters, and water in old-fashioned glass. Add 2 ice cubes; pour in liquor, and stir. To serve, slit orange slice, slip it onto rim of glass, and add a cherry.

WHISKEY SOUR

1 jigger bourbon
1 teaspoon sugar
1/2 jigger lemon juice

Orange slice
Cherry

Shake ingredients thoroughly with 1/2 cup cracked ice until chilled. Strain into a whiskey sour glass. To serve, slit orange slice, slip it onto rim of glass, and add a cherry.

ALEXANDER

1 jigger gin or brandy
3/4 ounce crème de cacao

1 tablespoon (1/2 ounce) fresh cream

Combine ingredients; shake well with 1/2 cup cracked ice; strain into cocktail glass.

STINGER

1 jigger brandy   1/2 jigger white crème de menthe

Shake ingredients well with 1/2 cup cracked ice, strain into cocktail glass. For stinger on the rocks, combine brandy and crème de menthe, stir lightly, and pour over ice cubes in old-fashioned glass.

GRASSHOPPER

1 ounce green crème de menthe   1-1/2 tablespoons cream
1 ounce white crème de cacao

Shake ingredients well with 1/2 cup cracked ice or mix in electric blender. Blend very thoroughly before straining into a cocktail glass.

GIN RICKEY

Juice and rind of 1/2 lime   Sparkling water
1 jigger gin

Squeeze lime over ice cubes in 8-ounce glass. Add gin, lime rind; fill glass with sparkling water. Stir.

GIN 'N TONIC

Juice and rind of 1/4 lime   Quinine water (tonic)
1 jigger gin

Squeeze lime over ice cubes in 8-ounce glass. Add rind, gin; fill with tonic. Stir.

MARTINI

4 parts dry gin or vodka   Green olive, pearl onion, or lemon peel
1 part French (dry) vermouth

Stir ingredients with 1/2 cup cracked ice until chilled. Strain into cocktail glass, serve with green olive, pearl onion, or lemon twist.

TOM COLLINS

1 teaspoon sugar   1 jigger gin
1/2 jigger lemon juice   Sparkling water

Dissolve sugar in lemon juice in a 10-ounce glass, and add ice cubes. Pour in gin. Fill with cold sparkling water, and stir.

GIMLET

4 parts gin or vodka | 1 part sweetened lime juice

Shake ingredients well with 1/2 cup cracked ice. Strain into pre-chilled cocktail glass.

DAIQUIRIS

1 scant teaspoon sugar or 2 scant teaspoons grenadine | Juice of 1/2 lime
1-1/2 ounces light rum

Dissolve sugar or grenadine in lime juice. Add rum and 1/2 cup cracked ice. Shake in cocktail shaker or put into electric blender. Strain and serve in 3-1/2-ounce cocktail glass. If electric blender is used, reduce amount of cracked ice.

RUM SWIZZLE

2-1/2 ounces light rum
Juice of 1/2 lime | 1 teaspoon sugar
4 dashes bitters

Mix ingredients in glass pitcher with plenty of finely cracked ice. Stir vigorously until mixture foams. Serve in double old-fashioned glass.

HOT BUTTERED RUM

Small piece stick cinnamon
1 lump sugar
Lemon peel | 1 jigger Jamaica rum
Small slice butter

Put cinnamon stick, sugar, lemon peel, and rum in a mug or short glass. Fill with boiling water. Float butter on top. (Place spoon in glass before pouring in hot water.)

RUM BOB NEWELL

1-1/2 ounces rum | 1/2 ounce pineapple juice

Combine ingredients. Serve over ice cubes in an old-fashioned glass. A pineapple cube in bottom of glass is attractive.

FOG CUTTER

1 ounce orange juice
2 ounces lemon juice
1/2 ounce orgeat syrup
2 ounces light rum | 1 ounce brandy
1/2 ounce gin
Sherry float

Pour all ingredients except sherry float into shaker with 1/2 cup cracked ice; shake. Pour into a 14-ounce chimney glass, or a bigger one if you can find it, and add ice to almost fill. Add sherry float. Serve with straws (and 2 aspirin).

RUM EASTERN SOUR

1/2 orange	2 ounces light rum
1/2 lemon	Fresh mint sprig
Dash orgeat syrup	Fruit
Dash rock candy syrup	

Squeeze orange and lemon juice into a 16-ounce or double old-fashioned glass with 1/2 cup shaved ice, and drop in fruit rinds. Add remaining ingredients. Add shaved ice to fill glass. Top with metal shaker and shake drink. Decorate with fresh mint and fruit. Serve with malt straws.

ROB ROY

1 jigger Scotch	Dash bitters
1/2 jigger sweet vermouth	Lemon peel

Stir ingredients with 1/2 cup cracked ice. Strain into cocktail glass; add twist of lemon peel.

SCOTCH ON THE ROCKS

1 jigger Scotch	Lemon peel
1/2 jigger water	

Pour Scotch over cracked ice in old-fashioned glass. Add water, stir, then add a twist of lemon peel.

HARVEY WALLBANGER

3/4 cup orange juice	1/2 ounce Galliano
1 ounce vodka	

Stir orange juice and vodka in old-fashioned glass with ice. Splash in Galliano.

BLOODY MARY NO. 1

1 jigger vodka	Dash Worcestershire sauce
2 jiggers tomato juice	Salt and pepper to taste
1/3 jigger lemon juice	Dash Tabasco sauce (optional)

Combine ingredients in shaker with 1/2 cup cracked ice. Shake until chilled, and strain into a 6-ounce cocktail glass.

BLOODY MARY NO. 2

2 jiggers tomato juice
2 jiggers vodka
Juice of 1/2 lemon

Dash Worcestershire sauce
Dash celery salt
Pepper to taste

Combine all ingredients and shake in a cocktail shaker with 1/2 cup cracked ice. Strain into a 6-ounce cocktail glass.

Variation: You may wish to add clam juice to taste or garnish with a thin lemon slice.

SCREWDRIVER

1 jigger vodka

Orange juice

Put ice cubes into an 8-ounce glass. Add vodka; fill with orange juice and stir.

MARGARITA

1 jigger white tequila
1/2 ounce Triple Sec

1 ounce lime or lemon juice
Salt

Moisten cocktail glass rim with fruit rind; spin rim in salt. Shake ingredients with 1/2 cup cracked ice. Strain into glass. Drink is sipped over the salted edge.

SCARLETT O'HARA

1 jigger Southern Comfort
1 jigger cranberry juice cocktail

Juice of 1/2 fresh lime

Combine ingredients in shaker. Shake with 1/2 cup cracked ice. Strain into cocktail glass.

BEE-BITES

Juice of 1/2 lemon
3/4 jigger grapefruit juice
3/4 jigger orange juice

1/2 jigger bourbon
Grenadine or sugar

Put all ingredients into shaker with 1/2 cup crushed ice, adding grenadine or sugar to taste. Shake well and strain into small cocktail glasses. Yield: 2 servings.

PARTY PUNCH

Bottle (4/5 quart) bourbon
2 quarts champagne
4 ounces Jamaica rum
4 ounces freshly squeezed lemon juice

8 ounces pineapple juice
8 ounces grapefruit juice
Orange slices

Pre-chill ingredients; mix in punch bowl, adding champagne last. Add ice; garnish with orange slices. Yield: 25 (punch-cup) servings.

ORANGE-CHAMPAGNE COCKTAIL

1 bottle (4/5 quart) champagne, chilled   4 cups fresh orange juice, chilled

Just before serving, combine chilled ingredients. Serve in champagne glasses. Yield: 12 (5-ounce) servings.

ORANGE SPRITZERS

2 (6-ounce) cans frozen pineapple
    juice concentrate
2 (6-ounce) cans frozen orange
    juice concentrate
3 cups water

1/2 teaspoon angostura bitters
2 (10-ounce) bottles sparkling water
    Gin or vodka (optional)

Empty concentrates into large pitcher. Add water and bitters; stir well. When ready to serve, add sparkling water and pour over ice in old-fashioned glasses. (If alcoholic beverages are desired, add gin or vodka — a small jigger to each glass.) Yield: about 11 (6-ounce) servings.

SCORPIONS

8 ounces light rum
8 ounces fresh orange juice
5 ounces freshly squeezed lemon juice

1-1/2 ounces gin
1-1/2 ounces brandy
3 ounces orgeat syrup

Mix all ingredients in an electric blender (or cocktail shaker) with a scoop of shaved ice. Pour into bowl filled with chopped ice and serve with long straws. Yield: 6 servings.

Note: We have found this drink to be an excellent starter for a bibulous crowd. The proportions may be altered to suit taste. Do try to find the orgeat syrup if you don't have it; if your friendly liquor dealer doesn't stock it, he can undoubtedly get it for you. If you could find a gardenia to float on top of the bowl, it would not only be authentic — like Trader Vic's — but also provide a nice conversation piece. — C. M.

SANGRÍA NO. 1
(Wine Punch)

1 unpeeled orange, seeded and sliced
1 unpeeled lemon, seeded and sliced
    Handful strawberries
    Handful raspberries (optional)
1 peach, peeled and sliced

2 teaspoons sugar
1 ounce orange or other
    fruit-flavored liqueur
1 ounce brandy
1 (27-ounce) bottle full-bodied dry red wine

Put all fruit into a large glass pitcher. Stir sugar into the liqueur and add to pitcher along with brandy. Let stand at room temperature for several hours. At serving time, add wine and generous amount of ice. Stir the Sangría with a wooden spoon until it is ice-cold and serve in chilled goblets. Yield: about 3/4 quart.

SANGRÍA NO. 2

Juice of 1 orange
Juice of 1 lemon
2 tablespoons powdered sugar
4 ounces Cointreau
4 ounces brandy

1 quart red wine
8 to 10 ounces club soda
1 unpeeled orange, thinly sliced
1 unpeeled lemon, thinly sliced

Put orange juice, lemon juice, and powdered sugar into a large glass pitcher. Add Cointreau and brandy, then about 8 ice cubes. Stir well; add red wine and club soda. Stir until ice-cold; pour into chilled goblets, and garnish with thin slices of lemon and orange. Yield: 8 servings.

DIAMOND HEAD COCKTAIL

1 ounce vodka or gin
1 ounce rum
1 ounce pineapple juice

1/2 ounce lime juice
Dash fine sugar

Combine ingredients and shake in a cocktail shaker containing 1/2 cup ice. Serve in tall cocktail glass with a straw.

HAWAIIAN COCKTAILS

Planters' Delight

2 ounces rum
1 ounce pineapple juice
1 ounce apricot juice

1 ounce orange juice
1 ounce lemon juice
Pineapple spear

Combine ingredients in a tall glass containing ice; serve with a pineapple spear and a straw. And in Hawaii, you might be served your drink with a small orchid floating on top!

Lelani Sour

2 ounces whiskey
1 ounce lime juice

1 teaspoon sugar
Orange slice

Mix ingredients in shaker with 1/2 cup cracked ice. Strain into highball glass containing shaved ice. Slit orange slice, slip it onto rim of glass, and serve with a straw.

Mai Tai — Wiki Wiki
("wiki wiki" means "quick")

2 ounces rum
Dash bitters
1 ounce lime juice

1 teaspoon sugar
Pineapple spear
Mint sprig

Mix first four ingredients in tall glass containing ice. Serve with pineapple spear, sprig of mint, and straw.

Potluck

Potluck is our potpourri chapter which presents a handful of hints and how-to's. Here you will find solutions or catalytic ideas for managing an entertaining household. There are notes on how to carve the tastiest morsels that go the farthest to please your guests. There are sauces to add savor to everyday fare. And the suggestions for Sunday night suppers will make this meal worthy of invited guests. For tea and coffee connoisseurs (and for those who simply enjoy a good cup of either), the methods to make both to perfection can be found in our "Potluck." It's a melage, a chapter we hope will bring interesting surprises that you will enjoy using. It's our final offering of tips and advice as you set about your entertaining ways.

SAUCE PREPARATION GUIDE

Every cook knows that the sauce makes the dish, and every good cook should have a knowledge of basic sauces. For your reference, the following recipes are for basic sauces and a few of their rich relatives.

Sauce	Ingredients	Directions
White Sauce	1/4 cup butter 1/4 cup all-purpose flour 2 cups milk or cream, scalded 1/2 teaspoon salt 1/8 teaspoon white pepper	Melt butter and gradually add flour. Cook the roux over low heat, stirring constantly, until it is foaming. Gradually add scalded milk and cook the mixture, stirring vigorously with a wire whisk, until it is thick and smooth. Add salt and pepper. Simmer for 5 minutes. Vary the flavor of White Sauce by adding any of the infinite number of herbs and spices that are available.
Rich White Sauce	2 egg yolks 1 cup White Sauce	Add egg yolks, one at a time, to White Sauce, beating well after each addition. Reheat the sauce without boiling.
Thin White Sauce	Follow recipe for White Sauce, but use: 1 tablespoon butter 1 tablespoon all-purpose flour for Each cup milk or cream	Same as for White Sauce.
Medium White Sauce	Follow recipe for White Sauce, but use: 2 tablespoons butter 2 tablespoons all-purpose flour for Each cup milk or cream	Same as for White Sauce.
Thick White Sauce	Follow recipe for White Sauce, but use: 3 or 4 tablespoons butter 3 or 4 tablespoons all-purpose flour for Each cup milk or cream	Same as for White Sauce.
Bechamel Sauce	1 tablespoon finely chopped onion 2 tablespoons butter 2 tablespoons all-purpose flour 3 cups scalded milk 1/4 teaspoon salt 3 white peppercorns Sprig parsley Pinch grated nutmeg (optional)	Sauté chopped onion in a saucepan in butter until soft. Add flour, mix well, and cook the roux slowly, stirring constantly, until it just starts to turn golden. Gradually add scalded milk, and cook the mixture, stirring vigorously with a wire whisk, until it is thick and smooth. Add salt, peppercorns, parsley, and nutmeg. Cook the sauce slowly, stirring frequently, for about 30 minutes, or until it is reduced by one-third. Strain through a fine sieve. Yield: about 2 cups.

Sauce	Ingredients	Directions
Cream Cheese Hollandaise Sauce	1 (8-ounce) package cream cheese 2 eggs 2 tablespoons freshly squeezed lemon juice 1/4 teaspoon salt	Add eggs, one at a time, to the cream cheese, blending thoroughly after each addition. Add lemon juice and salt. Place in top of a double boiler over hot water (not boiling). Cook, stirring constantly until the sauce is thick and fluffy.
Blender Hollandaise Sauce	3 egg yolks 2 tablespoons freshly squeezed lemon juice 1/4 teaspoon salt Dash cayenne pepper 2/3 cup butter	Combine egg yolks, lemon juice, salt, and cayenne in blender. Cover and blend on high speed for 3 seconds. Heat butter until it bubbles. Slowly blend into egg yolks over high speed. Serve at once or keep warm over hot water.
Foolproof Mock Hollandaise Sauce	3 egg yolks Freshly squeezed juice of 1 lemon 1 cup commercial sour cream, scant Salt, pepper, and sugar to taste	Add lemon juice to beaten yolks, add sour cream, and seasonings. Place in top of double boiler. Let cook until thick, about 5 minutes, stirring constantly. Sauce can be removed from heat over water, covered tightly, set aside, then reheated over hot water.
Veloute Sauce	1/3 cup butter 1/3 cup all-purpose flour 3 cups white chicken or veal stock 1/2 teaspoon salt 1/8 teaspoon pepper	Melt butter, add flour, and cook the roux, stirring, for a few minutes. Add the stock gradually, and cook the sauce, stirring constantly, until it thickens. Add salt and pepper, and continue to cook, stirring occasionally, until it is reduced to about 2-1/2 cups and is thick and creamy.
Blender Bearnaise Sauce	2 tablespoons white wine 1 tablespoon tarragon vinegar 2 teaspoons chopped shallots 2 teaspoons fresh tarragon, chopped; or 1 teaspoon dried 1/4 teaspoon black pepper 3/4 cup Hollandaise Sauce	Combine white wine, tarragon vinegar, shallots, tarragon, and pepper in a saucepan. Cook the mixture over high heat until almost all the liquid has evaporated. Pour the puree into the Hollandaise Sauce and put the mixture in a blender. Cover the container and blend the sauce at high speed for 4 seconds.
Mornay Sauce	3 egg yolks, lightly beaten 1/4 cup hot cream 2 cups hot Bechamel Sauce 2 tablespoons butter 2 tablespoons grated Parmesan or Swiss cheese	Mix lightly beaten egg yolks with cream and combine with hot Bechamel Sauce. Cook the sauce, stirring constantly, until it just reaches the boiling point. Add butter and grated cheese. Use the sauce with creamed foods that are to be browned in the oven. The top may be sprinkled with grated cheese just before browning. If a very golden brown is desired, reserve a few tablespoons of the sauce, fold in 1 tablespoon whipped cream, and spread this sauce on the creamed mixture.

BREW THE BEST COFFEE

Keep coffee pot clean. Oil residue from the coffee bean coats the pot and will contaminate a fresh brew. Clean with soap, rinse well, and scald with boiling water.

Accurate measurements are a must. Allow 6 ounces of water for 2 teaspoons (or a standard coffee measure) of coffee. Deviate from this measurement only for demitasse for which you add 3 teaspoons to each 6 ounces of water. Make coffee at its maximum strength to get the best flavor. If you prefer weaker coffee, dilute it after it has brewed. For the same flavorful reason, brew a full pot or no less than three-fourths the pot's capacity.

Use freshly drawn, cold water. Bring the water to just the boiling point before pouring it over the coffee and never, never let the coffee boil. Boiling leaches the bitterness from the bean and kills the flavor.

Watch your timing. Too little time and the brew is weak, too long and the brew is bitter. Finally, serve your coffee fresh and piping hot. And apply these basics to your favored method.

Drip. Rinse your pot with hot water to warm it. Measure the drip (medium) grind coffee into the filter section. Pour the just boiling water in the upper section and cover. When dripping is completed, usually four to six minutes, serve immediately while flavor is at its peak.

Percolator (non-automatic). Measure the cold water into the percolator and heat to just under the boiling point. Measure a regular grind coffee into the basket, place it in the percolator and perk gently — do not boil — for six to eight minutes.

Vacuum. Heat cold water to a boil in lower bowl. Put a filter in the upper bowl and fill with vacuum (fine) grind coffee. Reduce heat. When water rises into the upper bowl, stir. Brew one to three minutes. Remove from heat and allow coffee to return to lower bowl.

Filter. Put the disc and filter in the basket. Measure the coffee. Heat water to boiling point. Pour small amounts over the coffee allowing one to two minutes saturation. Then continue to add water slowly.

Good coffee for a crowd depends on the same rules; correct grind, measured amounts, and accurate timing. All you need to know is the amount of coffee to buy.

Number of Guests	Number of Servings (5-1/2 ounces)	Amount of Coffee (pounds)	Amount of Water (gallons)
25	40	1	2
50	80	2	4
75	120	3	6
100	160	4	8
125	200	5	10
150	240	6	12

BREWING TEA

An Englishman will tell you that a good cup of tea depends as much on the brewing as on the quality of the tea. If a connoisseur seems unduly miffed that you took the water to the pot instead of taking the pot to the water, there's a reason. So, for a large crowd, or for two, brew in the English manner for tea with a flavor to enjoy.

Bring freshly drawn cool water to a rolling boil. To release the full tea flavor the water must be boiling when it hits the leaves. Water that boils too long or that has been reheated makes a flat tasting drink.

Rinse the teapot with boiling water to warm it for the tea. Pottery or porcelain teapots are best as they hold heat well and don't interfere with the tea's flavor.

Measure into the pot a teaspoon of loose tea or a bag for each cup plus one for the pot. Reduce the proportions slightly for a large crowd or the brew may be bitterly strong. But for iced tea use 50% more tea to allow for melting ice.

Take the pot to the stove and add boiling water to cover the leaves. Let them steep for two minutes allowing the pores to open and the flavorful oils and aroma to be released. Fill the pot with briskly boiling water and steep three to five minutes more. Steep by the clock, not the color. Teas vary as to lightness. If you like weak tea, add water after brewing.

Serve at once with a pot of extremely hot water for those who prefer weaker tea. If you are making iced tea, cool to room temperature; then pour over ice cubes. Under refrigeration tea turns cloudy and soon loses its flavor.

When more tea is needed, rinse the pot and start from scratch. Never add fresh leaves to steeped leaves. Once the flavor has steeped from the leaves, they will only add bitterness.

CARVING

Pity the guest who watches a turkey leg wrenched in desperation, a standing rib trip across a platter and gravy dribble on the tablecloth. Carving, an easily learned skill, adds much to the success of a well served meal. Properly carved servings appeal to the eye and the economy — a well carved roast or chicken gives more mileage to the servings.

After removing meat or fowl from the oven, allow it to "set" a few minutes to make the carving easier. Place the meat on a hot platter that is large enough to accommodate the roast or turkey and the portions as they are cut. Garnishes are attractive but should not hamper the carver. Plates should also be warmed to keep food from cooling too quickly.

Carving may be done in the kitchen, the meat or fowl arranged on the hot platter and served piping hot. At the table, the carver may stand or sit, whichever is most comfortable.

The carving knife and fork are placed at the right side. After carving they may be laid together on the platter or one placed at each end of the platter. The importance being that they not drip on the tablecloth.

After the first incision has been made the angle of the knife should not alter. Each cut should be direct, sharp, and incisive made with a long sweeping stroke to give a smooth, even slice. A swaying motion gives a jagged, torn slice.

Cut across the grain of any meat to seal juices and give a tender slice. Steak is the exception but do slice steak at an angle to seal juices.

TO CARVE BEEF

Standing Rib Roast

1. Rib standing, place the heavy end to the carvers left.
2. Insert fork and with knife slice through crispy fat to bone.
3. Cut as many slices as desired before removing fork.
4. Draw knife along bone to separate slices. If the roast is small, one or two ribs, and won't stand, place it on its side with the ribs to the carver. Cut horizontal slices and loosen from the bone with a vertical slice.

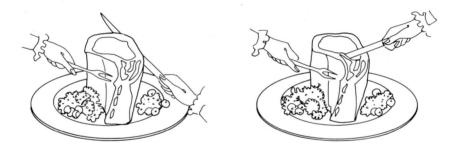

Rolled Roast

1. Place on platter with flat-side up.
2. Insert the fork with tines downward about half way down the roast.
3. Slice meat from right to left in 1/4-inch slices. Remove string and skewers as the meat is sliced.

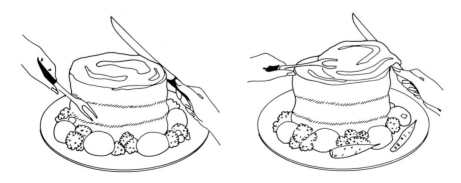

TO CARVE PORK

Roast Loin of Pork

1. Have the butcher free the backbone from the ribs. Leave in place for roasting and remove before placing roast on platter.
2. Place the roast on the platter so the smaller end is toward the carver's right.
3. Insert the fork, tines down into the heavy part of the meat between the ribs.
4. Beginning at the right, cut down between each rib bone, allowing one chop per person.

Crown Roast

1. Place roast on platter with rib bones up.
2. Insert fork between ribs and with knife, slice between bones, allowing one chop per serving.

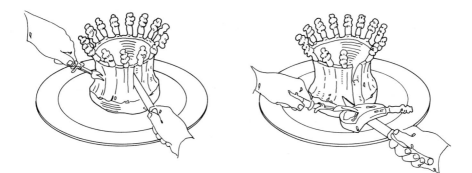

Ham

1. Place the glazed-side up, broad side away from carver.
2. Cut three or four thin slices parallel to the length of the ham from the thin side to form a solid base. Turn ham on this base.
3. Insert the fork where it gives the carver the firmest control of the ham, usually the butt end.
4. Starting at shank end, cut out a wedge-shape piece then carve perpendicular to the bone.
5. Release slices by slicing under them along the leg bone.
6. For more servings, turn ham to original position and make slices to bone. Release slices and serve. Country ham is rich and should be sliced extremely thin.

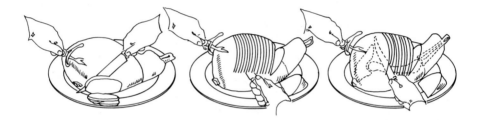

Ham Shank

1. Place shank on platter with bone to carver's right.
2. Hold with carving fork and with knife remove cushion of thick side, slicing close to the bone.
3. Slice this section, cut-side down, across the grain at right angle to platter.

TO CARVE LAMB

1. Place roast on platter with leg bone to carver's right and cut three or four lengthwise slices to form a base.
2. Turn roast so it rests on base.
3. Steady roast with carving fork.
4. Beginning at the leg bone end, slice meat at a right angle to the platter down to the bone.
5. Release slices by cutting along bone parallel to platter.

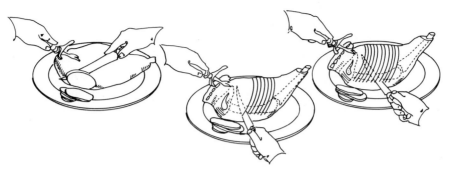

TO CARVE FOWL

Roast Turkey or Chicken

1. Place bird breast-side up with legs to carver's right. Remove strings and skewers.
2. Beginning with the side nearest the carver, insert the fork one prong through the drumstick, the other through the second joint (thigh).
3. Use the carving knife to cut around the second joint.
4. With the flat blade, press against the body of the bird and using the fork as a lever, draw the leg toward you. If necessary use the knife to cut through the flesh and skin from the underside of the leg.
5. Place drumstick and second joint on a side platter skin-side down so the joint may be clearly seen and more easily divided.
6. Cut the joint in lengthwise pieces and holding the drumstick heavy-end down, slice for serving.
7. Remove the wing at the joint in much the same manner.
8. Plunge the fork deeply across the breast bone and beginning at the left, carve long even slices of white meat from the breast. Under the back, attached at either side of the back bone, are found two choice bites of dark meat, known as the "oyster."
9. To carve the other side, turn the platter and repeat.

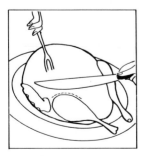

SUNDAY NIGHT SUPPER SUGGESTIONS

Some of our most memorable times turn out not to be parties in the usual sense. When friends drop in, usually on Sunday afternoon, and conversation is lively and the company stimulating, who wants to end it just because it's getting on toward evening? At such times you begin to squirm a little; it's Sunday-night-supper-time and you naturally want to say, "Do stay for supper. I promise not to go to any trouble; we'll just take potluck." But can you?

The foresighted homemaker develops a little repertoire of foolproof dishes which can really be produced at the drop of a pan or two, but which appear to have come about through hours of preparation. (Actually, many did require hours of preparation — but that was done on a leisurely day when she felt like cooking.)

Such dishes she reserves for Sunday nights only, meals that will satisfy the "It's-six-o'clock-so-what's-holding-up-dinner?" crowd and still not trap her in the kitchen long after a hearty noon dinner is polished off.

Here are a few recipes which, though not generally considered party fare, will enable you to fully enjoy those accidental parties — which are frequently more fun than the on-purpose ones.

SUNDAY NIGHT SHRIMP GUMBO
(prepare ahead of time)

2 tablespoons all-purpose flour	1/4 teaspoon leaf thyme
2 slices bacon, diced	Salt and freshly ground pepper to taste
2/3 cup chopped green onions, including tops	1 teaspoon grated lemon rind
1 (10-ounce) can or bottle clam juice	1 pound raw shrimp, peeled and deveined
1 (1-pound) can tomatoes (preferably plum or pear tomatoes)	1 (10-ounce) package frozen okra
1 bay leaf	Hot cooked rice
1 teaspoon Worcestershire sauce	Chopped parsley

First, brown flour in small dry skillet over very low heat. This may be done weeks ahead of time in quantity and kept in a jar for use in thickening soups, stews, etc.

Fry bacon in a deep pot or Dutch oven and when half done, add onion and cook over medium heat until translucent, about 5 minutes. Sprinkle browned flour over onions, stir well, and add clam juice. Cook over low heat, stirring constantly, until smooth and thick. Add tomatoes, bay leaf, Worcestershire sauce, seasonings, lemon rind, and uncooked shrimp. Cook 10 minutes, add frozen okra, stir until pieces are separated. Cover and simmer about 15 minutes, or until okra is barely done.

Serve in soup bowls with a mound of hot rice in center, garnished with chopped parsley. With a fresh grapefruit salad, this is a meal. Yield: 4 servings.

SOUTHERN RAILWAY BEAN SOUP
(may be prepared ahead of time)

1 pound navy beans
1 ham shank
1 (1-pound) can tomatoes
3 quarts water
3/4 cup chopped onion
1 cup chopped celery

1 teaspoon marjoram (optional)
1 bay leaf
Salt and pepper to taste
2 cups diced uncooked potatoes
1/2 cup mashed potatoes

Soak beans overnight in water to cover. Next day drain and put in deep soup kettle with all ingredients except diced and mashed potatoes. Cover and simmer at least 2 hours, until beans are tender.

Remove ham and bay leaf; skim off any fat on surface. Cut ham into small pieces and return to soup. Add diced potatoes, cover and simmer about an hour longer, or until potatoes are well done. Blend the mashed potatoes into the soup by stirring small amount of soup into the potatoes, then a little more, etc., then returning all to the pot. (This prevents the soup from being watery.) Freezes well. Yield: 8 to 10 servings.

Variation: This recipe may be used with a large beef bone instead of ham. A good combination is a knuckle bone plus some shank bones.

CHEESEBURGER HERO

1/4 cup butter or margarine, melted
1/4 cup grated Parmesan cheese
2 small loaves brown-and-serve French bread
1 pound ground lean beef
1 (6-ounce) can tomato paste
1/2 cup sliced green onions
1/4 cup chopped pimiento-stuffed olives

1/4 cup chopped green pepper
1/2 cup grated Parmesan cheese
1/2 teaspoon oregano
1/2 teaspoon garlic salt
1/8 teaspoon black pepper
About 8 triangles (about 2 x 2 x 2 inches) Cheddar cheese
3 tomato slices, halved

Combine butter and 1/4 cup Parmesan cheese; set aside. Cut bread loaves in half lengthwise; place cut-side down on baking sheet in 425° oven for about 10 minutes, just to finish baking. Remove from oven; brush cut-sides of bread with butter-cheese mixture and return to oven, cut-side up, for 5 minutes. Remove from oven; reduce oven temperature to 350°. Set top halves of bread aside.

While bread bakes, combine beef, tomato paste, onions, olives, green pepper, 1/2 cup Parmesan cheese, oregano, garlic salt, and pepper. Spread over bottom halves of bread. Place on baking sheet and bake 30 minutes. Remove; alternate 4 cheese triangles and 3 tomato halves on top of each meat roll. Cover with bread tops and return to oven for about 5 minutes or until cheese begins to melt. Serve immediately. Yield: 6 servings.

CUBAN BLACK BEAN SOUP
(a memorable soup for a cold winter's evening)

1 pound black beans (sometimes called "turtle" beans)	1 teaspoon oregano
2 quarts water	1/4 teaspoon dry mustard
1 tablespoon salt (for beans)	2 tablespoons olive oil
2 cloves garlic	2 onions, chopped
1 teaspoon salt (for soup)	1 or 2 green peppers, chopped
1 teaspoon ground cumin	1 tablespoon freshly squeezed lemon juice

Soak beans in water overnight. Next day, using same water, add the 1 tablespoon salt; bring to a boil, cover and cook until beans are almost tender. (These beans require longer cooking than other varieties.)

Crush together garlic, 1 teaspoon salt, cumin, oregano, and dry mustard. Heat oil and sauté onions about 5 minutes in large skillet; add green pepper and continue sautéing until onions are tender. Stir in seasoning mixture and lemon juice, then about 1/2 cup of the hot bean liquid. Cover and simmer about 10 minutes. Add to beans and continue cooking until flavors are thoroughly blended, about 1 hour.

To thicken soup, remove 1 cup of beans and liquid and put through electric blender or fine sieve, returning puree to soup kettle. Check seasonings and correct if necessary.

Serve in bowls with mound of hot dry rice in center. Garnish top with finely diced green onion tops; or soup may be garnished with diced hard-cooked egg with thinly sliced lemon floating on surface. Yield: 6 to 8 servings. The ideal accompaniment for this soup is Italian Bread Sticks (see Index).

PLAIN OMELET

3 eggs	1/8 teaspoon pepper
3 tablespoons water	1 tablespoon butter, margarine, or oil
3/8 teaspoon salt	

Mix eggs, water, salt, and pepper with a whisk or three-tined fork until yolks and whites are blended. Meanwhile, heat butter, margarine, or oil in a 7- or 8-inch omelet pan or heavy skillet until it is just hot enough to sizzle a drop of water. Pour in egg mixture all at once. Mixture should begin to cook immediately at the outer edges. With a fork, lift cooked portions at the edges so uncooked portions flow underneath. Slide pan rapidly back and forth over the heat to keep mixture in motion and sliding freely to avoid sticking. When the mixture is set properly, it no longer flows freely and is moist and creamy on top. Let the omelet cook for about 1 minute to brown the bottom slightly. Fold or roll, and serve promptly on a warm platter. The omelet should be tender and light, moist, and delicately brown on the bottom. Yield: 1 to 2 servings.

Index